TEACHER PREP

MERRILL
PRENTICE HALL

Teacher Preparation Classroom

See a demo at
www.prenhall.com/teacherprep/demo

Your Class. Their Careers. Our Future. Will your students be prepared?

We invite you to explore our new, innovative and engaging website and all that it has to offer you, your course, and tomorrow's educators! Preview this site today at www.prenhall.com/teacherprep/demo. Just click on "go" on the login page to begin your exploration.

Organized around the major courses pre-service teachers take, the Teacher Preparation site provides media, student/teacher artifacts, strategies, research articles, and other resources to equip your students with the quality tools needed to excel in their courses and prepare them for their first classroom.

This ultimate on-line education resource will provide you and your students access to:

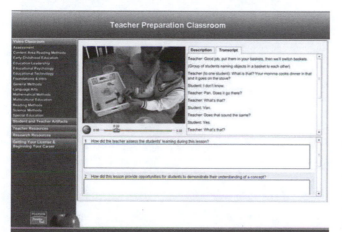

Online Video Library More than 250 video clips—each tied to a course topic and framed by learning goals and Praxis-type questions—capture real teachers and students working in real classrooms.

Student and Teacher Artifacts More than 200 student and teacher classroom artifacts—each tied to a course topic and framed by learning goals and application questions—provide a wealth of materials and experiences to help your students observe children's developmental learning.

Lesson Plan Builder Step-by-step guidelines and lesson plan examples to support students as they learn to build high-quality lesson plans.

Articles and Readings Over 500 articles from ASCD's renowned journal *Educational Leadership are available.* The site also includes Research Navigator, a searchable database of additional educational journals.

Strategies and Lessons Over 500 research-supported instructional strategies appropriate for a wide range of grade levels and content areas.

Licensure and Career Tools Resources devoted to helping your students pass their licensure exam, learn standards, law, and public policies, plan a teaching portfolio, and succeed in their first year of teaching.

How to ORDER *Teacher Prep* for you and your students:

For students to receive a *Teacher Prep* Access Code with this text, instructor **must** provide a special value pack ISBN number on their textbook order form. To receive this special ISBN, please email:
Merrill.marketing@pearsoned.com and provide the following information:

- Name and Affiliation
- Author/Title/Edition of Merrill text

Upon ordering *Teacher Prep* for their students, instructors will be given a lifetime *Teacher Prep* Access Code.

SIXTH EDITION

Diagnostic Teaching of Reading

Techniques for Instruction and Assessment

Barbara J. Walker

Oklahoma State University

PEARSON

Merrill
Prentice Hall

Upper Saddle River, New Jersey,
Columbus, Ohio

Library of Congress Cataloging-in-Publication Data

Walker, Barbara J.
    Diagnostic teaching of reading: techniques for instruction and assessment / Barbara J. Walker.—6th ed.
        p. cm.
    Includes bibliographical references and index.
    ISBN-13: 978-0-13-199586-4
    ISBN-10:   0-13-199586-3
    1. Reading—Remedial teaching. 2. Individualized reading instruction. 3. Reading—Ability testing. 4. Reading comprehension. I. Title.
    LB1050.5.W35 2008
    428′.407—dc22

                                                                                            2007018795

Vice President and Executive Publisher: Jeffery W. Johnston
Senior Editor: Linda Ashe Montgomery
Editorial Assistant: Laura J. Weaver
Production Editor: Mary Irvin
Production Coordination and Text Design: Carol Singer, GGS Book Services
Design Coordinator: Diane C. Lorenzo
Cover Designer: Jeff Vanik
Cover Image: Scott Cunningham/Merrill
Production Manager: Pamela D. Bennett
Director of Marketing: Ann Castel Davis
Marketing Manager: Darcy Betts Prybella
Marketing Coordinator: Brian Mounts

This book was set in Garamond by GGS Book Services. It was printed and bound by Hamilton Printing. The cover was printed by Phoenix Color Corp.

Pearson Education Ltd.
Pearson Education Singapore Pte. Ltd.
Pearson Education Canada, Ltd.
Pearson Education–Japan

Pearson Education Australia Pty. Limited
Pearson Education North Asia Ltd.
Pearson Educación de Mexico, S.A. de C.V.
Pearson Education Malaysia Pte. Ltd.

10 9 8 7 6 5 4 3 2 1
ISBN-13: 978-0-13-199586-4
ISBN-10:   0-13-199586-3

To Sharon and Chris

About the Author

Barbara J. Walker is professor of reading at Oklahoma State University-Stillwater/Tulsa where she teaches courses in reading difficulties and literacy coaching. Dr. Walker received her Ed.D. from Oklahoma State University in Curriculum and Instruction, specializing in reading difficulty. Prior to returning to Oklahoma, Dr. Walker was a professor in the Department of Special Education and Reading at Montana State University, Billings, where she coordinated the Reading Clinic. She was a reading specialist in the elementary schools of Stillwater, Oklahoma; organized and taught the college reading program at Vernon Regional Junior College in Vernon, Texas; and coordinated the educational program at the Hogar Paul Harris in Cochabamba, Bolivia.

Dr. Walker's research interests focus on teacher development, early literacy intervention, reading difficulties, and literacy coaching. Her publications include *Techniques for Reading Assessment and Instruction* (2005), *Supporting Struggling Readers* (2003), *The Supervisors's Handbook for the Reading Team* (1998) with Ronald Scherry and Lesley Morrow, *Tips for the Reading Team* (1998) and *The Reading Team: A Handbook for K–3 Volunteer Tutors* (1997) with Lesley Morrow and *Interactive Handbook for Understanding Reading Diagnosis* (1994) with Kathy Roskos. Dr. Walker received the College Reading Association's 1997 A. B. Herr Award for outstanding contributions to reading education and was a distinguished finalist for the International Reading Association's 1991 Albert J. Harris Award for research in reading disabilities.

Dr. Walker is the elected President (2008-2009) of the International Reading Association, an organization that influences over 300,000 reading educators worldwide. She is a state, national, and international professional leader, having served on the board of directors of the International Reading Association, the College Reading Association, the Montana State Reading Council, and the Oklahoma Reading Council. Most important to her, however, is preparing teachers to work with struggling readers. In this capacity, she has helped more than 3,000 struggling readers improve their literacy.

Preface

As our national diversity grows, teachers must increasingly celebrate our likenesses, empathetically discuss our differences, and resolve that we know of no *one best* way to teach all children to read. The Great Debate has continued, but the conclusions have been the same. No one approach is better in all literacy situations and with all learners, so that it should be considered the one best method. However, we have increasingly expanded our concepts of the instructional process. At the core of this knowledge has been the continued assertion that effective instruction is executed by effective teachers. This text provides a tool for teachers to understand the various instructional frameworks underlying diagnostic teaching techniques.

Text Purpose

Embodied within this text is the strong belief that as a nation of readers, our strengths lie in our individual differences. These individual differences need to be nurtured within our instructional programs, building upon the unique strengths that each student possesses. Furthermore, sensitive teachers use these strengths to expand students' conceptual knowledge, creating intelligent citizens.

Teachers are often keen observers and reflective thinkers. This text promotes the idea that teachers can make sophisticated diagnostic judgments and can identify appropriate instructional techniques through a process of diagnostic teaching. Using this knowledge to make informed instructional decisions leads to a renewal of teachers' decision-making power.

Diagnostic Teaching of Reading is designed to supplement course work in the diagnosis and remediation of reading difficulties. It can ultimately be used in a reading practicum or as a guide in reading clinic experiences. Furthermore, reading specialists, literacy coaches, school psychologists, special education teachers, and Title I teachers will find it a useful reference. The instructional techniques are written in a step-by-step fashion so that reading specialists and teachers can evaluate when and how they should modify their instruction. The book will help teachers and practicum students readily follow the designated procedures. The goal is to increase communication between the practitioner and various specialists as well as between the practicum student and the college professor.

Changes for the Sixth Edition

In this edition, you will find:

- An elaborated theoretical perspective including an explanation of constructivist learning theory.
- A new chapter on literacy coaching.
- Revision of Chapter 8, the portfolio chapter, to various kinds of assessment, which portrays a broader scope of assessments. New chapter topics include formal assessments and motivation assessments.
- Term change from problem readers to struggling readers. Soon after the first edition was published, I found (using the thesaurus) the word *struggling*, which seemed to me to be more consistent with the intent of this book. All individuals struggle at some point in their literacy lives, even college professors.
- New to each technique: at least one reference that is evidence based. Also referenced are websites that direct readers to more information about the technique.
- More than 65 instructional techniques that meet the diverse learning needs of students explained in easy, step-by-step procedures. Important diagnostic information accompanies each technique. New instructional techniques are *Internet Inquiry, Questioning the Author,* and *Concept Mapping.* Several techniques developed to focus on specific needs of readers have been combined in this edition—prediction logs and prediction maps can be found under the *Prediction Strategy; Herringbone* can be found under graphic organizers; *Echo Reading* can be found under *Impress Reading. Word Analogy Strategy* and *Word Probe Strategy* were combined to form *Decoding by Analogy. Webbing* went back to its roots and is now called *Semantic Mapping.*

Text Organization

This text is organized in two parts. Part One outlines the principles of assessment and instruction. Part Two includes the instructional techniques. The following is a description of the text's content.

Chapter 1 presents the decision-making process of diagnostic teaching. It outlines some common initial diagnostic decisions and lays the groundwork for the rest of the text. Chapter 2 describes the various influences on diagnostic decisions. Factors impacting a student's reading performance are the reader, the text, the task, the technique, and the context. Chapter 3 presents a framework for effective diagnostic teaching, while Chapter 4 develops a framework for a diagnostic teaching session, which now includes writing time.

Chapter 5 explains how to gather diagnostic data, including specific assessment for each stage of reading development; Chapter 6 shows how to formulate hypotheses using the collected data. Chapter 7 provides the procedures for using teaching (rather than testing) as a method of reading evaluation. The revised Chapter 8 discusses how different types of assessments influence the gathering and evaluation of diagnostic information.

Chapter 9 describes the various kinds of instructional materials available for a diagnostic teacher to use, and the new Chapter 10 focuses on literacy coaching. Chapter 11 classifies the diagnostic teaching techniques on the basis of several methods: the instructional framework implemented, the type of text used, the response mode used, the strategy taught, the targeted skill taught, the source of information targeted, the structure of instruction selected, and the cognitive process emphasized.

Finally, Part Two presents a simple description and the procedures for instructional techniques. Following each description is an explanation of when that approach is most effective in teaching reading. It describes the view of reading underlying the technique, provides a checklist for the diagnostic teacher to use in assessing its effectiveness with a particular student, and offers evidence-based references and websites.

Acknowledgments

This text represents a point of view developed over years of clinical experience. During that time, several people have been an inspiration to me. First, I want to thank Darrell D. Ray, Oklahoma State University, who has been my mentor and advisor. At the cornerstone of this text is his strong belief that children who experience reading difficulty need instruction that uses their strengths, which is continually adjusted to meet their changing needs. I thank him for initiating my quest to understand individual differences in learning to read. Also, I want to thank my knowledgeable friends who read parts of the text and offered suggestions, criticisms, and support for my efforts. I am especially grateful for the ideas and comments of Claudia Dybdahl, University of Alaska, regarding qualitative assessment, and William Powell, University of Florida, regarding quantitative assessment and classifying techniques. Their professional critique of my initial ideas set the course for the view of assessment in the text.

Special thanks are extended to my reviewers: Valerie Chapman, The University of Texas at El Paso; Alan M. Frager, Miami University; Betty Goerss, Indiana University East; Barbara Pettegrew, Otterbein College; and Timothy Shanahan, University of Illinois at Chicago. I have also appreciated the astute judgment of the staff at Merrill/Prentice Hall, especially Jeff Johnston for his encouragement and perspective as I have grown as an author; Linda Bishop, editor for many editions, for her innovative ideas for improving each edition and her continuing support of my work; and production editors Mary Irvin and Cindy Miller for their untiring efforts to keep the project moving at all times. I am especially thankful for the editorial work of Bruce Owens.

I owe a great deal to each of the eager students who willingly let me test my ideas about instruction. I am especially indebted to my own two children, Chris and Sharon, who let me teach them in different ways. They were especially patient in sharing their mother with the reading profession.

Adjusting instruction to meet the changing needs of students in our classrooms and clinics is a challenging and rewarding task. This text is designed to facilitate that decision-making process.

Barbara J. Walker

Contents

7   **Assessment Using Diagnostic Lessons** *121*

8   **Using Different Types of Assessments** *133*

Appendix A

NOTE: Every effort has been made to provide accurate and current Internet information in this book. However, the Internet and information posted on it are constantly changing, so it is inevitable that some of the Internet addresses listed in this textbook will change.

PART ONE

The Process of Diagnostic Teaching of Reading

Diagnostic teaching has a long history in reading. The learning methods (Mills, 1954) test based on sight-word recognition was a forerunner to this approach. The test taught children 10 words, and after a 20-minute wait period, the children were tested to see how many they remembered. However, as theories have grown, the use of teaching as assessment has not been developed to keep abreast of these advancements. Likewise, there have been few attempts to systematically organize procedures for using diagnostic teaching in today's classrooms. This book is designed to help teachers create lessons that serve as both instruction and assessment. To do this, the diagnostic teacher observes students' responses during instruction and measures learning. If the technique supports learning, the teacher continues instruction. However, if the technique does not work, the teacher adapts instruction until the students are learning and then measures students' responses to the adaptations.

The theoretical foundation of this book lies in the constructivist learning theory. This theory purports that readers build an understanding as they read. Readers are not blank slates that memorize information in order to repeat it back. They think about what they are reading. Sometimes they form images and schema to organize new learning. From a cognitive (dealing with the mind) view of constructivism, readers develop semantic networks (schema; Pearson & Anderson, 1984) that organize their experiences into structures so that their knowledge is more readily available. However, the constructivist theory is much more than schema theory. It has several perspectives. One proposes a basic cognitive perspective of how people learn (Piaget, 1968), while the another proposes a social view of how people learn (Vygotsky, 1978). Both share some similar tenets: (a) learning is active, (b) learning is meaningful, and (c) learning involves a situation. Where and how this learning occurs varies in these perspectives. In a cognitive view, the learning occurs when learners actively construct meaning in *response to a specific situation*. Thus, people actively and individually construct meaning in relationship to their own knowledge, culture, and past experiences. In this view, understanding stems from integrating one's own knowledge with new learning. However, in the social perspective (dealing with the mind in situations), learning is socially constucted *within a social interaction*, not as a response to a situation. That is, meaning is constructed as individuals interact with more informed others within society. In this view, the collaborative nature of learning means that every cognitive function stems from social interactions. In this book, both perspectives in constructivism are used, helping the diagnostic teacher view learning as both personal and social while realizing that readers actively construct meaning. More information can be found at http://gsi.berkeley.edu/resources/learning/introduction.html and http://leo.oise.utoronto.ca/~lbencze/Constructivism.html.

In part 1 of this book, there is an outline of the diagnostic teaching process (chapter 1) and its use in teaching students who find reading challenging (chapters 6 and 7). Diagnostic teaching requires teachers to constantly reflect on their observations within a reading event. They collect data about students as readers and writers (chapters 5 to 8) and use these data to design instructional routines (chapters 3 and 4). The students are viewed as active learners who build a model of meaning as they read and write. As students read and write, they are influenced by many factors, including the text, the task, the technique, their own strategies and approaches, and the situational context (chapter 2).

A diagnostic teacher must continually evaluate the influence these multiple factors have on students' literacy behaviors and plan effective instruction (chapter 3). Teachers orchestrate many facets that influence students as they interact during literacy events. A diagnostic teacher plans effective lessons and provides a supportive context for students. For this purpose, the diagnostic teacher uses an instructional framework (chapter 4) to guide her planning. Further planning is enhanced by knowledge of instructional materials (chapter 9) and knowledge about the purposes of instructional techniques. (chapter 11). Support and collaboration for implementing this complex process are needed for most teachers; thus, chapter 10 introduces basic concepts of literacy coaching.

The diagnostic teacher encourages the reader to use both what she knows and the text to construct meaning within the situational context (chapter 1). In the first part of this book, reading theories are discussed. The point of view of this book is that readers are active and constructive as they approach learning tasks. Although a teacher may select instructional techniques and materials that are based in other theories, the diagnostic teacher strives to balance her instruction within a constructivist framework.

Ways to Use These Chapters

Chapters 1 and 2 can provide a conceptual and theoretical basis for the subsequent chapters in this section. The information in chapter 2 can be used as a checklist of instructional conditions that might influence the reader's performance. Chapter 6 uses the case study of a reader, Jenny, to outline instructional conditions using the criteria suggested in chapter 2.

The information in chapter 3 can be used as a checklist for teaching behaviors. Often, teachers make a self-assessment measure using the guidelines in chapter 3 in order to evaluate their own performance. Likewise, they make a mental checklist of aspects of lesson planning found in chapter 4. Further, they use the information in chapter 4 to design instructional sessions for struggling readers. Using this framework for the instructional session (familiar text time, guided contextual reading, strategy and skill instruction, process writing time, continuous diagnostic assessment, and personalized reading and writing) provides a balanced approach to instruction.

Using the information in chapters 5 to 8, the diagnostic teacher designs her initial and ongoing assessments. In these chapters there are assessment techniques, including the following: informal reading inventory, miscue analysis, think-aloud assessments, skills assessments (e.g., letter identification), phonemic segmentation, and fluency assessments as well as other assessments, such as formal assessments, engagement assessments, student self-assessment, and authentic assessments (e.g., portfolios). The diagnostic teacher carefully selects assessments that will augment her instructional decision making.

Diagnostic teachers use chapter 9 to select and evaluate instructional materials. Being knowledgeable about instructional materials helps provide effective instructional conditions. Teachers need to collaborate with others to use the diagnostic teaching approach; therefore, the literacy coach explains the collaborative process of teacher development. Diagnostic teachers and literacy coaches use chapter 11 to select techniques to use during the lesson framework. By using the charts in chapter 11, the diagnostic teacher and coaches can readily select instructional techniques based on the analysis of assessment data and observations during teaching. If the diagnostic teacher and literacy coaches are searching for a technique for guiding reading for meaning, then they could use Table 11-1, where techniques are suggested according to when instruction takes place (before, during, or after) to promote meaning construction. Thus, the instructional technique as implemented by the diagnostic teacher supports meaning construction for the struggling reader. If the area of concern is fluency, the diagnostic teacher or literacy coach might use the matrix (Table 11-5) for skill development to select a technique by looking under the fluency column. Thus, during the strategy and skill section of the lesson framework, the diagnostic teacher can increase fluency development. When diagnostic teachers and literacy coaches use the tables in chapter 11, they facilitate instructional decision making and increase the likelihood of student achievement.

1 What Is Diagnostic Teaching?

Diagnostic teaching is an instructional lesson in which teachers use both assessment and instruction to figure out how struggling readers approach the reading event. Using this information, diagnostic teachers establish the instructional conditions necessary for struggling readers to learn. Diagnostic teaching, then, is the process of using assessment and instruction at the same time to establish the instructional conditions that enhance learning. Instruction that appropriately matches struggling readers' characteristics enriches their engagement in literacy activities and enhances the likelihood they will be strategic readers who construct meaning with text.

In this book, diagnostic teaching is based in constructivist learning theories. The constructivist theory has several basic tenets. First, learning is viewed as an active process where readers use what they know along with the text. They construct or build their own meaning. They do not respond passively to new information by simply absorbing it. They create a semantic network (see introduction to part 1) where they revise and reorganize their knowledge with each new experience. This is referred to active learning, thinking, reading or writing. Second, learning is viewed as making meaning. In other words, individuals are always searching for meaning in their lives and as they read. Readers have an incredible need to make sense of what they read and write. Therefore, from a constructivist view, readers actively construct meaning. Finally, constructivist theory holds that learning involves situations. In this last premise, there are differing perspectives on the role of the situation in learning. In a **cognitive** view that involves mainly the mind, it is proposed that learning occurs when individuals actively construct meaning in *response* to a specific situation. However, in the social perspective of constructivist learning theory, learning is viewed as socially constructed *within situations*, not as a response to a situation. That is, meaning is constructed as individuals interact with more informed others within society. In this book, both perspectives of constructivism are used. The premises and procedures of diagnostic teaching hold that reading is an active constructive process. Further, diagnostic teaching draws heavily on situational theories but also maintains that the individuals sometimes create a response as a result of a situation.

Not only do diagnostic teachers understand and use theories as they plan instruction, but they are also aware of the characteristics of effective teachers. The report *Preventing Reading Difficulties* states, "The critical importance of the teacher in the prevention of reading difficulties must be recognized" (Snow, Burns, & Griffin, 1998, p. 9). In an award-winning article about struggling readers in high-poverty schools, Taylor, Pearson, Peterson, and Rodriguez (2003) found several important characteristics of effective teachers that are in line with a growing body of research. An initial result was that students who had more effective teachers actually learned more and scored higher on achievement tests. In analyzing teacher behaviors, they found that effective teachers focused on higher-level questioning strategies like prompts to use background knowledge and figure out the theme. This possibly indicated that they believed that readers in high-poverty schools could actually read and think. Also, the effective teachers focused on strategy use in the context of reading events. They supported strategy use through demonstrations and coaching literate behaviors. With this knowledge about reading and reading instruction, teachers can adapt instruction to meet the needs of struggling readers and tailor it to their strategy use, which heightens students' engagement and enhances their understanding when reading.

The diagnostic teacher identifies specific instructional alternatives for struggling readers to enhance their literacy. As a reader begins to experience success, he attributes his reading improvement to using strategic processes. This attribution, in turn, increases his engagement during subsequent literacy events. The diagnostic teacher's task is to monitor this advancement and identify the instructional modifications that produced it. Therefore, she formulates her diagnostic hypotheses by observing the instructional conditions that enhance reading. This process is outlined in Figure 1–1.

The decision-making cycle of diagnostic teaching begins in the midst of a *reading event*, where the teacher can observe the reader's strategies for constructing meaning. From these observations, she develops various types of assessment activities (see chapters 5 and 8). She uses the information from the assessment activities and her observations within the reading event to *formulate diagnostic hypotheses* and select instructional techniques that will advance the student's reading. As she *teaches the diagnostic lesson*, the teacher adjusts her original plan to ensure learning. After the lesson, she *assesses the changes* the reader made and *evaluates* the effectiveness of the adjustments she made. Using this information, she either *establishes the conditions* for learning (how she will teach) or *recycles* (reformulates or makes new hypotheses). In this decision-making cycle, the diagnostic teacher shifts between assessment and instruction to create evaluations that emerge from and that immediately influence instruction within the reading event.

> Diagnostic teaching is the process of using assessment and instruction at the same time to identify the instructional modifications that enable struggling readers to become independent learners.

The diagnostic teacher is an active problem solver. She is much more than a test giver. She is first and foremost a teacher. As she teaches, she explores how a particular student reads and responds. She knows that his reading is affected not only by what he knows but also by the strategies he uses and within the situation where he reads. Thinking about what the student already knows and does when he learns, the diagnostic teacher selects techniques that will facilitate learning in the most efficient way. Rather than looking for causes of reading disabilities, the diagnostic teacher focuses on what students can do, then coordinates their strengths with suitable reading experiences.

Figure 1–1   *The Decision-Making Cycle of Diagnostic Teaching*

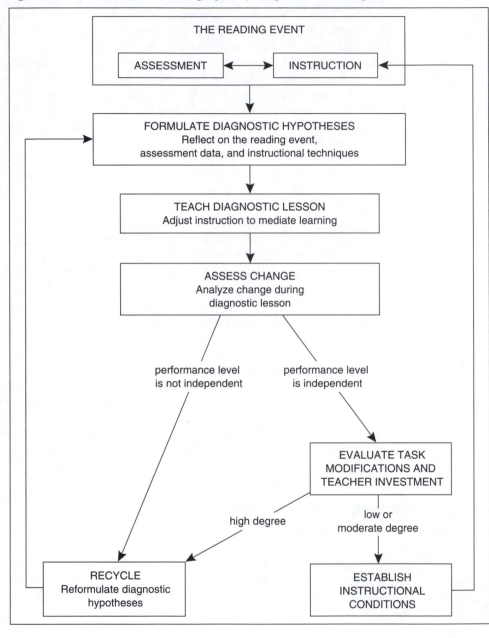

Active Reading

The diagnostic teacher makes instructional decisions based on her understanding of how reading occurs. In this book, reading is viewed as a constructive process that involves making meaning with text within a situation. Students employ strategic processes that help them monitor and elaborate their understanding. As they actively use these processes, they combine resources like their prior knowledge, the information they are reading, and their prior and present reading situations to construct meaning. **Active readers** use the following processes:

1. Active readers engage in the reading process, *combining both the text and prior knowledge* (Rumelhardt, 2004). While reading, such readers construct a tentative understanding based on inferences. They shift between using what they know (reader-based inferencing) and what the text says (text-based inferencing) to construct meaning. Both the reader and the text have many features that influence the reader–text interactions (see chapter 2, text and reader discussion).

2. Active readers elaborate what and how they read (Pressley, 2000). They connect information in the text to what they know to *elaborate* their understanding. In other words, they transform the new information and reconcile it with their **schema**, or structures of knowledge. At the same time, many readers elaborate the strategies they are using to construct their understanding. Thus, they notice how they are making connections that help them remember and interpret what they read. These connections, then, become part of what readers know. Like knowledge, strategies are embedded in schema. Thus, readers expand their strategy options as they read and embed new strategies within their repertoire of strategies.

3. Active readers monitor their understanding to see if it makes sense (Alexander & Jetton, 2000). They regularly monitor and therefore are aware of their understanding. They ask themselves if what they understand is making sense, or they monitor themselves by double-checking to see if they understand the important parts. If their interpretation does not make sense or is unclear, they examine where they lost meaning. Then they troubleshoot what interfered with understanding. As they revise their understanding, they actively monitor meaning. Sometimes they check what they know and compare it to what they are reading. Other times, they check their purposes to see if they are on the right track. As a result, they vary their strategies to remove difficulties as they construct meaning. The active readers use strategies like revising predictions, self-questioning, and clarifying as they monitor their understanding.

4. Active readers use their knowledge and perceptions within a situational context to select both their strategies and the information they use. In essence, literacy situations, both past and present situations (such as a home literacy interactions, the classroom group, friends talking on their way to school, a one-to-one tutoring session), frame how students interpret text. Active readers engage in literacy activities, so they define the literacy situation positively. Their situational interactions influence what students select as important to discuss, what they elaborate, what strategies they use, and their engagement in literacy (Au, 2002).

> Reading is an active process in which readers shift between sources of information (what they know and what the text says), elaborate meaning and strategies, check their interpretation (revising when appropriate), and frame their understanding within a situational context.

The following scenario illustrates the process of active reading when a reader encounters an unknown word. A text has a picture of a baseball diamond with a figure running toward second base at the top of a page and the following sentence at the bottom of the page: "The girl hit the home run."

From the picture of the baseball diamond and his past situations, Bobby guesses that the story is about a boy. However, when he reads the sentence, the graphic cue *g* instead of *b* helps him figure out that the story is about a girl rather than a boy. Bobby's initial hypothesis, that the story is about a boy, is based on his previous experiences with similar situations and stories.

The reader selects cues from the text and measures them against his own background knowledge and important textual information already established (*combines sources of information*). If the response is confirmed, or fits, reading continues. For example, when Bobby could not confirm the expected response in the baseball story because the word *girl* does not look like *boy*, he asked himself, "What word is like *boy* that begins with a *g*?" In other words, he wanted to know what word semantically and graphically fits (*monitors reading*).

Our experiences and the language used to describe them build our schema, or our personal worldview. Although in their own experience children may know that both boys and girls play baseball, they may view baseball as more associated with males because of the professional games they see on TV and the many baseball books available with male stars. Because of these experiences (*use of situational context*), Bobby, in the baseball story example, expected the main character to be a boy. He then revised the expected response of *boy* according to **grapho-phonic information**, and he read the sentence in the text as "The girl hit the home run." Reading this story caused the reader to refine the schema that "stories about baseball usually have boys for heroes" to be more specific, namely, that "stories about baseball usually have boys for heroes, but sometimes they have girls (*elaborate*)." With this experience, along with other similar experiences, Bobby began to elaborate strategies for reading and at the grading period was able to name some things good readers do when they read (*elaborate strategies*). See Figure 1–2.

The model just described can provide a framework for analyzing the behaviors of struggling readers. As Bobby did in the example, readers consider many factors within any given reading event to make sense of what they are reading. Thus, all readers "draw on their prior experiences, their interactions with other readers and writers, their knowledge of word meaning and of other text, their word identification strategies, and their understanding of textual features" (International Reading Association & National Council of Teachers of English, 1996, p. 3). This active process is at the heart of instructional decisions made by the diagnostic teacher. The report *Preventing Reading Difficulties* points out that "effective reading instruction is built on a foundation that recognizes that reading outcomes are determined by complex and multifaceted factors" (Snow et al., 1998, p. 313). Therefore, the diagnostic teacher examines the strategies and knowledge of struggling readers in

---

Figure 1–2   *Second-Grade Explanation of What Good Readers Do*

Name some things good readers do when they read.

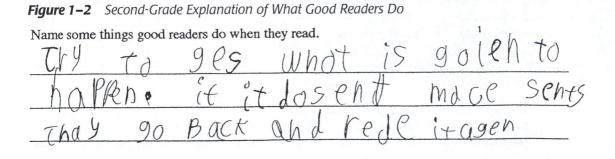

relation to active readers. Thus, a reading problem, rather than being a static deficit within the reader, is a set of strengths and weaknesses affected by interactions among many factors and instruction.

Struggling Readers

Struggling readers find constructing meaning with text overly challenging. While effective readers naturally combine sources of information, struggling readers vary in their use of strategies. The point of view of this text is that struggling readers often experience difficulty employing either a strategy or a skill, so they shift away from that information source. They compensate by using their strength and thus eliminate a need to use their troublesome knowledge source (Stanovich, 1986).

This overreliance on their strength often results in compensatory behaviors that actually inhibit rather than enhance the reader's understanding. For example, readers who easily learn to decode words and recall text-based information often develop the perception that reading is simply repeating a string of words from the text. They become bound by the text and *do not combine both the text and their experiences.* This behavior is often coupled with the likelihood that the student will be placed in demanding texts and asked to read fewer authentic texts (Allington, 2005). Effective readers elaborate both the content and their strategies, but when reading overly challenging texts, struggling readers cannot readily elaborate either the content or their strategy deployment. For example, if Bobby could not read the words *baseball* or *hit,* the sentence would have been difficult to read, and Bobby would have allocated most of his resources to constructing meaning. In this case, Bobby's *elaboration would be restricted,* and he would not expand his content knowledge (sometimes *girls* can be baseball heroes) and his strategy use ("When the word that I said doesn't look like the text, I can think of another word that fits").

After an extended period of failing to combine sources of information or elaboration strategies, struggling readers become accustomed to understanding only bits and pieces of what they are reading. They *refrain from monitoring* and passively read words without constructing meaning (Walker, 2003a). For instance, if Bobby had an extended period of time reading difficult text, he might have continued to read the story miscalling *boy* for *girl,* thus misconstruing a major character in the story. Habitual passive reading fails to build an expectation that reading is a strategic process in which readers bring together their resources to make sense of text. While effective readers readily monitor their understanding, struggling readers passively read text without checking understanding, thus compounding their reading difficulty.

If readers continually fail to construct appropriate meaning when reading, they alter how they perceive themselves within literacy situations (Schunk, 2003). They attribute their continued failure to an ability (a fixed characteristic) that they do not possess rather than to lack of a strategic process that they can acquire. This attitude reinforces the belief that if they try to read, they will fail; and if they fail again, they are admitting their lack of ability. Knowing they have strong capabilities in other academic situations, such as in mathematics, these struggling readers reduce their effort, cease to try, and thus disengage from literacy activities. By disengaging, they can attribute failure to "not having tried" rather than to their lack of ability. Effective readers can choose among different strategies as they read, while struggling readers come to view *literacy situations as self-defeating* and decrease their engagement.

> Rather than actively constructing meaning, struggling readers perpetually read with one or more of the following characteristics. They (a) overrely on a single information source; (b) read difficult text with little or no elaboration of content and strategies; (c) read without monitoring meaning, resulting in passive reading; or (d) define reading as a failure situation and decrease their engagement.

Instructional Process

The goal of diagnostic teaching is to establish exceptional and appropriate learning opportunities for struggling readers. If the students use effective strategies and make adjustments for themselves, reading varied texts and responding in groups may be sufficient for them. Struggling readers, however, have difficulty making adjustments and employing effective strategies. Less proficient readers often need to be shown exactly how to use effective reading strategies. They need instruction that is modified to fit their learning. The diagnostic teacher, as a result, continually assesses what and how struggling readers are learning and makes instructional adjustments to ensure successful reading. The process of adjusting instruction to ensure learning is called **mediating learning**.

> The diagnostic teacher mediates learning, which means she adjusts instruction to ensure successful interpretation of text.

The diagnostic teacher specifically selects activities that will directly mediate learning for each struggling reader. She establishes what the student already knows and adjusts instruction to overlap his present knowledge with new information. Furthermore, she evaluates how the students have learned to establish strategy strengths. A struggling reader often relies heavily on his strengths; therefore, the diagnostic teacher selects a technique that allows him to demonstrate these strengths. During instruction, the diagnostic teacher discusses these strengths with the student and shows him how to use these strengths in various literacy situations. As the student experiences success with the new reading task, the diagnostic teacher selects techniques that have a more balanced instructional approach. This approach allows the diagnostic teacher to use the learner's strengths (what he already knows and does) to show him how to use his weaker processes when reading.

Diagnostic teaching techniques were developed from different theories of reading and learning. Four are described briefly here:

- *Text-Based View.* Simply stated, this view of reading focuses on the text as the major instructional concern of teachers. Learning to read is viewed as a series of associative connections that are reinforced until they become automatic. Letters are linked to form words, words are linked to form sentences, and sentences are linked to form ideas; that is, the parts of reading are put together to form the whole. Making text associations shapes the learner's response.

  This theory is often associated with a skills model of instruction. In this approach, the teacher teaches letter sounds and their symbols first. Then she demonstrates how to put the sounds together to make a word. Next, she shows students how to use words to make sentences, then the paragraph and the passage.

- *Reader-Based View.* This view of reading focuses on reader-based processing where readers make meaning as they read. The reader is a major instructional concern of teachers. The reader is viewed as an active thinker who predicts what the author is saying. Then he samples textual information to check his predictions. Readers may actually verify their ideas about what the author is saying with a minimal amount of textual cues. Thus, reading is viewed as negotiating meaning between an author and a reader. In the reader-based view, the reader creates his response.

  The whole-language philosophy uses reader-based processing. The focus is on the child as an active learner who naturally seeks meaning. Therefore, this philosophy focuses on creating authentic learning experiences situated within a powerful literacy context. Within this context, learners make sense of the world and use their own understanding to figure out the multiple aspects of language. In this approach, the teacher provides a book-rich environment and responds to children as they make inquiries about language.

- *Interactive View.* This view stems from cognitive constructionism where readers actively construct meaning. The reader is viewed as using both reader-based processing and text-based processing to form interpretations of text. Although he is active, his predictions are formed on the basis of what the text says and what he already knows about this information; that is, reading is viewed as constructing meaning using various information sources. The interactive view focuses on the active–constructive nature of reading as the major instructional concern of teachers. In this way, they focus on how the reader strategically shifts between the text and his schema to construct his response.

  This theory is often associated with a balanced view of instruction. However, in this view of balanced instruction, teachers make sure students have time for various aspects of strategy development (figuring out meaning and words). Furthermore, in this approach, teachers focus on having children read complete stories and passages with the teacher guiding some of the learning and students using strategies to figure out words and meanings.

- *Socio-Cultural View.* In this view, learning and instruction involve social interactions among individuals. Therefore, it focuses on situating understanding as a major instructional concern of teachers. As a reader discusses his response, he uses his ideas about what he personally understands bearing in mind the advanced ideas of others. During discussions and verbal interactions, he reconstructs his understanding as a result of rethinking his ideas and those of his peers. Thus, reading is viewed as a socio-cultural process in which the reader along with others jointly construct an interpretation using their shared knowledge and personal feelings, framing and reframing responses according to the situational context.

  The diagnostic teaching techniques associated with differing points of view can be matched to learner strengths and needs. The diagnostic teacher *chooses* techniques for guided reading based on strengths and allows the student to read authentic literature to construct meaning. On the other hand, she is cognizant of techniques that would develop the strategies and skills the learner needs to learn. The diagnostic teacher's point of view for instruction is based on the classroom and student responses to instruction; however, as she plans for instruction, the diagnostic teacher *balances* her instruction.

■ *Balanced Instructional View.* Balanced instruction requires the thoughtful orchestration of instructional procedures. It requires not equal time for every type of activity but that teachers view the activities as equally important. Thus, the diagnostic teacher strives for *balance* in her instruction. She uses multiple views of reading and "makes thoughtful choices each day about the best way to help each child become a better reader and writer" (Spiegel, 1998, p. 116). The diagnostic teacher readily *balances* her instruction among the various views of reading, always mindful of learners' needs. The diagnostic teacher *balances* both text-based approaches and reader-based approaches to plan and modify her instruction. She *balances* supported, teacher-directed instruction with learner-centered, inquiry approaches. Likewise, she *balances* techniques that promote active discussion in a group of peers with settings in which the student responds on his own. The diagnostic teacher uses her understanding of students, instruction, and assessment to select instructional techniques that allow students to use their strengths. Then she uses these strengths to show students how to solve their reading problems.

Assessment Process

In diagnostic teaching, assessment is continuous. As the student learns, diagnostic information is immediately incorporated into the lesson. The teacher thus deals with the problem as she teaches, not after she has gathered the facts. For example, a teacher discovered at midpoint in her instruction that a student could not sequence the events of the story. Rather than continue trying to teach using the planned instructional format of predict, read to find out, and summarize, she introduced a story map (see "Story Mapping" in part 2), a visual arrangement of the sequence of events. Using the story map, the student and teacher reviewed information from the beginning of the story and placed it on the map. In the course of instruction, the lesson format was changed to summarize what was on the map, make a prediction, and read to find out what happened next. The final step became to add to the story map and tell how the new information fits into the story and how it fits with the previous prediction. The lesson format changed because the teacher assessed the difficulty during the lesson and *changed the instructional conditions*, or format. This modification increased student learning.

> Diagnostic teaching means that assessment is continuous as the student is learning. The diagnostic teacher adjusts instruction as she teaches, not after she has gathered the facts.

Diagnostic teaching means that assessment occurs during the lesson. Thus, the assessment information derived is both practical and valid because it is gained through authentic literacy activities. Furthermore, the assessment is efficient because learning does not stop in order to test. The assessment process becomes an integral part of the learning.

To lead students to more efficient reading, the diagnostic teacher looks for recurring patterns among the variables of the reading event (see chapter 2 for further discussion) and uses this information in her teaching. She changes her instruction in order to mediate learning, thus showing students how to use what they already know to solve more challenging reading tasks. This process leads readers to improved reading.

As materials and activities are adjusted to the needs of the struggling reader, the diagnostic teacher maintains a close match between the text and the student's reading, making sure that the text is not overly challenging. Although this precision permeates all instruction, the degree to which the diagnostic teacher uses continuous assessment is not practical for the classroom teacher. The immediate adjustments needed are often multiple and difficult for a classroom to manage on the spot. The classroom teacher, however, makes some adjustments as she teaches based on observation. Afterward, she records observations and collects classroom projects to evaluate student learning. Over a period of time, she uses portfolios and observations records to gather data on student learning. Whether in a large classroom, small groups, or individual tutoring, both classroom teachers and the diagnostic teacher assess how the readers are learning and adjust their instruction. These adjustments provide excellent sources for assessment data. Thus, assessment becomes an integral part of teaching.

Diagnostic Teaching Process

Diagnostic teaching is a dynamic process in which decisions about what the reader needs change as the student learns. Initial diagnostic information can be gathered through screening or from classroom instruction. This initial information is then expanded through informal assessment (see chapter 5). The informal assessment allows the diagnostic teacher to identify the major processing patterns and establish an instructional range that is challenging for the student. From this information, the diagnostic teacher makes tentative decisions about instruction.

As she teaches, the diagnostic teacher also analyzes the effects of the variables of the reading event (see chapter 2) to help her formulate her hypotheses. She gathers and analyzes further data about the strategies the student uses to construct meaning with text (see chapter 6). After the lesson, she reflects on the information she has gathered, the reading event where instruction occurred, and her role (see chapter 3) during instruction to formulate and refine her diagnostic hypotheses. Reflecting on this information, the diagnostic teacher selects materials (see chapter 9) and techniques (see chapter 10) to adjust instruction in order to mediate learning for the struggling reader.

The diagnostic teacher then instructs a lesson. The lesson can be conducted in an individual setting or within an instructional group. In any setting, the teacher assesses the specific reader's growth during instruction. To establish the amount of the reader's change, the teacher assesses the reader's growth that resulted from the instructional adjustment (see chapter 7 for the format to assess growth). If no change took place in the reader's performance, the diagnostic teacher cycles back through the process and instructs another lesson based on the new diagnostic information gathered during instruction. If the reader's behavior did change, then the diagnostic teacher establishes instructional conditions for this reader, which includes much more than whether the student's learning increased. Because the diagnostic teacher collects data as she teaches, she also analyzes how she modified her initial plan in order to mediate learning. After the lesson, she assesses the amount and type of support (**teacher investment**; Feuerstein & Feuerstein, 1991) the teacher needed to give in order to make a change in the student's reading behavior. As she teaches, the teacher alters her instruction systematically, providing support for student learning. The amount of teacher investment indicates whether the selected techniques are working and when they are not (namely, when a high degree of teacher investment is required). If a high degree of teacher investment is required, the diagnostic teacher also recycles through the process, selecting new instructional approaches. Likewise, the diagnostic teacher can orchestrate reading tasks in a variety of ways, such as introducing graphic aids (story maps) or asking students to read aloud. These changes are made to foster strategic reading. Again, the teacher records the adjustments (**task modifications**; Feuerstein & Feuerstein, 1991) that she devises during the diagnostic lesson. If a high degree of task modification is needed, the diagnostic teacher may choose to recycle and select a new instructional technique. In some cases, the task modification may be precisely what is needed to increase student learning, and the teacher then establishes these modifications as part of the instructional conditions for the student.

The decision-making cycle of the diagnostic teacher illustrated in Figure 1–1 is a continuous process where instruction informs the assessment and subsequent instructional choices.

Summary

The process of diagnostic teaching uses instruction to understand how the struggling reader approaches the reading event. As instruction is adjusted to ensure that readers construct meaning with text, the teacher gathers data. Furthermore, she views reading as an active process in which the reader uses what he knows to interpret what the text says within the social interactions of the literacy event. Therefore, the diagnostic teacher uses the student's strengths (knowledge and strategies) to lead the student to integrate new information as well as new strategies into his reading repertoire. She then assesses the reader's change as a result of her instruction. She uses her reflections about instructional adjustments to decide on further instruction. These decisions become increasingly more refined as the diagnostic teacher considers the reading event, evaluates the strategies of the struggling reader, and matches those with appropriate techniques.

2 The Reading Event

Diagnostic teaching identifies instructional alternatives that enhance reading performance for struggling readers. To do this, the diagnostic teacher focuses on the multiple aspects of the reading event. He looks at the patterns of interactions during all aspects of the reading event (see Figure 2–1). Reading difficulties can arise from interactions among the task, text, technique, and the situational context. These are the variables of the reading event the diagnostic teacher can adjust. Reading difficulty is not a deficit in a reader but rather results from interactions that occur among all variables in the reading event.

During instruction, the diagnostic teacher analyzes five variables of the reading event—task, text, reader, technique, and the situational context—and evaluates their effect on the reader's performance. The variables do not act in isolation but affect one another during the course of instruction. The diagnostic teacher evaluates how changing any one of them affects a reader's response. As he adjusts instruction, he establishes the instructional conditions for literacy learning.

Through repeated instructional opportunities, the teacher evaluates the interactions of these five variables. During the lesson he evaluates the diagnostic task (what he asks the reader to do) and the technique (how he asks her to complete the task). He evaluates the text (what is read) and how it affects reading performance. The diagnostic teacher evaluates the reader's knowledge, strategies, and engagement during the reading event. Equally important, he evaluates the situational context or where instruction occurs. As shown in Figure 2–2, these five variables influence reading performance during any given reading event and continuously interact as instruction occurs. This chapter elaborates on each variable.

Task

As teachers develop reading experiences in classrooms, they ask students to complete various literacy tasks. Sometimes, the task are easy to complete, but sometimes they are misunderstood, and the student gets off task. Other times, the task requires a student use a weakness rather than a strength. Thus, the literacy task affects the students' reading performance.

Figure 2–1   *The Decision-Making Cycle of Diagnostic Teaching*

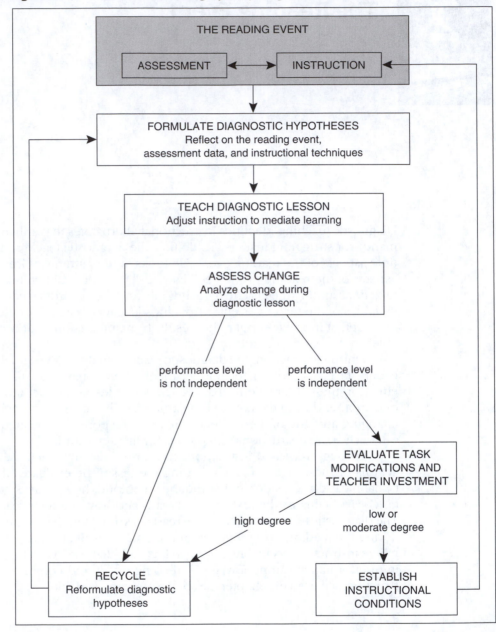

Purpose of the Task

Students are often mystified when trying to figure out the purpose of the task they are to complete during an instructional lesson. For instance, Bobbie finished a report on lime. Then she looked up and realized that she had written about lime, the stone, and she was in a nutrition class. Thus, knowing the purpose means approaching texts with a specific goal. If Bobbie had elaborated the purpose to include a report on lime, the fruit, as the goal, this situation would not have happened. When

Figure 2–2   *The Reading Event*

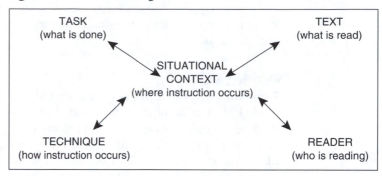

possible, the diagnostic teacher asks students to read a text from a specific point of view, depending on what the text might suggest. Thus, reading tasks come in many shapes and sizes. For instance, a teacher can ask a student to read a workbook page and complete the word recognition task. In one class, Rosa could not figure out this task because she was bilingual and did not know the English word for the pictures on the page. The task was a mystery to her. To demystify reading tasks, the diagnostic teacher needs to create authentic, functional tasks in his classroom. Authentic tasks have been found to provide opportunities for students to discuss ideas both before and after reading. This type of task is generally more cognitively challenging and engaging (Hiebert, 1994). Teachers need to choose activities that will show children the variety of functions that reading can serve: reading for pleasure, reading for information, or reading to remember. There are days we do all three. Many people read for pleasure at night, getting involved in an exciting novel. Others might read for information on a daily basis. People often read the newspaper to find out information about current events, new books and movies, and, of course, sports. On the other hand, doctors read their medical journals to remember the information in order to treat patients with the most current medical technology. Even though tasks have different purposes, they are often understood in terms of the context in which they are embedded. If learners complete authentic tasks that are familiar and functional, they will generate responses easily and view literacy as a challenging cognitive task (Turner, 1997). However, if the task is contrived to teach an isolated part of reading like a timed test to measure fluency, then students must define the task as well as its function. When Sharon did not know that her reading was timed, she read slowly to make sure she remembered important facts. However, she found out later she was being timed and became upset because she had not known what the task was. Thus, many teachers evaluate precisely this factor: the rapidity with which students can figure out the task. Later that day, in the context of assessment using an informal reading inventory, the teacher did not say, "I will ask you questions after you finish reading." He had Sharon read silently not realizing she had just completed a timed reading (different task). After Sharon quickly read the text (a previous task purpose), the teacher started asking questions. Sharon responded immediately, "I did not know I was going to answer questions on this. Let me read it again." Sharon did not know the purpose of the task and therefore read fast without paying attention to the meaning of the text. Thus, many contrived tasks make instruction less effective for the struggling reader. In daily reading tasks, people are not timed when they read, and they do not answer specific questions; rather, they read and discuss their interpretations with family and friends.

Mode of Task

The mode of task that students are asked to complete also affects their reading performance. For instance, the diagnostic teacher uses either *silent or oral reading* during the diagnostic lesson.

Oral Reading

Sometimes oral reading is performed for students to prove a prediction that they made before a silent reading of a text; thus, students are reading material aloud that they previously read silently. Therefore, they use already-obtained meaning to facilitate their oral reading. Other times students are asked to read aloud a poem or a play. This is a different task because the passage has usually been rehearsed, so their oral reading is fluent. At other times, however, the oral reading occurs on an initial reading of the passage, which places an additional demand on the processing of information (Allington, 2005). In this instance, readers must attend not only to meaning but also to oral production of the text. Whether the text is read orally or silently is a task condition.

Silent Reading

Silent reading is the most common mode of reading. People read the newspaper silently. They understand the passages because silent reading is more in line with constructing meaning with text. To understand how students comprehend material, it is better to evaluate silent reading. When the students read silently, they can devote their attention to the meaning of the text.

Writing

Within the reading event, teachers often have students respond to reading by writing. Writing changes the task mode from answering questions to creating a response. Writing a summary increases reading achievement by asking students to collapse information. Further, writing is a task used to respond personally. Writing about reading changes the mode of the task. Writing also changes the task demands.

Task Demands

As the diagnostic teacher varies the task demands, the students produce widely varied responses. These varied responses are a direct result of the task demands of questions and probes.

Question Type

As has been mentioned, after reading a paragraph and being asked *literal questions*, students often ask for a second chance once they know what the teacher wants for an answer. During the lesson, students who are repeatedly asked one type of question pay more attention to that type of information (Hiebert, 1994). Many teachers use comprehension questions to ask about the information in an undifferentiated way. This kind of questioning can be purposeful but unfortunately results in all content being viewed evenly, as if all aspects of the text were equally important. In short, this type of questioning does not help the student develop concepts about the content. For example, Tracy had only responded with information from the text in the early grades. Both the texts and the teacher required little more. Now in fourth grade, the teacher asked broad *open-ended questions and nonliteral questions* to encourage a deeper processing of text. Tracy did not know how to respond. This type of questioning required her to think in a different way. She was used to reading the text and answering questions that were directly found in the text. This required very little text processing. Research on effective teaching has also revealed that *higher-level questioning* increases student reading achievement. Higher-level questioning includes questions dealing with the theme, the characters, and events as well as asking for predictions (Taylor, Pearson, Peterson, Rodriguez, 2003). Thus, the type of question asked can narrow or expand a reader's purpose for reading, either limiting or opening up thinking.

Production Demands

Reading comprehension can be taught and assessed using different formats that require distinctive production demands.

Direct Questions

The teacher can use direct questions—"How did Johnny solve his problem?"—or he can ask students to retell the story—"Tell me this story in your own words." However, the kind of information required and the organization of the response make these tasks quite different. Direct questioning asks for information from the text that relates specifically to the stem of the question. For example, Janet was asked, "What is the main idea?" She was mystified because she didn't know exactly what "a main idea" was; therefore, she did not respond.

Retelling

However, when Janet was asked to tell the story in her own words, she began by telling a brief main idea and the theme before she proceeded to retell the story. An oral retelling asks students to organize a response according to what they think is important. Janet thought the theme was very important, so she started with this. Retelling a story usually involves an elaborated response.

Response

Personal response lets students talk freely about their reactions, thoughts, and feelings about the text they read. When giving a response, the students cannot be wrong, so they take more risks and actually talk more. They often connect their personal experiences with the characters and actions.

    These three types of task have different production demands. Answers to direct questions frequently require a short, constrained response, while retelling and response let the students use their own interpretations to discuss the passage or story.

Reasoning Requirements

Likewise, the type of response can require different types of reasoning. Sometimes the diagnostic teacher uses a series of direct, literal questions: "Who were the characters? What did they do? What was the outcome?" Answering these questions is different from answering questions about the overall theme: "What was the author trying to tell you in this story? Do you think the author has a reason for including this character?" The two types of questions require different kinds of reasoning. The first group of questions requires the students to recall factual information stated in the text. The second group requires that readers use inferential thinking about the author's intended meaning. The readers have to use several parts of the text to construct a rationale for their answers. For example, Kendra was asked to retell the story, and she told a short synopsis of the story. However, when asked about the theme, she simply said, "I don't know." She simply had not thought deeply about the story. To end instruction on a high note, the teacher asked Kendra if she had experienced a situation like the main character. She elaborated on her own experiences. Kendra could use both the text and background knowledge, but she did not connect the two in order to think deeply. These last questions ask students to respond personally to information in the text: "Have you had experiences similar to Jack's? Did you feel the same way?" Each of these formats required different types of reasoning.

Question Order

Besides the reasoning requirements, the order of the questions asked by the teacher can also change the task. Questions can probe a logical sequence of story development, they can require nothing more than a random recall of unrelated facts, or they can ask students to make an inference to their own experiences. These three tasks are quite different. Questions that probe a logical sequence of story events cause students to think about story development and, therefore, increase their comprehension of the story (Duke & Pearson, 2002) as well as increase their knowledge of story structure. For example, two teachers were teaching the same story. When the class finished reading, Bill asked his students to first discuss where the story took place and who were the important characters. Then he asked what problem the main characters had and so on. This promoted higher understanding because the questions were related to what had just been read. However, unrelated literal questions are harder to answer because they offer no relationship among the responses. Bob asked his students a series of questions about episodes he thought were very interesting and contributed to the problem resolution. The question-and-answer session went when fairly well, but the students did not understand how this story or other stories develop. Bob's ordering of the questions did not allow the students to construct a coherent explanation of the story as a whole. Furthermore, asking students to relate story comprehension to their own experiences can prompt them to associate what was read to what they already know and thereby increase their comprehension of the text. However, Mark asked students to retell the story in order with the facts only. Then he asked students if they had the same experiences. When Mark taught *The Stranger* by Chris Van Allsburg, Mark could have increased comprehension if he had asked about their similar experiences before the story. Mark could have begun the lesson by asking, "Does any know what a harvest is?" If most of the class knew, his discussion might be brief. But if the students lived only in an urban area, he would spend more time explaining a harvest. He could use pictures in the book, dowload photographs from the Web, or show a short movie. Many times, asking what students know about a topic before beginning to read rather than after reading increases their story understanding. The order of the questions that the diagnostic teacher asks change the task, making it harder or easier for the students to understand stories.

Text Availability

Likewise, the task changes if the readers have the text available for answers. The difference in the responses when the text is available and when it is not becomes a task condition. Many assessments are completed without the text available. However, in real-life situations, we often have the information in front of us when we talk with others. Therefore, if the teacher prompts the student to clarify a response or asks the student to search the text, he influences comprehension and changes the original task demands. This change often increases comprehension. When the teacher does not probe incomplete student responses, a valuable learning occasion may be lost. When possible, the diagnostic teacher probes the students' responses and records the task modifications that increase reader performance.

In summary, the task can vary during reading instruction. As tasks change, the way the reader perceives the purpose of the task and approaches the text may change. Likewise, the task can be oral or silent reading of sentences, paragraphs, or stories. After students read the story, the task can vary from answering direct questions to elaborate, unaided recall of textual information and free response. Questioning can also vary from literal teacher-generated questions to nonliteral student-generated self-questions. Furthermore, responses can require different kinds of reasoning; they can vary from factual recall to personal response. Sometimes responses require students to locate the answer in the text, while at other times they do not use it to answer questions.

Consequently, different task conditions result in various instructional procedures that can be modified by the diagnostic teacher. Altering any of the task conditions changes the nature of the information obtained during a diagnostic lesson. It is the diagnostic teacher's responsibility to analyze the major task features of the diagnostic lesson and vary them (when necessary) to enhance the students' ability to construct meaning with text. The following list provides task considerations that establish what the student is asked to do and can be used to focus the teacher's reflective thinking about the reading event:

- Purpose for the task
- Mode of the task
    Oral, silent, or written
- Question type
    Literal, nonliteral, open ended, and higher level
- Production requirements
    Short one-word answer, retelling, and personal response
- Reasoning requirements of task
    Factual recall, inference, and personal experience
- Availability of text

What the teacher asks students to do affects the kind of information he obtains about them. Many beginning teachers evaluate only oral reading and believe that students have no reading problem. If the teacher had asked questions after silent reading, he would have found that the students did not comprehend what they read silently. They did not know how to think about what they were reading. The diagnostic teacher thinks about what he asks students to do when they read. Then he formulates tentative decisions about the students' reading processes.

Text

Traditionally, variation in a student's reading is attributed to the difficulty of the text, caluculated by using a readability formula. Diagnostic teachers still use readability formulas (see chapter 9 for further discussion) to make an initial decision about how easy or hard the text is to read. However, the influence the text has on reading performance is much more complex. The diagnostic teacher, therefore, systematically evaluates what the student is reading, focusing on specific aspects.

Content and Background Knowledge Required

Content

The content of text varies greatly, from simple stories with familiar topics to the more complex information of content area texts. For example, the novel might be about a particular country and the narrative would involve accurate information about the country and time period in which the novel takes place. The cohesive framework of knowledge that is used also affects the text's readability. In sciences like physics, the content can be complex, making the text harder to understand. The content of the text can influence the student's reading performance.

Background Knowledge Required

Students differ in what they already know about the topic they are reading. Content that is familiar is easier to read and increases understanding of the new information. The diagnostic teacher analyzes the content of the text and how much prior knowledge students need to know before they read the text. For example, the sentence "She wore a parka" requires more prior knowledge on the part of the reader than "She wore a parka to protect her from the cold wind." The diagnostic teacher evaluates the effect that text content and required prior knowledge have on reader performance.

Density of Information

The diagnostic teacher thinks about the possible textual characteristics that affect reading performance. He thinks about the influences of the density of the information. The length and complexity of the passage as well as its coherence, words, and structure influence how dense the information load is. Many short passages are extremely dense, requiring an extraordinary amount of comprehension in a short span. Longer passages, on the other hand, often contain examples, diagrams, and explanations that aid comprehension. For some students, however, reading a long passage orally often reduces comprehension because of the attention demanded by oral production over a long period of time. Other students' strategies improve as they read longer passages. The diagnostic teacher thinks about the density of information and how passage length and use of examples affect how a student reads.

Text Formats

Reading performance also changes with different text formats (narrative or expository). Each text format requires different kinds of reading strategies.

Narrative Text

Narrative text is organized using characters who have problems that are solved. The story line is developed through characters' actions, consequences of their actions, and events that occur in solving the problem. Narrative text represents life situations that appear bigger than life so as to catch the reader's interest.

Expository Texts

Expository texts are organized around main ideas and the supporting details that explain the main idea. These aspects represent a framework for a knowledge base about the topic (e.g., Japan, river networks, or clouds). Even expository texts that adults read on a daily basis (e.g., newspapers and magazine articles) have the structure of main ideas and supporting details. Directions (e.g., cooking, setting up a television, or navigating a Web search) have a different structure-specific vocabulary of the parts, usually shown on a diagram, that are listed along with the steps. Students learn this organizational structure so that they can read directions more easily. Teachers and students also read textbook information, which is usually expository in nature. For example, these texts represent science, social studies, and mathematics information. Because each text format is organized differently, readers do not have the same experiences with them, thus increasing the variability of their performance (Pearson & Camperell, 1994).

Coherent Organization and Style

The way the text is structurally organized, moreover, influences what is remembered (Alexander & Jetton, 2000). Some texts are well organized using structure of the content, while others are more random in the organization.

Logical Organization

Authors who logically organize the text using the expected formats for narrative or expository text facilitate reader performance. If a text follows a logical organization, then it is easier to comprehend and remember. Thus, the style the author uses will affect reader performance. High-quality literature is usually well structured using the literary aspects of setting, characters, plot, resolution, and theme (Rasinski & Padak, 2004).

Style

Expository text is written in many different styles. When expository text is written in a more engaging style (more like a novel), it is also more easily remembered. Thus, coherent organization and engaging style affect reading performance.

Grammatical Complexity

Grammatical complexity also affects constructing meaning with text. Some texts are constructed of simple sentences that require the reader to infer causality. For example, the pair of sentences "The lamp fell" and "The cat ran" requires that the reader infer that the dog ran because the chair fell. Other texts are constructed with more complex sentences that reveal causality and thus facilitate comprehension. The wording "The cat ran because the lamp fell" describes the relationship between the cat running and the lamp falling. Sometimes the simple sentences do not tell a readily comprehensible story. If the sentences are combined to form a well-structured story and connections between ideas are explicitly made, text is easier to understand.

Predictablity of Sentences

Another aspect of grammatic complexity is the predictability of the sentences. Authors have their own style of writing, including their use of grammar and word choices. Many short novels by the same author have a predictable sentence structure that can improve reading. Texts that contain repeated language patterns also increase reading because the child can predict a word by using the pattern of the language (Fountas & Pinnell, 1996). For example, the language pattern in the following paragraph allows readers to use a minimal amount of visual cues to guess the words: "There was an old fisherman who swallowed a shark. He swallowed the shark to catch the piranha. He swallowed the piranha to catch the crayfish. He swallowed the crayfish to catch the gnat. He swallowed the gnat as he yawned on the shore."

Word Choices

Types of word choices affect comprehension of text. Some texts have words that are easy to read but do not convey the exact meaning. For example, "This boy had that" uses easy words, but it does not describe the exact meaning of the story. In another text, the words may be harder to read but more precise in conveying the intended meaning of the text: "The tall boy had the ice cream cone." This sentence uses harder words, but the meaning is clearer because the words are more precise.

During initial reading instruction, word choices are highly related to reading performance. Word choices including both meaning and word patterns can affect student learning. For children who have profited from instruction in phonics, a text that is decodable is easier to read ("The pig went to dig a hole") than a text that consists primarily of sight words ("The children have gone to the house") (Barr, Blachowicz, Bates, & Katz, 2007). As children apply the rules of the phonetic system to a text that has a high percentage of sight words, the error pattern will reveal a set of problems different from what might appear if the text contained decodable words that followed the rules they had been taught (see chapter 6).

The diagnostic teacher thinks about the words in the text. He evaluates whether the words can be easily decoded using phonic rules. If the students were taught to read using a sight-word approach (see "Sight-Word Approach" in part 2), the diagnostic teacher evaluates whether the words in the text are the words that students have been taught in the program. If so, students can use this knowledge to read the unfamiliar text. They figure out a word by thinking, "What word do I already know that starts with a *b*?" If the words are unknown, the diagnostic teacher checks to see if the new words have similar letter patterns to the words that the students already know. If the new words have the same pattern as the known words, students can figure out a word by thinking, "What word do I already know that looks like this word?" However, if many words are unfamiliar or words do not have patterns similar to known words, students will stumble over words, substituting words that make sense but do not look like the words in the story. Therefore, the diagnostic teacher evaluates the words in the text to assess their influence on student performance.

The text can help or hinder reading performance. The kind of text that is read will affect the information the teacher gathers about students' reading. For example, an informal reading inventory placed a student at the sixth-grade reading level; however, this same student had difficulty when she read the 10-page story in the sixth-grade reader. Three text characteristics had changed. The content had changed from information about sunflowers to a story about a boy who was cleaning his room. The text length had changed from short paragraphs to a long story. The text format had changed from expository to narrative.

A reflective teacher looks closely at the kind of text he has asked students to read. He asks himself, "Which features of the text will affect students' reading?" Then he asks, "Have these same features affected the reading before?" In other words, "Is it a consistent problem?"

In conclusion, a variety of textual characteristics affect student reading performance. Text content and the background knowledge of the reader—as well as the density of information and the elaboration of information by the use of examples, pictures, diagrams, and headings—influence student performance. Equally important are the passage format (expository or narrative) and the organizational structure of the text. Furthermore, an engaging style (whether the text is expository or narrative) facilitates comprehension of the text. Coherent organization, grammatical complexity, and word choices affect how the student constructs meaning. In other words, the diagnostic teacher examines the text to evaluate these features which that affect student reading performance:

- Content and background knowledge required
- Density of information
    Passage length and use of examples, graphic organizer, and so on
- Passage format
    Expository or narrative
- Organizational structure and style
- Grammatical complexity
    Predictable sentence patterns
- Word choices
    Distinctive meanings and word patterns

Reader

Bringing to the task and the text their own knowledge and strategies, learners construct meaning in distinctively different ways; therefore, the diagnostic teacher observes students' interactions and reading behaviors within the reading event to assess learner differences. Readers differ not only on what they already know (knowledge-based dimensions) but also on how they integrate new information into what they already know (strategy-based dimensions). Likewise, readers differ in their participation (engagement dimension) in literacy events.

Knowledge-Based Dimensions

Initially, the diagnostic teacher evaluates knowledge-based dimensions. As students talk in a classroom during an interview or as students retell a story, the diagnostic teacher develops a sense of the students' language facility.

Language Facility

Some students have a well-developed language system and use sophisticated language as they talk. Paula, who had many social interactions with her parents and their friends outside of school, used highly developed language when she related information about how chickens hatch an egg. Her language structures were precise, and her vocabulary was quite sophisticated. Cheryl, who lived on a farm and had many experiences raising chickens, used very stilted language and simple words. Both her mother and father had dropped out of high school. She had minimal daily interactions with other people, so she did not develop a vocabulary to express her experiences. She talked using short sentences, indicating that she had little knowledge of complex language structures. Rosa, on the other hand, speaks broken English because her family moved to the United States only a year ago. She speaks Spanish at home, and she has little practice with English-language structures. Rosa talks extremely slowly because she has to translate every word. Likewise, Rosa has many experiences raising chickens but does not know how to use the language to explain these experiences. Although she is familiar with eggs hatching and can describe it exceptionally well in Spanish, she does not have the same language facility to express it in English. These three students are very different in their language facility, but they are not different in their experiences. Others, however, do not have experiences with the topic. Rhonda, who lives in a condo in a big city, has no knowledge of chickens. She has never seen chickens except as meat in a grocery story. She could not discuss the topic because she lacked experience with it.

Word and World Knowledge

Some students have a rich variety of experiences but are not able to explain these experiences because of their lack of knowledge with language structures (language facility) and word meaning (word knowledge). On the other hand, Rhonda had very limited knowledge of chickens. She could not discuss the egg-hatching process because she had never seen an egg hatch or read about it in a book or magazine or on the Web. Rhonda, like many other students, simply lacked experience with topics discussed in school. Students with limited experiences are said to lack world knowledge. Consequently, when students have a wealth of experiences (world knowledge) and the ability to talk about the experiences (world knowledge), they are organizing and classifying their worlds of experiences using sophisticated language structures and precise word knowledge. When they read, they are able to use their prior experience and the words they know to express them. Other students have limited experiences or limited word knowledge, resulting in difficulty when reading. Students' knowledge of the world and the words they use to describe their experiences influence comprehension and word identification.

Reading Stage

A budding reader acquires certain knowledges of skills that place that reader in a specific stage of reading development. This stage represents a level of development for a student who understands certain major tasks. After meeting with students, the teacher establishes a range of performance that involves conducting an informal reading assessment to identify a reading level for instruction. This is often accomplished by giving an informal reading inventory (see chapter 5). The reading stage is identified by matching the readability of the text with the level of reading performance for the students. This instructional reading level can be matched to a stage of reading development (see chapter 5 for full discussion). For example, Rhonda's teacher gave her some initial assessments and found that she read at the second-grade level. She read the words fluently, but her comprehension of the passage was very weak. The teacher thought about the task in the second stage of reading (see chapter 5) because students reading at the second grade level are usually in the second stage of reading. For comprehension, this stage focuses on story organization. Therefore, the diagnostic teacher decided to use story maps (see part 2) to help Rhonda understand stories.

Skill Knowledge

As the instruction begins, the diagnostic teacher looks for patterns within the reading event to analyze skill knowledge. All students demonstrate some print identification skills (e.g., sight-word knowledge, phonic knowledge, context use, and fluency). For instance, many struggling readers have difficulty with using decoding (phonics) when they read. Jenny knew a lot of sight words and how to use sentence context to figure out words. Yet when she encountered several unfamiliar words in a row, she could not use context and could not recognize these words immediately. When evaluated, Jenny did not have the skill to take sounds in words apart or put sounds together, both of which are prerequisite skills for phonics. Jenny profited from a little bit of practice with phonemic awareness and a great deal of instruction using the language experience approach (see part 2). Language experience was initially used so that Jenny could regain a sense of fluent reading, as she had read at a frustration level for 2 years. Later the teacher adapted the directed reading/thinking activity to include a review of problem words before reading a passage so that the teacher could use Jenny's strength of predicting using her background knowledge. The diagnostic teacher compares skill knowledge in relation to how the student constructs meaning. Comprehension skills (e.g., identifying the main idea or problem, key details or events, and the theme or the resolution) are also evaluated during instruction. For instance, Jenny had a tremedous knowledge of the world because she had traveled many places and engaged in hands-on science projects with her father. These language strengths enhanced her comprehension, and she often appeared to her teacher as a wizard. Initially, the diagnostic teacher had no idea that Jenny had difficulty with word identification because her parents rehearsed spelling words and she scored perfectly. After she assessed Jenny, she realized that word reading was difficult and that Jenny was using her background knowledge when answering questions in the classroom. Students vary in the skills they know and how extensive that knowledge is.

Strategy-based Dimensions

The knowledge-based dimensions are accentuated by differences in readers' strategy deployment. Students differ in their strategy deployment (Paris, Lipson, & Wixson, 1994). Some students select meaning cues, while others select graphic cues. Some students rely heavily on their background knowledge, while others use only the text to form hypotheses while they are reading. Some students revise and monitor their model of meaning readily, while others need explicit information in the text before they revise their models.

Students' use of strategies can be evaluated by their patterns of verbal responses and miscues (words miscalled) as they read and answer questions. Looking for consistent patterns, the diagnostic teacher notices students' selection strategies (the way they find cues and use sources of information), monitoring strategies (the way they check their understanding), and elaboration strategies (the way they relate new information to what they already know).

Selection Strategies

Initially, the diagnostic teacher notices how the reader selects from a range of information sources to enhance comprehension and predict words. When students are reading for comprehension, they begin by predicting what the passage or story will be about. In this process, they select a few cues from the text, such as the title, picture, and headings, and use a great deal of their background knowledge to predict what the passage might be about. Efficient readers select appropriate cues and flexibly use sources of information; however, inefficient readers often use only a single source of information when selecting cues.

Monitoring Strategies

Readers also differ in their monitoring strategies, or when and how they check their understanding. Students' strategies for monitoring word identification and comprehension are evaluated through oral reading and story discussions. Young and less skilled readers monitor their reading less frequently (Paris et al., 1994). They tend to read a string of words without checking to see if the words they are reading make sense. When their understanding breaks down, students differ in their persistence to regain meaning. Many poor readers tend to give up when repeatedly encountering problems, while good readers persist in employing a variety of strategies to solve problems. For example, to repair word recognition mistakes, students can use the overall meaning ("Oops, that doesn't make sense") or the way the word fits into the sentence ("That doesn't sound like a sentence"). Sometimes students use what the word looks like or sounds like ("Oops, I didn't say what those letters say") to restore comprehension.

Elaboration Strategies

Finally, readers differ in the way they elaborate responses. During a discussion, some students answer literal-level questions with exact, text-based responses, while others answer questions by relying heavily on the overall theme of the story and inferring facts about the story rather than recalling specific information. Retellings can indicate students' ability to organize and elaborate verbal responses. In an oral retelling, the brevity or elaboration of the story theme is evaluated to determine how students differ in elaborating information. In some discussions, students will reflect on text using their personal experiences to think deeply. These students use several information sources simultaneously. In summary, students vary in the strategies they use and how actively and frequently they deploy these strategies.

Engagement Dimension

Through instructional interactions, the teacher notes the students' involvement in literacy activities. The students' engagement is based on the reasons and expectations that they have for participating in a reading event. They formulate these reasons from past experiences and their personal coping strategies. Chris, like any other child, went to kindergarten expecting to learn literacy skills like everyone else. In kindergarten, she learned about 60% of the letter names and scored high on tests of phonemic awareness. At this time, she placed a high value on reading, as her parents read themselves and read to her. Her father read to her every day. She was an emergent reader and began first grade expecting to learn to read. The following section describes aspects that influence engagement.

Interest

Interest in literacy activities, the tasks, and the topics contribute to increase engagement in reading. As a result of increased engagement and other factors, reading achievement increases. Literacy researchers have defined several categories of interests. Traditionally, interests have been thought of as individual or personal interest. These interests are often enduring preferences of an individual reader for a variety of special topics. By contrast, situational interest refers to interest generated by situational factors. Text-based situational interests are topics that are of universal or archetypal appeal (Hidi & Renninger 2006), such as danger, money, strong visual images, or perceived links to personal experience. However, interest alone does not account for readers' performance. Among other influential variables are strategic processing and knowledge. Readers' level of interest will help shape the reading process. For example, interest contributes to the frequency and form of strategic processing in which readers engage (Walker 2003a). In turn, readers' levels of interest are related to what they know about the topic with greater knowledge being linked to stronger interest in the topic (Hidi, 2001).

Value of Reading

The value that students have about reading is an important part of motivation and engagement. If students come from homes where reading is valued, they are likely to value it too. Chris valued literacy and wanted to read like her parents and older friends. However, values differ on the basis of students' experiences and how literacy was modeled within their environment. When students see parents, grandparents, and friends reading in their daily lives, then they too begin to value literacy as these role models do. Thus, if students value reading and see its usefulness, then they are more likely to engage in literacy activities.

View of Reading

The view of reading that students have contributes to their engagement. Most students view reading as a strategic process where they make sense with text. They continually search for meaning. These students are intrinsically motivated to read and experience learning as deeply personal. Their engagement is sustained by the ideas and emotions that emerge from constructing meaning. However, some students develop a different view of reading. A handful of students develop a view of reading that focuses on text-based knowledge. In fact, when asked, "What is reading?" they respond, "Reading is getting the words right" (Fortenberry & Walker, 2006). Another group of students view reading as filling in answers in workbooks. They actually love workbook exercises despite the fact that these exercises may have little substantial purpose. Such students believe that the teacher is right and are externally motivated to please the teacher. Although Chris valued literacy, she was extremely motivated to please the teacher and was able to sound out words readily. Eventually, her view of reading focused on getting the word right.

Social Interaction

Social interaction also plays a role in engagement. Students have different preferences for the social interactions within the classroom. Some students like to read and respond independently. They prefer to work alone or simply with a partner. Jan was one of those students. She was often working at her desk while others were gathered in a circle as the teacher read aloud. Chris, on the hand, loved to work in small groups. She learned as she discussed ideas with others. Like Chris, other students like social settings in which they share their learning with group members. They are constantly learning from their peers as they discuss ideas. In fact, most of these learners increase their engagement when they work as part of a group. The group offers support for ideas and a chance to share and modify thinking. According to Almasi (1996), students who talk with their friends about what they read are more active, engaged readers. Thus, social interaction and the expectation that others will listen to their views create increased student engagement.

Reader's Concept of Self as Reader

Readers' self-concept as readers or their belief in their competence as readers is also linked to engagement. These beliefs affect their perception of task success and students' engagement. If students believe that they can succeed in a reading task, then they are more likely to choose to read. The reader's perception of her success at a task influences the amount of effort she will expend and her persistence in reading (Wigfield, 1997). Because prior experiences with reading vary, as does reading success, students differ in their beliefs about their success or self-efficacy when they read. This belief, in turn, affects their engagement.

Attributions for Success and Failure

Linked with self-perception as a reader is how the students respond to their own successes and failures. Some readers persist when confronted with a difficult task, while others give up easily. As Chris progressed through first grade, she realized that she was not as successful as others. Since she was very sensitive to group interactions, she noticed immediately that she was slowly sounding out words, affecting how rapidly she could read. Her peers often finished with their work early. As the literacy tasks became more difficult, Chris began to give up easily and move on to a new activity. As this process continued, she began to lose the sense of when she was successful and when she was not. This began to change her belief that she was a competent reader. If students view themselves as unable to read, it is more difficult to change their perception of themselves as a reader.

Positive and Negative Attributions

Attributions are a powerful influence on engagement. Some students view reading as a strategic process and are reinforced simply by revising their thinking. Sharon was always making mistakes but corrected them. She viewed reading as a strategic process; therefore, she attributed her success to the strategic process of correcting her mistakes. Other students, however, view reading as getting the words right rather than as a strategic process. Attributions about their success and failure influence their engagement. Because Chris repeatedly failed in comparison to others, she began to believe that she would never read well. This led her to make negative attributions like "I am an awful reader!" even when she was engaged in reading an easy text. Students like Chris do not recognize their success. Even when they are sucessful, they attribute success to luck or an easy task. When Chris read an easy text, she said, "I could read that because it was a baby story." Thus, Chris began to disengage in literacy activities because she viewed literacy activities as a failure situation. These negative attributions affect students' subsequent engagement in literacy activities. Like Chris, when they falter, they lower their perception of themselves as readers and, in turn, decrease their engagement. They do not understand how to apply strategies when reading becomes difficult; therefore, they do not expect a successful outcome of their engagement. Through their repeated failures and negative attributions, they change their view of reading and their view of themselves as readers.

How readers approach the reading event affects the kind of information a teacher has about them. A teacher makes many diagnostic decisions about differences among the learners in his classroom on the basis of what his students know, how they learn, and their engagement. Although this assessment is appropriate, a teacher should also evaluate how the other variables of the reading event affect the reading patterns that the readers use. He asks, "Is what I am observing a pattern that I always see in these readers, or has something in the reading event affected their performance?" Therefore, to assess readers, he looks for consistent responses over different reading events.

In conclusion, readers differ not only in what they already know as evaluated by level of performance, skill knowledge, and content knowledge but also in the strategies they possess. These strategy-based differences include patterns of selection strategies, monitoring and shifting of these strategies, and as elaboration strategies.

Students also differ in their engagement. The interest students have in the content they are asked to read influences their engagement. Likewise, the value students place on literacy activities and their view of reading varies, as do their perceptions of themselves as readers. Their interactions within a social group can also increase their engagement. Students have different ways of responding to success and failure and their subsequent attributions of success or failure. Each of the attributes affects their subsequent engagement in literacy activities. The diagnostic teacher evaluates the following dimensions of reading performance:

- Knowledge-based dimensions
    Language facility
    Word and world knowledge
    Reading stage
    Skill knowledge

- Strategy-based dimensions
    Selection strategies
        Text or prior knowledge
    Monitoring
        Active or passive
    Elaboration
        One word or embellished
        Literal or nonliteral

- Engagement dimension
    Interests
    Value of literacy tasks
    View of reading
    Social interaction
    Self-perception as a reader
    Response to success and failure
    Attributions: positive or negative

Technique

A key to effective instructional decision making is an analysis of the instructional techniques used by the diagnostic teacher. During the lesson, the diagnostic teacher thinks about how the readers will benefit from instruction. Subsequently, he analyzes the literacy processes involved in each technique so that he can match readers' strategies with the most efficient instructional techniques. Several considerations inform the analysis of instructional techniques.

Instructional Frameworks

Techniques can differ in their function within the instructional framework. Techniques can be implemented before reading, others are implemented during reading, and others after reading a passage or story.

Before Reading

Some techniques develop prerequisite knowledge in order to understand the content of the passage. Techniques that introduce vocabulary and develop background knowledge are used before reading. Sometimes the technique introduces new word meanings and ways to decode the new words before reading the passage. Karen, a fourth-grade girl, had difficulty reading expository text because she did not know what many of the new words meant. The diagnostic teacher decided to use a directed reading activity (see part 2) where she introduced the important words and their meaning before reading. When definition information did not help, the teacher decided to use a semantic map (see part 2). He put the word "Volocano" inside a circle that was placed in a central place on the chalkboard. He asked for experiences and events that were similar to volocanoes and drew lines out from volocanoes to show the relationships among the students' responses. The students along with Karen used their background knowledge to describe a volcano. The teacher arranged their information conceptually on the map.

During Reading

Other instructional techniques focus on developing active reading during the reading of the text. Since Karen was an active reader when reading narrative text, the diagnostic teacher decided to stop and ask questions while reading. As Karen read the selection about why a volcano erupts, the teacher asked specific questions about important information that contributed to the definition of a volcano. This supported Karen as she was developing the concept of volcano. However, there are other ways to promote active comprehension that are used frequently by classroom teachers. Techniques such as the directed reading/thinking activity, reciprocal questioning procedure, and reciprocal teaching (see chapter 11 and part 2) are used during the reading of the story to promote active comprehension.

After Reading

After Karen read the passage, the diagnostic teacher referred back to the semantic map (see part 2) to help Karen as well as the other students elaborate the textbook definition with their background knowledge. New information from the textbook was placed alongside what the students already knew to develop an understanding of volcanoes. Thus, after a passage is read, techniques can extend comprehension (see "Semantic Mapping" and "Story Mapping" in part 2) or reinforce word identification and fluency (see "Repeated Readings" in part 2).

Text Types

Different techniques were designed to be used with different types of text. The two text types most used in classrooms are narrative and expository texts.

Narrative Texts

Narrative texts tell captivating stories where readers can relate to characters and their experiences. Some techniques fit narrative text and would not be appropriate for expository text. For example, it would be difficult to story map an expository passage about volcanoes. But responding to a book with the character Harry Potter lends itself to discussion.

Expository Texts

Expository texts provide information about specified topics and are used in the content areas. Making a semantic map or a K-W-L sheet (see part 2) is ideal for teaching volcanoes and other expository text. A novice teacher once used a K-W-L sheet with the story "The Gingerbread Man." It was very difficult to use the technique, as the repeated phrases in the story did not provide new information. "The Gingerbread Man" is a playful story that is often read aloud with children, as it is a predictable narrative story.

Mode of Response

Techniques also differ in the mode of response that readers are asked to use. Readers vary in their ability and preference for response modes.

Discussion

Some techniques ask students to discuss what they learn when reading. By sharing their thoughts through a discussion, students select what is important to retell about the story. They actually construct a response rather than merely recall events. Some students like to discuss what they have learned and share ideas and thoughts. Throughout Chris's educational carreer, she loved to talk with others. It was only in high school that some of her classes were based on discussion rather than recitation. The steady diet of recitation focused Chris on factual information and inhibited discussion.

Writing

Other techniques ask students to write about what they have read. This facilitates meaning making. Again, students must decide what is important as well as how they will communicate their responses and new information. Some students prefer to write what they are thinking so that they can revise their understanding before communicating what they think. Karen was one of those students. She preferred to jot down notes before she discussed so that she could make her points and clarify her understandings. The diagnostic teacher selects a response mode that will support learning for his students.

Strategy Instruction

The diagnostic teacher also decides whether a technique is to work on a strategy. The more common strategies are prediction, monitoring, and elaboration (see chapter 11 for a detailed discussion).

Prediction
Readers predict what is going to be communicated. Then they select and sort important information from the text and relate it to their prior knowledge. For example, Sandy could always make a prediction but went right on reading without selecting information to support the prediction.

Monitoring
Next, readers monitor their predictions on the basis of new textual information. They continually ask themselves if what they are reading is making sense. Sandy usually knew if text made sense but did not notice specific details. She sometimes skipped over important words but continued to make predictions with faulty information.

Elaboration
Finally, readers *elaborate* their understanding as well as their strategy use. Elaboration involves making connections between newly learned information and prior knowledge. It is a generative process where they expand their strategy and knowledge base.

Question-and-answer relationships (see "Question-and-Answer Relationships" in part 2) is a technique developed to teach how to answer comprehension questions. Students learn to analyze questions according to the source of information needed to answer the question. Not only are they taught how to answer comprehension questions that are literal or inferential, but they are given information on how to use the strategy.

Skill Instruction

Some techniques incorporate strategy instruction as they teach skills, while other techniques focus only on the skills. There are many skills in reading. This book focuses mainly on *word identification, word analysis (phonics), fluency, sentence structure, literal comprehension, and nonliteral comprehension.* A lesson to work on word analysis deals with teaching phonics. A typical synthetic phonics lesson (see "Synthetic (Explicit) Phonics" in part 2) often focuses only on the skill. The lesson teaches the letter sounds and the blending of sounds to form a word. This skill knowledge helps readers figure out unfamiliar words in isolation.

Source of Information

As discussed in chapter 1, techniques differ according to what source of information is emphasized during instruction. The two major sources of information are the text and what readers know.

Background Knowledge

Some techniques ask students to use their background knowledge, called reader-based inferencing. In using these techniques, the diagnostic teacher helps students focus on what they know to figure out what the text may say. In other words, they use a reader-based approach. The language experience approach is an approach that begins by using what students know (see part 2). In this approach, the students use what they know (reader-based inferencing) to dictate a passage or story about an experience. Once the dictation is completed, the students use this as a text to learn words by reading them over and over until they read fluently. This technique allows students to learn to read by using their natural language structures. In this type of approach, the students are continually asked to refer to their own experiences and what they said about them when problems for figuring out words occur.

Text Information

Other techniques, however, ask the student to use the information in the text. In using these techniques, the diagnostic teacher helps the student focus mainly on the text to figure out meaning and to learn words. For example, in the synthetic phonics approach (see part 2), the student is asked to decode words letter by letter, focusing on the text to figure out the words. After the word is decoded, the student is asked to think about what it might mean. In these approaches, the students are continually asked to refer to the text when problems in figuring out words occur.

Nature of Structure

Techniques also differ in the nature of the structure that is provided by the diagnostic teacher during implementation. The structure of instruction falls along a continuum from implicit to explicit instruction.

Implicit

Some techniques require that the teacher present the information in a rather implicit format (without much teacher direction) and simply provide thoughtful questions and support for reading. These techniques rely on students to construct their own meaning and rules. When using these techniques, the diagnostic teacher immerses students in reading and then facilitates their inquiry. It is assumed that students will be able to discover the meaning of the text on their own. Journal writing (see "Journal Writing" in part 2), where students write in a journal about their thinking, is based on an implicit, student-directed approach to learning. This technique allows students to learn by writing down their thinking before they talk with anyone else.

Explicit Instruction

Other techniques with a more explicit structure begin with explicit explanation and modeling by the teacher. Students follow the model as teachers support their learning. Finally, the students take control of the new learning or strategy and continue on their own. Reciprocal teaching (see "Reciprocal Teaching" in part 2) is a technique that uses explicit instruction. It begins with the teacher's demonstrating how to summarize, ask good questions, clarify difficult parts, and predict what the text is about. For example, Derek convened a small group and demonstrated the strategy of summarization; next, the students led the discussion following his model by summarizing while Derek offered encouragement and talked about when it is best to use the strategies. Derek repeated the process using how to ask good questions and so on. In this example, Derek is using explicit instruction where he gradually lets the students work on their own.

Instructional Sequence

Techniques differ not only in their functions as exemplified by their instructional frameworks but also in the cognitive demands placed on learners by the instructional sequence. These cognitive demands can be influenced by simultaneous or successive cognitive processes (Das, Parrila, & Papadopoulos, 2000).

Simultaneous Focus

Some techniques present reading tasks simultaneously as a whole and show students how the parts are organized within the whole. These techniques are called *simultaneous*. The shared reading approach (see part 2) is an example of a technique that introduces the story as a whole. Children read along with the teacher to discover the predictable pattern. After the story has been read as a whole several times, students are asked to identify individual words. The technique begins with the whole and then, depending on the task purpose, proceeds to the parts.

Successive Focus

Other techniques present the parts of the reading task in a sequential, step-by-step progression that leads to the formation of the whole. These techniques are called *successive*. They emphasize verbalizing the separate parts, logically structuring these parts into a whole, and explicitly stating rules for organizing the parts into a whole. Synthetic phonics is an example of a technique that is sequential in nature. The synthetic phonics approach begins by teaching the sounds of letters. These sounds are then blended to form words, and finally rules for the different sound combinations are given. In the end, the students decode words in whole stories.

How the teacher directs the reading event affects the information he gathers. Techniques vary in the demands placed on learners. For example, a teacher explicitly tells a student to look at the sounds of letters and blend the sounds together to form words; however, the student prefers to create her own rules, and thinking about sounds is her weakness. The ineffective teacher continues to teach the letter sounds, providing a high degree of feedback about her miscues and finally concluding that she is passive and a nonreader.

However, the effective diagnostic teacher probes further. He changes the technique to include predictable stories that have phonetically consistent words. When the student self-corrects, the teacher asks, "How did you figure that out?" The student then tells how she has used her knowledge of phonics: "I thought about other words that looked like this word and then I substituted the sounds. You see, 'hopping' looks like 'popping.' Words that look alike at the end usually sound alike." The diagnostic teacher changed the technique from explicit instruction in letter sounds to implicit instruction in a text that required the student to create her own rules for phonics. The reflective teacher thinks about how he is directing instruction. He asks himself, "In what other ways can this context be presented so that this student can learn more efficiently?"

Although evaluating techniques seems to present an either–or situation, in reality the techniques can be placed on a continuum of instructional features. For example, a technique is neither a totally explicit nor a totally implicit one; rather, each technique falls along a continuum with a tendency to approach instruction from a more or less explicit to a more or less implicit structure. The relative effectiveness of its approach depends on the learner's task knowledge and task independence as well as the teacher's execution.

In conclusion, the diagnostic teacher can use different teaching techniques to vary the manner in which instruction is implemented. The techniques can be more appropriately used either before, during, or after instruction. Some techniques are more appropriate for narrative text, while others are better for expository material. Likewise, some techniques require oral discussion, while others require a written response. Techniques are designed to teach strategies, skills, or both. Techniques vary in the source of information stressed during implementation (reader based or text based). Techniques also vary in the amount of teacher direction (implicit or explicit format) necessary for their implementation. Some techniques present information as a whole (simultaneously) and then show the parts, while other techniques present information in separate parts (sequentially) and then show how the parts fit into the whole. The diagnostic teacher evaluates the instructional features of each technique as well as the students' responses to the techniques. From this information, he makes some diagnostic decisions about the readers and then selects the most efficient techniques to generate learning for his students. Instructional features include the following:

- Instructional framework
    Before, during, or after reading
- Type of text
    Narrative or expository
- Mode of response
    Discussion or writing
- Strategy instruction
    Predict, monitor, and elaborate
- Skill instruction
    Word identification, fluency, vocabulary, and comprehension, etc.
- Source of information
    Reader based or text based
- Instructional structure
    Implicit or explicit
- Instructional sequence
    Simultaneous or successive (sequential)

Situational Context.

The situational context plays an important role in influencing the learning that occurs during any situation. The school classroom where many instructional events occur has a particular social context that often differs from real-life situations. Sometimes schooling enhances learning, and sometimes it does not. Complex social interactions as well as literate environments in schools and classrooms can serve an important role in reading and writing development. Thus, students' perception of their role in the literate environment of school is critical for literacy learning. A fifth grader explained it simply: "It is like school has a big circle around it. Once I walk into this circle, I don't talk. Outside this circle, I talk a lot. I talk with my friends about the ideas I have. But in school, I don't talk about the ideas that I have" (S. R. Walker, personal communication, February 17, 1982).

This example illustrates the status of schooling. Schooling has become a culture of its own where students are taught formal rules within well-structured activities. Unfortunately, literacy learning is a complex, dynamic activity that depends heavily on the social context in which it is situated. Vygotsky (1978) stressed that social interaction provides individuals with an opportunity to interact with more knowledgeable peers, thus increasing their level of understanding. Students "gradually internalize some of the interpretive behaviors that are associated with higher levels of thinking" (Almasi, 1996, p. 15). As they talk with more knowledgeable peers, their thinking is reconstructed within these experiences. In one study, for example, students' story retellings were more complete when conveyed to a peer who had not read the story than when they were told to a teacher who had already read the story (Harste, Burke, & Woodward, 1994). Jenny, for example, enjoyed group projects and often shared travel experiences to make points in the discussion. However, she did not respond when asked a question by the teacher, whom she presumed already knew the answer. The situational context, such as the authority structure of the classroom (whose understanding will count?), the teacher expectations, and the social dynamics (what are the question-and-answer patterns?), influences students' achievement and engagement (Ruddell & Unrau, 1997). Furthermore, the context is influenced by the kinds of assessments that are mainly used. Whether the teacher uses a standardized test or an informal discussion affects how students respond and engage in the instructional context. Therefore, as students read in a variety of situational contexts, they refine and generalize their understanding of text. Consequently, students' knowledge and strategies are constantly evolving within each new situation.

Format of Classroom Interactions

In classrooms where everyone shares their point of view, students engage in thinking and talking about the topic at hand. Often, however, instruction does not focus on an exchange of ideas about content used to construct meaning from texts. Much of the time, teachers ask questions to assess learning rather than discuss ideas. Continual random questioning after students read a story can inhibit an exchange of relevant information. By focusing on irrelevant facts without connecting them to the reader's knowledge, the teacher inhibits reading comprehension and reinforces a context of interrogation rather than discussion. This recitation format does not allow students to participate in engaging discussions where they can construct meaning.

Discussion

Rather than using a recitation format, the diagnostic teacher moves his interactions to a discussion where students naturally engage in constructing meaning. When a teacher participates in a discussion, he changes the situational context. He engages everyone in discussion rather than merely answering questions that he poses. Meaning is negotiated during the discussion with all students sharing and rethinking their ideas. The diagnostic teacher listens closely to the discussion, focusing comments on the students' ideas and encouraging reflection by saying, "Let's think more about that idea" or "How did you figure that out?" These open-ended questions encourage them to share ideas. For instance, Mickey started her fourth-grade year reading within the range of the end of first grade and the beginning of second. She made many oral reading errors (miscues); therefore, her reading was sluggish, and she did not improve. In the past, her extra reading instruction had focused on skills, but her new reading teacher, David, began by reading and discussing stories that she could read successfully. David taught in a small group and asked open-ended questions. After the students responded, he would discuss important points in the text. If an important detail were missing, he would have the students orally reread parts of the text to find the detail. On many days, Mickey would discuss ideas that were not related to the text. David simply asked her to prove her point of view by reading aloud the relevant passage. Mickey would read aloud and provide an elaborate explanation. If the explanations were logical, David would accept it. Within 3 months, Mickey was reading fourth-grade books in the classroom with her peers. Changing the situational context and text with a new teacher that focused on meaning and reading aloud to prove your thinking supported Mickey's reading advancement. Thus, meaning and shared understanding are cultivated by students' rethinking understanding and explaining their thinking.

Group Composition

As in Mickey's example, the diagnostic teacher thinks also about the composition of the instructional group and how he responds to students during the lesson. The context can vary in terms of who is a member of the instructional group and the students' perception of their role in that group. Mickey had always worked alone on skill sheets and had never been asked to discuss a story. The small group allowed her to view herself as a reader and explain her thinking. This had never occurred during whole-class or small-group instruction. Sometimes the diagnostic teacher uses whole-group instruction; however, sometimes he uses small groups, which can be heterogeneous (grouped by different traits) or homogeneous (grouped by similar traits). Heterogeneous small groups can be literature discussion groups or book clubs. Homogeneous groups often gather to teach a specific strategy, such as story retelling or summarization. At times, he might even decide to use partner reading.

Conferencing

Sometimes diagnostic teachers conduct conferences with students to explore understanding and strategy use. As the diagnostic teacher confers with a student, he probes for information about what the student uses to construct meaning. Through the conversation, the diagnostic teacher identifies the strengths and the needs of the child. Using this information, a diagnostic teacher might model his own reading strategies or develop deeper conceptual knowledge by helping the students integrate new knowledge into their knowledge base. Sometimes when conferencing, the diagnostic teacher conducts a mini assessment to identify problem areas. For example, when conferencing with Rose, a third-grade student, David found that although she understood the story, she could not write about it. She just didn't know how to start, so David gave Rose a story map to help her with story organization. She began not only to write more but also to understand stories more deeply.

Teacher Responsiveness

In addition to the format of classroom interactions, how the diagnostic teacher responds to students affects the situational context and the students' perception of it. Responsive teaching follows the students' thoughts and finds ways to engage students in expressing their own ideas. This requires openness and receptivity.

Teacher and Student Talk

Teacher and student talk proceeds in a conversational manner where both respond with interesting ideas and information that create a shared understanding. They are open to each other's ideas so that each interchange builds or extends a previous idea. The diagnostic teacher listens closely to students' ideas and fosters more appropriate student–teacher interactions. The reciprocity within these discussions increases both the teacher's and the student's learning. Further, the diagnostic teacher thinks about how he formed his questions and how that influenced the student–teacher interaction. For example, the diagnostic teacher can probe and rephrase his talk to promote more interaction. He can evaluate his receptivity to students' comments, examining their intended meaning and tailoring the conversation to meet the developing understanding (Roskos & Walker, 1998). These analyses can foster an engaging and dynamic relationship between the diagnostic teacher and his students.

Support for Thinking

Additionally, the diagnostic teacher decides at what points he needs to provide support for active thinking. If he provides support before the lesson, students might read the story with ease; however, they might profit more from talking about reading strategies as they read the story. As instruction continues, he considers whether his questions and comments truly support the students' learning, realizing that if he intervenes at the appropriate instructional points, he is able to support students' understanding. Sometimes the diagnostic teacher can rephrase the text, eliciting from the students what similar experience they might have had, and encourage the students to tie together their experiences with the text. These conversations can trigger the students to elaborate information from the text with background knowledge. If students cannot construct meaning, the diagnostic teacher thinks about how he can assist them. He asks himself, "Do I need to focus on what the word means, or do I need to reread the text with expression?" These on-the-spot analyses create a situational context that is responsive to students.

Prompting and Wait Time

Teachers also can change when and how they prompt students. When the teacher gives the student the word or tells her to sound it out, the student loses an opportunity to construct a meaning base for reading. The student will continue to focus on the words in the text without thinking about their meaning. Other times, teachers interrupt at the point of error and prompt with a word-level prompt. However, with some students, teachers wait until the end of the sentence and then say, "Try that again; that didn't make sense." Allowing students to read to the end of the sentence rather than interrupting at the point of error facilitates more active reading strategies and communicates to readers that they can think through problems when they read (Cunningham & Allington, 2007). Thus, the diagnostic teacher is aware of the silent time between responses (wait time) and the scaffolds, or prompts, he uses to promote meaning construction within the situational context.

Nature of Classroom Focus

In every classroom, the ambience is unique. Accepting relationships among the diagnostic teacher and students promotes higher levels of interaction and support. Creating a classroom focus where all ideas, cultures, and races are accepted for unique contributions to the whole community is a responsibility of both the diagnostic teacher and his students. When diagnostic teachers demonstrate respect, high expectations, and support for students, students respond to them in positive ways. In the same way, teachers' focus is influenced by the responses they get from students. Over time, their actions and commitment become mutually supportive. More information can be found at http://www.sedl.org/change/school/culture.html.

Teacher Expectations

However, teachers' expectations for individual students might differ even when the classroom culture focuses on accepting different cultures. Teachers' expectations about what students can do can also affect the situational context. Having high expectations for all learners improves student learning and the classroom environment. However, if teachers expect students to fail and to expend little effort, then teachers' language, wait time, and prompting will convey this expectation. Consequently, the readers respond according to the teachers' expectations (Ruddell & Unrau, 1997). They slowly change their perceptions of the literacy context and begin to judge themselves as unable to read, contributing to their associating reading events with failure.

Often school reinforces negative expectations by focusing on weaknesses. When teachers focus on skill weaknesses and repeatedly evaluate these skills using criterion-referenced tests, they reinforce readers' association of reading with failure. Likewise, when teachers use norm-referenced evaluations, they reward students who learn easily and quickly rather than assist struggling readers who may require adjustments in their learning. Although struggling readers try hard, they do not meet the standard created by other, rapid learners in the classroom. Over time, struggling readers change their perceptions of the context and view literacy events as experiences to avoid because their efforts do not result in positive evaluations by their teachers.

Focus on Strategies

A key to reversing students' association of reading with failure is a situational context where students focus on strategy use (Walker, 2003a) and discuss with their peers what and how they learn. These conversations refocus the classroom climate on the strategies each student uses to construct meaning rather than on how to get right answers to narrowly defined questions. Discussing the strategies that students use to interpret text increases the likelihood that they will define the context of literacy as a place where they can learn.

Collaborative Assessments

Along with focusing on conversations about strategies, the diagnostic teacher changes the classroom focus by using collaborative assessments rather than evaluating students against their peers using norm-referenced assessments (See chapter 8). Both the teacher and the students can construct self-assessments where students evaluate how they performed on a particular task. For instance, Randy had his students evaluate how they retold a story. They used a short "yes or no" format of story elements to evaluate their story summaries (see chapter 8). Then Randy and his students talked about how the students could improve their performance on retelling. Two of the students were going to pay more attention to main characters, while three were going to focus on key events rather than naming all the events. All the students were going to reread the last of the stories to figure out the resolution. This assessment focused on how the task was completed rather than on a comparison among students. It also shifted from the teacher making judgments to the students and teacher discussing performance and setting goals for improvement. This approach changed the classroom focus from simply looking at the number of points each student received to a collaborative process where individual goals were based on students' strategies and performance. Portfolios (see chapter 8 for further elaboration), where students need to think about how to show their expertise and reflect on selected pieces that show what and how they are learning, also change the classroom focus. When portfolios are used, the classroom climate changes from looking at how we are alike on a specific task to looking at how we all did the task well but differently. In portfolios, individual differences are highlighted by changing the context to one of accepting uniqueness rather than evaluating sameness.

> The context of the reading event is a powerful influence on readers' performances. The situational context affects the information the teacher gathers about students' reading. For example, an informal assessment that used only factual questions after silent reading placed a student at the third-grade level; however, this same student was able to answer inferential questions at the eighth-grade level. When she discussed the same story with her peers, she recalled 80% of the facts, as she needed them to support her interpretation. In this case, the context had changed from silent reading and answering factual questions in a relatively sterile context to reading and discussing the story in an interactive instructional group.

In conclusion, the situational context (or where instruction takes place) influences diagnostic decision making. A format that promotes positive classroom interactions and lots of student talk is encouraged. The situational context, therefore, can vary by who is a member of the instructional group and the students' perception of their membership in that group. The form and timing of teacher support are influential factors in creating a situational context for learning. Teacher expectations and the classroom focus also influence the situational context. The diagnostic teacher evaluates all these aspects of the situational context:

- Format of classroom interactions
    Discussion
    Group composition
    Conferencing

- Teacher responsiveness
    Teacher talk
    Support for thinking
    Prompting and wait time

- Nature of classroom focus
    Teacher expectations
    Focus on strategies
    Use of collaborative assessments

Summary

In summary, five interrelated variables of task, text, reader, technique, and situational context establish the instructional conditions for learning. By varying any one of these conditions, the diagnostic teacher can improve student learning. Thus, by evaluating these five variables, the diagnostic teacher identifies elements that affect student learning. Reading instruction and assessment are redirected to the interrelationship of the variables rather than just student deficits.

3 Roles of Diagnostic Teachers

Effective diagnostic teaching engages students in literacy activities throughout the school day. As she teaches, the diagnostic teacher decides when to step in to coach and model literacy strategies. As she modifies her instruction, she encourages students to realize their individual potential as learners. The diagnostic teacher continually thinks about her role within the situational context of the reading event. At the core of effective teaching is a teacher who reflects on her instruction, rethinking her instructional adjustments. As she does this, she reviews the many roles that she assumes: reflecting, planning, mediating, supporting, and responding. These roles and the eight instructional guidelines help the diagnostic teacher focus her instruction. As the effective teacher assumes these roles, she views readers from different perspectives. As she reflects on her decision making, therefore, she considers each of these roles and its influence on her instruction. Figure 3–1 suggests the interrelationships between the roles and guidelines discussed in this chapter.

The first role of the effective diagnostic teacher is reflecting. Teaching as reflecting means that every interaction is analyzed so that appropriate instructional adjustments can be made. The second role of the diagnostic teacher is planning. As the diagnostic teacher plans for instruction, she thinks about the literate community and selects experiences where all students can share their ideas (Johnston, 2004). She is sensitive to multiple cultures in her classroom and how that enhances the literate community. As she plans her lessons, she selects activities that not only will be challenging but also will *ensure success*. The third role of diagnostic teaching is mediating. The effective diagnostic teacher *encourages active reading* by asking high-level questions using what students already know. During the lesson, the diagnostic teacher *assesses while she instructs* so that she can modify her instruction to meet students' changing instructional needs. The fourth role of effective diagnostic teaching is supporting. The diagnostic teacher supports the students' learning, phasing in to support reading and phasing out to *build students' independence*. She models her own internal thinking and coaches students' reading strategies as they independently use new strategies. As they succeed, she provides appropriate praise so that they can develop a *concept of themselves as readers*. Immersing her students in relevant and successful reading experiences, she attributes their success to the effective strategies they use. In the fifth role, the diagnostic teacher views teaching as responding to individual human needs. An effective diagnostic teacher *accepts the individual differences* among her students. She knows that the experiences of her students vary widely and

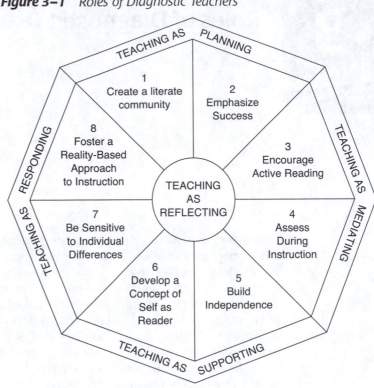

Figure 3–1   *Roles of Diagnostic Teachers*

instruction to account for the differences in what her students already know and the culture they live in. In accepting their individual differences, the effective teacher *fosters a reality-oriented environment* by accepting individuality but expecting all students to read. She uses humor and laughter to develop a relaxed atmosphere where students learn to cope with their mistakes and produce well-thought-out ideas. Teaching as a human response means that the diagnostic teacher treats individuality and making mistakes as human conditions.

These roles and the instructional guidelines they represent work together to create an instructional environment where all students learn. This model fosters instructional interactions that create a coherent learning experience for struggling readers.

 **Reflecting**

The reflective diagnostic teacher considers and selects among instructional alternatives and, at the same time, anticipates the consequences of differing decisions on student learning. This reflection helps teachers know why they teach and facilitates their explanations to others (Roskos & Walker, 1994). The diagnostic teacher shifts between immersion in the reading event and distancing herself from it in order to critically analyze the experience. This distancing helps the diagnostic teacher reconsider reasons for her instruction and refocus on the theoretical framework that underpins these decisions (Walker, 1990a). In other words, she reflects on her instructional decisions, comparing them with her personal assumptions about reading and cross-checking her plans with students' learning and her personal assumptions. Thus, in reflecting, the diagnostic teacher continually evaluates her guiding theory of reading (see chapter 1) and expands her awareness of individual differences among students. Daily, she reflects about her instruction before, during, and after she teaches.

Before the lesson, the diagnostic teacher plans her instruction on the basis of her guiding theory of reading. She thinks about students' strengths and needs in relation to students' knowledge, strategies, and engagement. She reflects on the instructional sequence as she plans each lesson. Diagnostic lessons are much more than a set of activities selected because they are fun. Diagnostic teaching involves the systematic orchestration of reading instruction. At this stage in the teacher's thinking (*reflections before teaching*), the students' attributes are matched with an instructional framework (see chapter 4), and her plans are cross-checked with her guiding theory.

As the lesson is taught, the diagnostic teacher observes how the student is responding to the lesson (*reflections during instruction*). Using these observations, the diagnostic teacher changes original plans to modify instruction and thus to mediate student learning. Every day, teachers make decisions that are intuitive and unconscious. These changes help struggling readers employ independent strategies. For example, after a fourth-grade teacher finished working with a student, she reflected in this way:

> *During the lesson, I discarded the story map, modeled self-talk, self-questioning, and especially prediction. I used the story map as a summary.... The student elaborated and answered with background knowledge the comprehension questions today. (Jordan, 1989)*

In this example, the teacher makes adjustments during the lesson to improve the student's reading. The teacher is constantly sensitive to how the student–teacher interactions affect the goals of the lesson.

After the lesson, the diagnostic teacher evaluates what specific part of the lesson produced the desired reading behavior, and she considers how the on-the-spot adjustments fit into the overall diagnostic lesson. She considers the amount of energy expended in order to encourage student understanding. Likewise, she reflects on the scaffolding, or prompts, she used to improve reading performance. Then she makes adjustments in subsequent lesson plans as she reflects on what occurred and how the interactions were consistent with her plans as well as her beliefs about reading.

The reflective teacher analyzes her own preferences for learning and how these preferences affect her teaching. She focuses on how she learns and how she teaches, not only on what she is teaching. She watches herself to cross-check strategies for teaching with personal beliefs about reading. The teacher's beliefs about reading affect how she teaches (Ruddell & Unrau, 2004). Reflective teachers review their assumptions about literacy.

Finally, the diagnostic teacher thinks about how this instructional event brought a new understanding to her theory of reading instruction. For example, one diagnostic teacher was uncertain how to measure students' comprehension when they did not respond. She had a student who was not constructing meaning but simply repeating the words in the text. After teaching, she decided to review several articles on passive (non-active) behavior in reading. She later commented, "I understand that there is no testing that particularly tests this element. It is determined by observation and analysis of the reader and the reading event." After analyzing the characteristics described in the research literature, she felt she knew enough to identify one of her students as a **passive reader**. These reflections led the diagnostic teacher to become more confident in her own knowledge. By reflecting on the various aspects of an instructional event and thinking about how they fit together, the diagnostic teacher elaborates and changes her model of the reading process. Through reflection, she actively constructs her theory of reading and reading instruction.

Thus, the diagnostic teacher reflects on her plans (the diagnostic session), her observations during instruction, and her intuitive decisions (adjustments). She uses these reflections as she plans lessons, mediates learning, supports reading and writing, and responds personally.

Planning

Prior to the reading event, the diagnostic teacher thinks about the variables of the reading event: task, text, reader, and situational context. Then she selects teaching techniques that focus on reading stories or passages that ensure student success. As teachers focus on the broad aspects of reading, they talk with students about why and how the strategies of reading will improve their reading performance. Through these interactions, they create activities that are both challenging and successful.

With thoughtful planning, the effective teacher has high expectations that the students are engaged in reading, writing, and thinking. Teaching as planning means that the teacher sets up her lessons to create a literate community and to ensure success. These two planning guidelines are delineated in the following section.

Guideline #1: Create a Literate Community

The diagnostic teacher plans for the *engagement of all individuals* in the literate community. Realizing that learning is a social activity, the diagnostic teacher creates a classroom that invites all cultures, all types of learners, and all types of disabilities to engage in literate activities as she honors their personal histories. Diagnostic teachers understand how various cultures and diversity affect the learning environment. Thus, she creates a literate environment by being sensitive to the culture and learning diversity in her classroom. Furthermore, she realizes that students learn what teachers teach. If she creates a culture that respects differing views, students will learn to value each others' understanding. However, if she emphasizes literal understanding, students will, in fact, become excellent fact finders and comprehend the literal information. But if teachers focus on students' responses within a literate community, students will actually become comprehenders who flexibly shift their thinking about what they know, the information in the text, and the present and past situational context. After creating a literate community where all learners can participate in literate activities, the diagnostic teacher thinks about her conversations within the literate community. The diagnostic teacher can create a literate community by *creating instructional conversations* (Goldenberg, 1992–1993) and focusing on the social context where the teacher respects variation in cultural and personal learning experiences. The diagnostic teacher creates an open setting where the students and teachers talk about their ideas rather than the traditional recitation format used in many classrooms. Thus, an instructional conversation is embedded in a supportive and collaborative environment. Conversations build not only knowledge structures but also a sense of community.

As they talk about ideas, the diagnostic teacher connects the students' statements to each others' thinking. She interjects open-ended comments that encourage rethinking of ideas, and she invites students to expand their thinking by saying "tell me more," encouraging them to connect new ideas with their own knowledge, experiences, and cultures. Diagnostic teachers believe that the students have something to say that will benefit every member of the community. They listen carefully to what students say, engaging them in the conversation. This lessens the distance between themselves and their students by constructing interactions from a common understanding of each others' experience, ideas, and cultural values.

Having vibrant conversations depends heavily on the quantity and quality of what is read. Diagnostic teachers plan on having students *read entire stories and passages* and relate them to relevant personal and cultural experiences. Engaging in reading and discussing text for an extended period of time often creates thoughtful responses and increased perspective sharing. However, studies have shown that not all students receive the same amount of time engaged in contextual reading. A longitudinal study that investigated children's reading progress in first through third grade (Juel, 1988) found that struggling readers read less than half as many words each year as good readers. Other studies found that in Title I and special education programs, the amount of contextual reading was reduced rather than increased when students were placed in these special programs (Johnston & Allington, 2001).

GUIDELINE #1: CREATE A LITERATE COMMUNITY

- Plan for the engagement of all students
- Create instructional conversations
- Focus on reading entire stories

Guideline #2: Emphasize Success

As the diagnostic teacher creates a literate environment, she must at the same time ensure successful reading for all students. Students' reading achievement is directly related to their engagement in a literate community. Not only is it their high engagement in the literate community that matters, but they also need to experience a high level of success. To encourage their involvement in a literate community, students must first experience numerous successful reading experiences. When students have success, they tend to repeat the literate activity. Obviously, success is a powerful motivating factor.

On the other hand, if students experience numerous failures within a literate community, such as reading inappropriate texts that do not respond to their cultural perspectives or that are too difficult for them to read or engaging in an activity beyond their present knowledge base, these students often disengage from school-based literate activities (Walker, 2003a). These unsuccessful reading experiences contribute to an unhealthy attitude toward reading.

To encourage a healthy attitude toward success, the diagnostic teacher creates a series of consistently *successful reading activities.* She keeps a close match between the students' abilities, their cultural interactions, and the texts that she chooses for reading instruction. When choosing texts, the diagnostic teacher considers not only an appropriate reading range but also the extent of students' prior experiences and culture. She chooses material that contains familiar and universal concepts so that students can readily use their prior knowledge to generate understanding. She then plans for the students to read a greater amount of material and to express ideas based on what they have read.

Not only does the diagnostic teacher plan successful reading experiences by placing the students at the appropriate reading level, but she also carefully selects *authentic texts that are familiar and interesting* to her students. Good children's literature presents characters who share similar experiences with readers, thus promoting students' ability to read for meaning. When children's literature is matched with students' experiences, the struggling readers readily identify with the main character's conflict and can successfully predict solutions out of their own experiences. Therefore, the diagnostic teacher selects high-caliber children's literature and reads with students to establish a successful reading experience. Likewise, she looks for trade books that contain information about the topics the students are studying. These usually have highlighted vocabulary, key concepts in headings in the text or pictures, and well-structured paragraphs (see "Text" in chapter 2). The students can continue to read on their own and feel the success of reading an entire book. This success can spill over into other literacy activities by giving students confidence in writing or in taking on other reading tasks.

The purpose for reading can also influence students' success. In the classroom and tutoring, the diagnostic teacher sets aside time for children to *read for their own purposes* and then share their reading. When students read for their own purposes, their interactions with text are perceived as real and relevant reading. The teacher provides time to share the understanding and response with their peers. She creates a "read and tell" time that reinforces individual variation in text interpretation. This activity allows students to have ownership of their own responses to the text and builds success.

When readers are successful, they actively engage in text interpretation. The sensitive teacher creates readers by creating successful reading activities, having them read a lot of familiar and interesting text, and having them read relevant materials for their own purposes

---

GUIDELINE #2: EMPHASIZE SUCCESS

- Create a series of successful reading events
- Use authentic texts that are familiar and interesting
- Encourage easy reading for individual purposes

Mediating

The diagnostic teacher mediates learning by phasing in and out of the reading event as she adjusts her instruction to students' understanding. She asks questions that help students actively interpret the text. She listens to the students and uses what they understand about the story to elicit more elaborate interpretations. She gives them time to think about what they read and formulate responses. When students are unsure of a response, she asks them what they know so far about the story. Then she asks them to explain how they came to that conclusion. From this information, the teacher develops leading questions or examples that will guide the students' interpretation. Teaching as mediating means that the teacher phases in and out of the reading event in order to encourage active reading as she teaches and assesses student understanding. These two mediating guidelines are detailed in the following section.

Guideline #3: Encourage Active Reading

Reading is an active, problem-solving process. The diagnostic teacher engages students in this active problem-solving process so that they can construct meaning as they read. From a young age, children strive to make sense of their world, and the diagnostic teacher builds on this natural aptitude by encouraging students in *making sense of reading and writing events*. The diagnostic teacher, then, encourages students to evaluate their responses from a sense-making perspective. She assists students in extending ideas, revising misunderstandings, and developing opinions. In their search for meaning, students invent their own explanations, examine and justify hypotheses, and finally refute or rework their explanations. To mediate learning, the diagnostic teacher constantly engages students in an active meaning search.

To do so, the diagnostic teacher checks her behavior with both proficient and struggling readers to see whether her prompts focus on meaning. Research shows that teachers treat their less proficient readers differently from struggling readers (Allington, 2005). When working with proficient readers, teachers are more engaged using meaning-level prompts and letting good readers continue reading to see whether they are going to recover meaning. However, when working with less proficient readers, teachers often allow more interruptions, interrupt struggling readers at the point of error, and use more word-level prompting. These teaching behaviors often cause struggling readers to miscall words or ideas and continue reading without checking these words or ideas against an overall meaning to see whether they fit. For these readers, the diagnostic teacher needs to frame her prompts from a sense-making perspective that is culturally sensitive. As students miscall a word or miscomprehend an idea, she indicates her inability to make sense of their response and encourages them to rethink their explanation. This approach focuses the struggling reader on making sense of text. For example, the teacher might say the following:

> What would make sense and start with an *s*?
> Think about the story; what would make sense and start with the sound *s-s-s*?
> Look at the picture; what would make sense and fit with the picture?

The diagnostic teacher combines these responses in a variety of ways to help the reader focus on making sense of text.

As the diagnostic teacher responds to the discussion, she thinks about how to orchestrate her support. The effective diagnostic teacher *phases in to support the students' sense making, and phases out to allow students to think independently.* Initially, she allows 3 to 5 seconds between her probes and the student's response. Increasing the wait time from 1 second to 3 seconds positively affects the number of student responses as well as the organization of the response (Allington & Cunningham, 2006). Furthermore, the amount of time between the students' responses and the teacher's response affects the elaboration of meaning. Thinking takes time. Silence may mean that students are constructing thoughtful responses.

Not only should the diagnostic teacher increase her wait time, but she must also deal effectively with inappropriate responses. Initially, the teacher uses part of the student's response to probe reasoning. Sometimes she rephrases or repeats part of the student's response to clarify the interpretations. At other times, she asks students to justify their answers by supplying information from the text. She probes student reasoning by asking, "How do you know that?" and "What makes you think that?" Finally, if the line of reasoning is justifiable, the diagnostic teacher accepts the response as a valid point of view. As the diagnostic teacher increases her wait time and deals creatively with inappropriate responses, she develops an atmosphere that promotes active interpretation of text.

As teachers focus on a literate community, they talk with students in an open way, encouraging everyone to express their views. Rather than giving right or wrong answers, students are encouraged to express themselves. The social interaction is critical to the process of constructing knowledge, and the diagnostic teacher supports students, helping them build a cohesive understanding of textual information. Classrooms with high reading achievement in high-poverty schools are characterized by reading of selections followed by small-group discussions where students exchange ideas about meaning (Taylor, Pearson, Peterson, & Rodriguez, 2003). Through the small-group discussions, students justify their interpretations by relating the text to what they already know, which focuses instruction on meaning rather than recitation. As students actively explain and defend their ideas, they refine, reorganize, and situate their understanding. The diagnostic teacher plans time for discussing stories in both small- and large-group settings so that students can explore their own interpretation with others in an open atmosphere.

The effective diagnostic teacher encourages students to discuss ideas. She explains the process of shifting between reader-based knowledge and strategies, the information in the text, and the situational context and how this will influence understanding when problems in text interpretation arise. The diagnostic teacher carefully orchestrates these discussions to engage all students.

In summary, the diagnostic teacher encourages active reading by focusing students on making sense of text and probing student responses in order to support their active reflection. She phases in and out of the lesson to create an atmosphere that promotes thinking rather than interrogation. To increase students' understanding, she engages students in discussions about text where they elaborate their thinking.

GUIDELINE #3: ENCOURAGE ACTIVE READING

- Focus on sense making with text
- Phase in and out to support active thinking
- Create open discussions about the text

Guideline #4: Assess During Instruction

As the diagnostic teacher implements the lessons that she planned, she keeps a mental log of the students' responses. Her instruction, therefore, not only creates active readers but also provides a means for assessing their progress. As the diagnostic teacher mediates learning, she observes how she modifies the initial reading task to create learning. In other words, she *assesses changes in the readers' performances occurring as she mediates learning*. This record of students' responses to instructional modifications is called **dynamic assessment**. Dynamic assessment evaluates students' performances as they are coached to use more effective reading strategies. This type of assessment focuses on the students' acquisition of strategies during instruction rather than unaided levels of competence.

During dynamic assessment, the teacher *probes responses*. For example, when a student read a story about two mountain climbers in Chile, South America, he miscalled the word *Chile* (actually, he pronounced the *ch* sound and then mumbled). In the oral retelling, he referred to Chile as the location. When the diagnostic teacher probed how he knew the country was Chile, the student said, "Well, the author talked about the Andes Mountains, and I know the Andes Mountains are on the west coast of South America . . . so I decided that the country must have been Chile."

From this information, the teacher assessed that this student had a wide range of prior experiences and used them to interpret text. He was also able to mentally self-correct word recognition errors. This sign told her that he was an active rather than a passive reader. When reading, he often struggled because he used too much of his own background knowledge when he encountered several words that he could not recognize. Probing the student about how he arrived at a response gave the diagnostic teacher a more accurate picture of the student's potential for learning new information.

Finally, as the diagnostic teacher assesses learning while she teaches, she evaluates whether her instruction is appropriate for her learners. She evaluates the reading event and *asks whether there is another way* to interact with the students. She asks herself the following:

1. Am I leading students through the task according to their present strategy use? If not, should I try another way?
2. Is this text appropriate for these students? If not, should I try another text?
3. Am I using the students' strengths as I am teaching? If not, should I try another way?
4. Is this technique appropriate for these students? If not, should I try another way?

5. Is this situational context appropriate for these students? If not, should I try another situation?

As key variables of instruction are changed, assessment is based on the resulting response. The diagnostic teacher evaluates students' improvement as a result of her instruction. If students do not progress, the diagnostic teacher looks for another way to modify instruction in order to enhance literacy.

GUIDELINE #4: ASSESS DURING INSTRUCTION

- Assess reading change as a result of mediated learning
- Probe students' responses to understand their thinking
- If reading behavior does not change, try another adjustment

Supporting

During the reading event, the diagnostic teacher supports students as they read so they can be independent learners and therefore think of themselves as readers. To support students, the diagnostic teacher helps them develop independence by sharing how she thinks while she is reading. The students and teacher work together to figure out a story or understand the passage. As the teacher shares her thinking and works with the students, she supports when they take charge of their own learning and talk through their own understanding. To build students' independence, she finds ways to show them that they can read and think. She acknowledges the effective strategies they use when they read efficiently. At times, she allows students to read for their own purposes without teacher questions and discussion. They simply respond in their journals (see part 2). These guidelines for enabling students are elaborated in the following section.

Guideline #5: Build Independence

The fifth guideline requires that the teacher both instruct the strategies of reading and systematically plan how students will assume responsibility for their own learning. Not only does the diagnostic teacher direct the learning process by explaining the steps and guiding the practice, but she also gives students ownership of their learning by encouraging them to think about their thinking. Efficient readers monitor their understanding. As they are reading, they actively choose alternate strategies when the words or passages do not make sense. Struggling readers, on the other hand, are characterized by disorganized strategies and failure to spontaneously self-monitor. Consequently, they continue to rely on the teacher to monitor reading performance.

Struggling readers, therefore, need instruction in effective monitoring behaviors so that they can move from teacher-directed to self-directed learning. The initial step is to redirect assessment from the teacher to the student, with the teacher demonstrating how to self-monitor reading. To do so, the teacher purposely makes mistakes while reading so that she can *demonstrate* how she monitors an active meaning search. Too often, struggling readers perceive proficient reading as error-free reading. By making mistakes, the teacher can demonstrate her own coping behaviors.

To do this, the teacher begins by saying, "Oops, that doesn't fit or make sense." Then she demonstrates alternative strategies. She shows readers that they can ignore the mistake and read on to see whether they can figure out the meaning or that they can reread the sentence checking the overall passage meaning to see what might fit.

As she continues to demonstrate this active meaning search, the teacher illustrates the self-questioning process that goes through the mind of an active reader. For instance, *If I lose meaning, I ask myself a series of questions. Most of the time I need to figure out either a word I don't know or what the author was trying to say. I can use two different sequences to figure out words or meaning.*

TO FIGURE OUT A WORD, I ASK MYSELF QUESTIONS

"What would make sense? (sematic fit)

"Does it make sense in the sentence?" (semantic fit)

"What word does it look like" or "Does the word I said look similar" (graphic fit)

"What does it sound like" (phonic fit) and

Sometimes, I prompt myself with two questions combined:

"Does that make sense (semantic fit) and start with the letter *s*?" (graphic fit)

There are similar questions when problems occur as students are figuring out meaning. Initially, the teacher models this in the following way:

TO FIGURE OUT MEANING, I ASK MYSELF,

"What does the text say, and I reread to gain meaning?"

"What do I already know about what the text says, and I think about what I know related to the topic?"

"What is the important information?"

"How does this information fit together?"

"What are the purposes for reading this text?"

After modeling the self-questioning process, the teacher and students work through a couple of examples. The students follow the teacher's model and think aloud, asking themselves questions about their reading. The students actually talk about how they solve the reading task. As the students talk aloud, the teacher *supports their thinking by giving them hints and encouraging them to talk through their thinking.* As the students talk aloud, the teacher names the strategies that they are using. She comments, "Did you notice how you reread that sentence to see whether it made sense? That was very effective." One student reflected on her self-talk when she wrote her portfolio reflection, as shown in Figure 3–2.

Figure 3–2   *Portfolio Reflection on Self-Talk*

I like this because, I could write what I was thinking. This shows that you can get off track & stay on track. Self-talk helps me think of what I am thinking wail I read

As processes are demonstrated and practiced, the teacher explains when it is most appropriate to use them. For example, for different types of text, the teacher explains why or why not to use the particular reading strategy she is teaching. If the teacher is demonstrating how to formulate predictions based on prior knowledge, she explains that if the student does not know anything about the topic, he must read two or three paragraphs, summarize the information, and then create a prediction based on the just-learned information. Teacher and student thus *collaborate in thinking* about various ways that strategic reading changes in different situations.

The diagnostic teacher builds student independence by coaching the process of active reading and the corresponding troubleshooting strategies that proficient readers use. In addition, the teacher thinks out loud, showing students how she knows what she knows. In turn, students think out loud using the steps of active reading, and the teacher supports their thinking process rather than focusing on right or wrong answers. Finally, the teacher and students collaboratively discuss how they use strategic reading in various situations. In these ways, the diagnostic teacher supports students' independent engagement in literacy activities.

GUIDELINE #5: BUILD INDEPENDENCE

- Demonstrate thinking
- Coach thinking by encouraging self-talk
- Collaborate in thinking about when to use strategies

Guideline #6: Develop a Concept of Self as Reader

Children come to school with well-developed problem-solving abilities; they have learned to walk, to talk, and so on. Through their everyday living, they have learned many of the principles of communicating their ideas through language. However, students differ in their evaluation of how they are doing. Some students easily evaluate their performance, and if the evaluation is positively related to their effort, they increase engagement (Schunk, 2003). Other readers have a rather hazy notion of what constitutes proficient reading. Therefore, they often have a confused idea of their performance and disengage in literacy activities. Because these readers repeatedly fail when reading, they develop a concept of themselves as nonreaders. This self-evaluation is difficult to change.

While listening to such readers, the diagnostic teacher notices that they read as if they do not expect the text to make sense. They read as if they believe that getting every word right is reading (Goodman, 1996). This attitude is also exhibited when comprehending text. These readers seem to monitor their reading less frequently and accept whatever argument is presented in the text without applying their prior knowledge. They seldom reread text to check initial interpretations, and they try to maintain interpretations even in light of contradictory information (Paris, Lipson, & Wixson, 1994). These ineffective strategies can be altered by the teacher who is sensitive to her influence on the students' concept of themselves as readers. This concept can be developed using three teaching strategies: immersing students in reading, attributing success to effective strategy use, and allowing time for personal reading.

To be engaged in the actual reading of text is the first important prerequisite for developing a concept of self as reader. *Immersing students in relevant reading* will increase their concept of themselves as readers. As students read material that is relevant, culturally appropriate, and at their instructional reading level, they can feel themselves reading. Struggling readers, however, have few opportunities to read contextual information. In first-grade classrooms, Allington (2005) reports that children in high-reading groups read three times as many words as children in low-reading groups. Therefore, increasing the amount of fluent contextual reading students engage in each day is the first step toward helping them develop a concept of self as reader. Difficult reading material causes students to focus on the word level of reading, precluding an active search for meaning. Reading text fluently and at an easy level allows students to read enough words correctly so that they can engage in an active search for meaning.

Struggling readers, however, need more than easy reading material to change their concept of themselves as readers. As the children build their self-concepts as readers, a second major task of the teacher is to talk about the strategies used to derive meaning from text and *attribute active reading to effective strategy use and effort* (Linnenbrink & Pintrich 2003). Because of the repeated failures of struggling readers, they do not recognize the effective strategies they do use. When asked how they got an answer, students often respond with "I don't know." These students do not have enough experience with successful reading to recognize when and how their effective strategies work. Often, they attribute their reading performance to forces outside their control rather than to effective use of strategies. To change this attitude, teachers show students how their strategies influence reading performance. As students engage in reading, the teacher points out or names the strategy they are using. The teacher follows this up by attributing success to effective strategy use and effort. When effective strategies are supported, students can attribute their comprehension not only to the product but also to the process of active reading. They begin to see themselves as active readers who can construct meaning from text.

However, many struggling readers do not recognize their effective strategy use. These readers need more than teachers evaluating their performance and strategy use orally. Thus, the diagnostic teacher *encourages **self-assessment***, which helps readers evaluate and recognize their strategy use. They need a way to see their progress and attribute it to strategy use. Using self-assessment charts (see chapter 4), the students' attention is refocused on those behaviors they can control. Students can also evaluate their strategies use by using teacher-developed check sheets related to the task. For example, a check sheet was designed with story grammar questions (see "Story Mapping" in part 2). The students marked whether their retelling included main characters, setting, problem, major events, and problem resolution. Using the check sheet, the students and teacher assess literacy and strategy use. These self-assessments help struggling readers develop a more systematic evaluation of reading performance and attribute their performance to internal factors such as knowledge and strategies rather than to luck or easy materials.

GUIDELINE #6: DEVELOP A CONCEPT OF SELF AS READER

- Immerse students in reading
- Encourage students to attribute active reading to effective strategy use
- Encourage self-assessment

Responding

In all her interactions, the teacher responds as a person. She responds to the different students in her classroom and challenges them according to their individual needs. She uses what they already know to present concepts matching the way they learn best. Using the unique strengths of the individual learners in her classroom, she reduces stress for each learner. Furthermore, she acknowledges the realities of the educational situation. Using personal statements about her own reading process and laughing about her own mistakes increase students' awareness that reading is constructing a response rather than getting the answer right.

Guideline #7: Be Sensitive to Individual Differences

Students bring to the reading task their own sets of experiences and knowledge that affect their reading behavior. At the same time, they bring their own strategies for dealing with the world. Some children are impulsive, some are extremely verbal, and some are quiet. Even though each of them is different, seldom do these differences affect instruction in public schools, partly because the exploration of how learners are alike and different is limited. Understanding human similarities can increase one's sensitivity to human differences.

People learn new information in two ways. First, they use what they already know to formulate hypotheses about new information. Second, they use their reading strategies to learn the information. Therefore, in a state of disequilibrium (new learning), people use what they already know to make sense of the new information. However, people differ not only on *what* they already know (knowledge-based differences) but also on *how* they integrate new information with what they already know (strategy-based differences).

Knowledge-based differences are evident in the scope of vocabulary knowledge and the variety of experiences that students have. Some children come to school with a rich variety of experiences and well-developed oral language. Some children have had repeated experiences with books and have developed concepts about print. Other children come to school with limited experiences with reading events and require more exposure to a variety of experiences with both print and concepts.

These knowledge-based differences are accentuated by differences in problem-solving strategies. All students do not learn the same way. Some students select meaning cues, while others select graphic cues. For example, Clay (1993) found that many young readers did not integrate cuing systems. Some of these students used a visual cuing system: they matched the missed word with the initial letters of other words they knew. Other students used the phonic cuing system: they matched the missed word to the sounds they knew.

Some students rely heavily on their background knowledge to form hypotheses while they are reading. These students check what they already know without thinking about the text. Other students rely heavily on the text to form their hypotheses while reading. Some students summarize stories, giving the overall gist of the text, while other students give explicitly stated information. Some students revise and monitor their model of meaning readily, while others need concrete facts before they revise their model of meaning. Some students organize information within broad, overlapping categories, while others organize information in discrete, hierarchical categories. Being sensitive to individual differences, the diagnostic teacher *adjusts instruction, incorporating not only what students already know but also what they can do.*

The diagnostic teacher thinks carefully about the individual students in her classroom. Because the reading event is more stressful for struggling readers, the demand for instruction using strengths, i.e., background knowledge and personal reading strategies, is more critical for them. The diagnostic teacher *reduces stress by using students' strengths*. By using appropriate instructional methods, the diagnostic teacher can reduce the stress and increase learning. For example, teachers have differentiated prompting by using language that emphasizes the preferred cuing system and then encouraging the integration of other cuing systems (Clay, 1993). For instance, the student using the visual cuing system can be prompted to use meaning-based and visual cues by asking, "What makes sense?" or "What begins with the letter . . . and makes sense in the sentence?" Teacher prompting can effectively focus instruction on using students' processing strengths and then encouraging them to incorporate more flexible strategies.

Furthermore, *individual sense making is encouraged through the use of* I *statements.* The teacher models "I think . . . ," talking about her own reading and thinking aloud about how she figured out a particular answer. Showing the *how* and modeling "I think . . . " releases students from the necessity of having to do the process in the same way. "I do it this way" implies that others can do it a different way. Furthermore, this attitude eases the need to conform and acknowledges that even though a particular process or strategy for solving problems is not an effective strategy for reading, it may be effective in other situations. For the impulsive child, the teacher often remarks, "Someday your rapid-fire decision making may help you become a great artist, but when you are reading text, you need to think about what the author is trying to say."

Being sensitive to individual differences requires that the diagnostic teacher evaluate and use students' strengths in background knowledge and strategy deployment. First, she evaluates what the students already know because using what they already know will increase what is learned. Second, she assesses the way the students learned what they already know so that new information can be presented using the students' strategies. These two categories, knowledge-based differences and strategy-based differences, help the diagnostic teacher adjust instruction for individual students. As the teacher learns to meet the needs of her students, she uses their strengths and models *I* statements (which releases everyone from doing things in the same way). Thus, she encourages individual variation in problem solving.

GUIDELINE #7: BE SENSITIVE TO INDIVIDUAL DIFFERENCES

- Adjust instruction to what students already know and do
- Reduce stress by using students' strengths
- Use *I* statements to acknowledge individual variation in problem solving

Guideline #8: Foster a Reality-Based Approach to Instruction

Even though each child is different and some are harder to teach than others, the diagnostic teacher interacts with each of her students as a person. She is a participant in the learning process, sharing with them her reactions to reading events and student learning. Honest communication and sharing of the knowledge of the students' reading strategies set the stage.

The diagnostic teacher helps students develop a realistic assessment of their own reading behavior, as opposed to a tense, perfectionist view of their learning. Continually, she demonstrates that *real life requires coping with mistakes.* She becomes human as she talks about her own mistakes and coping behaviors, focusing on the process rather than the products of reading. As the teacher finds humor in her mistakes and proceeds to correct them, so too will her students learn to reflect on their mistakes in a lighthearted manner, realizing that they can correct incongruencies as they read. Mistakes become a tool for learning rather than an indication of failure. Modeling self-correcting strategies in a relaxed atmosphere helps students develop a risk-taking attitude toward reading (Goodman & Marek, 1996) and increases their active reading behavior.

Likewise, effective teachers expect students to think, cope with their mistakes, and resolve problems as they read. As such teachers adjust instruction, they *maintain high expectations* (Taylor, Pearson, Clark, & Walpole, 2002). They expect students to read lots of words and to express ideas based on what they have read. A major characteristic contributing to the success of all readers is the teacher's expectation that all students can read and learn. Maintaining appropriate expectations is extremely demanding for the diagnostic teacher. It is important, however, to maintain high expectations and to share with students how those expectations are to be met. Once the diagnostic teacher has made adjustments during instruction, she tells students she expects them to complete the necessary reading. She emphasizes that real life involves coping with limitations and using one's strengths to solve difficult problems.

Finally, the diagnostic teacher engages students by personally responding to literature, *discussing her own personal change as a result of reading and writing experiences.* In other words, she shares how literacy has changed her life. This personal response draws students into discussing their own individual reactions to literature. Consequently, both the students and the teacher talk about how their worldview is changing as a result of being literate. In this way, she fosters reality-based instruction that gives the student more than a reading experience; it provides a model for how literacy stimulates people to expand their own knowledge.

In her classroom, the effective teacher creates a relaxed environment where students can take risks and correct mistakes as they try out new ideas. She expects that all students will grow and learn from their mistakes. She interacts with her students, personally sharing with them her own interpretations and growth. Thus, a reality-based approach to instruction is just that: it makes reading a real, personal event.

GUIDELINE #8: FOSTER A REALITY-BASED APPROACH TO INSTRUCTION

- Teach that real life requires coping with mistakes
- Maintain high expectations
- Discuss personal change as a result of reading and writing

Summary

Effective diagnostic teaching creates a situational context where all students can share ideas and learn together. She welcomes multiple viewpoints and multiple cultures weaving a tapestry of learning. Thus, the diagnostic teacher plans for a literate community, the emphasis of which is success. She mediates learning to create active, engaged readers while assessing responses while she teaches. She is sensitive to the individual differences among her students and accepts the uniqueness of each reader's experiences and cultures. The diagnostic teacher provides support for students giving them the resources to become active, independent readers and writers who positively engage in literacy activities. Thus, she reflects on instruction not only as the planner, mediator, and supporter but also as a participant. She acknowledges her own personal response to literature and fosters in her classroom sincere responses and thoughtful sharing.

4 The Diagnostic Teaching Session: An Overview

The diagnostic teaching session* places a premium on tailoring programs that specifically fit problem readers. It provides a structure for lesson planning that uses the processes of assessment and instruction to identify instructional alternatives and monitor their effectiveness. The session is composed of the following six elements: (a) familiar text time, (b) continuous diagnostic assessment, (c) guided contextual reading, (d) strategy and skill instruction, (e) process writing time, and (f) personalized reading and writing. Each element performs a distinct function and combines with the others to form a complete diagnostic teaching session that can be completed in an hour and a half. However, the session may be spread out over several days or a week, depending on the amount of individual contact the teacher has with the student.

Each of the six elements has specific purposes within the session framework. *Familiar text time* provides a time for students to flexibly use their reading strategies and skills while reading easy material. It provides a balance between easy reading and the challenging tasks that lie ahead (Roskos & Walker, 1994). *Continuous diagnostic assessment* uses the principles of dynamic assessment to monitor the effect of instruction on students' learning. It is a way for the teacher to assess growth by gathering data about students' unaided performance in the text that is used for guided contextual reading. In this way, assessment occurs during an instructional setting, a critical aspect of diagnostic teaching. *Guided contextual reading* focuses on meaningful interpretation of entire stories and informational passages while allowing students to demonstrate their strengths. It involves the planning and mediating roles of the diagnostic teacher. The diagnostic teaching session also includes the other two elements embedded in the reading event. *Strategy and skill instruction* focuses on specific areas of concerns that might be inhibiting students' active reading. By engaging in strategy instruction, the teacher promotes student independence. During *process writing time*, the teacher supports writing by demonstrating writing conventions and encouraging the student to write. During *personalized reading and writing*, both the students and the teacher engage in reading and writing for their own purposes and self-fulfillment. This element extends aspects of the diagnostic teaching

---

* The diagnostic teaching session is based on a teaching procedure developed by Darrel D. Ray and used in the Oklahoma State University Reading Clinic. The author is grateful for the perceptive insights gleaned from her work in that clinic.

session by helping students develop concepts of themselves as readers and ensuring success. The students define their own goals during this element. This chapter explains the instructional premises of the diagnostic teaching session and discusses its features, which are further elaborated on in the chapters on instruction and assessment that follow.

Premises

In addition to the components of the reading event and the roles of the diagnostic teacher described in previous chapters, the diagnostic teaching session is based on concepts related to *balanced* reading instruction.

1. Effective diagnostic teaching results in a *balance* of contextual reading with strategy and skill instruction. Guided contextual reading uses entire stories and informational passages to teach reading as the students interpret and discuss text. Strategy and skill instruction provides minilessons in specific strategies or skills that could enhance a student's active reading.

2. Effective diagnostic teaching results from monitoring the effect that instructional adjustments have on reading performance. The diagnostic teacher *balances* assessment and instruction. Continuous diagnostic assessment provides baseline data about students' reading performance prior to instruction and is done prior to guided contextual reading. During this phase, the reading lesson is adjusted so that the reader can construct meaning with text. The difference between performance without aid (continuous diagnostic assessment) and performance with aid (guided contextual reading) is recorded using the data from these two elements. Thus, the diagnostic teacher *balances* assessment with instruction.

3. Effective diagnostic teaching results from a *balance* of guided (implicit) instruction and direct (explicit) instruction. Personalized reading and writing is characterized by implicit instruction during which the teacher acts as a participant in the learning process. The focus is on constructing meaning with text. Strategy and skill instruction, on the other hand, is characterized by minilessons that explicitly demonstrate needed strategies and skills.

4. Effective diagnostic teaching is supported by a *balance* between text selected by the student and text selected by the teacher. In familiar text time and personalized reading and writing, students select the texts. In guided contextual reading and strategy and skill instruction, the teacher usually selects texts with student input.

5. Effective diagnostic teaching allows students to demonstrate their strengths (what they already know and do) by overlapping what is known and done with new information and new strategies. In other words, the diagnostic teacher *balances* instruction using the students' strengths with instruction in areas of need.

6. Effective diagnostic teaching results from a *balance* of challenging and easy reading tasks. Thus, reading materials are validated by the diagnostic teacher, and texts are chosen to maximize student success on both independent and mediated reading. Guided contextual reading provides instruction in material that is moderately challenging for the student, while personalized reading and writing are characterized by easy reading material. During strategy and skill instruction, the diagnostic teacher uses a combination of moderately challenging texts and easy texts, depending on the instructional needs of the learners.

These premises underlie the elements of the diagnostic teaching sessions. Taken together, the elements provide a vehicle for monitoring the effect of instructional adjustments and the *balance* of instruction using strengths and instruction in areas of need, of contextual reading and strategy lessons, of implicit and explicit instruction, of challenging and familiar reading tasks, of self-selected and teacher-selected materials, and of assessment and instruction.

Familiar Text Time

Familiar text time (FTT) is the rereading of books and poems that the student enjoys. These easy and often predictable books are authentic children's literature that can be read repeatedly because of the rhyme, rhythm, and repetition. Like singing a favorite song over and over again, this procedure engages the readers in active reading and sets a supportive tone for the entire session.

In this part of the diagnostic session, the diagnostic teacher invites the reader to choose among four or five familiar stories. Allowing the reader to choose what she will read increases engagement. By choosing, the reader establishes a reason for reading the selected text. She might think, "I like how the bird scares the spider, so I will choose this one." Thus, the student is in control of this aspect of the diagnostic session.

Familiar text also increases the amount of easy reading that the student accomplishes during the diagnostic teaching session, which establishes a balance between easy and challenging tasks. During FTT, students use their developing strategies and skills within the context of already-known material. As they try out and refine their new strategies and skills while immersed in known information, readers concentrate on implementing the new processes. The interactions, among the teacher, the student, and the text provides a safety net for making and correcting mistakes, in turn increasing the active engagement of readers. They enjoy the risk-taking activity that begins the session and continue the rest of the session with this same attitude.

Continuous Diagnostic Assessment

Continuous diagnostic assessment (CDA) is an unaided assessment taken from the text used during **guided contextual reading** (GCR). It is the vehicle used to monitor reading performance. During the other elements, the diagnostic teacher adjusts instruction as the students read; therefore, this element assesses students' reading performance. No teaching is done at this time. Continuous diagnostic assessment allows the diagnostic teacher to collect a sample of reading behavior prior to or after instruction. Then the diagnostic teacher compares performance data without guided instruction (CDA) and reading performance during GCR. These samples of reading behavior allow the diagnostic teacher to develop hypotheses about the changing reading needs of the students.

Conducting Assessment Prior to Reading for Guided Reading Approaches

The assessment before GCR provides two kinds of information. First, it provides information about the appropriateness of the text that is being used during the GCR element. If the material proves too difficult (at frustration level) or too easy (at independent level), an alternate text is selected and checked for an appropriate match (see chapter 5 for procedures to determine performance level). The teacher asks himself, "Am I using an appropriate text (moderately difficult) in GCR?" Second, this assessment provides baseline data so that the teacher can analyze the difference between unaided reading performance and the students' reading performance with instruction. He asks himself, "Is the student profiting from my instruction? Is there a difference between the reading performance in GCR and CDA?"

To monitor progress, the teacher follows the procedures found in chapter 5. First, a segment from the text to be used in GCR is read without prior instruction (at sight). A passage about 50 to 125 words long is selected, and questions are written that focus on the main idea or problem, key facts or events, key vocabulary words, and inferences. The selection is read orally or silently, depending on the focus of instruction (see chapter 5). Error or miscue rates and percentage of comprehension are calculated. These data are compared to the criteria of performance for instructional level found in Table A–6 in appendix A. Decisions are made as to the appropriateness of the text. If the selection is at frustration reading level (more than 1 miscue out of every 10 running words and comprehension below 50%), the teacher immediately moves to easier reading material in the GCR segment. For example, Chris reads a selection from a trade book with a rate of one miscue every seven words and a 50% comprehension rate on constructed questions. Since these results indicate frustration-level reading, the diagnostic teacher selects an easier text to use during GCR.

If the selection reflects the instructional reading level, the diagnostic teacher continues using the material and records miscues to establish a pattern of reading performance. For example, Sally reads a selection from a novel with a rate of 1 miscue every 15 words and 80% comprehension. After three samplings in this text, the error pattern indicates that the substitution miscues most prevalent are on key vocabulary words, limiting comprehension. The diagnostic teacher develops a program of word identification based on word meanings related to both the text to be read and background knowledge. He adapts instruction during GCR by using a semantic map of key words to increase both word identification and word meanings of those words (see "Semantic Mapping" in part 2). After the story is read, he returns to the map and adds new understandings to reinforce word meaning with word identification.

If the selection is at an independent level, a more difficult text needs to be evaluated in the CDA phase. The diagnostic teacher then selects a more difficult text and prepares a segment for evaluation. For example, Toni, whose instructional focus is on meaning processing, can silently read a segment from a third-grade text with 100% comprehension. No previous instruction was provided before this segment was read. Therefore, a text at the fourth-grade level is selected. To evaluate suitability of that text, an on-level assessment is conducted and scored. Toni reads the on-level evaluation silently with 70% comprehension on the constructed questions. As a result, the text used in GCR with Toni is changed to the fourth-grade text, which reflects a level that is challenging to her and has a moderate success rate.

Conducting Assessment After Reading for Supportive/Shared Reading Approaches

When a student and teacher read a story together before the student reads the story on her own, the teacher uses a different approach to monitor progress. This supportive beginning allows students to read text beyond their instructional reading level; therefore, the teacher assesses performance after instruction, waiting at least 20 minutes before asking the student to read part of the selection for an assessment. The student should be able to read the text at independent level. The assumption is that if the student is learning, a text that initially would have been at frustration level will convert to independent level when taught using the supportive reading techniques of shared reading, language experience, and collaborative reading (see part 2).

To monitor progress, the teacher follows the procedures found in chapter 5. A segment from the text already taught in guided contextual reading is read orally. A passage about 50 to 125 words in length is selected, and questions that focus on the main theme are written. Error or miscue rates and percentage of comprehension are calculated. These data are compared to the criteria of performance for independent level found in Table A–6 in appendix A. If the selection is read at independent level, then the procedures and the level of difficulty are probably creating the appropriate cognitive stretch for the learner. The diagnostic teacher carefully reviews the amount of support given to attain independent level. If support is moderate, he continues his approach. If a high degree of support is needed, such as rereading the text together six times rather than just once or twice, then the diagnostic teacher considers selecting easier material (see chapter 9). However, if the diagnostic teacher is giving the student very little support, then he might consider moving to a more difficult text or changing the technique. For example, Jenny was reading together with the teacher, keeping a fairly good pace. After reading the selected text together, they briefly discussed the story, and then Jenny read alone. The next day, Jenny read the entire story again with no miscues. The diagnostic teacher decided that rather than move to a more difficult text, he would try an "at sight" assessment (see "Using Guided Assessments" this section) in the trade book *Frog and Toad*. Jenny read this sample passage at an instructional level. Thus, the diagnostic teacher changed his instructional approach to increase the cognitive stretch for Jenny.

In all the elements, the diagnostic teacher is assessing the response of students to instruction. As a more systematic monitor of progress, however, the students read a segment of a text without immediate instruction. Continuous diagnostic assessment is an integral part of the diagnostic teaching session because it provides the framework for dynamic assessment by providing immediate data about the students' performance in the selected text without instruction.

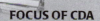

FOCUS OF CDA

- Monitor reading behavior
- Analyze patterns when reading
- Analyze reading growth

Guided Contextual Reading

Each teaching session includes a GCR lesson, which focuses instruction on the communication of ideas gleaned from reading entire stories and informational passages. Therefore, the focus of this element is constructing meaning with text. Guided contextual reading encompasses 60% of the instructional time in the diagnostic teaching session; therefore, students are reading contextual material for the majority of the time. The reading selection is of sufficient length to allow for comprehension of story-line and character development; however, it is short enough to provide a sense of closure for the reader. During GCR, the diagnostic teacher differentiates instruction according to the strengths and reading levels of the students. Texts are moderately challenging and are chosen to maximize student performance.

The diagnostic teacher thinks about the kind of instruction needed before, during, and after the student reads the selected story or chapter. He considers the support needed before the story to enable the student to construct meaning with text. The teacher asks himself, "Can I provide support before reading to help the student anticipate the meaning?" If support is needed, he reviews the charts that suggest techniques to use before reading a story (see Tables 11–1 and 11–2 in chapter 11). Then the student's attention is focused on the key concepts of the story prior to reading. These concepts are related to the student's own experience. Together, teacher and student develop predictions related to the story theme, thus increasing the student's active reading of the story. Open-ended questions need to focus on predictions that will engage the student in active reading through the entire length of the story. Therefore, purposes or predictions that can be answered on the first page of the story hardly represent the main story theme.

During this brief discussion, the teacher anticipates problem vocabulary words and, if needed, provides instruction in either word identification or word meaning. This instruction needs to be directly related to the story to be read, predictions that have been made, and the key concepts or story theme. Time is of the essence in diagnostic teaching. Consequently, only the important words, meanings, and concepts need to be stressed.

The second step of guided contextual reading occurs while the students are reading and includes silent reading to construct meaning. The diagnostic teacher thinks about what kind of support is needed as the students read the story or chapter. If support is needed, he reviews the charts that suggest techniques to use during instruction (Tables 11–1 and 11–2 in chapter 11). While discussing the story, the teacher needs to elicit responses from students that focus on the main theme. Rather than focusing on responses and questions that are text-based, literal, and unrelated to the story theme, the teacher can use questions and lead discussions that focus students on understanding the purposeful actions of the characters to resolve the problems in the story. In other words, a thematic focus and logical questions help students summarize the main actions or ideas and themes that occur.

After the text is read, the students respond to the passage as a whole. This requires the students to analyze the story in terms of the characters' motivations, the author's purpose for writing the story, and other stories and experiences with similar themes. A key component of this phase is students relating the story to similar personal experiences and analyzing the effect these experiences have on comprehending the story. Experiences may include other stories, movies, and songs that the students have encountered with similar plots and characters, as well as personal experiences. Students should focus on the similarities and differences among these cases, using textual and nontextual information to support statements.

These aspects form the framework for GCR, the major component of the diagnostic teaching session. Basic to the development of GCR is an instructional sequence that uses the students' strengths; therefore, specialized techniques are selected so that the reader can construct meaning. In other words, the diagnostic teacher asks, "What can I do to make these stories more understandable for my students? Do I need specific reading techniques to ensure active reading At what point in the instructional sequence do I need to adjust my instruction?"

For example, students who have a limited ability to deal with oral language could receive vocabulary development and direct experiences with the prerequisite concepts that are necessary to read a particular selection with understanding. For these students, GCR requires an increased amount of instruction before they read the story. Semantic maps (see "Semantic Mapping" in part 2), which require students and teacher to construct a visual diagram relating the students' background knowledge to unfamiliar words, are used to introduce the story. In this case, the instructional adjustment occurs prior to reading the story. This approach facilitates the students' understanding of the concepts in the story and increases their ability to construct meaning.

When students experience little difficulty with understanding what the words mean, however, the instructional adjustments are different. For students who show extreme difficulty with recognizing the words, the diagnostic teacher spends more time on word identification and less time on developing word meanings. Before a story is read, for example, a language experience story (see "Language Experience Approach" in part 2) might be written using the targeted vocabulary words. The teacher encourages rereading of this story so that the students encounter the vocabulary in text. After the selected story is read, readers theater scripts (see "Readers Theater" in part 2) could be constructed from the story so that increasing oral reading fluency becomes purposeful. The diagnostic teacher incorporates specialized techniques both before and after the students read the story. The adjustments facilitate their ability to construct meaning with text. During GCR, the diagnostic teacher differentiates instruction according to learner strengths. The ultimate goal is to focus on reading in connected text that will allow the students to integrate their prior knowledge with the text and to develop personal interpretations.

FOCUS OF GCR

- Have the students read entire stories
- Focus on meaning
- Support active reading before, during, and after the lesson
- Differentiate instruction so that the reader can construct meaning

Strategy and Skill Instruction

Strategy and skill instruction (SAS) consists of a series of minilessons planned to develop and modify reading strategies. As such, the diagnostic teacher selects texts to teach a designated strategy or skill. He carefully selects varying levels of text difficulty to provide for an interplay of easy and challenging reading. Three requirements form a basis for the effective execution of strategy and skill instruction. First, prior to teaching a strategy or skill, the teacher conducts a task analysis. Task analysis of reading performance pinpoints specific strategies or skills that could increase students' reading (McCormick, 2007). Second, after the task analysis has identified those strategies and skills that if developed could enhance proficient reading, lessons that explicitly teach those strategies are developed. Strategy instruction (see part 2) is a minilesson that is constructed so that the teacher can easily explain and model how to use a particular strategy or skill. Finally, the targeted task is monitored by the students and teacher, using a graphic representation of progress that calls for self-assessment.

Analysis of Patterns of Reading Development

The analysis of reading patterns identifies strategies and skills that could enhance the student's reading. Using the constructs of informal reading assessment, miscue analysis, and think-aloud procedures (see chapters 5 and 6), the diagnostic teacher identifies particular reading strategies and skills that if learned would readily increase students' reading performance.

An initial informal assessment of Mary, for example, identifies fluency of word identification as a concern that if developed could enhance her reading performance. Further analysis indicates that she can decode words in isolation. During the diagnostic lesson, however, it is evident that when miscues are made, Mary does not use what the word looks like or means in the story to correct the miscue. In other words, she does not ask herself, "What makes sense and starts with the letter(s) . . . ?" This analysis indicates that she would benefit from instruction in applying a sense-making framework or in using the overall context to self-correct errors. Therefore, the reading analysis results in recommending strategy instruction in self-correction.

Strategy and Skill Instruction

After the reading analysis has identified those strategies and skills that could enhance proficient reading, lessons that teach those strategies are created. For most mini-lessons, the diagnostic teacher selects an easy text to introduce the targeted strategy or skill, limiting other possible problems in text interpretation. As the new strategy or skill is learned the diagnostic teacher increases the difficulty level of the text so as to lead students to use the targeted strategy or skill in reading situations that are moderately difficult. The activities need to be carefully chosen so that the teacher can model active reading. The strategies and skills of reading development are explained in Chapter 11 and techniques to support their improvement are found in Table 11-4 and 11-5. For Mary, therefore, an effective diagnostic technique would be an adapted repeated reading (see Modification #2 in "Repeated Readings" in part 2) that incorporates the strategy instruction of self-talk ("What would make sense and starts with a . . . ?") as an intervention between the first and second readings.

Initially, students are informed of their inefficient strategies and shown the efficient counterpart (see "Strategy Instruction" in part 2). After stating how the strategy or skill works, the teacher gives students a rationale for its inclusion in their program and tells them why doing these specific activities will increase strategic reading. Then students are led systematically through a series of short activities. In the first examples, the teacher demonstrates the active reading process. Then students use the teacher's example to modify their previous strategy use.

In Mary's case, after the first reading of a selection, the teacher reviews miscues and suggests that reading would be more effective if Mary would check the miscue to see whether it made sense. Then he explains how he would self-correct those miscues using a sense-making framework and checking the initial letter of a word. For example, before the second reading, the teacher explains that when reading breaks down, Mary should ask what would make sense and start with the same letter as the word in the text. "If I had made this mistake," says the teacher, "I would have asked, 'What would Dad use that starts with a *sh?* Then I would have corrected the sentence to read, 'Dad shoveled the garden,' and said, 'That's good! I can make sense of my reading by fixing up my mistakes.' Then I would continue to read. Now *you* try the next sentence with a miscue." As Mary rereads the next sentences, the diagnostic teacher scaffolds her attempts with strategy conversations. He focuses the conversations on the targeted strategies and discusses the active thinking process involved in using a particular strategy or skill. Furthermore, he encourages self-evaluation. For Mary, the teacher says, "I like the way you reread that sentence to correct your mistake. What did you think about as you changed your original response?" This approach engages Mary in describing her thinking. The teacher responds by supporting active thinking and highlighting Mary's strengths in strategy deployment. These on-the-spot conversations help Mary talk about her strategy use as well as expand her strategy options. These conversations lead into the third aspect of strategy and skill instruction: self-assessment.

Self-Assessment

The third aspect of strategy and skill instruction is helping students evaluate their increasing use of strategic reading processes. Self-assessment, therefore, directs the students' attention to the use of various strategies and to the effect their implementation has on their reading. It also helps students draw relationships among their strategy use, skill knowledge, and personal effort.

Constructing a graph or self-assessment rubric of strategy use provides an avenue for the students and teacher to discuss the strategies that the students are using and how the strategies or skills will enhance active reading. For example, using the chart in Table 4–1, Mary evaluated her fluency when she completed her second reading. This evaluation encouraged her to discuss how the strategies she was acquiring were influencing her reading fluency. Thus, Mary, like other students, assumes increasing responsibility for changing her reading behaviors. Charts can be skill oriented, as in the fluency chart in Table 4–1, or they can be charts of strategy use, such as the chart in Table 4–2. Self-assessment charts can vary in complexity; however, the focus of charting should be the evaluation of strategy and skill use and discussing how changing strategic reading enhances constructing meaning with text. Thus, the students assume the role of monitoring strategic reading; the teacher discusses their troubleshooting strategies, thus encouraging self-assessment.

Strategy and skill instruction is like many regular classroom lessons; however, it is different because it is specific to the readers' targeted concerns in reading. In diagnostic teaching, it is important to identify those strategies and skills that are limiting active reading. The diagnostic teacher asks, "What strategies and skills are limiting reading improvement? Will instruction in these strategies or skills advance active reading?" Identifying and working with these strategies and skills will improve overall reading. Therefore, the key characteristic of SAS is the identification of specific strategies and skills that problem readers need and that, when taught, will enhance constructing meaning with text.

TABLE 4–1 *Chart for Self-Evaluation of Fluency*

How I Read Today	M	T	W	Th	F
Fluently in Phrases					
Mostly in Phrases				●	●
Sometimes Word by Word		●	●		
Mostly Word by Word	●				

TABLE 4–2 *Chart for Self-Assessment of Comprehension Strategies*

Today when I read,	Not at All	Sometimes	Most of the Time
I made predictions throughout.			
I revised my predictions as needed.			
I justified my thinking.			
I thought about the information in the text.			
I thought about what I knew.			
I used important information.			
I used the text information and what I knew together.			

Today my reading was _____ because _____
_____.

FOCUS OF STRATEGY AND SKILL INSTRUCTION

- Conduct an analysis of patterns of strategy and skill development
- Implement strategy and skill instruction
- Encourage students to employ self-assessment
- Converse about strategy use

Process Writing Time

Each teaching session includes a specified time for writing that focuses instruction on the communication of ideas through writing. Writing is a constructive process. Writers envision what they want to say, and as they write, they revise the content by checking ideas to see whether they are making sense. As they write, students elaborate what was written, making connections between what they wrote and what they know to create new ideas. Writing also supports using the convention of written language. As students revise their work, they not only change and confirm their ideas but also edit their work by revising their work, expanding their knowledge of written conventions.

Writing time includes a minilesson and time to write at each session. The diagnostic teacher demonstrates how to write. Sometimes he uses his life to model how to write, but other times he uses interactive writing. Using interactive writing, the teacher and students create a written piece of information together. As they create the piece, the teacher interjects information about idea development and written conventions. These models help children understand and use the writing process. Pappas, Kiefer, and Levstid (2006) suggest that minilessons can include modeling writing techniques, such as sketching characters, using imagery, or working on specific conventions of writing.

FOCUS OF PROCESS WRITING TIME

- Provide time for writing
- Conduct minilessons
- Share products

Writing time also includes a time to share writing. During sharing time, students share works in process in a one-to-one setting, in small groups, or as an entire class. As students read their work, others find where they need to clarify their writing. The share sessions are sometimes called Author's Chair (Short, Harste, & Burke, 1996). At other times, students share their work to celebrate their completed writing product. Everyone gathers to listen to each others' writing.

Personalized Reading and Writing

In personalized reading and writing, students are engaged in 10 or more minutes of self-selected reading and 10 or more minutes of self-selected writing. This element offers students a time of quiet reflection to respond personally using the language arts. Writing and reading influence each other, and both develop from children's desire to communicate. In this phase, time is set aside for the students and teacher to read and write for their own purposes. Easing the structure of the teaching session and shifting the control to the students are crucial aspects of situating literacy. If the students do not experience "choosing to read and write," they may not define literate activities as a part of their lives. Personal reading and writing allows time for students to define their literacy interest, to read and write for their own purposes, and to read and write without failing because they establish their purposes. In this way, they are defining themselves as literate individuals.

For the silent reading time (see "Sustained Silent Reading" in part 2), students select books, magazines, newspapers, or their own writing to read during the designated time period. Encouraging students to read books for their own enjoyment rather than instructional purposes develops the desire to read. They learn to ask themselves, "What do I want to read about? What kind of stories do I find more interesting?" This facilitates habits of book selection and defining interests (Gambrell & Marinak, 1997).

Students are taught to match the book to their reading levels by using the rule of thumb (Morrow & Walker, 1997). To determine whether it is a good match, they read a page from their selected book and put a finger on each unknown word starting with the little finger. If they reach their thumb before the end of the page, the book is too difficult, and another should be selected. Therefore, personalized reading encourages students to select books they can successfully read and moves the control of the selection of reading material from the teacher to the students. In fact, during this element, the students are in control; they have no "have-to" reading. If the students want to skip pages, look at pictures, laugh, or cry, they can read and think whatever they want. The students control what they learn from books.

For personal writing (see Modification #1 in "Journal Writing" in part 2), the students and teacher communicate through writing. During each session, students write to the teacher about anything of interest or importance to them. Following the journal entry, the teacher comments with a brief, personal, and honest reaction to what was written.

The teacher responds during each session to what the students have written. The teacher's comments can be an empathetic response or can ask for more information. Such comments (e.g., "That sounds like fun, I would like to know more about . . . " or "Can you describe what it looked like?") allow the diagnostic teacher to encourage the fluent writing of ideas without evaluations. The focus is communication between students and teacher; therefore, the teacher should not correct any spelling or grammatical errors.

The teacher encourages the writing of ideas as he models writing in his responses to the student. This stream-of-consciousness communication is based on the students' personal, real-life experiences. The topics, length, and format are self-selected. As students compose text, they think about ways to express ideas. This thinking about how ideas are expressed sensitizes students to the visual aspects of text (how words are spelled and the order of words in sentences); consequently, students become more aware of how words are used.

In fact, personal reading and writing are both major sources of knowledge about word meaning and sentence and text structure. Both are major vehicles for self-reflection because they encourage students to think about what they want to read and learn as well as what they want to communicate in written form. Further, once students have written their thoughts on paper, they can reflect on their thinking, elaborating on their personal ideas.

Thus, personal reading and writing develop within students an interest in reading and writing for their own enjoyment. It releases students from the "have-to" assignments made during explicit and guided instruction, thus placing them in control of their interests, ideas, and emotions. By setting aside time for personal reading and writing, teachers are inviting these readers to be members of the literacy club. As problem readers continue to read and write for their own purposes, they set their own goals and thus control their responses. A student selects her journal writing to include in her portfolio (see chapter 8). Figure 4–1 shows her reflection about why she selected the journal. This activity has no wrong answers (in fact, *no* answers); thus, students cannot fail. This time gives students an opportunity to pursue their interests, responding personally to literacy.

FOCUS OF PERSONALIZED READING AND WRITING

- Evoke a personal response
- Choose reading and writing purposes
- Provide a failure-free situation

Figure 4–1   *Portfolio Reflection About Journal Writing*

> this a Journal. and this good because I cant be right and I cant be wrong. and I can write about anything I want to. And I also gave me good practice on my writeing things. My favorite writing was my one on the corus consert that we had at school. and I like this one because that day all the periods where shortened for it.

Summary

Reflecting on his roles as a diagnostic teacher and the variables of the reading event, the diagnostic teacher plans a teaching session that allows him to assess and instruct at the same time. *Familiar text time* begins each session with familiar activities that are chosen by the student. It provides time for easy, familiar reading, allowing the student to use the strategies and skills she has just learned. During *continuous diagnostic assessment,* the diagnostic teacher monitors the effects of his instruction by comparing unaided reading performance and mediated reading behavior. During *guided contextual reading,* he guides students' learning; therefore, he is constantly asking what will make this reading event successful for the students. As he teaches the planned lesson, he encourages students to read actively by focusing their attention on constructing meaning with text. He probes with leading questions: "What did the author mean when she said that? Does that [the answer] make sense in relation to the other ideas presented in the story?"

During *strategy and skill* instruction, the diagnostic teacher decides which strategies and skills would, if taught, result in higher reading achievement. Then he develops short demonstration activities to teach strategic reading and converses with students about using both strategies and skills. He uses charts to encourage self-assessment and continues the discussion about strategy use. Therefore, he builds responsibility within the students by gradually giving them the control to monitor their own reading behavior. From the folder, they select a piece to develop, revise, and edit. During *process writing time*, the students contribute written text to their writing folders. During *personalized reading and writing,* the diagnostic teacher allows time for students to read and write for their own purposes, thus inviting them to participate in the literate community.

The format of the diagnostic teaching session allows the diagnostic teacher to develop instructional alternatives that fit the strengths and needs of problem readers. By systematically planning instruction, the diagnostic teacher provides learning opportunities that enable problem readers to become independent learners.

5 Gathering Diagnostic Data

When reading and writing, students are constantly striving to construct meaning. In turn, the diagnostic teachers are constantly gathering data to formulate diagnostic hypotheses about what the reader uses to construct meaning (see Figure 5–1). Diagnostic decisions are made on the basis of data gathered before any instruction and also after instructional adjustments have been made. This chapter focuses on data acquired before the student has received instruction. Such data provide needed information about the independent literacy strategies of the learner.

In the decision-making cycle of diagnostic teaching, data are gathered to make initial decisions about instruction through standardized assessments, writing samples, word identification assessment, comprehension assessments, and informal assessments. Traditionally, the informal reading inventory (a collection of graded passages) has been used to determine a level of instruction that is moderately challenging for the students. The diagnostic teacher also establishes whether it is print or meaning that is a concern by comparing performance when students read orally and silently. Using this information, the diagnostic teacher extends her diagnosis by conducting an on-level assessment using a story or passage that she is going to teach. The data gathered from it are later used to monitor the student's changes. This assessment can be taken from the first phase of the diagnostic lesson, which establishes baseline data (see chapter 7), or it can be the baseline information that is continuously gathered (see chapter 4 for a discussion of the continuous diagnostic assessment element of the diagnostic teaching session). These procedures provide detailed information about the reader's strategies for constructing meaning with text. The diagnostic teacher uses these data to formulate hypotheses about a particular student's instructional needs. This chapter elaborates on these factors in the diagnostic process: the processing pattern and an appropriate text level for instruction and the reader's strategies and skills.

Identifying the Processing Pattern

The ultimate goal of reading is to construct meaning with text. Therefore, constructing meaning while reading silently is used by nearly everyone for daily, adult reading. However, diagnostic teachers use both oral and silent reading to assess students' reading processes. Both print and meaning processing occur simultaneously. Students

Figure 5–1   *The Decision-Making Cycle of Diagnostic Teaching*

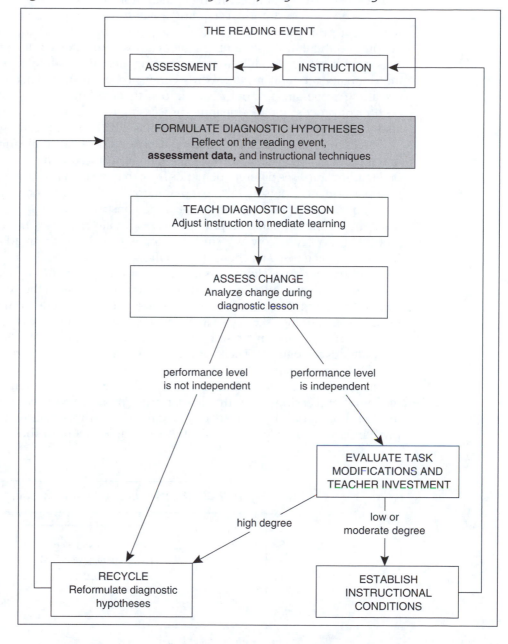

combine sources of information and shift among the text, print knowledge, and personal knowledge to figure out what the text says. Meaning processing involves predicting, monitoring, and elaborating on the author's intended meaning. When meaning becomes unclear, the reader cross-checks his own knowledge with information in the text. On the other hand, print processing involves predicting, monitoring, and elaborating on what the words on the page look like. When the meaning becomes unclear, the reader shifts his attention to a close examination of single words, that is, to print processing. When students read, they strategically combine all their resources to construct and reconstruct the author's message.

Based on an informal reading inventory, the diagnostic teacher decides whether a print processing or meaning processing pattern emerges when reading becomes difficult for a student. As the diagnostic teacher works with a student, she asks herself, "What is inhibiting constructing meaning with text? Is the student having difficulty recognizing the words (print processing), understanding the content (meaning processing), or both?" She knows that reading requires that the student use both print processing and meaning processing to construct meaning with text. She also realizes that oral reading is a different task from silent reading.

When reading orally, the reader must attend not only to meaning but also to the oral production of the text. According to Allington (1984), "The instructional setting for oral reading imposes different demands from that of silent reading (e.g., public vs. private performance, personal vs. external monitor of performance, emphasis on accuracy of production vs. accuracy of meaning construction)" (p. 853). If the diagnostic teacher needs information on print processing ability, she uses an oral reading assessment. She observes how the student attends to print when reading breaks down. Further, the diagnostic teacher listens to the student read orally and asks him to retell the passage—a process known as *oral reading analysis.* Some students call words fluently but need assistance in how to construct meaning with the words that they recognize (meaning processing). If the diagnostic teacher needs further information on meaning processing, she uses silent reading analysis and asks the student to think aloud at critical points in the story. She breaks a story into segments and discusses the story after each segment. These procedures are known as *silent reading analysis.*

By looking at the pattern in oral reading and silent reading on an informal reading inventory, the diagnostic teacher can decide the processing pattern—print or meaning processing—that the reader uses most effectively. For the diagnostic teacher, this initial decision merely begins her analysis of how the student is approaching reading. Figure 5–2 illustrates the assessment of the processing pattern.

Figure 5–2   *Assessment of Print and Meaning Processing*

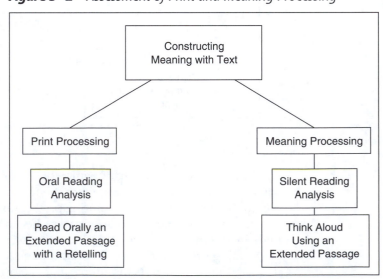

The diagnostic teacher establishes the processing pattern by thinking about how print processing and meaning processing affect the student's reading.

Establishing the Level of Student Performance

To begin gathering data, the diagnostic teacher samples reading behavior across levels of text difficulty to identify the student's level of performance. To make this assessment, the teacher uses a series of graded passages that range in difficulty from first grade to junior high. This procedure is known as *informal reading assessment.* A reader's responses on easy, moderate, and difficult texts can be used to determine a level at which the student will experience success in classroom instruction. In the initial assessment, the diagnostic teacher evaluates both oral and silent reading performance to establish appropriate instructional ranges for oral and silent reading.

Categories of Performance

To determine the level, the diagnostic teacher can administer passages from a standard **informal reading inventory**, such as the Basic Reading Inventory (Johns, 2005). Levels of performance can be established for both oral and silent reading because the inventory has equivalent forms for both types of reading. Therefore, the diagnostic teacher administers one form for the oral reading analysis and another form for the silent reading analysis. Three estimates of reading performance are derived:

1. The student's **independent reading level** provides an estimate of the level at which the student can read fluently with a high level of comprehension. The student reads and understands enough of the text to monitor his own reading performance. He applies appropriate revision strategies when reading breaks down, using both reader-based and text-based processing; therefore, teacher-directed instruction is not necessary.
2. The student's **instructional reading level** provides an estimate of the level at which the student experiences a mild amount of stress between the text and his present reading strategies. It is assumed that classroom instruction would increase the student's understanding of the text and ability to obtain new information from a text.
3. The student's **frustration reading level** provides an estimate of the level at which the reader is not fluent and has little recall of textual information. It is projected that at this level, guided instruction would be extremely demanding and time consuming because the reader does not know enough about what he is reading to make adequate connections between the new information and prior knowledge.

These levels are derived by having the student read passages from the informal reading inventory.

Scoring the Informal Reading Inventory

After each passage has been read, comprehension is evaluated by computing the percentage of correct answers to various types of comprehension questions, such as main idea, supporting details, inferences, and vocabulary. As the student reads

---

Figure 5–3   *Scoreable Errors (to be used in computing error rate)*

Substitutions or mispronunciations (the replacement of one word for another): Mark the mispronounced word by drawing a line through it and writing the substitution above the word.

want
"The man went to the store," said Ann.

Omissions (leaving out words): Circle the word omitted.

"The man went to (the) store," said Ann.

Insertions (adding extra words): Draw a carat and write the inserted word above it.

away
"The man went ‸ to the store," said Ann.

Transpositions (changing the word order): Mark with a ‿‿‿‿‿‿ .

"The man went to the store," said Ann.

Prompted words (words that have to be prompted or supplied by the teacher): Write the letter *P* above these words.

P
"The man went to the store," said Ann.

---

orally, errors or miscues (deviations from the text) are recorded. These errors are used to compute an error rate, or percentage of word recognition. Although variation exists in what types of errors or miscues are used to compute a score, generally substitutions, mispronunciations, omissions, insertions, and unknown words are used to compute the error rate (see Figure 5–3). Other reading behaviors, such as repetitions and self-corrections, are analyzed when a qualitative assessment of oral reading performance is conducted and indicate that the reader is constructing meaning. (Further directions for conducting informal reading assessments can be found in appendix A.)

Establishing Instructional Level

From the information derived from the informal reading inventory, the diagnostic teacher identifies a level that would be moderately challenging for students. She thinks again about the criteria for frustration and independent reading level and mentally pictures the ranges shown in Figure 5–4. Word recognition and comprehension criteria for *independent* reading are 1 miscue in 100 words ($\frac{1}{100}$, or 99% accuracy) and 90% comprehension accuracy. When readers know most of the words and concepts, they can then focus their attention on constructing meaning. In other words, they can independently read the text, making a variety of connections between what they know and what's in the text. Other criteria are used to identify text that is extremely difficult for a reader. Word recognition and comprehension criteria for *frustration* reading are 1 miscue in 10 words ($\frac{1}{10}$, or 90% accuracy) and 50% comprehension accuracy. Clay (1993) believes that more than a 10% error rate represents a "hard" text

Figure 5–4 *Performance Ranges*

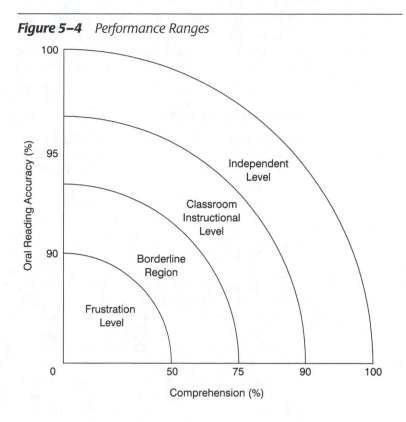

for a young child. At this frustration level, readers have extreme difficulty construct-ing meaning for two general reasons. Either they don't recognize enough words to correct their miscues and thus regain meaning, or they don't understand enough of the concepts to relate what they are reading to what they know. In either case, read-ers struggle to regain meaning, but the attempt is futile because they don't have enough knowledge to engage in active processing of text.

The range of performance between frustration level reading and indepen-dent level reading is called the *instructional level* or, more appropriately, the *In-structional range*. The instructional level is an estimate of the level at which the student would have some problems when reading classroom texts at sight, but most of these problems can be overcome after the student has a chance to read the same text silently (Johns, 2005). Therefore, the guidelines for regular classroom instruction are more in line with traditional scoring criteria in informal assessment. These crite-ria use 94% accuracy at word identification and 75% on comprehension as an esti-mate of instructional reading level. However, the range between independent and frustration level includes both (a) the acceptable instructional level used within a classroom setting and (b) a borderline range, which is often used in one-to-one tu-toring or for extended diagnosis. In this borderline range, the reader typically uses active, constructive processes to regain meaning, which often reveal their strengths and strategies in meaning construction. As Barr, Blachowicz, Bates, and Katz (2007) suggest, when students read within their borderline region (between frustration and acceptable instructional level), tailored instruction that is sensitive to their particular reading profile might result in increased student learning. This borderline region represents a text level (90% to 94% on oral reading accuracy and 50% to 74% on comprehension questions) that is moderately difficult and is appropriate for one-to-one tutoring. The diagnostic teacher uses this information to select appropriate materials for instruction (see chapter 4) and extended assessments.

Adding a Fluency Rating

While analyzing the student's performance using the traditional criteria on the informal reading inventory, the diagnostic teacher can also evaluate the student's fluency as she listens to him read orally. To do so, she asks herself three questions:

1. Is the student's reading fairly smooth?
2. Does the student read words in meaningful phrases?
3. Does the student's pitch, stress, and intonation convey the meaning of the text?

Using these questions, the diagnostic teacher rates the student's fluency on reading each paragraph and adds this information to that obtained from the traditional informal reading assessment. Sometimes the informal reading inventory does not reveal a problem with oral reading (few substitutions, omissions, or prompts), but the phrasing seems atypical. These students read like their word recognition is not automatic enough to pay attention to phrasing and expression typical of fluent reading. Thus, print processing must also be evaluated by rating fluency. The diagnostic teacher notes how the student's oral reading miscues and comprehension interact with his reading fluency on the informal reading assessment. Teachers have used a 4-point fluency scale to evaluate upper elementary school children's reading fluency (Zutell, 1988). This scale is a valid and reliable measure of the student's fluent reading and correlates with overall reading ability (Zutell, 1988). The scale includes ratings to reveal patterns of oral reading fluency (see Figure 5–5). Using this scale, a student's rating of 1 would indicate that the student is experiencing a great deal of

---

Figure 5–5 *Ratings for Oral Reading Fluency*

---

1. Clearly labored and disfluent reading, marked by very slow pace (less than 60 wpm), word-by-word reading, numerous pauses, sound-outs, repetitions, and/or lack of intonation and expression.
2. Slow and choppy reading, marked by slow pace (roughly 60–80 wpm), reading in two- and three-word phrases, many pauses, sound-outs, and/or repetitions, some difficulty with phrase, clause, and sentence boundaries and/or intonation problems at the ends of sentences.
3. Poor phrasing and intonation, marked by reasonable pace (roughly 80–105 wpm), but with some choppiness and possibly several repetitions, sound-outs, and/or run-ons.
4. Fairly fluent reading, marked by good pace (more than 110 wpm), longer phrases, and a good sense of expression and intonation. While there may be some difficulties with aspects of fluent reading behavior, this reader is aware of the need for appropriate phrasing and intonation; repetitions may be used to correct phrasing/expression errors.

Source: From *Developing a Procedure for Assessing Oral Reading Fluency: Establishing Validity and Reliability,* by J. Zutell, May 1988. Paper presented at 33rd Annual Convention, International Reading Association, Toronto, Canada. Reprinted by permission.

stress and is reading at frustration level. A rating of 2 or 3 would indicate a mild amount of stress and that the student would profit from instruction at this level. A score of 4 would indicate fluent, independent reading. After listening to the students read, the diagnostic teacher uses the fluency rating in conjunction with the information obtained from the informal reading assessment to identify performance levels and processing patterns.

Analyzing the Results from the Informal Reading Inventory

After administering the informal reading inventory, the diagnostic teacher analyzes the student's reading performance for both oral and silent reading by summarizing the data on a summary sheet (see Table A–8 in appendix A). For oral reading, she records the fluency rating, miscue rate, and comprehension percentage for each paragraph given. Likewise, she records comprehension percentages for the silent reading paragraphs given. When she has each paragraph recorded on the summary sheet, she reviews the data to establish an instructional level for both oral and silent reading. This level is indicated by the highest paragraph the student reads at the instructional level before reaching frustration. Using the criteria for performance on the chart in Table 5–1 or the charts in appendix A, the diagnostic teacher establishes independent, instructional, and frustration levels for oral and silent reading as she begins her analysis of oral and silent reading.

When the instructional level for both oral and silent reading has been established, the diagnostic teacher compares the performance on each set of paragraphs. She thinks about the instructional level for oral reading and silent reading, realizing that she needs to establish a level at which the student will profit from instruction. In the following example, if she uses silent reading, she wonders whether Ricardo will read the words or just skip words and guess at the meaning. She knows that the overall instructional level at which the student will profit from instruction must be established in order to select material. Ricardo's scores are given in Table 5–2.

Reviewing Ricardo's performance, the diagnostic teacher established the instructional level at the end of first grade. The processing pattern indicated a strength in silent reading because oral reading was lower than silent reading. Thus, Ricardo's processing pattern indicated that print processing is inhibiting his reading. At the end of first grade, Ricardo read at least 90% of the words correctly and used meaning clues to revise his miscues. To be sure that Ricardo is using both print and meaning processing to construct meaning with text, the diagnostic teacher looks for instructional material at the end of first grade to use during

---

TABLE 5–1   *Criteria for Determining Instructional Reading Levels*

Grade Level of Paragraph	Fluency	Miscue Rate	Oral Comprehension	Silent Comprehension
1–2	2–3	$1/10-1/16$	65–80%	65–80%
3–5	2–3	$1/13-1/26$	65–80	65–80
6+	3–4	$1/18-1/35$	70–85	70–85

Source: Adapted from Powell (1986).

TABLE 5–2   *Ricardo's Scores for Informal Reading Inventory*

	Oral Reading	Silent Reading
Independent level	1.25	2
Instructional level	1.75	3
Frustration level	2	4

guided contextual reading. At this instructional level, Ricardo will be able to use both print processing and meaning processing. She selected *Marvin Redpost: Lost at Birth,* with a reading level estimated near the end of first grade. She hypothesized that at this level Ricardo would be able to use both print and meaning processes as he reads. From the data, she can also conclude that Ricardo is more proficient at silent reading than oral reading. Reviewing Figure 5–2 at the beginning of the chapter, the diagnostic teacher hypothesizes that the student's strength is in meaning processing and that he needs support for print processing. She begins to build a program of instruction using his strength in meaning processing during guided contextual reading (see chapter 4) and works on print processing during strategy and skill instruction.

As the diagnostic teacher gathers data about performance levels, she is also thinking about the strategies the student is using. However, the short paragraphs on the informal reading inventory are used for screening and are not long enough to reveal the student's pattern of use of reading strategies. The diagnostic teacher then conducts an extended assessment to analyze the readers' strategies when constructing meaning with text (see chapter 6).

 Further Assessments

After the diagnostic teacher has completed the informal reading inventory, she continues gathering diagnostic data and begins to interpret her initial findings. The first interpretation is likely to be the stage of reading development indicated by the informal reading inventory. Using the instructional reading level ascertained by the informal reading inventory, the diagnostic teacher determines the stage of reading development for the child. To do this, the teacher reviews the informal reading inventory for patterns of strengths and decides on the highest-level paragraph that met the instructional criteria. She then compares this level to the stages of reading development. As she compares the information from the informal reading inventory, matching it with the stages of reading development, she asks herself if further assessments would add information for adjusting instruction to meet the needs of the readers. If the further assessments are too time consuming, she continues with an instructional plan, observing the characteristics of the readers at that stage. In other words, she can gather information while observing children within the instructional event. However, other times she may want further assessments to elaborate on her decisions about instruction. In this case, the diagnostic teacher reviews the informal reading inventory and the stages of reading development to find a level and stage of reading for a child. From this information, the diagnostic teacher selects further assessments that will inform her about the children's abilities.

Stages of Reading Development

Teachers can use stages to represent ways to group the progression of understandings that occur during reading development. Five stages help the diagnostic teacher understand the tasks confronting her students as they develop as readers (Walker, 2003b). The stages are not static but rather are overlapping stages of development that flow along a continuum. During the transition from one stage to the next, critical learning occurs. At this time, readers refine and build on their experience with previous tasks, fitting the resulting insights into the new framework as it develops. During this overlap or interface, students begin to take control of their learning while at the same time they encounter text that requires new strategies. They are assimilating new strategies while taking control over familiar strategies. Figure 5–6 elaborates on the stages.

The first stage of reading, often called the *emergent literacy stage,* begins at a very young age and continues to the middle of first grade. Children at this stage encounter literacy in social situations with their families and teachers. As they interact with others, they begin to understand what literacy is. Children read along with parents and friends and begin to understand what a book is. After memorizing a few books, often students can recognize a few words. This is the beginning of a recognition or sight vocabulary. Thus, their literacy emerges out of the social situations in which they encounter literacy.

As developing readers begin to encounter more unfamiliar words and longer stories, they develop new strategies to meet the challenges of the second stage, which begins during first grade and continues through second grade. To figure out unfamiliar words, they use decoding analogies where they match consistent letter-sound patterns in words they know with unfamiliar words. Likewise, their literacy development becomes grounded in textual conventions, such as patterns in stories, and their comprehension relies less on understanding the situational context and more on the story organization.

As learners encounter longer passages and chapter books where word meanings are embedded in complex sentence structures, the simple strategies of using sight words, decoding by analogy, and retelling the facts of a story are no longer sufficient. They are entering the third stage, which begins during third grade and continues through fifth grade. At this stage, the sentences have expanded, becoming longer and more complex. During this stage, students develop an understanding of

Figure 5–6   *Stages of Reading Development*

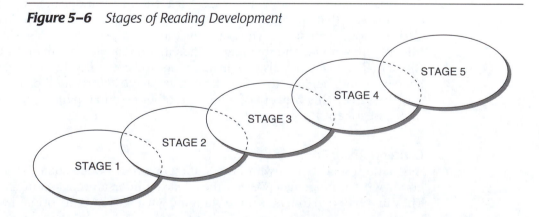

more thought-provoking sentence structure and use them to figure out sophisticated understanding in word and overall passage meaning. As sentence structure becomes more complex, students focus on predicting sentence meaning to increase fluent reading of words and phrases within sentences. As students continue to progress and read more challenging text, they find that the strategies that deal primarily with textual information are no longer adequate.

In the fourth stage, which begins in sixth grade and continues through eighth grade, texts are more difficult because authors develop complex ideas. Thus, readers assert new control over their thinking as they begin experimenting with ways of thinking. Readers must begin to shift strategically between text-based and reader-based processing, synthesizing their understanding of text. The final stage is where readers use reading and writing to construct and reflect on meaning. In this stage, readers begin to look beyond their own point of view and recognize that others exist. They also begin to link information from a variety of sources into a cohesive point of view. This synthesis requires an increasingly reflective stance that involves use of reasoning strategies as well as skill knowledge in an organized and perceptive fashion.

In the next section, each stage is discussed, and a few selected assessments are suggested that augment the diagnostic teacher's understanding of the readers' approach to literacy.

Stage 1

Many younger children may not have scored within the independent or instructional range on any paragraph on the informal reading inventory. Thus, they fall within stage 1. They need further assessments to ascertain what they know. During this stage, young readers' knowledge about printed texts expands as parents read books to them. Children begin to read along with their parents, memorizing the book. As they do this, they begin to understand that they are reading from the left side of the page to the right side of the page. They also begin to notice that books are read from the top of the page to the bottom. These new associations are what we term *concepts of print* and are important features of emergent literacy. As young children watch TV and go out to eat with their families, they begin to read signs based on distinctive features like the *M* in *McDonald's*. They know that when they go to the golden arches, they are going to eat hamburgers and french fries. This is an indication they are noticing that print carries meaning. Their knowledge grows as young children move the awareness that the golden *M* in *McDonald's* stands for *M* to understand that *m* is in many words and that we call it a letter. This understanding of letter names demonstrates that children know letters are a component of print. Young children also memorize nursery rhymes and in this way begin to hear sounds in words. Initially, they notice the rhyming sounds in words and how many sounds are in a word. In this stage, they also begin to understand concepts about words—that words have meaning, begin with certain letters, and have letter-sound patterns that always stay the same. This concept of word is another essential part of the concepts about print assessment.

Concepts About Print

As children read books with others, they begin to notice some basic conventions about written language. We call these early understandings *concepts about print*. They involve such things as understanding what we read (the printed words), where

---

Figure 5–7 *Concepts About Print Interview*

---

1. Holding the picture book by its spine, ask the child to show you the front of the book, or where it begins.
2. Say that you are going to read the story. Ask the child where to begin the story. This indicates that you are going to read the print, not the pictures in the story.
3. On the next page, ask the child to point where you should begin and in what direction should you go. This indicates the child's understanding about directionality or that print is read from the left side of the page to the right side.
4. After you have read that line, ask the child to indicate where to go next. The child should indicate that you should make a return sweep and begin on the next line. This indicates that print is read from top to bottom.
5. You can also ask where to stop reading on this page, which also indicates going from top to bottom.
6. Next, turn the page to a double spread of print. Ask the child which page you read first.
7. A child who is more advanced should be able to indicate information about words. Ask the child to frame one word, then two words.
8. Ask the child to point to the beginning letter in a word, any letter in a word.
9. Finally, ask the child to name any letters they know and any words they know.

---

the print begins, what a word is, and reading left to right. They also involve the notion that print carries meaning. In assessing concepts about print, teachers can use any simple picture book. While looking at the book, the diagnostic teacher asks the child a series of questions about book knowledge (see Figure 5–7).

Speech to Print Match

There are two ways of evaluating voice to print match. The first is more in line with concepts about print, and the other way is leading into knowledge of letter names. One way is simply to read a line of print and have the student follow along, pointing to each word as you read it. This indicates an understanding that words are the unit that we read. The young child understands that the marks on the page are related to what you are reading. Another similar emerging ability that precedes actual reading is being able to repeat a line of print with the appropriate number of words. Reading all the words correctly is not important; the child simply repeats the sentence, retaining the meaning and sentence length. This knowledge is prerequisite to understanding that individual words make up sentences.

Knowledge of Letter Names

Another assessment for young children is knowledge of letter names. As they noticed the distinctive features within their social environment, young children also notice the distinctive features of words, which are the letters. At the outset, they learn the letters in their own name so that they can write it. As parents and teachers talk about letters in words and the alphabet, young children begin to associate the various letters with their names. They often know that "S-T-O-P" spells stop and spell it every time they see a red octagonal sign with the same letters. They learn from various encounters where their parents or teachers repeatedly point out the letters and say the letter names. As they learn the letters, they are able to read a few words. The

---

Figure 5–8 *Knowledge of Letter Names*

The teacher points to a letter and asks the child to say its name.

t	n	d	f	a	s	k	b	m	g
c	r	l	h	p	x	v	o	z	y

---

diagnostic teacher assesses letter names to indicate how the child is noticing the features of words (see Figure 5–8).

Knowledge of letter names assessed before first grade has consistently been the best predictor of success in reading at the end of first grade. Many informal reading inventories include an informal assessment for letter names where the child simply says the name of the letter as the diagnostic teacher points to the letter and records the student's response. This assessment indicates how the child is using the distinctive features of words to differentiate knowledge about letters that are found in words. If the student is not attending to the distinctive features of letters within words, particularly the initial letter, then all words look alike, and the student has difficulty figuring out individual words.

Phonological Awareness

Another area the diagnostic teacher can assess is the young child's phonological awareness. This awareness develops on three levels, the syllable, the rime–onset level, and the phoneme level (Goswami, 2000). As children hear familiar stories read repeatedly, they begin to associate certain words with certain sound chunks. This ability leads to hearing the syllables in words like "he huffed and he puffed." Children recognize that *huffed* has more syllables than *he*. This is the first level of phonological awareness. Children also begin to hear the rhymes in words. As children listen to nursery rhymes and jingles, they begin to associate the singsong quality heard with the rhymes they hear. As they repeatedly chime in with the nursery rhyme "Jack and Jill went up the hill," they begin to notice that *Jill* and *hill* share some of the same sounds, /ill/. The more stories and rhymes they memorize, the more they begin to recognize the sound structure of language until they notice that both *Jack* and *Jill* begin with the same sound. Recognizing the initial sound leads the way to noticing the initial phoneme and rimes in a word. This is called the *onset* (the initial phoneme) and *rime* (the letters following the initial phoneme) in words. Onset and rime awareness is another aspect of acquiring the alphabetic principle. This second level of understanding phonological awareness adds to the young child's ability to develop a fund of readily recognized words. Later, in the next stage of reading development, the third level of phonological awareness will develop. The child will recognize more individual phonemes in words as he begins to read more words in stories. However, this is far more abstract than noticing rhymes. As the individual sounds in words often merge together, understanding individual sounds is difficult at this stage and develops during the next stage.

The diagnostic teacher assesses phonological awareness to ascertain what levels of sound knowledge the young child has. Phonological awareness indicates that the young child has developed understandings about how sounds work in words. Many informal reading inventories include an informal assessment for phonological

---

Figure 5–9 *Assessment of Phonological Awareness—Syllable Level*

Say the word and ask the child how many syllables he hears.

pat	patting	hot	puddle	batter	mat	walking	giraffe

---

awareness. The teacher simply says a word and asks what the beginning sound is or how many sounds they hear in the word (see Figure 5–9).

To continue the assessment, the diagnostic teacher says two words and asks if they rhyme. The diagnostic teacher records the student's responses. This assessment indicates how the child is using his knowledge of sounds in words to understand one of the concepts about words: words have sound patterns that stay the same every time the word is said or read (see Figure 5–10).

Putting Stage 1 Assessments to Work

Using these assessments along with the informal reading inventory, the diagnostic teacher plans literacy activities within the diagnostic session. Since a child at this stage usually does not have a score from the informal reading inventory, the diagnostic teacher selects easy, predictable books for shared reading or uses language experience (see part 2 for shared reading and language experience techniques) for the guided contextual reading (see chapter 4) part of the diagnostic session. Using the information from the assessment, she may decide to do some letter-naming activities or sound-building activities or both during the strategy or skill lesson (see chapter 4). In addition to these activities, she selects easy, predictable books that can be learned quickly and read repeatedly to develop a fund of words recognized by sight.

Stage 2

Because the students can read longer stories, they encounter unfamiliar words that are not contained in their sight vocabularies. Therefore, emerging readers develop new ways to figure out unfamiliar words. As children participate in literacy activities, their recognition vocabulary increases. Along with this increasing word identification, children begin to read longer stories; therefore, reading changes from a shared oral experience to silent reading and discussion. Initially, the children are familiar with most words in stories because many of the stories are encountered during shared oral reading before reading alone. These known words represent their sight-word vocabulary. This ability to identify words allows the children to figure out unfamiliar words using the oral context created by the shared experience. If they use

---

Figure 5–10 *Assessment of Phonological Awareness—Rime–Onset Level*

Do the two words rhyme? Do they have the same sounds at the end of the word?

pat, hat	hot, not	bat, sit	cake, snake
went, sent	pit, bark	toad, road	cat, cake
sheep, soak	meet, sweet	rain, pain	boy, toy

distinctive features of words, they usually look at only the initial letter and then think about what the story means or glance at the picture to figure out the word.

With longer stories, children can no longer rely on pictures, as there are fewer of them, and many of them do not represent the words on the page. Neither can young children rely on shared understandings to figure out the words, as the stories are much too complex for the shared understanding to signify specific words. Therefore, children begin to look for letter patterns in unfamiliar words and map those letter patterns to familiar sound patterns in already-known words. This is known as *decoding by analogy.*

As more and more stories are read silently, young children want to communicate their understanding by discussing with others. This discussion initially focuses on retelling what happened in the story; therefore, children's knowledge of story grammar is important to assess.

Word Identification

As young children read along with adults, they begin to recognize a few words. These words become more familiar as they repeatedly appear in the text that is read together. Finally, these words become part of the child's sight-word vocabulary. Recognizing these words is known as *word identification.* Word identification ability is often used to estimate a reading level. Thus, using an assessment of word identification can provide guidance for instruction. Most informal reading inventories include a word identification assessment, which includes lists of words representing frequent words at a particular grade level. To administer the assessment, you simply ask the child to pronounce each word on the word list. These lists are read until the student misses around 7 to 10 words in a row. This usually indicates that few words at the more advanced levels will be recognized. The score is the number of words prounounced correctly. The highest level before the student stopped is usually considered the grade level where instruction would be most appropriate. This level is where you can begin your informal reading assessment, or this can be used to monitor progress in word identification. This ability to identify words provides an understanding of how the student can recognize words in a passage or a story and an indication of the fund of words that can be used to develop phonemic awareness.

Phonemic Awareness

As children begin to look for letter patterns in unfamiliar words and map those letter patterns to familiar letter-sound patterns in already known words, they engage in decoding by analogy. Thus, young children begin to develop phonic knowledge by recognizing rime patterns in words. This builds on their oral phonological abilities that developed in stage 1. As children begin to recognize more words at sight, their spontaneous use of decoding analogies grows. Knowledge of the printed words helps to develop a fund of decoding analogies based on onset and rime patterns that are needed to decode unfamiliar words automatically.

Children are also increasing in the third level of phonological awareness—that is, the recognition of more individual phonemes in words. This is far more abstract than noticing rhymes. As the individual sounds in words often merge together, understanding individual sounds is difficult. However, the increase in rime analogies and word recognition facilitates the awareness of phonemes. Phoneme awareness and phonic knowledge in this stage depend highly on both analytic and synthetic phoneme strategies. Segmenting words into their single letter sounds (analytic) and

---

Figure 5–11 *Yopp–Singer Test of Phoneme Segmentation*

Name _____   Date _____

Score (number correct) _____

Directions: Today we're going to play a word game. I'm going to say a word and I want you to break the word apart. You are going to tell me each sound in the word in order. For example, if I say "old," you should say "/o/-/l/-/d/." (Administrator: Be sure to say the sounds, not the letters, in the word.) Let's try a few together.

Practice items: (Assist the child in segmenting these items as necessary.) ride, go, man

Test items: (Circle those items that the student correctly segments; incorrect responses may be recorded on the blank line following the item.)

1. dog	_____	12. lay	_____
2. keep	_____	13. race	_____
3. fine	_____	14. zoo	_____
4. no	_____	15. three	_____
5. she	_____	16. job	_____
6. wave	_____	17. in	_____
7. grew	_____	18. ice	_____
8. that	_____	19. at	_____
9. red	_____	20. top	_____
10. me	_____	21. by	_____
11. sat	_____	22. do	_____

Source: Yopp (1995). A test for assessing phonemic awareness in young children. The Reading Teacher, 49(1), 20–29. Reprinted with permission of Hallie Kay Yopp and the International Reading Association. All rights reserved.

synthesizing the sounds to form words are strategies used when decoding unfamiliar words. These abilities lead the way to decoding words by using single letter sounds. Children use this ability in combination with decoding analogies to figure out longer, more complex words. The ability to segment sounds and synthesize sounds can be easily measured. Hallie Yopp and Harry Singer (Yopp, 1995) prepared an easy-to-administer test for phoneme segmentation that includes 22 words and asks students to say the individual phoneme (see Figure 5–11). The diagnostic teacher says the word *sat,* and students say the sounds /s/ /a/ /t/. Each word where the phonemes are correctly identified receives a point. Students who correctly respond to 10 items are still developing their understanding of individual phonemes, while those who score 20 are capable of using individual phonemes to decode unfamiliar words.

Spelling Assessments
One of the best ways to evaluate phonic knowledge is to analyze children's spelling. As they spell words, children must think about each letter and its sound and then synthesize these sounds into words. Thus, spelling is closely linked to phonic knowledge.

Children's early spelling that differs in systematic ways from standard spelling can provide some indications of their thinking about how sounds work in words. Thus, the level of spelling development gives insight into their knowledge and use of phonics. The diagnostic teacher uses the levels of spelling development to ascertain the child's spelling patterns and use of phonic knowledge. Gillet and Temple (1994) suggest four levels of spelling development. The first level of spelling development is the prephonemic level, where no letter-sound relationships are present. Children denote words by letters, but the spellings have no similarity to correct spellings. They often write a single letter or number to indicate a word. This does show that they understand that print carries meaning. Children at the second level, the early phonemic level, represent some of the sounds in words in a systematic way. They might represent the word *net* with the letters *nt*. Vowels are seldom present in their writing. At the third level, the letter-naming level, letter sounds represent more than half the sounds. The actual word produced when saying the letters actually sounds like the word, as in spelling *pet* as *pit*. The transitional stage is where spelling is fairly standard, with a vowel in every syllable; however, the spelling does not conform to the correct spelling. Finally, the diagnostic teacher recognizes that some words can be spelled correctly. To assess spelling, the diagnostic teacher has the students write a paragraph or two and collects this writing sample. Then the diagnostic teacher can rate each word according to the rubric based on the levels of spelling development (see Figure 5–12).

In this rubric, the prephonemic level equals 0, the early phonemic level equals 1, the letter name level equals 2, the transitional level equals 3, and the correct spelling level equals 4. After rating each word, the teacher can add the ratings together and divide by the number of words in the written passage. The average score gives an approximate level for spelling and phonic knowledge. Children in this stage can show any type of pattern. However, most children in this stage will have the majority of the spellings at the letter name level.

Figure 5–12 *Spelling Assessment Rubric*

---

0 = Prephonemic Stage
Random letters depict a message and show some knowledge of top-to-bottom and left-to-right concept.
No letter-sound relationship present.
Uses and repeats known letters and numbers (prefers uppercase letters).

1 = Early Phonemic Stage
Words are depicted by one or more letters showing a left-to-right order.
The letters represent some of the sounds in words but not all.
This letter naming strategy is erratic and restricted.

2 = Letter-Naming Stage
Entire words are present with a majority of the letters.
The word has more than half the sounds in the word.
Letters are based on sounds as student hears them (invented spelling).

3 = Transitional Stage
Conventional spellings are used properly but not accurately (e.g., *candel* for *candle*).
Spelling is based on standard spelling rather than invented spelling.
Vowels appear in every syllable.

4 = Correct Spelling

Another way to assess spelling is for the diagnostic teacher to give a list of spelling words and compare the individual spellings of the words to levels of spelling development and figure out a spelling level. Bear, Invernizzi, Templeton, and Johnston (2004) have developed a test that uses 22 words to evaluate spelling through the grades. For the purposes of identifying phonic knowledge during this stage, only the first 10 words need to be used. They are *bed, ship, drive, bump, when, train, closet, chase, float,* and *beaches.* How students spell these words can be compared to the stages of spelling development mentioned previously. The diagnostic teacher also can use the detailed analysis provided in the book *Words Their Way* (Bear et al., 2004) to interpret the spelling test and decide on instructional procedures.

Story Retelling

Another assessment for this stage of literacy is to find out how children understand a story. As children move from oral shared reading, they begin to read silently and, therefore, communicate their story understanding by retelling the story. This is a developing ability, and the teacher wants to ascertain whether the student is continuing his literacy development by also understanding the meaning of the story. The diagnostic teacher has the student orally retell the story or has the student write a story summary. This retelling can be evaluated by observing and rating the story retelling using a retelling rubric (see Figure 5–13).

Using the rubric, the teacher evaluates what information the students tell about the setting, including the place and the characters. The teacher also evaluates how elaborate the students' retelling of the problem is and how extensive is the understanding of key story events. Finally, the teacher evaluates how students end the retelling. In addition to listening to an oral retelling, the teacher can have the class write a story summary and use the same rubric to evaluate the written story summary.

Putting Stage 2 Assessments to Work

Using these assessments along with the informal reading inventory, the diagnostic teacher plans literacy activities within the diagnostic session. Since the student is at the second stage of reading development, the diagnostic teacher reviews the informal reading inventory to decide the level of text to be used during guided contextual reading (see chapter 4). She selects a story, chapter book, or basal reader whose range is near the end of first grade or second grade, depending on the results of the informal reading inventory. If the student is at the second-grade level, the diagnostic teacher has the student read silently. Using the information from the assessments, she may decide what to do during the strategy or skill lesson. If the processing pattern indicates further support for print processing, then she would look under the word analysis column in chapter 11. She might select "Making Words" (see part 2) to work on phonic knowledge and phoneme awareness. If the processing pattern indicates the student needs work on literal comprehension, then she would look under literal comprehension. She might select the story map technique (see part 2).

Stage 3

In stage 3, children associate their knowledge about print and a particular topic with what is written in sentences. As they progressed through the first two stages, they developed extensive knowledge about the use of decoding analogies and patterns in stories. Now their focus shifts from developing this knowledge to using it as they

---

Figure 5–13   *Retelling Assessment*

Setting

4   Has an elaborated explanation of setting, including introduction, names of major characters, important places, and times
3   Has major character and other characters; briefly describes place and time
2   Has major character and mentions times or places
1   Contains only one idea, such as place, or names minor characters
0   Does not contain any ideas related to setting

Problem

4   Describes the major character's main goal or problem to be solved, including theme of the story; also describes the event that sets up the problem in the story
3   Describes main problem the major character needs to solve
2   Mentions briefly the problem
1   Has an insignificant problem
0   Does not describe any problem

Events

4   Elaborates key story events. Most events are related to working out the problem, are a consequence of this event, or are a character's reaction
3   Has key story events, some of which are related to working out the problem, a consequence of this event, or a character's reaction
2   Describes briefly some key story events
1   Has only a few insignificant events
0   Has no events

Resolution

4   Ends with a feeling of continuity and tells how the problem was solved
3   Ends with a feeling of continuity and briefly tells how the problem was solved
2   Ends with a feeling of continuity, but does not tell how the problem was solved
1   Ends abruptly
0   Ends in the middle of the story

Source: From *Interactive Handbook for Understanding Reading Diagnosis: A Problem-Solving Approach Using Case Studies* (p. 123) by K. Roskos and B. J. Walker, 1994, Upper Saddle River, NJ: Merrill/Prentice Hall. Copyright 1994 by Prentice Hall. Adapted by permission.

read. During this stage, readers use sentence sense to increase both their fluency and their sentence comprehension. In particular, students learn that words can be grouped together to make thought units and that sentences have predictable structures that influence meaning. Sentence comprehension also enhances print processing; therefore, students use sentence context as well as decoding by analogy to figure out unknown words. Using sentence context to figure out unknown words and simultaneously associating appropriate word meanings becomes a major challenge during this stage.

Miscue Analysis

After analyzing the child's reading, the diagnostic teacher might want to know how the student flexibly uses the cuing systems, particularly the use of sentence sense to self-correct miscues. The diagnostic teacher prepares a passage at the student's instructional level and has the student read it orally while marking miscues. Then the diagnostic teacher evaluates how the miscues affect meaning constuction (see chapter 6 for further discussion).

Fluency Assessment

After analyzing the results from the informal reading inventory, the diagnostic teacher might want to analyze the student's fluency. The diagnostic teacher prepares a passage that is at the student's instructional reading level and asks the student to read it orally. The diagnostic teacher can use the same 4-point fluency scale (Zutell, 1988) that was used while gathering information using an informal reading inventory. The scale includes ratings to reveal patterns of oral reading fluency (see table 5–1). Using this scale, a student's rating of 1 would indicate that the student is experiencing a great deal of stress and is reading at frustration level. A rating of 2 or 3 would indicate a mild amount of stress and that the student would profit from instruction at this level. A score of 4 would indicate fluent, independent reading.

The multidimensional fluency scale (Zutell & Rasinski, 1991) might be preferred to the 4-point scale, as it measures dimensions of fluency that could lead to the development of an instructional program. In this scale, the diagnostic teacher assesses the following aspects of fluency: phrasing, smoothness, and pace. For each of these areas, there is a 4-point scale. The diagnostic teacher has the child read orally and records the reading so she can use the tape to score the dimensions of fluency. Figure 5–14 shows how to rate the three dimensions.

Figure 5–14 *Multidimensional Fluency Scale*

Phrasing
1. Monotonic with little sense of phrase boundaries, frequent word-by-word reading.
2. Frequent two- and three-word phrases giving the impression of choppy reading; improper stress and intonation that fails to mark ends of sentences and clauses.
3. Mixture of run-ons, mid-sentence pauses for breath, and possibly some choppiness; reasonable stress/intonation.
4. Generally well phrased, mostly in clause and sentence units, with adequate attention to expression.

Smoothness
1. Frequent extended pauses, hesitations, false starts, sound-outs, repetitions, and/or multiple attempts.
2. Several "rough spots" in text where extended pauses, hesitations, etc., are more frequent and disruptive.
3. Occasional breaks in smoothness caused by difficulties with specific words and/or structures.
4. Generally smooth with some breaks, but word and structure difficulties are resolved quickly, usually through self-correction.

Pace
1. Slow and laborious
2. Moderately slow
3. Uneven mixture of fast and slow reading
4. Consistently conversational

Source: "Training Teachers to Attend to Their Students' Oral Reading Fluency," by J. Zutell and T. Rasinski, 1991, *Theory into Practice,* 30(3), 211–217. Reprinted by permission. Copyright 1991 by the College of Education, The Ohio State University. All rights reserved.

Using either of these scales, the diagnostic teacher can readily select techniques for instruction. If phrasing is low, the diagnostic teacher selects techniques like chunking (see part 2) to focus on thought units to group words so that meaning is held intact. If smoothness is low, the diagnostic teacher selects techniques like choral reading (see part 2) where the smoothness carries the message of the text. If pace is low, the diagnostic teacher selects techniques like repeated readings (see part 2) to improve the rate of readings.

Cloze Test

Using sentence context to figure out unknown words and simultaneously associating appropriate meanings is important at this stage. Children at this stage need to learn how the sentence structure influences meaning. To evaluate sentence comprehension, a cloze test can be used. A cloze test consists of a passage with blanks so that the reader uses the sentence context to supply the most credible response. To construct a cloze test, the diagnostic teacher selects a passage that is 300 words long and is at the beginning of a chapter so that previous text knowledge will not be needed. The diagnostic teacher then deletes every fifth word after the first sentence. The first and last sentences are left intact. The diagnostic teacher makes sure the blanks are a consistent length. Readers are provided sufficient time to complete the task so that they work at their own pace. To score the cloze test, the diagnostic teacher counts only the verbatim responses as correct. Misspelled words are acceptable. Finally, the diagnostic teacher calculates the percentage of exact responses by dividing the number of correct responses by the number of deletions, which should be 50. This percentage is compared with the criteria for performance-independent (60% to 100%), instructional (40% to 59%), and frustration (0% to 39%).

Putting Stage 3 Assessments to Work

Using these assessments along with the informal reading inventory, the diagnostic teacher plans literacy activities within the diagnostic session. The diagnostic teacher reviews the informal reading inventory to decide the level of text to be used during guided contextual reading (see chapter 4). She selects a story, chapter book, or basal reader that is at the instructional level from the informal reading inventory. From the specific assessments, she may decide what to do during the strategy or skill lesson (see chapter 4). If the processing pattern indicates support for fluent print processing, then she would look under the fluency column in chapter 11. She might select the repeated reading technique (see part 2) to work on print and meaning processing simultaneously. If the processing pattern indicates support for comprehension, then she would look under literal comprehension and word meaning columns in chapter 11. She might select the contextual processing (see part 2) to improve sentence comprehension and word meanings.

Stage 4

As students read more difficult text, they find that strategies dealing primarily with information that is in the text are no longer adequate. As they reach this level of text difficulty, they need to use a deeper processing of text. In texts at this level of difficulty, readers construct complex ideas that require an interpretation of text-based information within a reader's personal worldview (Alexander & Jetton, 2000). These processes require the flexible control of strategies. During this stage, children assert new control over their thinking. According to Pressley (2000), sustained strategy instruction produces better test scores for comprehension and more thoughtful readers. The strategy instruction programs focus on multiple strategies for understanding and interpreting texts. Although readers have been using some basic strategies, this stage marks the onset of taking control over multiple strategy use. Some of these strategies include using the pictures and title to predict what's going to happen, revising predictions, making new predictions, imagining pictures of information, picking out important points, summarizing important ideas, and rereading to clarify confusing parts. One of the more powerful strategies is the readers' ability to take control of the shift and integration of prior knowledge and the text.

The informal reading inventory provided information about literal and nonliteral comprehension. However, at this stage of literacy development, a key focus is assessing readers' strategies. Therefore, it is important to evaluate the strategies that students do possess. However, the underlying strategies used to construct meaning are internal processes. Since these are internal actions, they are more difficult to assess.

Think-Aloud Assessment

One way to assess the reader's strategic control of meaning construction is to evaluate the shift between prior knowledge and the text. To do this, the diagnostic teacher can have students think aloud as they read. In this procedure, the teacher divides a story into sections. After the student reads a section silently, he thinks aloud about the story. The diagnostic teacher prompts by asking him questions and making statements such as, "Tell me what happened. What do you think will happen next? Why do you think that?" The teacher records the student's responses to these questions after each section and then reviews the think-aloud to evaluate whether the student used the text or background knowledge when he summarized, predicted, and elaborated understanding (see chapter 6).

Self-Report of Strategy Use

Another way to assess strategy awareness and use is by using a self-report. In a self-report, students are asked which strategies they use and how often they use these strategies to understand and remember information. Teachers can make a checklist with the names of strategies to have students report about their strategy use (see the example in Figure 5–15).

Figure 5–15   *Strategy Self-Report*

When I read, I

_____ thought about my purpose for reading.
_____ made predictions.
_____ checked the text.
_____ summarized important points.
_____ compared what I knew with the text.
_____ revised my thinking as I needed.
_____ elaborated what was in the text with what I knew.

Figure 5–16 *Metacognitive Awareness of Reading Strategies Inventory (MARSI, Version 1.0)*

Directions: Listed below are statements about what people do when they read *academic* or *school-related materials* such as textbooks or library books. Five numbers follow each statement (1, 2, 3, 4, 5), and each number means the following:

- **1** means "I **never or almost never** do this."
- **2** means "I do this **only occasionally**."
- **3** means "I **sometimes** do this" (about 50% of the time).
- **4** means "I **usually** do this."
- **5** means "I **always or almost always** do this."

After reading each statement, **circle the number** (1, 2, 3, 4, 5) that applies to you using the scale provided. Please note that there are **no right or wrong answers** to the statements in this inventory.

Strategy	Scale				
1. I have a purpose in mind when I read.	1	2	3	4	5
2. I take notes while reading to help me understand what I read.	1	2	3	4	5
3. I think about what I know to help me understand what I read.	1	2	3	4	5
4. I preview the text to see what it's about before reading it.	1	2	3	4	5
5. When text becomes difficult, I read aloud to help me understand what I read.	1	2	3	4	5
6. I summarize what I read to reflect on important information in the text.	1	2	3	4	5
7. I think about whether the content of the text fits my reading purpose.	1	2	3	4	5
8. I read slowly but carefully to be sure I understand what I'm reading.	1	2	3	4	5
9. I discuss what I read with others to check my understanding.	1	2	3	4	5
10. I skim the text first by noting characteristics like length and organization.	1	2	3	4	5
11. I try to get back on track when I lose concentration.	1	2	3	4	5
12. I underline or circle information in the text to help me remember it.	1	2	3	4	5
13. I adjust my reading speed according to what I'm reading.	1	2	3	4	5
14. I decide what to read closely and what to ignore.	1	2	3	4	5
15. I use reference materials such as dictionaries to help me understand what I read.	1	2	3	4	5
16. When text becomes difficult, I pay closer attention to what I'm reading.	1	2	3	4	5
17. I use tables, figures, and pictures in text to increase my understanding.	1	2	3	4	5
18. I stop from time to time and think about what I'm reading.	1	2	3	4	5
19. I use context clues to help me better understand what I'm reading.	1	2	3	4	5
20. I paraphrase (restate ideas in my own words) to better understand what I read.	1	2	3	4	5
21. I try to picture or visualize information to help remember what I read.	1	2	3	4	5
22. I use typographical aids like boldface and italics to identify key information.	1	2	3	4	5
23. I critically analyze and evaluate the information presented in the text.	1	2	3	4	5
24. I go back and forth in the text to find relationships among ideas in it.	1	2	3	4	5
25. I check my understanding when I come across conflicting information.	1	2	3	4	5
26. I try to guess what the material is about when I read.	1	2	3	4	5
27. When text becomes difficult, I reread to increase my understanding.	1	2	3	4	5
28. I ask myself questions I like to have answered in the text.	1	2	3	4	5
29. I check to see if my guesses about the text are right or wrong.	1	2	3	4	5
30. I try to guess the meaning of unknown words or phrases.	1	2	3	4	5

Source: "Assessing Students' Metacognitive Awareness of Reading Strategies" by K. Mokhtari and C. Reichard, 2002, *Journal of Educational Psychology, 94*(2), 249–259. Copyright 2002 by the American Psychological Association. All rights reserved.

Similar to a teacher-made checklist where students use self-report to reveal their strategy use is the *Metacognitive Awareness of Reading Strategies Inventory* (Mokhtari & Reichard, 2002), which is based on responses from a large sample size. While taking the instrument, the students become aware of the strategies they use as they read. The diagnostic teacher uses the information to get a general sense of the students' awareness and use of reading strategies as well as over- or underreliance on particular strategies. For example, a student who reports overusing the dictionary may have a limited view of reading, while a student who reports rereading may not know how to use other strategies, such as summarization. The scale provides a rating for global strategies like setting a purpose, problem-solving strategies like reading slowly and carefully, and support strategies like paraphrasing (see Figures 5–16 and 5–17).

Along with the self-report, teachers can interview students and observe their strategy use. The following questions can guide the interview:

1. What do you do before reading to help you understand?
2. While you read, what do you do if you don't understand something?
3. After you read, what do you do to help you remember ideas?

These questions along with self-report checklists and observations during think-aloud can help the teacher identify strategy use.

Putting Stage 4 Assessments to Work

Using these assessments along with the informal reading inventory, the diagnostic teacher plans activities within the diagnostic session. Reviewing the informal reading inventory, the diagnostic teacher identifies an instructional range and selects texts within that range for guided contextual reading (see chapter 4). Using the information from the think-aloud and self-report assessments, the diagnostic teacher selects specific strategies to work on during strategy and skill instruction (see chapter 4). For instance, using information from a think-aloud, she might focus on justifying predictions using textual information (see "Think-Aloud Approach", in part 2). Using information from the self-report, she might decide to instruct students in how to use summarization (see part 2) to identify important information to remember.

Stage 5

The fifth stage is where readers begin to look beyond their own point of view and elaborate the author's point of view. Students select critical information from various sources to extend their own point of view. They also begin to link information from a variety of sources into a cohesive point of view. This synthesis requires an increasingly reflective stance. The thoughtful procedures used during this period are the ability to summarize and organize information from multiple sources, reorganize information to support a premise or point of view, and reflect and analyze others' points of view and one's own point of view. Thus, readers use information to construct personal points of view and increase reasoning about a particular topic.

Since few poor readers reach this stage, there are no appropriate assessments. The diagnostic teacher relies on self-report and teacher observation to ascertain if the students are operating at this level of sophistication.

Figure 5–17 *Scoring Rubric for MARSI*

Student name: _____ Age: _____ Date: _____
Grade in school: ❑ 6th ❑ 7th ❑ 8th ❑ 9th ❑ 10th ❑ 11th ❑ 12th ❑ Other

1. Write your response to each statement (i.e., 1, 2, 3, 4, 5) in each of the blanks.
2. Add up the scores under each column. Place the result under each column.
3. Divide the subscale score by the number of statements in each column to get the average for each subscale.
4. Calculate the average for the whole inventory by adding up the subscale scores and dividing by 30.
5. Compare your results to those shown below.
6. Discuss your results with your teacher or tutor.

Global Reading Strategies (GLOB subscale)	Problem-Solving Strategies (PROB subscale)	Support Reading Strategies (SUP subscale)	Overall Reading Strategies
1._____	8._____	2._____	GLOB_____
3._____	11._____	5._____	PROB_____
4._____	13._____	6._____	SUP _____
7._____	16._____	9._____	
10._____	18._____	12._____	
14._____	21._____	15._____	
17._____	27._____	20._____	
19._____	30._____	24._____	
22._____	28._____		
23._____			
25._____			
26._____			
29._____			
_____GLOB score	_____ PROB score	_____SUP score	_____Overall score
_____GLOB mean	_____ PROB mean	_____SUP mean	_____Overall mean

Key to averages: 3.5 or higher = high   2.5–3.4 = medium   2.4 or lower = low

Interpreting your scores: The overall average indicates how often you use reading strategies when reading academic materials. The average for each subscale of the inventory shows which group of strategies (i.e., global, problem solving, and support strategies) you use most when reading. With this information, you can tell if you score very high or very low in any of these strategy groups. Note, however, that the best possible use of these strategies depends on your reading ability in English, the type of material read, and your purpose for reading it. A low score on any of the subscales or parts of the inventory indicates that there may be some strategies in these parts that you might want to learn about and consider using when reading.

Source: "Assessing Students' Metacognitive Awareness of Reading Strategies" by K. Mokhtari and C. Reichard, 2002, *Journal of Educational Psychology, 94* (2), 249–259. Copyright 2002 by the American Psychological Association. All rights reserved.

Summary

The diagnostic teacher gathers data by asking questions that focus her evaluation of the strategies of the problem reader. First, she evaluates both oral and silent reading performance and determines the processing pattern (print or meaning) using an informal reading inventory. Next, she evaluates the student's performance across levels of text difficulty using the informal reading inventory. From this information, she designates a level that is moderately challenging for the student. She match this with the stage of reading and establibhed a level of performance She decides whether print processing or meaning processing is inhibiting constructing meaning with text Then, she conducts further assessments in areas of need and plans a daignostic teaching session.

6 Formulating Diagnostic Hypotheses

To formulate the diagnostic hypotheses, the diagnostic teacher analyzes the information he has gathered through the assessments in chapter 5 and within the reading event (see Figure 6–1). He uses data from an informal reading inventory to assess the student's reading patterns across a range of difficulty levels for both oral and silent reading. He performs an on-level reading analysis to assess the student's reading pattern when she reads a text either orally or silently that is moderately difficult.

Reflecting on Print and Meaning Processing

To formulate hypotheses about a reader's strategies, the diagnostic teacher selects a text that is expected to be in the borderline area, or moderately difficult (90% oral accuracy and 60% comprehension), for the student. He also decides whether the major concern is print processing or meaning processing. Then he prepares an extended passage that is to be read either orally or silently. In either case, he constructs questions that require the student to understand the main idea or theme, identify supporting details or events, infer relationships between ideas, and explain how the key words are used in the text.

In the discussion that follows, the premises for each analytic process are laid out together with the kinds of diagnostic data collected. After collecting the data from the extended analysis of oral or silent reading, the diagnostic teacher reflects on the diagnostic questions. This analysis provides detailed information about the strategies the reader uses to recover from difficulties in processing print or meaning. The diagnostic teacher uses these data to formulate hypotheses about the most advantageous instructional design for the student. How a diagnostic teacher uses the data is described in this section within the framework of a case study of a hypothetical third grader named Jenny, who is experiencing difficulty in fluent oral reading.

To analyze the pattern of reading performance, the diagnostic teacher looks at the data collected when the student reads without assistance. He prepares an extended assessment to evaluate a pattern of reading behaviors for constructing meaning. The diagnostic teacher analyzes the miscues and miscomprehensions to evaluate the student's patterns of strategies when reading breaks down and the strategies she uses to recover meaning while reading. Both oral reading analysis (of print processing) and silent reading analysis (of meaning processing) result in a more

Figure 6-1   *The Decision-Making Cycle of Diagnostic Teaching*

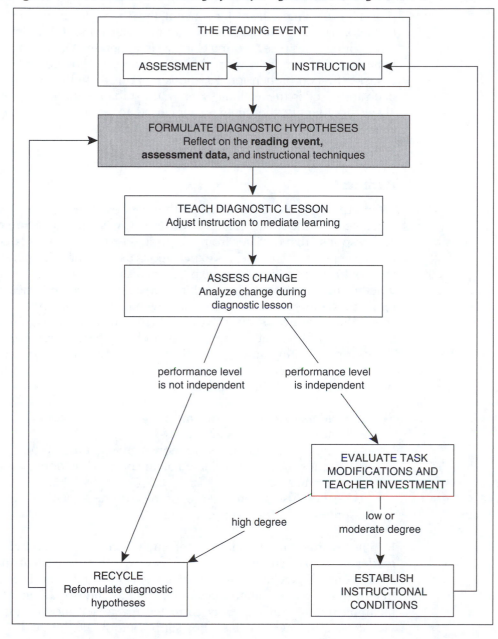

comprehensive understanding of the strategies students use to interpret the text *as* they are reading. However, the diagnostic teacher usually evaluates either print processing or meaning processing, depending on the student's major concern. If print processing is a major concern, the diagnostic teacher conducts an *oral reading analysis using a miscue analysis* to ascertain the reader's characteristics for print processing. If meaning processing is the major concern, however, the diagnostic teacher conducts a *silent reading analysis using a think-aloud assessment* to evaluate meaning processing.

Analyzing Oral Reading Using Miscue Analysis

If print processing is the major concern, the diagnostic teacher interprets oral reading behavior. He asks the student to read the selected text aloud while he records the errors or miscues (see "Scoring Criteria" in appendix A). To cross-check oral reading behavior with comprehension, the oral reading is followed by an oral retelling. Then he asks the comprehension questions he constructed (those that have not already been answered in the retelling). Finally, the student's reading errors or miscues are analyzed to identify the cuing system used to repair the reading miscue (for detailed procedures, see Goodman & Marek, 1996) and the pattern of reading behavior employed.

Premises

To interpret oral reading behavior, the diagnostic teacher uses miscue analysis to evaluate how the reader miscalls words as she is reading. A **miscue**, or error, is an oral response that deviates from the printed text. The reader is viewed as an active interpreter of text. She creates expectations using her background knowledge. Then she confirms or revises these expectations as she reads and checks the text to see whether her interpretation is making sense. A reader's miscues, therefore, are systematic attempts to construct meaning with text (Goodman, 1996).

   Miscue analysis is a tool for evaluating the relative significance of miscues in the context of both the entire passage and the reader's experiences. Several frameworks for evaluating miscues have been developed; in this text, an adaptation of the procedures suggested by Goodman and Marek (1996) is used. This analysis is based on several theoretical assumptions:

1. Readers read to construct meaning.
2. Reading is not an exact process.
3. Some miscues or errors are more significant than others.
4. Miscues should be evaluated on the basis of the degree to which they change meaning.
5. Readers use a consistent pattern of correction strategies that indicate their preferences for text processing.

In other words, miscues indicate the cue selected or the source of information the reader tends to use to construct meaning with text. Miscues that change meaning and remain uncorrected are viewed as diagnostically significant. They indicate what happens when a reader cannot regain meaning as she is reading. Miscues that change meaning but are subsequently corrected reveal self-monitoring strategies that are viewed as efficient strategies. They supply information about how readers construct meaning. Miscues that do not alter the meaning of the text are viewed as insignificant. Evaluating the nature of the information used to regain meaning reveals the student's approach to text interpretation.

   The student may use various sources of information when she encounters an unknown word in her reading: (a) the situational context and her experience; (b) the way words sound in conversational speech, that is, whether the words make grammatical sense; (c) graphic information; and (d) phonic information. Using the situational context and her own experience, she might try various words to see if they make sense in the context of the sentence and the story.

Sentence:	The girl hit the baseball.
Reader:	The girl bit the baseball. (*Oops, that doesn't make sense. I'll try again.*) The girl hit the baseball. (*Yes, that makes sense because people hit baseballs, not bite them.*)

Sometimes, she might check to see whether the way she is reading the sentence sounds like a real sentence.

Sentence:	The girl hit the baseball.
Reader:	The girl hitted the baseball. (*Oops, that's not the way we talk. I'll try again.*) The girl hit the baseball. (*Yes, this sounds like the way we talk.*)

At other times, she might check the graphic information by asking herself how the word begins and how long it is.

Sentence:	The girl hit the baseball.
Reader:	The boy hit the baseball. (*Oops, the word is not* boy *because it starts with a* g *not a* b, *but it is the same length. It must be* girl *instead of* boy. *Yes, that looks right.*) The girl hit the baseball.

At still other times, she might check the phonic information to decipher unknown words by asking herself what sounds these letters make.

Sentence:	The girl hit the baseball.
Reader:	The girl hit the brassball. (*Oops, that doesn't sound right. Let's see* bbb--aaa-ss-bbb-all. . .baseball. *Yes, that sounds right.*) The girl hit the baseball.

Thus, analyzing oral reading involves watching how the student reads and what strategies she uses when combining information sources.

Diagnostic Questions

Using these premises, the teacher can develop diagnostic hypotheses. The diagnostic questions that follow are used to analyze oral reading behavior:

1. How close is the reader's interpretation (i.e., how much meaning change results from the miscue)?
2. Does the reader monitor oral reading (i.e., does she self-correct miscues that do not fit the context)?
3. Does the reader use reader-based or text-based strategies to regain meaning?
4. How has previous instruction influenced the student's miscue pattern?
5. Do the words in the text influence the miscue pattern?

The pattern of strategies revealed by these questions indicates the student's application of reading strategies. Each of the questions elicits data that contribute to a comprehensive analysis of the student's reading behavior.

1. How Close Is the Reader's Interpretation?   Proficient readers' text interpretations maintain the basic intent of the author. Although they make miscues and continue reading, their miscues are insignificant in terms of the context of the entire selection. However, struggling readers make miscues that change the meaning. Instead of correcting themselves, they continue reading, acting as if they did not expect the story to make sense.

The diagnostic teacher evaluates each miscue as to the degree it changed the author's intended meaning. She uses this information to determine the significance of the miscue. As she continues her evaluation, she thinks about what the student did when the miscue changed the meaning. Those miscues that did not change meaning are not evaluated.

Meaning Change

The diagnostic teacher analyzes the amount of meaning change that results from the student's miscues or errors. If the miscues do not significantly change the meaning of the passage, then the student is reading for meaning; however, if the meaning of the text is substantially changed because of the miscues, then the diagnostic teacher designs lessons that encourage sense making while reading.

1. First, the diagnostic teacher investigates whether the student is familiar with the concepts in the text. This requisite knowledge helps the student decode the words by asking what would make sense. If the student is not familiar with the concepts, the teacher carefully selects texts that include familiar topics that are easy to read, enabling the student to make sense of the story and use her understanding to correct miscues.
2. If the text is familiar, then as the student reads, the diagnostic teacher prompts the student using sense-making comments such as "Did that make sense?" or "Try that again, I didn't understand" or "Oops, what did you say?" These questions and verbal prompts can help students monitor their reading.
3. The diagnostic teacher selects techniques that naturally encourage students to predict and monitor their print processing (see the "Print Processing" column of Table 11–4 in chapter 11). These teaching techniques are coupled with sense-making prompts.

- *How Close Is Jenny's Print Processing?* When reading orally, Jenny reads to make sense of text as long as the topic is familiar. When Jenny makes a string of miscues, she misconstrues meaning and makes up the text. She ceases checking to see if what she is reading fits with the words in the text (monitoring print processing).
- *Diagnostic Hypothesis:* Jenny reads for meaning. However, if she reads a string of miscues, she reverts to word calling rather than sense making. Jenny needs to read interesting, familiar material so she can check her print processing by asking what makes sense.

2. Does the Reader Monitor Oral Reading?   Proficient readers typically correct those miscues that change meaning but pay little attention to those oral reading miscues that do not change the meaning. Inefficient readers, however, do not distinguish between the miscues that affect meaning and those that do not. Little difference is observed in the frequencies with which they correct either type of miscue. Therefore, inefficient readers do not *consistently* read for meaning and do not monitor their oral reading behavior. As a result, inefficient readers make more miscues and correct them less often.

The diagnostic teacher summarizes the number of miscues that are corrected and those that are not corrected. He uses this information to decide which miscues to evaluate further. Miscues that change meaning and are corrected are closely evaluated to predict how the student combines sources of information when reading is efficient and to show how the student attempts to troubleshoot when reading problems occur. The miscues that are left uncorrected and change meaning are evaluated to look for further concerns in reading.

Strategic Print Processing and Monitoring Oral Reading

The diagnostic teacher analyzes how students predict, monitor, and elaborate their model of meaning using the printed words in the text. Using miscue analysis, she evaluates how actively students attend to what they read. Effective readers actively monitor their print processing, correcting miscues that significantly change meaning by rereading or predicting what comes next. In fact, effective readers have twice as many self-corrections as ineffective readers (Allington, 2005). Ineffective readers often exhibit one of the following patterns:

1. Some students simply call words and fail to correct miscues. They believe that reading is orally reading words without constructing meaning. They are unaware of the mistakes they make because they are not reading to make sense of text. When students exhibit this behavior, the diagnostic teacher constructs reading experiences in which the student will naturally make sense of text. Language experience is an excellent technique to help the student use prediction and to elaborate print processing strategies. Other techniques in the "Print Processing" column of Table 11–4 in chapter 11 can also improve self-correction strategies.
2. Other students guess at words but fail to check if the words they say match the words on the page. They continue to read, changing the story to fit the miscue rather than actively monitoring their print processing. When students exhibit this behavior, the diagnostic teacher constructs reading experiences that encourage them to monitor and elaborate print processing. The use of repeated readings with conversations about strategic processing is an excellent technique for this purpose. Other techniques in the "Print Processing" column in Table 11–4 can also improve these strategies.

- *Does Jenny Use Strategic Print Processing?* Jenny predicts what words are by using overall textual meaning and her background knowledge. However, if she miscues, she does not check the print in the text to confirm her guesses. If her miscues don't make sense, she begins to decode every word and ceases to predict or recover meaning. Because this process has continued over a period of time, Jenny has not elaborated flexible strategies for print processing.
- *Diagnostic Hypothesis:* Jenny would profit from instruction that helps her monitor and elaborate strategies for processing print. Reading predictable books and then writing a new story using the same pattern would focus Jenny's attention on elaborating how print works.

3. *What Source of Information Does the Reader Use to Regain Meaning?*   Proficient readers flexibly shift between sources of information when what they are reading does not make sense. They use what they already know (reader-based inferencing) as well as what the text says (text-based inferencing) to check and revise their miscues. However, inefficient readers use only one source of information to correct problems when reading orally (Allington, 1984). Whether they rely too much on what they already know or how the text looks, they invariably limit their strategy use to one source of information. This limitation leads to one of three diagnostic hypotheses.

The first hypothesis is that when reading breaks down, the student makes her miscues fit *her* interpretation and background information without referring to the information in the text. For example, a student who consistently substitutes a word that does not resemble the text but retains the meaning reflects a processing preference for a reader-based meaning search. She does not revise a miscue on the basis of the words in the text but relies solely on her background knowledge. If this is the pattern, the diagnostic teacher works with the student to encourage her to use how the words look as well as what she already knows. He chooses techniques that teach word identification and emphasize monitoring print processing.

The second hypothesis considered is that when reading breaks down, the student's miscues are similar to the graphic form of the text. For example, a student who depends on the graphic form for figuring out unknown words often produces a miscue that has the same initial letter and is approximately the same length as the word in the text and is a word she has been taught. This reader is using what the text looks like but does not ask what the word would mean in this sentence. She needs to check not only the words she has been taught but also what word would fit in the meaning of the story. In this case, the diagnostic teacher chooses techniques that demonstrate using both text cues and meaning cues simultaneously.

The third hypothesis evaluated is that when reading breaks down, the student's miscues reflect an attempt to employ sound–symbol (phonic) associations. For example, a student who depends on grapho-phonic information produces miscues by sounding out a word one letter at a time, blending those sounds to form a nonword, and continuing to read. She often sacrifices meaning for inaccurate decoding. This reader is said to be bound by the text because she uses only letters in the words and not her own knowledge. In this case, the diagnostic teacher decides whether decoding is an efficient strategy. If it is, he uses techniques that incorporate strategy instruction for word identification. On the other hand, if decoding is an inefficient strategy for this reader, the diagnostic teacher looks for strategies that use overall meaning of the text rather than sounds of letters to decode unknown words.

Sources of Information

Through print processing analysis, the sources of information a student uses can be identified. The diagnostic teacher can then describe a consistent pattern of how the student uses information sources and how the student is processing information. From this pattern, the diagnostic teacher can make hypotheses about instruction. Although students vary in their use of the sources of information, three of the predominant patterns used by ineffective readers and appropriate instructional responses follow:

1. If the student uses her background knowledge at the expense of text-based information, the diagnostic teacher uses prompts that focus on sense making (a strength) and the letters in the text (a weakness) at the same time.

Additionally, the diagnostic teacher selects techniques that emphasize monitoring print processing using reader-based information. The shared reading technique used in combination with repeated readings encourages combining sources of information. The diagnostic teacher selects other techniques that emphasize monitoring print processing using reader-based information by cross-checking selections from the "Print Processing" column in Table 11–4 with the information in Table 11–6.

2. If the student uses graphic clues from the text but fails to supply a word that makes sense, the diagnostic teacher prompts using "What word do you know that would make sense in this text?" Additionally, the diagnostic teacher selects techniques that emphasize predicting what would come next in the sentence. Predictable books coupled with cloze techniques would be useful for this type of reader. Other techniques can be found in Tables 11–4 and 11–6.

3. If the student overrelies on phonic information (a strength) without integrating this strength with sense-making strategies, the diagnostic teacher prompts using "What word has those same sounds (a strength) and would make sense in this story (a weakness)?" Repeated readings and charting miscues helps these students combine text-based information with reader-based information as they reread the text. The diagnostic teacher selects other techniques that emphasize monitoring print processing using text-based information by cross-checking selections from the "Print Processing" column in Table 11–4 with the information in Table 11–6.

- *What Source of Information Does Jenny Use When Solving Print Problems?* Jenny predicts what the text will say using her own ideas about the story. When she is on the right track, reading progresses. However, when Jenny has misconceptions about the story content, she adds words to fit her understanding.
- *Diagnostic Hypothesis:* Jenny would profit from instruction that shows her how to monitor her predictions using the words in the story. Repeated readings in interesting and predictable texts can encourage Jenny to monitor her print processing using her own knowledge.

4. How Has Previous Instruction Influenced the Reader's Miscue Pattern? Young readers use the strategies they have been taught. Therefore, readers differ in their use of strategies to construct meaning because of the instructional emphasis in their initial reading programs (Barr, Blachowicz, Bates, Katz, & Kaufman, 2007). This emphasis affects a student's correction strategies through the third-grade reading level. Some reading programs emphasize using meaning and the initial letter of the word to remember words (meaning-emphasis programs). Other programs emphasize blending sounds together to remember words (phonics programs). Miscue patterns often reflect the type of initial reading instruction a student has received.

Sometimes the student is using a system she has been taught effectively. In a meaning-emphasis program, the student's attention is focused on the initial letter and word length along with context to figure out unknown words. As she reads for meaning, she develops fluent and appropriate phrasing while checking her guesses with the initial letter and word length. However, in a structured phonics program, the reader's attention is focused on the letter-sound relationships to identify words. Therefore, she sacrifices meaning for phonic decoding, reflecting less use of text context and a higher tendency to focus on individual words to correct reading miscues.

The diagnostic teacher evaluates whether the student is effectively using the system she has been taught. If so, he plans a program to help her refine this system and integrate it with other cuing systems. In other words, if the student was taught phonics and is using it well, the diagnostic teacher continues to emphasize this cuing system while simultaneously asking the student to double-check her responses to see whether they make sense.

At other times, however, the student may try to use a system she has been taught but reverts to using sources of information more in line with her personal strategy use. When a mismatch occurs between the way a student has been taught to read and her personal strategies, often the student tries to use the cuing system she has been taught but usually abandons it to rely on a source of information that seems more natural to her. For example, if a student has been taught to sound out words letter by letter but cannot synthesize sounds, she will try to sound out the word but abandon this strategy in favor of using meaning cues and the initial letter. Because she has been taught a system she cannot use, the student reverts to a strategy that is more natural to her.

If the diagnostic teacher observes these phenomena, he can change his instruction to match the reader's strengths in print processing. He reinforces these strengths and plans a more integrative use of cuing systems. For example, a reader who was taught phonics continually miscues by substituting a word that makes sense in the context without regard for the letters in the word. The teacher notes that she is overriding her instruction and using her preference. Therefore, he chooses techniques that develop word recognition using the overall meaning of the text. As the student becomes more accurate with this system, he calls attention to the initial letter and word length.

Previous Instruction

Sometimes, the student overrides her previous instruction, reverting to her natural ways to figure out words. In these cases, reading problems often grow out of confusion about how to approach print processing and result in a disorganized set of strategies. The following patterns are most prevalent:

1. The student has been taught to sound out words but often abandons this strategy in favor of using meaning cues (a strength). If the student is somewhat successful in using phonics, the diagnostic teacher focuses his prompting and instruction on first using meaning cues and then phonics when the student encounters difficulty in a text. The predictable language approach allows the student to easily combine these two sources of information. Predictable books such as *The Hungry Giant*, where many of the words are decodable, facilitate combining these cue systems.

2. The student has been taught to think about the meaning and how a word begins but guesses wildly using only the meaning. These students need to be encouraged to look at more of the letters in the word to regain meaning. The diagnostic teacher prompts using "What would make sense?" (a strength) and "Look closely at the letters" (a weakness). The language experience approach and message writing as well as other techniques that encourage monitoring and elaborating print processing are excellent techniques for this type of reader.

- *How Has Previous Instruction Influenced Jenny's Print Processing?* Jenny has had 3 years of a structured synthetic phonics program. Thus, Jenny often tries to sound out words at the expense of using her natural cue system of meaning processing. Since sounding out is a laborious process for Jenny, she gives up using her strength and simply calls words, only halfheartedly searching for meaning.

- *Diagnostic Hypothesis:* Jenny needs experiences where she can first use meaning cues and then use her learned strategy of sounding out words. Techniques that encourage the student to use reader-based processing while focusing on printed words are the most appropriate.

5. Do the Words in the Text Influence the Miscue Pattern?   The type of words in the text can affect the miscue pattern. If a text has predictable rhythmic sentence patterns, the student who has language facility can figure out words easily using the sentence patterns. Likewise, a text that contains many decodable words is easier to read for the student who has had phonics instruction. However, if the text contains high-frequency words with a mixture of regular and irregular decodable words, the student who uses initial-letter and word-length cues has more success in reading the text. Consequently, before making final decisions about the student's correction strategies, the diagnostic teacher checks the text to see whether it has caused an atypical error pattern.

Textual Influence

Because the type of text can influence the miscue pattern, the diagnostic teacher thinks about the reading strategies the struggling reader uses and selects texts that will extend those strategies so they become more integrated and automatic (see Table 11–2 for a more complete analysis).

- *How Does the Text Influence Jenny's Print Processing?* Jenny has had numerous experiences reading decodable words in isolated word practice; however, she does not efficiently use phonic analysis when reading authentic texts.
- *Diagnostic Hypothesis:* Jenny would profit from reading many meaningful stories where she can use both reader-based inferencing and phonic knowledge at the same time. The diagnostic teacher needs to look for predictable stories that contain an abundance of decodable words.

In conclusion, oral reading patterns give insight into how the student is monitoring her reading behavior. The student's reading errors or miscues are analyzed to identify patterns of strategy use. The strategies that the student uses are affected by previous instruction, her natural abilities, and the text being read. The sensitive teacher considers all these influences when interpreting the student's oral reading behavior.

Analyzing Silent Reading Using a Think-Aloud Assessment

If meaning processing is the major concern, the diagnostic teacher conducts a *think-aloud* assessment. These assessments are ways for students to think aloud as they are performing higher-level tasks, such as predicting and revising their understanding. In this way, diagnostic teachers are able to collect systematic observations about a student's thinking. To begin, the teacher selects a passage and divides it at strategic points. First, he asks the student to predict what the story is about and to read silently to strategic points in the story. Next he asks the student to respond to the information read. When the diagnostic teacher is uncertain whether the student can read the text silently, he asks the student to find support for the response in the text and read it out loud, permitting him to assess whether word identification is interfering with comprehension. Then he asks the student to predict what will happen in the next segment of the story and why she thinks it will happen. He asks her to evaluate her previous prediction in light of the new information read and to decide whether she wants to change the prediction, keep it, add to it, or discard it. When the student finishes reading the selected text, the diagnostic teacher asks any prepared questions that have not yet been answered. Each exchange during the think-aloud period is analyzed to identify patterns of reading behavior (for detailed procedures, see Glazer & Brown, 1993).

Premises

To analyze comprehension, the diagnostic teacher evaluates how the reader thinks through the comprehension of a passage. Using a think-aloud format of interrupted reading, the teacher observes how the student uses the text and what she knows to interpret the passage. Analysis of a **think-aloud**, therefore, is a tool for evaluating the reader's comprehension strategies in the context of the entire passage. Although several researchers have outlined think-aloud procedures, the approach discussed here has been drawn from the work of Glazer and Brown (1993).

A think-aloud analysis is based on three theoretical assumptions:

1. Reading is an active process (i.e., a reader constructs a model of meaning as she reads).
2. To construct this model, the reader uses what she already knows (reader-based inferencing) and the information in the text (text-based inferencing).
3. Reading is a strategic process (i.e., the reader checks her model of meaning to see whether it makes sense).

In other words, the reader is viewed as actively constructing meaning with text. She predicts what is going to happen. Then she confirms or revises these expectations, using both what she already knows (reader-based inferencing) and the important information from the text (text-based inferencing). Finally, she checks her interpretations to see whether they are making sense.

Asking the student to think aloud gives an indication of how the student is processing text. The think-aloud process shows the diagnostic teacher the strategies that the student uses to make sense of what she is reading (Glazer & Brown, 1993). As with the oral reading analysis, interpretations that change the author's intended meaning and that the reader does not revise are seen as diagnostically significant. They indicate what the reader does when she cannot interpret the text. Interpretations changing the author's intended meaning that the reader later revises are viewed as efficient strategies, revealing the comprehension strategies the reader is using. They offer information about how the reader regains meaning. Interpretations that do not alter the author's intended meaning are viewed as insignificant. Basically, the student uses various sources of information for text interpretation: (a) what she already knows, (b) facts stated in the text, and (c) a connections between both the text and what she already knows.

Diagnostic Questions

Based on these premises, the teacher can develop diagnostic hypotheses using the following questions:

1. How close is the reader's interpretation (i.e., how elaborate is the summary, and are the important points covered)?
2. Does the reader monitor comprehension (i.e., how does she use new information to predict and revise her model of meaning)?
3. What sources of information (reader based, text based, or both) does the reader use?
4. How has previous instruction influenced the think-aloud process?
5. Does the text influence the think-aloud process?

The diagnostic teacher uses these questions to analyze silent reading during the think-aloud experience. The pattern of answers indicates the student's application of reading strategies. When the student's interpretation changes the meaning, a careful analysis is needed to assess the strategies she uses to regain meaning. Each of these questions is designed to elicit the particular kinds of data necessary for a complete assessment of a student's silent reading behavior.

1. How Close Is the Reader's Interpretation? During the think-aloud assessment, the student is asked to retell what she read silently. This retelling asks the student to select information important in illustrating the message as she perceived it. It reveals the student's ability to recall textual information and to make inferences using her own experiences. For narrative text, a good summary includes the important elements of story grammar: setting (characters and place), problem, key events, and resolution (for procedures, see Figure 5–13). For expository text, a good summary contains the main idea and key details. During the discussion, the diagnostic teacher evaluates how inclusive or narrow the summary is, the completeness of verbal responses, and the cohesiveness of the summary. After the student has finished her summary, the teacher uses questions to probe higher-level thinking, to focus on key ideas in the text, and to assess the student's knowledge of the meaning of the key words.

The diagnostic teacher uses this information to determine the significance of the miscomprehension. As he continues his evaluation, he thinks about how the reader's interpretation affects how she constructs meaning. Summaries that do not change the intended meaning of the story are considered the result of effective strategy use. However, summaries where the student changes the meaning of the text are evaluated to form hypotheses about the reader's strategies. Often poor readers do not organize textual information as they read. The details or events they include in their summaries become increasingly random and show a decreasing relationship to the text. Thus, summaries can alert the diagnostic teacher to problems in text processing that will be uncovered as he continues his analysis.

Meaning Change

The diagnostic teacher analyzes the degree to which the students' summaries differ significantly from the author's intended meaning. Effective readers use the critical information when summarizing text, while ineffective readers fail to recount important information. If the student changes the meaning substantially, the diagnostic teacher designs lessons that encourage selecting important information when reading:

1. First, the diagnostic teacher makes sure the student is familiar enough with the topic to construct summaries. If the student is not familiar with key vocabulary words or larger concepts, then the teacher carefully selects texts that include familiar topics and less challenging vocabulary.
2. If the text is familiar, then as the student reads, the diagnostic teacher prompts using leading questions that encourage the student to integrate the major concepts within the framework of the story. Techniques such as graphic organizers like story mapping, retelling, and summarizing help students develop a textual framework for selecting important information and elaborating concepts (see the "Meaning Processing" column in Table 11–4).

- *How Close Is Jenny's Meaning Processing?* When Jenny was asked to retell the story section by section, her interpretation was extremely close, indicating that she strives to make sense of text. However, she omitted some information in her summaries. This information was later evaluated as containing words that were difficult for her to decipher.
- *Diagnostic Hypothesis:* Jenny's desire to make sense of text and ability to select important information are processing strengths and should be included in all instructional activities.

2. Does the Reader Monitor Comprehension?

The diagnostic teacher uses this question to evaluate how the student uses new information to predict and revise her model of meaning. At each interruption, the teacher asks her to predict what will happen next in the story and why she thinks so. He asks her to evaluate her previous prediction in light of the new information read, and then he gives her the option of changing the prediction, keeping it, or discarding it. As the student makes predictions and evaluates them, the teacher observes her strategies for monitoring comprehension. He observes the inclusiveness of the prediction and the amount of textual information used up to the point of interruption.

Basically, inefficient readers have been found to be less active than more efficient readers. They change their predictions less often than more proficient readers. Some students rely too heavily on their initial prediction and make the entire story fit it. These readers do not use new textual information to revise predictions; rather, they keep a prediction when it is no longer supported by the text. When they do revise their predictions, passive readers change only one part of their predictions. Less active readers hold on to previous predictions rather than become more tentative about their approach to text.

Active readers seem more comfortable keeping their models of meaning tentative. If the text provides no new information, they delay making a prediction (Dybdahl & Walker, in press). Moreover, during a think-aloud experience, they change their predictions, adding and revising new information provided in the text as part of a continuous process.

This phase provides diagnostic information about how the student is monitoring her reading comprehension. The teacher notes the point at which the reader realizes that her model of meaning does not fit the stated information in the text. Since the story has been presented in segments, the diagnostic teacher can easily observe strategies such as rereading previous segments to check the text, modifying predictions, or remaining tentative until more information has been read. He uses this information to decide which summaries and predictions to evaluate further. Those interpretations that changed meaning but were subsequently revised are closely evaluated to predict how the student combines sources of information. The interpretations that were not revised and changed meaning are further analyzed to evaluate how the student attempts to make sense of what she is reading.

Strategic Meaning Processing and Monitoring Silent Reading

The diagnostic teacher analyzes how students construct a model of meaning by analyzing how they predict, monitor, and elaborate their model of meaning during the think-aloud procedure. Effective readers actively predict and revise their understanding, clarifying difficult areas by rereading and reading ahead. Ineffective readers passively read without revising or elaborating their understanding. These readers may demonstrate one of the following patterns:

1. Some students hang on to an initial incorrect prediction or change it infrequently by ignoring information that does not fit their interpretation. When a student fails to revise prediction effectively, the diagnostic teacher models his own predictions and how they change as the story progresses. Techniques such as think-aloud and prediction show students how to monitor their comprehension (see the "Meaning Processing" column in Table 11–4). Ambiguous scary stories and mysteries where the plot twists near the middle and end of the story are excellent materials for these activities.

2. Some students refuse to predict because they don't want to be wrong. Often their instruction has focused on getting answers correct. These students need to learn how to guess, realizing they can change their predictions when they get new information. To help these students, the diagnostic teacher encourages them to predict more frequently and to make several guesses at a time. Techniques such as request and prediction aid them in predicting a model of meaning (see the "Meaning Processing" column in Table 11–4).

- *Does Jenny Use Strategic Meaning Processing?* During a think-aloud, Jenny was able to predict and revise her understanding, elaborating ideas using her personal knowledge. Sometimes, however, her elaborations included tangential information that had little to do with the theme or main idea.
- *Diagnostic Hypothesis:* Using Jenny's active processing strength, the diagnostic teacher needs to help Jenny focus her attention on key ideas and concepts. Although elaboration is a strength, Jenny should be encouraged to use her knowledge selectively.

3. What Sources of Information (Reader Based, Text Based, or Both) Does the Reader Use?

Beginning the think-aloud procedure by using the title of the text, the diagnostic teacher can assess the student's prior knowledge about the topic. Questioning the student about how she arrives at a prediction from just the title allows the diagnostic teacher to probe background knowledge and begin to assess how the student uses this background knowledge as she reads the text. As the student reads the text, the teacher can observe the student as she constructs a rationale to support her prediction and evaluate whether the support is text based or reader based. This process leads to one of three diagnostic hypotheses.

The first hypothesis is that when reading breaks down, the student's interpretation fits something she can understand instead of what the whole text says. Some readers ignore information they do not understand. (They actually do not *know* that they do not understand.) When this happens, their responses are marked with an elaborate interpretation of the one or two events they were able to comprehend. No line of reasoning connects these students' responses to the story because they lack sufficient knowledge to interpret the text. If this pattern occurs, the diagnostic teacher needs to be cognizant of what the student knows about each topic. The teacher then develops the necessary background knowledge for this particular student before she reads a story.

The second hypothesis suggests that when reading breaks down, the student's interpretations fit what she already knows and not what the text says. Some struggling readers rely too heavily on their own knowledge and actually make their interpretations fit what they already know (McCormick, 2006). For example, some students consistently respond with information they know, using it to explain a line of reasoning for their answers rather than using information provided by the author. In these cases, the student understands what she reads but relies too heavily on her own experiences to develop reasons that are close to but not exactly like what the author intended. When this pattern occurs, the diagnostic teacher uses techniques that show the student how to use what she knows in combination with what the text says.

The third hypothesis proposes that when reading breaks down, the student's interpretations fit what the text says without tying together information. Some struggling readers rely too heavily on the text and fail to use their own knowledge to interpret or envision the text. They have too narrow an interpretation because they view reading as simply restating the text and thus do not draw relationships between information in different parts of the text. If this pattern occurs, the diagnostic teacher uses techniques that first allow the student to discuss what the text says and then shows her how to use what she knows to elaborate on it.

Sources of Information

Through the think-aloud analysis, the sources of information a student uses can be identified. Effective readers combine information sources (text and background knowledge), while ineffective readers overrely on a single source of information. From the think-aloud, the diagnostic teacher can make hypotheses about instruction to help readers combine information sources strategically. Two predominant patterns and suggestions for appropriate instruction follow:

1. If the student uses her background knowledge at the expense of text-based information, the diagnostic teacher uses prompts that focus on sense making (a strength) and uses the information in the text to verify guesses. A directed reading-thinking activity (see part 2) that includes reading aloud text that supports the prediction would facilitate this type of instruction. The diagnostic teacher selects other techniques that emphasize predicting and monitoring meaning using reader-based information by cross-checking selections from the "Meaning Processing" column in Table 11–4 with the information in Table 11–6.
2. If students rely heavily on the text without thinking about what they know, the diagnostic teacher asks them to restate the text and then think about what they know that relates to the text. He selects techniques that emphasize predicting

what the text might say and elaborating textual meaning. Using story mapping (see part 2) during reading to encourage students to predict using information from the map will facilitate combining sources. The diagnostic teacher selects other techniques that emphasize predicting and monitoring meaning using text-based information by cross-checking selections from the "Meaning Processing" column in Table 11–4 with the information in Table 11–6.

- *What Sources of Information Does Jenny Use for Meaning Processing?* When constructing meaning, Jenny relies heavily on her own knowledge about the topic. She does use the text to verify her response. Occasionally, however, she overrides the text by supplying information she already knows to support her interpretation. Most of the time, this strategy is effective for Jenny.
- *Diagnostic Hypothesis:* Because meaning processing is a strength, Jenny is asked to explain her reasoning and then orally read sections of the text that support the explanation. This refocuses on using text and background knowledge.

4. How Has Previous Instruction Influenced the Think-Aloud Procedure?   Some students have participated in literature discussion groups where the teacher participated as a member encouraging students to discuss how they constructed a response. However, other students have participated only in discussions where the teacher does the question asking. In the latter instructional situations, the types of questions teachers ask students affect their comprehension. Teachers who used higher-level questions, such as theme questions, increased student learning (Taylor, et al 2003). Furthermore, studies indicate that when teacher-generated questions are posed prior to reading, comprehension narrows because students read to answer those specific questions rather than to construct meaning. Some students have learned to rely on the teacher's direction rather than to think independently. The diagnostic teacher analyzes the focus of previous instruction to find out how that focus has affected comprehension.

Previous Instruction
The instruction students receive affects how they strategically read text. Some students rely on the teacher's direction rather than constructing their own meaning. The diagnostic teacher decides whether previous instruction has affected the strategic application of meaning processes. The following may be found:

1. The student has been taught to answer questions literally using the text and therefore fails to infer or elaborate meaning. In these cases, the diagnostic teacher uses text-based techniques such as story mapping and then asks the student to retell the story using what she knows.
2. The student's use of extensive background knowledge when retelling or responding has been previously reinforced. Therefore, she tends to disregard the text. In these cases, the diagnostic teacher uses reader-based techniques such as the DRTA (see part 2) but focuses on using the text to verify answers or completing a story map (see part 2) after discussion.

   - *How Has Previous Instruction Influenced Jenny's Meaning Construction?* Previously, Jenny has been rewarded for embellishing the text with her own topic knowledge. This instruction, however, has caused Jenny to rely too heavily on her own topic knowledge when reading. She needs to learn to verify her answers using the text.

- *Diagnostic Hypothesis:* Again, Jenny is asked to verify her explanations using the text. She is also asked to write new questions for other students to answer. This technique uses her strength of meaning processing to develop attention to text through writing.

5. Does the Text Influence the Think-Aloud Process?   The diagnostic teacher evaluates whether textual characteristics affect the active reading process. He reviews the density of information as well as the elaboration used. Likewise, he double-checks the background knowledge required, the grammatical complexity, and word choices as well as the textual organization. Poor story construction affects the student's think-aloud process. The choice of interruption points also affects the think-aloud. When story plots are engaging enough to motivate readers to find out what happens, then the teacher–reader interactions during the analysis period are elaborate; however, bland and boring texts give the students no reason to read (Schallert & Reed, 1997). The diagnostic teacher needs to construct a story map of the selected story to determine whether the story actually lends itself to a think-aloud process and is engaging enough to elicit an elaborate interaction. Some initial ambiguity of the story plot allows the diagnostic teacher to observe the student's approach to problem solving when reading. The type of text also affects the think-aloud analysis. Narrative text lends itself to prediction, revision, and monitoring, while expository text lends itself to summarizing, clarifying, and discussing the line of argument used by the author.

Textual Influence

Because the type of text can influence meaning processing, the diagnostic teacher thinks about the reading strategies that struggling readers use and their preference for narrative or expository texts. He selects texts that build on preferences and then extends strategies so they become more integrated and automatic (see Table 11–1 for a more complete analysis).

- *How Does the Text Influence Jenny's Meaning Processing?* Jenny enjoys reading information about science concepts. Her reading is more fluent, and her retellings are more elaborate in science text. Jenny also has a high need to read authentic text.
- *Diagnostic Hypothesis:* Jenny would profit from reading science texts about familiar topics that are well constructed so that the information makes sense.

After the diagnostic teacher has reflected on print and meaning processing, he thinks about how the student has responded during an instructional event. He reflects on the reading event and how these factors have influenced the data.

Reflecting on the Reading Event

After collecting the data, the diagnostic teacher reflects on the reading event. He returns to the model of the reading event discussed in chapter 2 and uses it to evaluate the influence of the variables on the student's reading behavior. He remembers that the information he has collected is a result of the interactions that occurred in the reading event. He systematically evaluates the influence of the task, the text, the reader, and the situational context of the reading event on the data. He looks for key factors by asking, for example, "What task did the student do? Is this task an important consideration in establishing this student's instructional program?" He considers the relative strengths of the student's oral and silent reading in constructing meaning with text. From this analysis, he formulates diagnostic hypotheses and selects teaching techniques to enhance reading growth.

How the diagnostic teacher uses the data from the initial assessments and relates them to the elements of the reading event is described in the pages that follow. The case study of the hypothetical third grader named Jenny, who is experiencing difficulty in fluent oral reading, is continued in this section. As the teacher reflects on the reading event, he makes observations about the student's performance, using the data he has collected. The asterisks (*) in the following figures indicate key factors he has to consider when establishing Jenny's instructional program.

The Task

The diagnostic teacher analyzes the reading tasks that the student completes during the reading event. He carefully considers the range of possibilities related to the task and looks for key factors that might affect the student's reading behavior. During the informal reading assessment, he has already decided on the major concern; now he uses this information to evaluate the effect that the question type is having on the reader's responses and to evaluate reasoning requirements. He compares the reader's performance on the informal reading inventory and the extended passage. From this comparison, he ascertains whether the task segment is affecting reading performance and whether production requirements are affecting reader response.

- *How Does Jenny Approach Reading Tasks?* Task analysis for Jenny is given in Figure 6–2.

Figure 6–2 *Task Analysis for Jenny*

Purpose for the task: Teacher-directed reading was used for evaluation. Informal conversation revealed that Jenny liked to control her own learning.

Mode of task: Both oral and silent reading behaviors were evaluated, with the student comprehending all passages where she could decode the words. Oral reading was the difficult task. At the instructional level, silent reading comprehension was not a concern. Jenny has poor handwriting and did not engage in writing unless absolutely necessary.

Question type: Literal and nonliteral responses were evaluated. Jenny performed equally well in both cases.

Production requirements: Retelling was used to assess comprehension, followed by inferential questions. Responses were elaborate in both cases.

Reasoning requirements of the task: Factual recall and applicative reasoning were required. Jenny did well in both types of tasks.

Availability of text: The text was not available for referral when responding; however, Jenny's responses were elaborate.

> ■ *Diagnostic Hypothesis:* Jenny reads with moderate difficulty at the second-grade level (¹⁄₁₁ error rate and 75% comprehension) on an informal reading inventory. Oral reading presents the most difficulty for the student. Although she prefers silent reading, Jenny needs to read orally to improve fluency. Her informal comments ("I hate these stories") indicate that she prefers to choose her own stories.

The Text

The type of text read during a reading evaluation can significantly influence the data being analyzed. The diagnostic teacher routinely assesses the text and its influence on reading behavior to identify which characteristics are affecting the student's reading. Again, he seeks the key factors about the text that affect this student's reading behavior. To do so, he looks at the information from the informal reading inventory, the extended passage, and the final question of the oral/silent reading analysis (does the text influence the results of this procedure?).

> ■ *How Does the Type of Text Affect Jenny's Reading?* The text analysis for Jenny would contain the material covered in Figure 6–3.

Figure 6–3 *Text Analysis for Jenny*

Content and background knowledge required: Jenny read various subject content. It did not seem to affect her responses because she always had extensive background knowledge.
Short passages produced more oral reading miscues.
Density of information: The high density of information did not affect understanding, but it did affect Jenny's miscue pattern. When too much information was presented in short paragraphs, she could not self-correct. The extended passage gave Jenny more opportunities to use content and passage context to self-correct miscues. Comprehension remained high on all passages.
Passage format: Both expository and narrative passages were read. Jenny made fewer miscues on expository text.
Organizational structure and style: When the story structure did not reflect the title of the passage, Jenny's miscues were affected because she tried to make the title fit the text. Jenny needs coherent text. Jenny also made fewer miscues on more engaging, predictable text.
Grammatical complexity: The more complex the sentence structure, the better Jenny read.
Word choices: Short words that fit the text were used. Elaborate word meanings were not required for comprehension. Decodable words were easier to read.

> ■ *Diagnostic Hypothesis:* Jenny needs a text that is coherently organized, and she appears to prefer expository text. Increasing the complexity of the sentence structure seems to have a positive effect on miscues (i.e., the longer the sentence, the more she is able to correct her miscues). Another possible influencing factor may be the word choices in the text. Since the student was taught phonics, words that are more decodable might improve performance.

The Reader

The reader is the major focus of traditional assessment. In diagnostic teaching, however, the reader is assessed in relation to herself as well as to the variables of the reading event. The teacher looks at the knowledge-based requirements of the tasks and how the student responds to them. From the informal reading inventory, the diagnostic teacher evaluates general skill proficiencies and deficiencies. Returning to the extended passages, the diagnostic teacher uses the answer to the first question ("How close is the reader's interpretation?") to assess general knowledge. He must judge whether the reader changes the meaning of the selection because she has no similar experience. In addition, he uses data from the extended passage to evaluate the strategies the student employs as she reads. He specifically analyzes the data on self-corrections and revisions during oral and/or silent reading. Finally, he evaluates data on the sources of information used.

- *How Does Jenny's Reading Performance Relate to Her Knowledge, Strategies, and Engagement?* Jenny's reader analysis is shown in Figure 6–4.

Figure 6–4 *Reader Analysis for Jenny*

Knowledge-Based Dimensions

Language facility: The student used language well and often engaged in elaborate descriptions related to the story. She had a wealth of prior knowledge.

Word and world knowledge: Jenny has many life experiences to draw on, and she has the verbal knowledge to express her experiences.

Reading stage: On the informal reading inventory, Jenny read at the borderline level (moderate difficulty) on the second-grade paragraph.

Skill knowledge: Answering comprehension questions and retelling a story were Jenny's strengths. However, she needed work on oral reading fluency. Phonic knowledge was inappropriately applied.

Strategy-Based Dimensions

Selection strategies (text or background knowledge): As she constructed meaning, Jenny used an integration of both textual knowledge and reader knowledge; however, during oral reading, she used either textual knowledge or reader knowledge but not both when she encountered difficulty.

Monitoring: Context of the story was used to help identify unknown words. Many miscues were semantically based. Jenny needs to self-correct during oral readings using *both* the semantic and the graphic cuing systems. Jenny actively monitored her reading comprehension when needed.

Elaboration: All responses were elaborate except when Jenny encountered frustration-level reading. She used both literal and nonliteral.

Engagement Dimensions

Interests: Jenny was interested in information whether it was in picture form, hands-on learning, or on television. She was not interested in reading.

Value of literacy tasks: Jenny does not value literacy tasks. She does value her own knowledge, but it is not the same as reading and writing.

View of reading: Jenny views reading from a sense-making perspective. She also has a high need to learn information from what she is reading. Thus, she expressed disdain for the second-grade stories. When she is learning from a science passage, she is more engaged, even when she miscues frequently.

Social interaction: Jenny learns while discussing information with her peers. She uses their text references to embellish her own understanding.
Self-perceptions as a reader: Jenny believes she is smart in world knowledge. But when it comes to literacy tasks, she believes she can't compete with her peers; therefore, she often shuts down when she has to write as a response to reading.
Response to success and failure: Jenny often gives up when reading orally because she views her miscues as indications that she is a failure. Her response changes when she talks about familiar topics related to a reading passage or story. She then views her response successfully.
Attributions of success or failure: When reading aloud, Jenny attributes her failure to baby reading material and dumb stories rather than active strategies. When reading silently, she skips many words but still believes she can construct some meaning from the discussion and uses active strategies to figure out meaning.

- *Diagnostic Hypothesis:* Using her meaning processing strength, Jenny would profit from instruction in word identification and fluency. She needs to be shown the effective strategies that she uses (e.g., self-correction from background knowledge). She tries to use phonic knowledge but is consistently unsuccessful in her attempts. Jenny, therefore, relies too much on her background knowledge and general story meaning. When she does, she reads a string of miscues that make some sense. Her unsuccessful attempts at self-correction reflect the use of either meaning cues or phonic cues without the integration of both cuing systems. She appears to like to direct her own learning rather than have the teacher tell her what to do. Because of her continual failure, Jenny needs to identify her strategy strengths and attribute her success to the combination of strategy use and effort.

The Situational Context

The diagnostic teacher evaluates the situational context in which the assessment occurs and how much influence that is having on the reader's response. At the same time, he evaluates how previous instructional experiences might have affected the student's responses. He reevaluates the patterns of performance, thinking about how the student's previous instructional experiences have influenced her reading patterns. He double-checks his data, focusing on the situational context of the reading event.

- *How Does the Situational Context Affect Jenny's Reading?* An analysis for the of Jenny's reading behavior is shown in Figure 6–5.

Figure 6–5 *Situational Context Analysis for Jenny*

Format of Discussion
Discussion: Jenny participates in group discussions, using her extensive background knowledge. However, previous learning situations have focused on completing workbook pages and not discussing. The present classroom placement encourages collaboration in thinking.

Group composition: Jenny prefers group instruction where she can participate in the discussion, using her background knowledge. However, previous learning situations have included an extensive pullout program with one-on-one instruction.

Conferencing: Jenny does not like individual conferencing because she is usually asked to read aloud. She is easily annoyed if she makes a mistake.

Teacher Responsiveness

Teacher talk: Although Jenny responds when asked questions, she prefers to create responses without teacher input. She prefers open-ended environments where she can use her extensive background knowledge.

Support for Thinking

Jenny needs support for recognizing words. Since Jenny uses word meaning to figure out words, the teacher can support recognizing words before reading the story by presenting the words in the context of the story. For her concern in strategies of decoding, the diagnostic teacher creates strategy and skill lessons that focus on the strategy of using multiple cues systems rather than just one.

Prompts and wait time: Instruction needs to have minimal feedback from the teacher and maximal from other students. The teacher needs to prompt with this question: "What would make sense and start with a _____?" The teacher needs to allow time for Jenny to figure the word after the prompt.

Nature of Classroom Focus

Teacher expectations: In previous literacy situations, Jenny was expected to sound out words in isolation. She prefers teachers who expect her—think and discuss higher-level questions and ideas. She also wants to the teacher to draw on her extensive background knowledge, particularly in science activities—a strength.

Focus on strategy use: Jenny would profit from a classroom focus on strategies of monitoring oral reading. Previous instruction focused on grapho-phonic skill knowledge including a 2-year program of intensive synthetic phonics instruction. By teaching only phonics, her weakness, she developed some of her negative attributions.

Use collaborative assessments: Jenny has started keeping a portfolio so that she can evaluate her work. It has helped her focus on her effort and meaning construction. Previously, she was simply assessed on her skill weaknesses; therefore, she had not been engaged in literacy activities.

- *Diagnostic Hypothesis:* Jenny's previous learning experiences in a one-to-one pullout program that focused on weaknesses affect both her perception of reading and her miscue pattern. When she miscues, she tries to sound out unknown words because that is the way she has been taught (instruction in synthetic phonics). This strategy usually fails, however, and Jenny becomes discouraged. Having forgotten the meaning of the story, Jenny creates a string of miscues that make sense for the sentence but not for the entire story. However, when Jenny participates in a group discussion, she circumvents her weakness and uses her extensive background knowledge to infer meaning from what she reads and what others say. This strategy allows her to discuss freely in an open-ended discussion.

Summary

Formulating Hypotheses for Jenny

When cross-checking the elements of the reading event, the diagnostic teacher remembers that some of the factors may not be important in examining the particular reading event under scrutiny. Only the key factors affecting the student's reading performance are analyzed. For Jenny, the analysis resulted in the following key factors:

1. The type of text (expository) facilitates constructing meaning and heightens interest.
2. The student has a negative attribution to reading (she states that she hates reading).
3. The student uses only one cuing system at a time when reading breaks down. (She tries to use phonics, and if this strategy fails, she uses sentence sense. She does not combine the sources.)
4. The more grammatically complex the sentence structure, the more the student can self-correct her miscues.
5. The student would rather direct her own learning than have the teacher tell her what to do.
6. The student overrelies on reader-based sources when constructing meaning when text becomes difficult.
7. The student has a well-developed background of information that she uses when responding to text.

Having identified these key factors, the teacher is then able to select an appropriate diagnostic teaching technique.

Reviewing the Steps

To formulate the diagnostic hypotheses, the diagnostic teacher reflects on the reading event, considering each variable and its relationship to the reader's performance. He looks at the interactions among the task, the text, the reader, and the situational context to establish patterns of reading performance.

 After he has formulated hypotheses, he selects instructional techniques to advance the student's reading (see chapter 11). To verify the hypotheses that have led to this selection, the teacher conducts a diagnostic lesson. The guidelines for conducting this lesson are found in chapter 7.

7 Assessment Using Diagnostic Lessons

Although the diagnostic teacher uses informal assessments and extended assessments discussed in chapters 5 and 6, she needs to constantly reinterpret the information in the light of student performance. She uses the informal reading inventory as a measure of what the student can do when he reads independently (without instruction). However, she also establishes how the student constructs meaning with text as she is teaching. Therefore, she continues her assessment and establishes a level at which the student profits from her instruction. From this knowledge, she derives her hypotheses for the student's instruction.

After the diagnostic teacher formulates her hypotheses, she teaches a lesson using techniques based on the hypotheses (see Figure 7–1). Diagnostic lessons provide a tool to assess the amount of growth that actually occurs as a result of the instruction and instructional adjustments. Through the *diagnostic teaching assessment*, the teacher assesses the student's changes in reading behavior and establishes the student's optimal *instructional conditions* (see Figure 7–1), including the student's mediated reading level.

Establishing Mediated Reading Level

The student's **mediated reading level** determines the level at which the student can efficiently be taught. This level is determined by evaluating the "distance between the actual developmental level as determined by independent problem solving and the level of potential development as determined through problem solving under adult guidance or in collaboration with more capable peers" (Vygotsky, 1978, p. 86). First, the diagnostic teacher identifies at what level the student can incorporate the targeted reading strategies as a result of specified instruction. This level is determined by calculating the "difference between the level of unaided performance a child can achieve, and the level he could achieve with aid" (Powell, 1984, p. 248). Therefore, the diagnostic teacher establishes the highest difficulty level at which the student profits from instruction.

Because the goal is to determine how instruction improves reading performance, a text that is moderately difficult (90% oral accuracy and 60% comprehension) provides a more appropriate measuring tool. Using a moderately difficult text (within the borderline range in Figure 5–2) allows the teacher to assess the student's change

Figure 7–1 The Decision-Making Cycle of Diagnostic Teaching

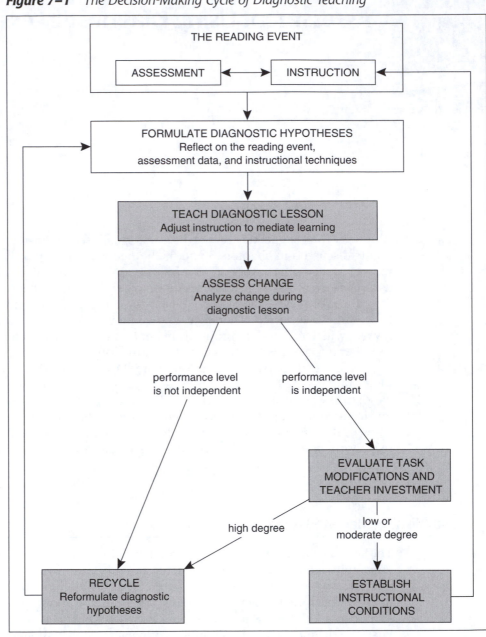

in reading as a result of instruction. She wants to observe how the student learns from her instruction. After instruction, the selected text should be read at the independent level (98% accuracy and 90% comprehension). If this level is achieved, the diagnostic teacher selects a more difficult text and teaches another lesson. She continues this process of selecting more difficult texts until the student does not achieve an independent reading level after instruction. Placement is thus determined by identifying the highest difficulty level at which the student profits from instruction.

For example, a teacher took two short segments from a story in a text that was designated as moderately difficult for a student. Using the passages, she developed two assessments according to the constructs of informal reading assessment. Without teacher instruction, the student read the first segment with an error rate of $\frac{1}{11}$ words and 60% comprehension. After the targeted vocabulary words were introduced and a discussion about how these words related to the selection was conducted, the second segment was read with an error rate of $\frac{1}{50}$ and 90% comprehension. For this student, a text that was read near frustration without teacher direction could be read at independent reading level with instruction by the teacher.

The diagnostic teacher continued this procedure with a more difficult text. The highest level of text that the student read fluently after instruction was designated as the text to use during instruction. The level was then called the mediated reading level, the highest level of text that can be read meaningfully after instruction (Powell, 1986).

> The diagnostic teacher establishes the mediated reading level, the highest level of text that can be read fluently after instruction.

For the diagnostic teacher, decisions about placement involve more than just establishing at what level the student will profit from instruction.

Amount of Task Modification

Because she is actually teaching during her assessment, she also evaluates the amount of task modification (Feuerstein & Feuerstein, 1991) necessary to create the desired change. Prior to instruction, the diagnostic teacher decides on certain task conditions that will enhance learning for a particular student. Some of these decisions include these questions:

> *Will I segment the selection? If so, how will I do it—sentence by sentence, or paragraph by paragraph? Will the instruction be entirely silent reading? Or will oral rereading be necessary? How many new vocabulary words will be introduced before reading the selection, and how will instruction occur? Should part of the discussion be written down so it can be referred to later?*

These decisions involve how she will modify the task so that learning will occur. If a high degree of task modification is required, the diagnostic teacher needs to select either a less difficult text or a different teaching technique. If a low degree of task modification takes place during the lesson, a more difficult text can be selected. Therefore, placement can be determined by the amount of task modification needed to ensure constructing meaning with text.

> The diagnostic teacher evaluates the amount of task modification (change in the reading task) that she makes during instruction, such as changing from oral to silent reading or from one technique to another.

Amount of Teacher Investment

A third consideration is the amount of teacher investment (Feuerstein & Feuerstein, 1991) necessary to engage the student in an active interpretation of text. As she teaches, the diagnostic teacher adjusts her instruction to the needs of the student. She asks herself these questions: How can I elicit responses so that the student will understand the main idea? What does the student already know that will help him understand the story? How much time do I need to wait before I assist? What kind of assistance (prompting, questioning, or modeling) will be most helpful? These questions focus the teacher's involvement during instruction.

During instruction, the diagnostic teacher evaluates the amount of her investment. If the investment is extremely high, changes in instruction are needed that decrease complexity (an easier text or a different teaching technique). If the investment is low, changes are needed that increase the complexity (a more difficult text or higher-level questioning).

The diagnostic teacher uses three criteria to determine the mediated reading level, the highest level at which the student can profit from her instruction. She finds a reading level that is moderately difficult and teaches a lesson at this level. Then she evaluates the amount of change in reading behavior due to instruction as well as the amount of teacher investment and task modification needed to ensure active meaning construction.

> The diagnostic teacher evaluates her investment or the changes she makes regarding her interaction with the student, which includes an array of interaction possibilities, such as prompting, rephrasing, and feedback.

After establishing a student's mediated reading level, the teacher continues her diagnostic lessons at this level. To begin, she chooses a reading passage that is at the student's mediated reading level.

Procedures for Diagnostic Lessons

The goal of conducting a diagnostic lesson is to establish the instructional conditions that promote active reading. As the lesson is conducted, the diagnostic teacher evaluates not only the success of the reader in terms of traditional criteria, such as miscues and comprehension, but also the degree of task modifications and teacher investment that are needed to produce the reading change. Two formats have been used to conduct diagnostic lessons. One format assesses the reader prior to instruction (at sight) and compares this information to an after-instruction assessment. This format is used when the student's reading level is near the end of first grade or above. The other format is used when students cannot read enough words fluently to successfully evaluate their reading prior to instruction. In these cases, the diagnostic teacher compares the reading change after several lessons using different techniques that have been taught. The procedures for both are outlined in this section.

Diagnostic Lesson Using Baseline Data

The diagnostic teacher selects a story and divides it into three sections and uses the first section to assess students' reading performance without assistance. It is read *at sight*—either orally or silently—without any period of familiarization and without assistance to establish baseline data. The middle section of the passage is taught using the selected technique (see chapter 11 and part 2). This part of the lesson is the actual implementation of the hypotheses and requires keen observation of the changes that improve students' interpretation of text. To assess the degree of change in reading as a result of instruction, the student reads the third section of the text at sight and without assistance. As a result of the mediated instruction, changes in the students' reading should be apparent. If the instruction has been appropriate, the student should now be able to read the third section of the text at the independent reading level and exhibit patterns of performance that reflect a more integrated use of reader-based and text-based processing. Using the information from the diagnostic teaching lesson, the diagnostic teacher establishes the conditions that result in improved learning for the student. The following discussion delineates the purpose for each of the three sections of the diagnostic lesson.

Establishing Baseline Data

Having the student read the first section at sight and without assistance serves two functions: (a) to add information to the diagnostic hypotheses (see chapter 6) and (b) to establish baseline behaviors so that the effectiveness of instruction can be evaluated. The section should be about 100 to 200 words long and may be read either orally to evaluate print processing or silently to evaluate meaning processing (see chapters 5 and 6). The data are analyzed by computing the percentage of comprehension and error rate as well as evaluating the patterns of the reading performance.

The diagnostic teacher reviews the data to expand her diagnostic hypotheses. However, her primary purpose for collecting baseline data is to measure growth as the result of instruction. Baseline data reflect the student's reading performance without aid and before adjusted instruction. During the instructional lesson, the teacher establishes the instructional conditions that mediate learning. To assess this change, the diagnostic teacher compares the student's reading without aid and his performance after specified instruction. During the third section of the diagnostic lesson, the baseline data are used to evaluate reading growth as the result of instruction.

Establishing the Conditions of Learning

After the baseline data have been established, the teacher designs a diagnostic lesson based on her hypotheses about the student's reading. She selects a technique (see chapter 11) that matches the reader's profile. The second section is used to establish the optimal conditions for learning new reading strategies. As she teaches the lesson, her modifications are summarized and become part of the diagnostic data collection. Unlike the first section, where the teacher constructs diagnostic hypotheses based on a relatively static assessment of reading performance, during the instructional lesson, the teacher's assessments are dynamic. Modifications of hypotheses can occur as the teacher responds to the student's needs during instruction.

When using repeated readings with Ted, a second grader, for instance, the diagnostic teacher found that simply discussing the miscues did not result in decreased miscues, so she modeled her own self-correction process by saying, "Oops, that doesn't make sense; let's see what would make sense and start with a *g*. Oh, *girl* starts with a *g*. *The girl hit the home run.* Yes, that makes sense and sounds like it looks." Then Ted read the passage again, and the teacher recorded the miscues and evaluated the amount and kind of change evidenced in the reading performance. Because the number of miscues decreased and fluent reading increased, the teacher recommended the procedure with the modifications be tried during the diagnostic lesson.

On another occasion, a fourth-grade student named John needed assistance in how to read silently and construct meaning with text. The diagnostic teacher formulated her hypotheses while she conducted a think-aloud assessment on the first section, which indicated that John had difficulty making predictions (see chapter 6). During the second section, the teacher used a directed reading activity. During the lesson, John could not answer an inferential question, so the diagnostic teacher rephrased the question to include some factual information to facilitate his response.

John still had no clue about how to respond, so she asked him to find the part of the story that told about the factual information and to read it aloud. The ability of the student to perform this action indicates whether he understands the sequence of the story as well as his ability to read the words without difficulty. He easily found the part of the text that contained the answer and read it without difficulty. Therefore, word identification did not present difficulty.

Again, the teacher began to elicit a response; however, this time she began with a factual question. Then she asked John to relate relevant personal experiences to the facts. After this discussion, the original inferential question was rephrased. John was able to respond to the inferential question, using the factual information and his personal experiences. Because this instructional sequence facilitated comprehension, the teacher hypothesized that John comprehends better when the instructional sequence begins with the facts and then develops an inferential understanding of the story.

During the diagnostic lesson, records of the instructional modifications are kept so that the amount and kinds of teacher intervention can be identified. When the teacher conducts a diagnostic lesson, however, her primary goal is to teach the student. Her second goal is to identify those instructional modifications that result in increased reading performance. In effect, the diagnostic teacher establishes the instructional conditions necessary to increase the reading.

Evaluating Change

To evaluate the effect the instructional adjustments have on the student's reading, the diagnostic teacher conducts a final assessment using the third section of the passage. She uses the same format as for the first section, either recording oral reading responses or a think-aloud experience. The final assessment, in which the students read at sight and without assistance, provides a systematic method for assessing the effects of the instructional adjustments on the student's reading. The teacher assesses reading change during the lesson as well as the amount of task modification and teacher investment needed to produce that change. These measures not only determine placement but also establish optimal instructional conditions.

Reading Growth as the Result of Instruction.   First, the diagnostic teacher must establish the amount of growth (Feuerstein & Feuerstein, 1991) that has occurred as a result of instruction. If the instruction was appropriate, the resulting scores should indicate an independent reading level (98% word identification and 90% comprehension). Because the student received instruction adjusted to mediate learning, the number of questions answered correctly should increase and miscues decrease. Reading progress should be evident.

> Reading progress is indicated by a decrease in miscues and an increase in the number of questions answered correctly.

Next, the diagnostic teacher compares the student's patterns of reading behavior on the first section with those on the third section. The student's oral reading of the third section should reflect more semantically and syntactically appropriate miscues and an increase in self-corrections. This pattern indicates that the student is using his knowledge of the story theme to figure out unknown words. A student's think-aloud on the third section should reflect a more integrated use of textual and nontextual information as well as more elaborate responses to questions. Spontaneous self-monitoring and the student's awareness of the sources of information he uses to construct responses should also be increasingly evident.

Reading progress is also indicated by an increasing use of both reader-based processing and text-based processing and by more self-monitoring for understanding.

Figure 7–1 highlights the final steps involved in assessing reading change using diagnostic lessons. When the diagnostic teacher analyzes change in this last phase of the decision-making cycle, two conclusions can result: a positive change in reading behavior (independent level obtained) or no change in reading behavior (independent level not obtained). These two outcomes necessitate different responses from the diagnostic teacher. If mediated instruction produces an independent reading level, the diagnostic teacher carefully evaluates the task modifications and teacher investment, or assistance, to establish the instructional modifications that produced the change. If mediated instruction does not produce reading progress, the diagnostic teacher eliminates those techniques and modifications that were used. She returns to her diagnostic hypotheses, adds any new information collected during the diagnostic lesson, and reformulates her hypotheses. Then she selects a new technique and conducts another diagnostic lesson.

Determining the Amount of Task Modification. Prior to instruction, the diagnostic teacher selects a technique to implement during the diagnostic lesson. She determines how she is going to promote active reading. She decides whether the reading task will be silent or oral and whether the story will be read as a whole or in segments. She decides whether she will introduce new vocabulary words and how to do it. As she teaches the lesson, the teacher modifies these original plans so that the student can construct meaning with text. It is these modifications that the teacher records and evaluates.

For example, the diagnostic teacher decided to use self-directed questioning (see "Think-Aloud Approach" in part 2) with Luis, a third-grade student who was relatively passive when reading. He did not make guesses about the story or revise the few predictions he did make. The teacher began instruction by demonstrating the steps of self-directed questioning. As she silently read the text, she thought aloud when important information was presented. Next, she asked Luis to read silently and then to think aloud about the text. Luis readily began to talk about his interpretations. The teacher and student continued this process by alternately thinking aloud about the text. Luis began to make guesses and then to revise his thinking about the text.

In this example, the teacher needed to make relatively few task modifications. The student learned the new task and readily applied it. The teacher concluded that the passive reading behavior was due to a lack of experience with the task. It was evident that Luis had not transferred his active stance in other problem-solving situations to silent reading behavior.

When evaluating Terry, another passive reader, the diagnostic teacher decided to use think-aloud again. As with the other student, the diagnostic teacher demonstrated the steps of self-directed questioning by thinking aloud about the text. Then she asked Terry to read silently and think aloud about the text when important information was presented. Terry read a long segment silently, then stopped and looked at the teacher for questions. However, he could not talk about the text. The teacher asked him to read the segment aloud and think out loud about the text. Again he read the words without stopping to think about their meaning. Therefore, the teacher demonstrated the same segment of the text, emphasizing how she thought about the text as she read out loud. Terry followed the teacher's example. However, he mainly recounted exactly what was stated in the text. He did not tie together events to make predictions or revise any previous thoughts.

The teacher demonstrated the next segment of the text. Terry was asked to follow the example, but he again read the words without thinking. The teacher, therefore, modified the task by segmenting the section into sentences. Reading sentence by sentence, she demonstrated her thinking about each sentence. Finally, Terry began to think aloud about the sentences and draw relationships among the sentences in the paragraph. During this segment, the teacher modified the procedures by asking questions such as, "What makes you say that? Was this character important? How do you know?"

To help this passive reader learn more active strategies for constructing meaning, the diagnostic teacher needed to modify a number of instructional areas. She changed the task from silent to oral reading when Terry could not talk about what he had read silently. She segmented the passage into sentences when he could not follow the paragraphs that she demonstrated. Moreover, she shifted from simply demonstrating to demonstrating with inquiry questions in order to help Terry see relationships among the ideas in the text.

The diagnostic teacher evaluates the amount of modification necessary to create a change in the student's reading performance. Luis required little task modification for the original task and learned the task readily. Terry, however, required substantial modification. The degree of task modification becomes a key factor in determining future instructional interactions. If a high degree of task modification is required, a less difficult text or a different technique should be selected. If a low degree of task modification is needed, however, a more difficult text or task can be employed.

> The degree of task modification is considered when establishing the conditions necessary to produce reading change.

Determining the Amount of Teacher Investment.   During assessment, the diagnostic teacher becomes a powerful determiner of active reading. She thinks about how she set up instruction according to the procedures for the technique. Were these procedures sufficient for improving a student's text interpretation? Or did she have to change the procedures, draw out of the student his own knowledge, and then show him how to relate this information to what he was reading? She evaluates how many times she had to rephrase questions and how many clues she needed to provide for the student.

Sometimes relatively little teacher investment, or assistance, is needed. For instance, Bobby could not recognize the word *skated* in this sentence: "The girl skated around the rink." The teacher told him to read to the end of the sentence. Bobby did so, thought for a minute about the word, and then read, "The girl skated around the rink." In this case, very little teacher investment was needed to encourage self-correction. With the simple prompt "read to the end of the sentence," the student was able to figure out the word.

Another student had the same difficulty, but he needed more teacher investment. With the same prompt, Fred read to the end of the sentence but could not recognize the word *rink* either. In this case, the teacher had to probe further. She asked Fred to think about the story and what the girl might be doing. Still there was no response. The teacher then said, "In the picture, there is an ice rink. Now, what do you think the girl is doing?" "Skating" was his reply. The teacher instructed him to read the sentence again. Fred now read, "The girl . . . skated around the . . . rink."

The diagnostic teacher assesses modifications in terms of the amount of teacher investment necessary to create a change in the student's reading. Bobby required relatively little assistance, so there was minimal teacher investment. However, Fred required a great deal of assistance, so there was a higher degree of teacher investment.

> The amount and kind of teacher investment are evaluated to identify the conditions that produce reading change.

The diagnostic teacher assesses reading change as a result of instruction by selecting a reading passage that is moderately difficult. She follows the procedures for the diagnostic lesson: establishing baseline data on the first section through the student's reading at sight, instruction during the second section, and establishing postinstructional data on the third section through more reading at sight. She evaluates whether the third section was read at an independent level. When the third section does not produce reader change, she reformulates her hypotheses and conducts another lesson. When the student reads the final section at an independent level, the diagnostic teacher assesses the amount of task modification and teacher investment that produced that change.

Diagnostic Lessons Using After-Instruction Assessments for Beginning Readers

When using techniques such as the shared reading procedure or language experience approach, the diagnostic teacher initially reads aloud to the student before the student is asked to read on his own. In these techniques, the diagnostic teacher does not have the student read without extensive support, so conducting an assessment before instruction would not be appropriate. In these cases the diagnostic teacher begins by teaching a lesson and *later* conducting an oral reading analysis of the student's reading. If the technique was effective, the passage should be read at the independent level even after a delayed period of time. These procedures are similar to the learning-methods tests developed by Mills (1956) and Ray (1970). After the lessons, the diagnostic teacher compares reading change under several different techniques as recommended in the preceding section.

A diagnostic teacher was working with Neil, a second grader who was a nonreader (he knew only five words by sight). The diagnostic teacher began her diagnostic assessment with a language experience lesson (see "Language Experience Approach" in part 2). She created an experience, Neil dictated a story, and they read the story together numerous times. The story was chunked onto cards, and the cards were flashed in story order. Then Neil read the story on his own and performed at the independent level (error rate $1/50$). Later during the day, he read the story with an error rate of $1/10$. This technique could be used for Neil in future instruction, but it required a high degree of teacher investment to achieve the recorded growth, and he seemed to memorize the story without looking at the words. Neil could, however, correct many of his mistakes when the teacher repeated the preceding part of the sentence (moderate teacher investment). Therefore, the teacher wanted to explore another approach.

For this diagnostic lesson, the teacher used the shared reading approach (see "Shared Reading Approach" in part 2). Neil and the teacher read the story simultaneously; however, he did not look at the text. Neil did, however, begin to read the text as the teacher omitted words in the language pattern. As she omitted more words, Neil paid more attention to the words on the page and reread the text with an error rate of $^1/_{50}$. He also corrected many of his miscues by rereading sentences on his own. Later in the day, Neil still read the story with only 1 miscue every 50 words. The diagnostic teacher concluded that this technique was more effective than the language experience lesson because he was able to use the language pattern to self-correct his miscues.

To see whether another technique would require less teacher time but have similar results, the teacher conducted another diagnostic lesson. This time she used the talking books technique (see "Talking Books" in part 2). Neil listened to a short story on a tape recorder until he had the story memorized. Then he read the story to the teacher, producing an error rate of $^1/_{15}$ and losing his place many times. Listening to the book repeated, Neil had memorized the words but not associated them with the printed words. Later that day, he read the book with an error rate of $^1/_{10}$. In this case, the diagnostic teacher continued using the shared reading technique and placed Neil in a small group where he was still able to maintain the reader change that he exhibited in the one-to-one assessment.

Using a series of modified diagnostic teaching lessons, the diagnostic teacher selects the most appropriate technique to teach the beginning reader. These lessons use two readings of the text—one immediately after instruction and another several hours later—to establish a learning rate for that particular instructional technique. For the beginning reader, the diagnostic teacher pays special attention to the teacher investment and task modification needed to create reader change. This assessment determines under what conditions subsequent instruction will be conducted:

1. If little task modification and teacher investment were used to produce the desired change, the diagnostic teacher considers using a more difficult text for instruction.
2. If a moderate amount of task modification and teacher investment were needed, the diagnostic teacher continues to use those adjustments in the same level of text.
3. If a great deal of task modification and teacher investment were required, the diagnostic teacher reformulates her hypotheses and selects either another technique or an easier text.

Special Considerations

The procedures outlined are used when considering only one or two techniques or instructional modifications for the student. In many instances, however, the diagnostic teacher needs to consider several options before establishing the optimal instructional conditions. Therefore, she compares growth under different techniques, uses several adapted lessons, and combines techniques to increase her effectiveness.

Comparing Reading Change Under Different Techniques

At times, the diagnostic teacher will conduct a series of diagnostic lessons so that she can identify the most efficient instructional procedure. After the final assessment with each technique, the diagnostic teacher compares how the reader constructs meaning under the different instructional conditions and evaluates the effectiveness of each technique. For example, Jason, a third-grade reader, was identified as having an oral reading fluency problem. In working with the student, the diagnostic teacher first formulated her hypotheses. From the data collected, the teacher designed a program of repeated readings (see "Repeated Readings" in part 2), including a discussion of the miscues after the first reading. She selected a text and conducted a reading-at-sight evaluation to establish baseline data. For the second section of the passage, she instructed Jason using a repeated readings format and discussed his errors with him. On the last section of the selected text, she conducted another reading at sight but without assistance. Jason decreased his error rate from $1/10$ on the first section to $1/15$ on the last section.

Because this technique resulted in only minimal change in reading performance, the diagnostic teacher designed another lesson. She decided to use the talking books technique (see "Talking Books" in part 2) during the instructional phase of the diagnostic lesson. She followed the same procedure: first establishing baseline data through unaided reading at sight, next instruction, and finally establishing postinstructional data through more unaided reading at sight. This time Jason decreased his error rate from $1/10$ on the first section to $1/50$ on the last section.

The diagnostic teacher compared the resulting changes from the two sets of readings to decide which technique was more effective. The talking books technique produced the most change; moreover, it required less teacher investment because the tape recording provided the words that would have needed the teacher's prompting under the repeated readings approach. As a result, the teacher used taped stories in the diagnostic teaching program. Whenever the diagnostic teacher can conduct a series of diagnostic lessons to compare the effectiveness of several techniques, she increases her ability to confirm the diagnostic hypotheses and select the best possible instructional approach for the reader.

Using More Than One Technique at the Same Time

Sometimes the diagnostic teacher needs to combine several techniques to produce the desired change. In these cases, the combined techniques are more effective than using either one of them alone. The decision-making process that results in combining techniques is illustrated in the case of Charles, a fourth-grade reader who had difficulty with silent reading comprehension. Initially, the diagnostic teacher designed a program using think-aloud procedures (see "Think-Aloud Approach" in part 2). She selected a story, divided it into three sections, and conducted a think-aloud assessment that was unaided. She recorded her data. Next she instructed the lesson using self-directed questioning. She modeled the process, using the concepts missed during the first section. Charles had a great deal of difficulty remembering the steps in self-directed questioning, even after the diagnostic teacher had written them down (task modification). Charles was never able to do the task independently (without a high degree of teacher investment). The final section of the story was read like the first, as an unaided think-aloud assessment, but provided only minimal change (improvement from 55% to 65% in comprehension).

The diagnostic teacher decided to try the reciprocal teaching technique (see "Reciprocal Teaching" in part 2), which is similar to the think-aloud approach but is more structured. She again conducted an unaided think-aloud assessment on the first section of the selected text. Next she instructed the lesson using reciprocal teaching, returning to concepts missed during the first section of the text to model the process and to clear up misconceptions about the story. Charles was to follow her model and summarize, ask a good question, clarify difficult parts, and predict what the next segment would say. However, he had a great deal of difficulty learning this task, so the teacher used a high degree of modeling on each segment. Charles was not able to do the task independently. The final section of the story was read like the first, as an unaided think-aloud assessment. When this technique resulted in only minimal change in reading performance (improvement from 55% to 75% in comprehension) despite a high degree of teacher modeling, the diagnostic teacher decided to add another technique to her procedure.

The teacher selected another story and followed the same procedure: having the student read at sight to establish baseline data, instruction, and having the student read at sight again to establish postinstructional data. During the instructional phase of the diagnostic lesson, the diagnostic teacher introduced a story map (see "Story Mapping" in part 2) along with reciprocal teaching. First, she modeled the combined sequence: add new information to the story map, summarize using the story map, use the story map to ask a good question, clarify any difficult parts that do not fit on the map, and, finally, use the components of the story map to predict what will happen next.

Following instruction in this combined approach, Charles began to take over the teaching. He began to teach the lesson independently. For him, using the story map was more concrete than either think-aloud or reciprocal teaching alone. During the final third of the lesson, the diagnostic teacher conducted a think-aloud assessment that revealed a change in his monitoring of understanding. Charles had begun to revise his predictions as he encountered new information. This new approach resulted in a growth from 55% to 90% in reading comprehension. As in this case, the diagnostic teacher may combine reading techniques to evaluate whether the new combination results in greater reading growth. If it does, she uses the combined, approach rather than either technique alone.

Summary

The job of the diagnostic teacher is to identify appropriate techniques for instruction. By teaching a lesson using selected materials and techniques, the diagnostic teacher assesses the student's learning as she teaches and evaluates reading growth as the result of her instruction. She also measures the task modification and teacher investment needed to ensure reader change. Then she establishes the most appropriate instructional conditions for the student. Once these conditions are in place, the diagnostic teacher introduces more difficult tasks or texts and observes the student as he learns the task or reads the text. The diagnostic teacher becomes both teacher and evaluator. Her purpose during the diagnostic lesson is to record changes in reading behaviors and the instructional adjustments that produced them. She focuses on teaching rather than testing to reveal those instructional adjustments that produce reading change for a particular student.

8 Using Different Types of Assessments

This chapter provides an explanation of the multiple types of assessments that are considered by diagnostic teachers. Many different tests and evaluations can be given to define students' literacy behaviors; however, diagnostic teachers tend to rely heavily on teaching as assessment. As they change their instruction, they make their diagnosis through their observations and the data they collect as they teach. Although different from the traditional forms of assessment, diagnostic teaching produces practical, efficient, and valid information about the learner:

1. It is practical because suggestions for instruction can be incorporated immediately into the instructional program.
2. It is efficient because reading instruction and learning do not stop in order to test; instead, they become an integral part of assessment.
3. It is valid because diagnostic teaching assesses reading in the same kind of instructional situation that is used throughout the student's classroom experience.

Diagnostic teachers have learned to interpret their teaching behaviors and the student's consequential response to guide instructional decision making and provide accurate descriptions of students' reading.

However, assessment is used not only for instructional decision making but also to evaluate progress over time and in relation to other children the same age. These teachers focus on a variety of assessments rather than relying on a single score. From multiple assessments, they create a profile of the students' learning that includes a multiplicity of aspects. The assessments include process-oriented assessments that produce a description of literacy behaviors and product-oriented assessments that often produce a score for achievement. They balance these assessments as well as others to create a comprehensive view of readers' literacy (Afflerbach, 2006). They use these assessments to get a clearer picture of the students' performance in literacy. Because of space limitations, this chapter provides only an overview of various types of assessments used by diagnostic teachers.

Process-Oriented Assessments

Many of the assessments in this book focus on process-oriented assessments that collect data during reading and reading instruction. The following provides a brief description of several ways process-oriented assessments work.

Diagnostic Teaching Assessment

As teachers conduct a reading lesson, they observe individual students' strategy use and background knowledge. A diagnostic teaching assessment is a process of collecting data of students' reading behaviors during instruction. These observations are made as the students are reading and interacting with teachers and peers. Afterward, the diagnostic teacher analyzes how he adapted instruction and the readers' behaviors as a result of instructional adjustments. From this analysis, he makes decisions about the readers' strategies for constructing meaning as well as the appropriateness of instructional techniques. Chapter 7 describes the diagnostic teaching lesson as an assessment.

Miscue Analysis

Analyzing how students monitor their reading is an invaluable way to understand their reading process. Miscue analysis is an accepted tool to help diagnostic teachers describe word identification processes in action. As readers construct meaning with text, they create expectations for what the words are in the text. When their expectations and the words they read orally do not match, they miscue. A selection of miscues can be analyzed to figure out how a student reads. Miscue analysis is a tool for evaluating the relative significance of miscues in the context of the entire passage, the sentence, the graphophonemic symbols, and the reader's experiences. Analyzing oral reading and miscues is described in chapter 6.

Think-Aloud Analysis

Analyzing how readers' construct meaning is a critical means to understand their unique reading process. Think-aloud analysis has been used extensively by teachers to help describe the students' thinking. To analyze comprehension, the diagnostic teacher evaluates how the reader thinks through the comprehension of a passage. Using a think-aloud format of interrupted reading, the teacher observes how the student uses the text and what she knows to interpret the passage. Analysis of a think-aloud, therefore, is a tool for evaluating the reader's comprehension strategies in the context of the entire passage (for further description, see chapter 6).

Running Records

Running records are intended to assist the diagnostic teacher as he monitors the progress of students and help him identify skills and strategies used by students. Running records provide evidence of the children's reading behaviors as they read. The diagnostic teacher uses a standardized system to record words read correctly and errors such as substitutions, omissions, insertions, deletions, repetitions, and self-corrections. When completed, the running record provides insight into the students' strategies and their cuing systems. It also allows the teacher to determine if a given book, either a student's own choice or a book considered for instruction or pendent reading, is at an appropriate level for the student. As in the informal reading inventory, the student should be able to read a book with at least 95% accuracy in order to learn in a classroom setting. In a running record, Marie Clay (1993) suggests that instructional level has an accuracy rate of 90% to 95% where a student can learn with assistance of the teacher in a small group or individually. Below 90% accuracy (frustration level), the student misses too many words to construct meaning and is not able to employ enough reading strategies to experience success (for more information, see http://www.readinga-z.com and http://pages.us.edu/reading/runrec.htm).

Informal Assessments

Informal assessments are used by many classroom teachers to make adjustments in their instruction. Informal means that assessment does not follow standardized procedures but rather has an informal protocol to follow.

Informal Reading Inventory

In the informal reading inventory (see chapter 5 for detailed discussion), the diagnostic teacher asks the student to read various levels of paragraphs, scoring each one. He gets a score for oral and silent reading that represents a product of reading. He uses these scores to decide on the independent, instructional, and frustration levels of reading for that particular reader. During the assessment, the teacher also makes many observations as the student reads. As diagnostic teachers evaluate the passages read and questions answered, they look for reader patterns among levels of text difficulty and describe the readers' behavior and fluency at various levels.

Rubrics

Rubrics have become popular ways to evaluate reading and writing. Rubrics are a printed set of scoring standards for evaluating a performance or a product. The rubric rates specific aspects of a literacy task, such as orally retelling a story or writing a summary of expository text. The standards are described qualitatively, making differences between excellent performance and weaker performance.

Sometimes, a group of teachers evaluate a specific strategy such as summarization. Often, teachers decide to use rubrics so that each teacher evaluates the student's literacy behaviors in a consistent manner. For example, a diagnostic teacher developed a series of questions based on research (Irwin & Mitchell, 1983) similar to the one in Figure 8–1 to evaluate written summaries of expository text.

Figure 8–1   *Questions to Evaluate Summaries*

Did the summary have—
Relevant content and concepts?
A focus on important information?
An organizational structure?
Clear language?
A connection to prior knowledge?

developed a series of questions based on research (Irwin & Mitchell, 1983) similar to the one in Figure 8–1 to evaluate written summaries of expository text.

From these questions, the diagnostic teacher created a rubric using an online rubric maker (see Table 8–1). Diagnostic teachers store rubrics on specialized discs. These assist teachers in creating criteria to rate the quality of student performance on each designated question.

Using the rubric, the teachers evaluated a students' work and were able to describe the student's written summaries. For example, a diagnostic teacher reflected on

TABLE 8–1   *Rubric for Summarization*

Category	Not Apparent	Adequate	Thorough	Exceptional
Includes relevant concepts	There are no relevant concepts in the summary.	There is a relevant concept that is supported with one detail.	There are several relevant concepts that are elaborated on with details.	There are appropriate relevant concepts that are elaborated on with both details and examples.
Focuses on important information	The summary does not include any important information stated in the text. It only has irrelevant details.	The summary includes some important information stated in the text and some irrelevant detail.	The summary includes most of the important information in the text and is somewhat elaborated on.	The summary includes all the important information in the text and is elaborated on with coherent textual information.
Has an apparent organization structure	The summary rambles without having any organizational structure.	The summary has some organization but becomes disorganized in parts.	The summary has clear organization throughout.	The summary is extremely clear in organization so the reader can easily follow the line of thought.
Uses clear language	The summary does not state anything clearly.	The summary has some clear language and some fragments making it difficult to understand.	The summary has clear language and appropriate language use.	The summary has excellent language use and is clearly written.
Evidence of using prior knowledge	The summary states only information in the text.	The summary uses prior knowledge to organize the information.	The summary uses prior knowledge to reorganize information into larger conceptual categories.	The summary uses prior knowledge to elaborate concepts and reorganize them into discrete and distinctive categories.

Note: Made with Rubistar.

evidence that she used her prior knowledge about snakes. However, Sandy's organization was exceptional since main ideas were supported by key facts revealing an overall theme in the summary." These statements describing Sandy's summaries were derived by analyzing the rubric. Rubrics help diagnostic teachers and their students reflect on how each student was developing the summarization strategy.

In schools, groups of teachers at a particular grade level often collaborate to develop a rubric to evaluate each student's work. For example, a group of second-grade teachers decided that story retelling, which is similar to summarization, was a critical task for their students. They developed a rubric similar to the one in Figure 5–12 to evaluate students' retelling (Roskos & Walker, 1994). After they read stories, the teachers had their second-grade students write a retelling as if they were telling the story to a friend. Then they took three pieces from their classes, and each teacher rated the pieces based on the rubric.

After the teachers had individually rated each retelling, they met to compare their ratings. The teachers discussed the differences and finally agreed on an adaptation of the rubric and designated standard pieces that represented each rating. This provided a consistent way to assess students' retellings.

Together, they evaluated each student's retelling, attaching the retelling rubric and a written reflection together. For example, a reflective analysis of Jeri's writing by a teacher included, "Jeri elaborates both the setting including the main characters in great detail; however, she only briefly mentions the problem but describes many events, some of which were not important. She does end her retelling so it makes sense but doesn't tell how the problem is solved. Jeri's strengths are in describing the setting and events; however, she needs to work on elaborating the problem and resolution."

The rubric provided not only a consistent form for evaluating retellings but also the language to write an analysis of the data. Several things happened in the collaborative design of the rubric. First, the teachers were developing their understanding of what was important in a retelling. Second, they were developing a standard for what a second-grade retelling would include. Third, the teachers learned how to evaluate differences within a rubric. They realized that not every retelling had to be alike but rather that a coherent and elaborate representation of the story was needed. Further, they began to use this evaluation as a way to inform instructional goals for individual students.

Finally, this group of teachers realized that this evaluation represented fairly text-based reading; therefore, they created another assessment that included an affective response to reading. They used this with narrative texts that were highly engaging. Then they asked the students to write their responses and what they liked about the story. This became the information evaluted by the new rubric.

Formal Assessments

The diagnostic teacher uses formal assessments along with other assessments. Formal assessments are administered under standardized conditions to measure reading and writing achievement, a product of learning to read and write. Standardized reading tests report a student's performance in relation to the performance of a representative group. Thus, a score on a given standardized test tells where a student stands in relation to a population of readers who have taken the test. In other words, these tests represent a snapshot of a student's reading on a specific day, and then the scores are compared to the norms that were already established. Tests that use normalized data are constructed using a large group of diverse students, so test creators are able to calculate the average performance of many students in differing age-groups (Barr, Blachowicz, Bates, Katz, & Kaufman, 2007). Using raw scores, the text makers create a normal distribution that is represented by a bell-shaped curve so that approximately 68% of the scores represent those scores closest to the average (see Figure 8–2). If a group of students scored from 15.9% to 84.1% on a standardized test, they would represent how the average student performed in the sample. They would not be failing in reading because they missed half the test questions (for further information, see http://en.wikipedia.org/wiki/Normal_distribution).

In fact, these standardized achievement tests and survey reading tests are designed with average students in mind. They often do not represent the less proficient reader's capabilities because so much of the test is read at frustration level. In using standardized tests, diagnostic teachers realize that these tests are not perfect, but they need to have a degree of reliability and validity. A test is considered reliable by the degree the scores of individuals are consistent over repeated applications, while a test is considered valid when it measures what it was intended to measure. That is, the test's content is representative of the actual reading the students do.

Standardized Achievement and Reading Tests

One of the most frequently used formal assessments are standardized achievement tests where reading is a major aspect. Standardized reading tests normally consist of a vocabulary and comprehension subtest. Comprehension is measured by selecting predetermined answers to questions, while vocabulary is measured by selecting a definition of the target word from a list of four alternatives. The tests give you a score that is based on the standardization sample so that a diagnostic teacher can measure such things as yearly progress. Often, these assessments are given at both the beginning and the end of the year to evaluate adequate yearly progress.

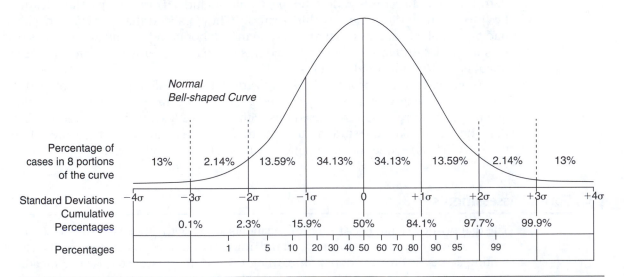

Figure 8–2 *Normal Curve with Percentiles*

Source: Wikipedia, the free encyclopedia (reviewed December 12, 2006, from http://en.wikipedia.org/wiki/Normal_distribution.

such things as yearly progress. Often, these assessments are given at both the beginning and the end of the year to evaluate adequate yearly progress.

Criterion-Referenced Tests

This type of assessment is designed to measure student performance against a defined set of criteria or expectations. Scores on criterion-referenced tests indicate what individuals *can* do in relation to the standard or criterion, not how they have scored in relation to others. Criterion-referenced tests usually have a passing standard that is sometimes set by a committee outside the classroom when the assessment is used by a large group of students in a school district. If the test is designed for classroom use, the teacher decides on the passing score. Either way, the passing score is a subjective decision, not an objective one. For more information, see http://www.fairtest.org/facts/csrtests.html. Criterion-referenced tests are preferred by standards-based educational reform and accountability efforts.

Engagement Assessments

As pointed out in chapters 2 and 3, engagement is a key factor in reading achievement. When individuals engage in extensive reading, they tend to improve as readers. Likewise, when students disengage from reading, they read less and begin to lower their perception of themselves as readers. Thus, attitudes, self-perception, and motivation are critical to being engaged in reading. To many teachers, struggling readers appear to lack motivation to learn because they are often off task or asking unrelated questions. Thus, engagement and motivation go hand in hand. Several different types of assessments have been designed to evaluate aspects of motivation and engagement in literacy. Certainly, a students' attitude toward reading affects their motivation, but also their value of literacy activities and their perception of themselves as readers and writers affect their motivation. Furthermore, if they are interested in a topic, they are more motivated to read about that topic. The following are frequently used indicators that give information about engagement in reading.

Attitude Toward Reading

Diagnostics teachers have always known that attitude toward reading plays a key role in reading engagement. When students view reading as a positive activity, they are more likely to engage in literacy activities and to read and write for longer periods of time. Although there are many scales designed to measure attitudes, one that is easy to administer and used frequently has been developed by McKenna and Kear (1990). The *Elementary Reading Attitude Scale* is geared to elementary-age students but also has been used with middle school students. It delineates a percentage score for attitudes for recreational and academic reading and can be downloaded from http://www.reading.org/publications/journals/rt/selections/index.html.

Concept of Self as Reader

When students think of themselves as readers, they actively engage in text interpretation and view themselves positively when reading. A positive view of self as a reader or writer increases their engagement in literacy tasks. For instance, Chris proficiency. However, she had extremely immature handwriting and therefore avoided activities that required writing. She gave very little effort when writing and gave up easily.

Although there are many self-perception scales, ones designed to evaluate self-perceptions as a reader and writer are the most important to the diagnostic teacher. Two that are exceptionally useful are *Reader Self-Perception Scale* (Henk & Melink, 1995) and *Writer Self-Perception Scale* (Bottomley, Henk, & Melink, (1997–1998). These self-perception scales are based on the theory that a student's judgment of their ability to read or write affects their engagement and depth of interpretation of what they read. In other words, how students perceive themselves as readers and writers influences whether they would engage in literacy activities or if they avoided them. A positive self-perception indicates that students will engage in literacy activities, thus improving their literacy.

Interviews

Interviews follow a predetermined set of questions. Perceptions of literacy interviews are commonly conducted during the initial meeting with readers. The following set of questions reveals students' perceptions and values of reading (Gambrell, Palmer, Codling, & Mazzoni, 1996). The questions are similar to the following:

1. *Who do you know that can read? Tell me about someone that you know or have seen reading.*
2. *What is reading? What do readers do?*
3. *Can you read?*
   a) *If "yes," ask, "Are you a good reader? What kinds of things do you do that make you a good reader?"*
   b) *If "no," ask, "Are you learning to read?" If student says "no," ask "When do you think you will be able to read?"*
4. *Do you like to read? Why?* (Or, Do you want to learn to read? Why?)

These kinds of questions provide interesting information about students' perceptions of reading.

Motivation to Read Profile

High motivation for reading is connected to achievement. If students are motivated to read and write, they will engage in reading and writing more frequently and subsequently increase their achievement. Motivation to read also involves a student's concept of self as a reader but also adds an assessment of the value that readers place on the act of reading. In addition, the assessment instrument provides both quantitative and qualitative information by combining the use of a survey instrument and an individual interview (Gambrell, Palmer, Codling, Mazzoni, 1996). Members of the International Reading Association can download this at http://www.reading.org/publications/journals/rt/selections/abstracts/RT-49-7-Gambrell.html.

Interest Inventories

Interest inventories are usually lists of statements or questions developed to indicate students' interests. Students' interests influence how they interact in various situations.

Interest is an engagement part of the situational context because it affects what students pay attention to in text. Students differ in their interest. Some students differ in their interest in the topic based on their level of knowledge related to the topic. In other words, they engage more intensely in topics where they have more background knowledge and, in turn, more interest. Interest also influences the frequency and form of strategic processing students use. The following Web site use student interest for book selection: http://www.teachers.ash.org.au/bookzone/thanks.htm.

 ## Student Self-Assessments

Diagnostic teachers have used student self-evaluation as assessment tools for many years. In fact, progress charts used in remedial programs for more than two decades are the forerunners of self-assessment. The power of flashing word cards was not in the rapid recognition of words but in the charting of progress so that the teachers and students could concretely discuss progress. Granted it was a very narrow perspective of literacy, but it put the students in charge of evaluating reading growth and establishing their own goals for learning. There are many ways to engage students in evaluating their own reading performance.

Strategy Self-Assessments

In self-assessments, students evaluate how well they are doing on acquiring the targeted strategy or strategies. They have to think about their reading strategies and how they construct meaning with text. For instance, one student evaluated her own prediction strategies using a yes/no check sheet (see Table 8–2). As she read a story, she completed a prediction log as she used the prediction strategy (see "Prediction Strategy Instruction" and modification #1 in part 2. Then she reread her prediction log and used the self-assessment prediction check sheet to evaluate how she predicted.

After evaluating her prediction logs, Mae, a fifth grader, reviewed the self-assessment prediction check sheet to complete a reflection sheet like the following: "Today my reading was _____ because _____. Next time I will work on _____." With this structure, this student wrote, "Today my reading was great because I actually read the words in the story and predicted what would come next. Next time I will work on using what I know and what's in the story." Using this type of self-assessment helped her identify her strategies for this particular story. It also helped her think about the targeted strategy (prediction) and how she used prediction. These types of check sheets can be developed collaboratively among the diagnostic teacher and the students.

TABLE 8–2   *Self-Assessment Prediction Check Sheet*

	Yes	No
I make predictions easily	X	
I use prior experiences		X
I use textual information	X	
I check predictions	X	
I change predictions as needed		X
I justify my responses	?	

Figure 8–3   *Assessment Letter*

Dear _____,

   This letter tells about my reading and writing.

When I read, these are the things I do well. _____

I am learning how to _____

So far I can _____

One of my favorite books is _____

because _____

I think my best piece of writing is _____

because _____

Thank you for coming to my conference.

Assessment Letters

Teachers make observations about student learning but so do students. Many know what their strengths are and how they are doing during reading instruction. Assessment letters help students conceptualize their progress in positive terms. When the assessment is written down, the students and the diagnostic teacher can readily discuss new goals for learning. During these conversations, the diagnostic teacher and the student fill out a summative check sheet or an assessment letter explaining how their reading is progressing (see Figure 8–3). The assessment letter describes the student's literacy. Using self-assessments, students can evaluate their own literacy, and thus the power of student self-assessment lies in the reflective process by which students evaluate their strengths and strategies, thus making changes in how they orchestrate the reading process.

Student-Led Conferences

Parent and teacher conferences provide information about student learning and growth. But a more powerful assessment is a student-led conference. A student-led conference is where a student and her teacher select artifacts from authentic and classroom experiences to demonstrate what the student knows and can do. The student then leads the parent conference with the teacher standing nearby ready to step in if necessary. Teachers often comment that when they prepare for student-led conferences, they can view the work and discuss with students their thinking and their strengths and areas to work on. They often comment that the conversation often showed them that the students learned more than what was measured through traditional assessments (for futher information, see http://www.educationworld.com). In a student-led conference,

Figure 8–4 *Student-Led Conference Outline*

1. Go over assessment letter.
2. Read a favorite part of a story and tell why it is a favorite.
3. Demonstrate a strategy to the parents.
4. Have parents use the strategy.
5. Present portfolio (see next section).
6. Have parents write a note to their child describing two things they liked.

the teacher and the parents can observe and converse about student learning and their strategy use rather than simply what books and activities the entire class is doing.

To prepare for the conference, an outline of what to present is developed between the diagnostic teacher and the students. This outline can include numerous literacy activities. Some teachers use the assessment letter as the core, while others use other activities, such as having students read a favorite passage from a story, informational text, or a piece of writing. Sometimes the conference includes a conversation and demonstration of a newly learned reading strategies. This activity can become even more powerful if the students teach the parents the newly learned reading strategy. For example, Cherie showed her father how she had learned to study by asking self-questions on key points and writing them in the margins. During the conference, she demonstrated the technique and had her father use it with a textbook. He asked a question and then stumbled when answering. Cherie piped in immediately, "Dad, it is Okay to make a mistake or stumble, it doesn't matter. The important thing is that you are thinking while you are reading. Later, you can go back and check and change your thinking." In any case, the students review their work with their parents and teacher. Here again they explain their literacy development. Such conferences serve to help students describe their reading and writing progress. An outline for student-led conferences can be used to help students remember what they plan to do (see Figure 8–4).

The student-led conference helps students distinctly see how they are progressing as a reader and a writer. They help students attribute their progress to the strategies they have learned and the effort they have expended, thus increasing engagment in further literacy activities.

Authentic Assessments

Authentic assessments involve tasks in which students must use reading and writing for real-world purposes. Reading the newspaper and retelling interesting information is a real-life activity, as is telling about favorite parts of books and movies. Reading and writing reports is also very much a part of many occupations. So assessing these activities needs to represent authentic tasks. For further information, see http://jonathan.mueller.faculty.noctrl.edu/toolbox/index.htm.

Assessment Talks

One of the most authentic assessments is asking the student about how reading is proceeding. This conversation can reveal much about the inner dialogue the student is having while reading. Student conferences about books and writing serve as assessment talks. It is during these interactions that teachers can probe student thinking about both content and process. As students and teachers discuss their literacy behaviors, students think about how they read and write. In this way, students think and talk about their reading strategies and how they constructed meaning with text. In real life, people often explain their thinking and how they thought through an idea. Likewise, assessment talks encourage students to talk about their thought process in terms of reading and writing.

Observations

In this authentic assessment, the diagnostic teacher looks for the strategies the students use to make meaning. Many teachers can "read" their students, observing when they are frustrated or motivated. As a teacher observes these cues, the diagnostic teacher can adjust the instruction accordingly. They make adjustments and record their observations afterward. Teacher notice how students use their use of knowledge sources. Teachers look at how active they are as they read orally. Here are some questions that can guide initial observations when a student is reading orally. Do students go back and correct significant miscues, or do they just read on trying to make sense of what they are reading? What do they do when they make significant miscues? If these questions indicate the student is making many significant miscues and not reading for meaning, the diagnostic teacher completes a miscue analysis (see the section "Miscue Analysis"). As the student is reading, the diagnostic teacher can make jottings about the sources of information the child is using. When teachers write down their observations, they are creating anecdotal records. This helps them collate continuous information for an individual child yet teach within an instructional group. Therefore, some teachers record their observations by using sticky notes that can later be put with other notes about this particular reader.

Portfolios

As schools have used portfolios, it has become increasingly clear that student-centered portfolios are important aspects of assessment. They shift the control of learning from test makers' and teachers' manuals to students and teachers collaborating on reading growth. Like diagnostic teaching lessons, which evaluate reading during actual learning experiences, portfolios assess literacy using artifacts from authentic activities in which students construct meaning. The artifacts represent what the student knows and can do. Each artifact includes a reflection about what it shows or what was learned; by this means, both the students and teachers begin to describe the process of learning. The contents of the portfolio are not items completed on a single day but rather items collected over a period of time that demonstrate the student understandings during literacy activities. For example, a teacher included in a portfolio an example of students' story writing (see "Story Writing Approach" in part 2) from each of the months of October, February, and April. Then he analyzed each student's growth in writing over the year and placed the artifacts and the reflective analysis in the portfolio. For example, his reflection for Jose was the following: "The three pieces of writing show that Jose is becoming more fluent and on task during writing time as his stories have increased in length. Jose's vocabulary knowledge is growing because he is increasingly using varied words appropriately in his writing. However, even with lots of writing experiences and editing pieces, Jose" spelling is inconsistent, and his paragraph organization needs work." Portfolios place the focus on the student's learning rather than a specific score on one single day.

Portfolios organize artifacts and information in a convenient format to demonstrate literacy. Therefore, portfolios document and evaluate literacy using multiple sources of information (oral reading recorded on tapes, written think-alouds, writing, retelling, and so on) and multiple contexts (alone, with a partner, with a teacher or parent, with a group, using the author's chair, and so on) in a collaborative fashion (Glazer & Brown, 1993; Stowell & Tierney, 1995). In fact, artifacts can be drawn from many different aspects of the student's day. For instance, students might include a vocabulary map about China or excerpts from a response journal. Sometimes students include poetry they have written at home. In fact, teachers have found that placing nonschool items in the portfolio served to build a bridge between school and society, thus creating a more elaborate view of literacy learning (Hansen, 1995).

Consistent with the focus of diagnostic teaching, portfolios focus on strengths rather than weaknesses (Glazer & Brown, 1993). As the diagnostic teacher and his students evaluate progress, they choose items that demonstrate what students know and can do. Thus, as they mutually discuss what to put into the portfolio, the students think about what they want to show about their literacy. Through deciding how to show strengths, the diagnostic teacher and his students begin to evaluate student strengths and see how to use them in literacy events. For example, Jenny decided to put a videotape of her oral science report, which was a demonstration about fossils, into her portfolio. For her report, she had collected fossils with her father and labeled them. This activity showed that she did, in fact, have extensive background knowledge about the fossils even though she had difficulty reading about the topic in her textbook. As Jenny reflected on her science project, she began to understand that she could participate in many literacy activities as she developed as a reader. Likewise, her teacher could assess Jenny's science knowledge through the medium of the videotaped demonstration rather than a paper-and-pencil test.

Evaluating Student Performance Using Multiple Assessments

The diagnostic teacher takes the information gathered from multiple sources (process-oriented assessments, product-oriented assessments, informal assessments, and authentic assessments) to target specific reading behaviors to monitor over time. For instance, a diagnostic teacher noticed that Erin was overrelying on the text when predicting and retelling stories. He used a prediction rubric to evaluate the student's performance, further verifying his observations. He cross-checked this with a standardized test that indicated that comprehension was lower than vocabulary development. He then double-checked the informal reading inventory and found that consistent questions missed asked the student to infer from the title the meaning of the passage. Taken together, all the data indicated that the student was not using background knowledge to make inferences from the text. This analysis led to the development of techniques to improve the student's ability to infer by assisting Erin in making predictions using background knowledge, the basis for making an inference. Once a week, the diagnostic teacher had Erin read a short story and keep a prediction log (see "Prediction Strategy Instruction" and modification #1 in part 2) where Erin wrote predictions and rationales at designated points in the story, thus creating a written think-aloud. These predictions and rationales were rated using a simple rubric (see Table 8–3) and placed in a working portfolio.

TABLE 8–3   *Prediction Rubric*

	Yes 3	Somewhat 2	No 1
Predicts			
Uses textual information			
Uses prior experiences			
Monitors			
Evaluates predictions			
Revises predictions as needed			
Uses text examples			
Uses prior experiences			

Using the prediction log, the diagnostic teacher talked with Erin about the strategies she was using in this particular story and jotted a reflection at the bottom of the page. It said, "Erin is still using more of the text to make a prediction. She realizes she needs to use her own knowledge but doesn't access it very frequently. Although I model this for her, she continues to repeat text information to make a prediction." The check sheet helped focus the conversations on the student's strategy use and how the text or her background knowledge might have affected her predictions. Erin kept saying, "I just want to be right, and that means using the information in the text. It is always right." The prediction log, coupled with the prediction check sheet and a conversation about creating a prediction, allowed the diagnostic teacher to have a concrete representation of how the student was thinking. At the end of a month, the teacher and the student reviewed the prediction check sheets to ascertain growth as well as the change in prediction strategies used. Looking over the check sheets with the prediction log, they found that Erin used increasingly more background knowledge. Often she used just one word and misconstrued the meaning; however, she was beginning to revise her predictions on the basis of textual information and a little of her own knowledge. This review allowed them to evaluate growth in a targeted strategy over time. Stapling the prediction logs and rubric together, the teacher wrote a reflection about the student's strategy development for that month. He wrote the following: "Erin is using a little of her background knowledge to recognize that her thinking is off track. This clues her to revise her understanding; however, she still relies on the text most of the time." These artifacts were placed in her portfolio to be reviewed at the end of the next month. The diagnostic teacher decided to model his thinking more specifically as he made a prediction. In this way, diagnostic teachers can use multiple assessments to decide on specific areas of reading that a student needs to work on. In this case, the diagnostic teacher used a strategy, a check sheet, and portfolios to monitor growth in reading development over time. At the end of the year, he would again give the standardized reading test and an informal reading inventory to confirm growth.

The diagnostic teacher wanted to compare reading strategies among several reading tasks to evaluate Jenny's reading strategies (for a description of Jenny, see chapter 6). Although in group standardized tests Jenny scored in the average range, when Jenny read orally on an informal reading inventory, her reading was marred with miscues even though she could retell the story in complete detail. After completing a miscue analysis (see chapter 6), the diagnostic teacher noticed that Jenny was mainly using the initial consonant as a cue and then was guessing what an unfamiliar word was. Reviewing a written summary, the teacher evaluated each word using the spelling assessment rubric (see Figure 5–12). The evaluation indicated that Jenny was just beginning the letter-naming stage, where she wrote many of the letters in the words but their spelling resembled the way they sounded (invented spelling) rather than conventional spellings. Looking more closely, the diagnostic teacher noticed that more than half the words simply had the initial part of the word with little resemblance to the final part of the word. This assessment was also consistent with Jenny's miscue analysis.

Next, the diagnostic teacher evaluated the written summary, using the retelling assessment (see Figure 5–13) to evaluate comprehension. This evaluation revealed that the student could retell a story but often embellished the story events with her own knowledge of similar situations rather than the actual events in the story. Additionally, the student had been keeping prediction logs, so the teacher evaluated these logs using the prediction rubric (see Table 8–3) to assess active reading strategies. These assessments showed that Jenny actively predicted what might happen in a story, sometimes missing the point because she used too much of her background knowledge. By comparing assessments across these tasks, the diagnostic teacher observed a consistent pattern of overrelying on background knowledge when reading. Using this strength, the diagnostic teacher and the student discussed this trait and developed a plan to help her monitor her reading, checking the text more frequently, particularly to correct miscues that might have important clues to story meaning.

Summary

The diagnostic teacher and his students evaluate how their literacy is progressing in the classroom. The use of multiple types of assessments provides a view of students' literacy. The various assessments allow the diagnostic teacher and the students to describe and measure reading achievement. Assessments can be informal and formal; they can be product oriented or process oriented, and they can be authentic or student driven. They can also evaluate engagment. Using a variety of assessments gives the diagnostic teacher a more comprehensive view of the students in a class, in a school, or when tutoring.

9 Selecting Materials

One of the decisions the diagnostic teacher makes is to select instructional materials that fit the students' reading performance. In fact, much of her initial diagnosis is directed toward finding an instructional range to inform decisions about instructional materials (see chapter 5). Once this level is established, the diagnostic teacher selects material within this range that would be appropriate for the students she is teaching. As she plans instruction, the diagnostic teacher thinks about the various kinds of instructional materials and their influence on students' learning (see chapter 2). Teachers have a myriad of materials available, including basal reader series, trade books, predictable books, magazines, skills books, computer software, Internet information, videotapes of classic stories/songs, and student-produced work. Teachers, however, often persist in using inappropriate materials because they lack the knowledge of how to make suitable selections. Knowledge about instructional materials allows teachers and students to make changes that can advance student reading performance.

Finding instructional materials that will improve the student's learning is an essential task of the diagnostic teacher. When the material is too difficult, students cannot construct meaning or flexibly use reading strategies. If too many words are unknown or the concepts too dense, students become flustered and decrease their attention. The students may instead worry about "how" to make sense with the text and develop negative emotions related to reading (Schallert & Reed, 1997). In fact, Roller (1998) found that as students read easier books, their word recognition accuracy increased, and children began to discuss the meaning of the text more readily. When reading easier text at least at their instructional level, poor readers can flexibly use multiple strategies. Thus, finding the optimal match between students' instructional level and the selected material can increase students' reading performance.

In the past, many teachers, including diagnostic teachers, used materials organized by others. This approach is convenient and time saving, but teachers need to make sure these materials align with the strengths and needs of the readers. The diagnostic teacher uses information about the reader to organize materials rather than a prescribed plan. Such an approach does not exclude the use of an organized sequence of materials published by others. It does, however, exclude the mindless completion of all units and tasks in the organized program. The diagnostic teacher asks, "How does the type of text affect the student's reading?" She is mindful of the individual progress of each student and selects material accordingly, constantly double-checking how successful the reader is.

Basic Types of Materials

Instructional materials often align with specific views of reading. Specifically, materials often are associated with either a text-based view or a reader-based view of instruction. However, the way the text is used is what makes the *instruction* text based, reader based, interactive, or socio-interactive. It is essential, however, that the diagnostic teacher find a text that fits the reader and will advance his reading using strengths. The basic types of materials offer options for the diagnostic teacher. No matter which type of material is selected, however, the key is to find material that is an instructional match for the reader.

Basal Readers

Basal readers are anthologies of stories arranged by grade level and packaged for each grade along with an instructional manual, workbooks, computer and technology resources, and sometimes classroom libraries. They are associated with more traditional methods that use a text-based approach to instruction. However, the most recent basal reader series include high-quality literature or excerpts from classic literature for their specific grade level. They also often include cognitive strategy instruction so that all students can learn to read strategically. An advantage to using a basal reader is that the difficulty of the story has been calculated and will be approximately at the third-grade range if the basal reader is classified as a third-grade reader. However, these designations often do not include story-specific vocabulary such as difficult names and places. Nevertheless, using a basal reader at the expected grade level can reduce the problem of identifying a text that will fit a reader. Major basal reading and structured literature-based programs are published by the following companies:

Houghton Mifflin Reading
 http://www.hmco.com/divisions/school_division.html
Harcourt Trophies
 http://www.harcourtschool.com
Scott Foresman Reading
 http://www.pearsonschool.com
Macmillan/McGraw-Hill Reading
 http://www.mhschool.com/reading/
Kendall-Hunt Pegus II
 http://www.kendallhunt.com/index.cfm?PID=252&PGI=0
SRA Open Court Reading
 https://www.sraonline.com/index.html?PHPSESSID=8fba06488f7428759a12b0
5eb3978d9f

Chapter Books

The term "chapter books" usually refers to narrative literature that tells a story through a sequence of chapters. These books are more closely aligned with reader-based approaches to instruction; however, it depends on how the chapter book is used. Chapter books do not have an instructional manual, nor are they designated to a specific grade level. Sometimes, publishers have indicated the reading level on the spine or back cover by using a readability formula (see the section "Readability Formulas" in this chapter). Chapter books tell stories similar to everyday life events, but the author captivates the imagination by making these events larger than life (Schallert & Reed, 1997). Yet at the same time, readers engage with a text to see whether the stories the author tells ring true in their own lives. This engagement becomes an inner conversation between the author and the reader. Thus, chapter books are often used in literature discussion groups so that students can share their experiences and interpretations, creating shared understanding of the world. Award-winning chapter books can be found at http://www.ucalgary.ca/~dkbrown/awards.html and http://www.factmonster.com/ipka/A0768701.html?utm_source or in the International Reading Association Children's Choices list at http://www.reading.org/Library/Retrieve.cfm?D=10.1598/RT.60.2.7&F=RT-60-2-ChildrensChoices.html.

Focused Lesson Books

To work on specific strategies and skills, some publishers have produced material in workbook-type format that will help readers focus on a specific area of need. These books usually reflect a text-based theory of reading because the readers focus on a single part of the text in order to improve their overall reading. Sensible decisions must be made with this type of material because it has decontextualized the specific strategy or skill to be learned. Thus, the reader is not using the skill or strategy in naturally occurring text. However, newer, focused lesson books provide both text and the skill activity. For example, *25 Read and Write Mini-Books That Teach Word Families* (Sanders, 2001) has both easy-to-read texts and word family activities. A list of Web sites for focused lesson books can be found at http://www.homeroomteacher.com/index.asp?PageAction=VIEWCATS&Category=43

High-Interest, Low-Readability Books

Some publishers have designed books specifically for readers who are reading below grade level. These books are stories that would appeal to an older student but are written at an easier level to provide interesting stories that help improve literacy. Many of the classic stories, such as "To Build a Fire" by Jack London, have been rewritten so that these readers can experience the story without having to struggle with complex vocabulary and language structure. These materials are based on the text-based approach to reading, in which the text is the driving force in comprehension. The topics of these books range from adventure and mystery to sports, history, and science fiction. There are several Web sites that have lists of books. The following sites can lead to titles and publishers of high-interest, low-readability books: http://www.indiana.edu/~reading/ieo/bibs/hilo.html and http://childrensbooks.about.com/cs/reluctantreaders/a/reluctantreader.htm

Internet Materials

There are numerous materials on the Internet that students can read, summarize, and analyze. These materials expand options for students who are trying to locate information from multiple sources. Encyopedias are now online, including Encyclopedia.com, Encyclopedia Britannica, and Yahoo! Encyclopedia. Other encyclopedias are also dictionaries, such as Encarta, Wikipedia, and Infoplease, while others focus on special topics, such as the Encyclopedia Mythica. Other materials that can advance learning are sites like Global Earth, which locates places and tells about geography. The federal government has a national site that has content for all subject areas (http://www.free.ed.gov/?sid=8). Other sites, such as the National Science Teachers Association (NSTA), include text for students to read as well as lessons for teachers NSTA (http://www.nsta.org/classroomdoors). Social studies topics are found in various places on the Internet; however, newspaper and current events Web sites are exceptionally useful for middle and high schools. The Web sites that update the news constantly are an invaluable resource for learning. The list could go on and on. Searching for information using a search engine is another alternative (See list in appendix D).

Media

Use of media is growing as a result of technological advances that make these products readily available to classrooms. Television, compact discs, videos, and podcasts can offer new media for teaching reading. For example, many sing-along videos or compact discs can provide support for the beginning reader. Using these forms of technology, young students can sing along and learn the words and the sounds in words. For comprehension lessons, other media can enhance understanding. Web newscasts and podcasts can help students develop a critical analysis of today's important issues as well as various cultures. Most important for this book is that media are often essential for struggling readers to get a sense of the whole topic or story. They often benefit from watching a video of a book before reading it. Using videos with struggling readers helps them (a) predict what the words are, (b) understand word meanings, and (c) understand the story organization or content information. Likewise, many early books are based on songs so that children can sing along and learn the words and the sounds in those words. These newer technologies are motivational and provide another avenue to promote positive attitudes for reading instruction. Many lessons that use media sources are now avaiable online. These are just a few: http://www.readwritethink.org/lessons/lesson_view.asp?id=887, http://www.readwritethink.org/lessons/lesson_view.asp?id=901, and http://www.readwritethink.org/lessons/lesson_view.asp?id=256.

Picture Trade Books

Many trade books are well-illustrated books that are designed to be read aloud to young children. The difficulty of the vocabulary and concepts varies greatly; therefore, it is hard to estimate the reading level of these books. However, these books can be used to demonstrate minilessons to intermediate and middle school students or as an introduction or extension of a lesson. If the story is engaging, as in Chris Van Allsburg's *The Wretched Stone*, students can learn sophisticated strategies when engaged in an authentic story. Typically, reading aloud picture trade books are associated with the reader-based or interactive approaches to reading instruction. There are many lists of picture books online. A Web site for various populations of children is http://childrensbooks.about.com/gi/dynamic/offsite.htm?zi=1/XJ/Ya&sdn=childrens books&cdn=parenting&tm=116&gps=231_1212_1063_847&f=10&tt=14&bt=0&bts=1&z u=http%3A//kids.nypl.org/reading/recommended2.cfm%3FListID%3D61.

Poetry Anthologies

Poetry is a type of material that is effective for developing readers. Many poems have rhyme and rhythm that invite students to read them again and again. An easy poem is a good way to begin tutoring sessions for older readers. When read chorally, the poems provide a successful experience that starts off a session well. Many anthologies of poetry can be used in classrooms and tutoring. Some of the favorite anthologies are those by Shel Silverstein and Jack Prelutsky. Many of their poems provide not only success but also humor because of the absurd actions and ideas. Web sites also have excellent poetry for reading and space for writing. Try these sites: http://www.poetry4kids.com/poems, http://www.houghtonmifflinbooks.com/features/poetry/children.shtml, and http://falcon.jmu.edu/~ramseyil/poehumor.htm.

Predictable Books

Predictable books have repeated language patterns that make them easier to read because of the repetition of words and language structures. Associated with reader-based approaches, predictable books invite young children to read them again and again. The colorful illustrations are interesting and help children figure out words using their own interpretation of the pictures. These books have been so successful that many of them are set as big books to allow the whole class to read them together. They have also been used to encourage writing innovations around the language patterns in these books. The following Web sites dealing with predictable books have several lists of various aspects and the book titles: http://clerccenter.gallaudet.edu/Literacy/srp/magazines/perspectives/1995-11-12.html and http://www.monroe.lib.in.us/childrens/predict.html.

Series Books

Series books are often easier for readers because the authors use the same characters and same language structures in each book. (See appendix D for a list of series books. Also see http://www.kidsreads.com/series/index.asp.) Students in the second- and third-grade ranges readily profit from series books because they provide predictable characters and actions. The chapters provide the predictability that the patterned language of predictable books did for younger readers. Many adults remember reading books in the Nancy Drew and the Hardy Boys series. These series books helped them gain fluency in reading. However, the books written by the same author with the same characters can provide support for struggling readers. In fact, some of these series books appeal to older readers and can be used to develop fluency.

Software Programs

Software programs provide another source of reading material. A variety of software programs from various views of reading development can be used to promote reading growth. Some of the newer interactive predictable book programs can be a substantial assistance to teachers who work with more than one student at a time. On these CD-ROM programs, an entire predictable book appears with illustrations on disk. The student can listen to the book read aloud as the words are highlighted in the text (Wood, 2005). Elaborate, structured programs, such as Wiggle Works, (http://teacher.scholastic.com/products/wiggleworks/index.htm), offer computer-assisted learning within the total approach to literacy instruction, including framed innovations on predictable books (see part 2). They can add writing as a way to develop reading. Not only are CD-ROM storybooks supportive for beginning readers, but they are also supportive for English-language learners (Bus, de John, & Verhallen, 2006). As these learners hear the words read aloud, they are learning how the words sound in English, how to say the words, and what the words mean through animations and comprehension by hearing the whole text read. Likewise, many computer programs help students with reading skills, such as fluency and word identification in context. Teachers and students can use speech recognition software programs. These programs recognize the students' voices as they read aloud and record their oral reading. If they miss a word, the program will pronounce the miscue for the student. When finished reading, some calculate the rate and make a record of reading progress (see the reading assistant at http://www.soliloquylearning .com/product/drJager.html_). Word processing programs can help students compose texts when their writing is labored. These programs are also used by teachers when students dictate stories for language experience. Publishing software also assists students in making their written work into a publishable piece. Teachers use other software programs like Inspiration to make concept maps and graphic organizers to present important information showing the relationships among concepts. Software programs provide various ways to construct databases. The advent of technology is certainly a valuable aid in the teaching life of diagnostic teachers. See appendix C for a listing of some quality computer programs and check out suggestions in an online article at http://www.readingonline.org/articles/art_index.asp?HREF=/articles/balajthy2/index.html.

Textbooks

Textbooks refer to expository books that are used for gaining information in the content areas. These books contain content-specific information and abstract concepts that make comprehension difficult. Students generally need some prior understanding of the concepts or at least an overview before they begin reading. As they read, they learn new information and study this information to be able to understand a topic. Textbooks are usually designated to a certain grade level because of the topic; however, textbooks often have a readability level more difficult than their designated grade level. Some Web sites give hints for reading textbooks. The following are examples: http://www.how-to-study.com/pqr.htm and http://www.bcit.ca/learningcommons/studyskills/readingtextbooks.shtml.

 ## Selecting Material for a Particular Reader

The diagnostic teacher evaluates the type of material she is using and considers factors that will help her match the material to the instructional level, interests, and needs of the reader. A teacher may use numerous ways to investigate whether certain instructional material will be an instructional match. The first consideration is the level of difficulty of the text, which can be assessed by matching the text to the reader using a mini-IRI or a cloze test. Another way is to assess the reading ease of the text by using a readability formula or a leveling procedure. In addition to the level of difficulty, the diagnostic teacher considers how interesting the text is, whether to give the reader choice, what background knowledge is needed to understand the text, and how long the text is.

Matching the Text to the Reader

The diagnostic teacher realizes that having the student read the actual text under consideration is the most effective way to ensure an appropriate level of text. This assessment can be done using a sample informal reading passage or a cloze test.

Mini-IRI for Assessing a Match

As indicated in chapter 4, the most effective way to match a story to a reader is to let the reader try it out. The diagnostic teacher collects a sample of reading behavior in the text she is going to teach. She selects about 50 to 120 words from the story and writes questions focusing on the main ideas and key facts or events. After the student reads the passage, the diagnostic teacher computes error or miscue rates and a percentage of comprehension to decide whether the text is at the student's instructional level (see the discussions of CDA in chapter 4 and of IRI in chapter 5 for further details). If the text falls within the instructional range, then it is appropriate for that reader. However, if the text has too many unfamiliar words and concepts and falls at the frustration level, then this text is too difficult for most instructional formats. When using shared reading and language experience, the assessment is conducted after instruction (see the discussion of CDA in chapter 4). When using an assessment such as a mini-IRI, the diagnostic teacher has confidence that the material fits the student she is teaching.

Cloze Passage for Assessing the Match

Using a selected 300-word passage is another way to evaluate whether a text will match a reader. In a cloze passage, 50 words of the selected text are deleted and replaced with blanks. The student reads the passage and fills in the blanks with an appropriate word. The passage fits the reader if he can replace at least 40% of the blanks accurately. This type of assessment is most appropriate for older readers and particularly useful in content area classes because it can be administered to an entire class at once. To construct a cloze test, use the following guidelines:

1. Choose a passage that is typical of the text and free of references to illustrated information.
2. Do not delete words in the first sentence of the passage.
3. Retype the passage, replacing every fifth word with a blank of equal length.
4. For reliable results, use at least 50 blanks. Fifty blanks easily convert to percentages. Figure 9–1 provides an example of a cloze test using an excerpt from *Sam, Bangs, and Moonshine.*
5. Before carrying out the assessment, have the students practice a cloze example to become familiar with the procedure.
6. Allow students to complete the text untimed.

The following guidelines are necessary for scoring:

1. Score only exact replacements as correct responses.
2. Convert score to a percentage by making a ratio of correct responses over total number of blanks (50). For example, 15/50 would equal 30%.

Figure 9–1 *Shortened Cloze Test from Sam, Bangs, and Moonshine, by Evaline Ness*

> Sam started to explain, but sobs choked her. She cried so hard _____ it
> was a long _____ before her father understood _____.
>   Finally, Sam's father said, "_____ to bed now. But _____
> you go to sleep, _____, tell yourself the difference _____ REAL
> and MOONSHINE."
>   Sam _____ to her room and _____ into bed. With her
> _____ wide open she thought _____ REAL and MOONSHINE.

3. Use the following criteria to rate the match of the material to the student:

Independent level	60% or higher
Instructional level	40% to 59%
Frustration level	39% or lower

Using the criteria, the diagnostic teacher decides whether the material is at an appropriate reading level for the student. See the following Web site for information on the cloze: http://mason.gmu.edu/~lshafer/ELL-LD/ELL-LDcloze.shtml.

Evaluating the Text

To evaluate the reading ease of the text, the diagnostic teacher can use a readability formula for textbooks and chapter books or a leveling system for predictable books.

Readability Formulas

Using a readability formula is another way to help the diagnostic teacher select the material that would fit the student's instructional reading level. As mentioned in chapter 2, text difficulty can be a result of various factors: grammatical complexity, vocabulary (word choices), structural organization, abstractness, density of ideas, background knowledge required, and so forth. Many readability formulas, however, are based on only two of the factors that affect text difficulty. The formulas mainly use words (vocabulary) and sentence length (grammatical complexity). Vocabulary difficulty is measured primarily by the number of syllables or letters in the word or how many words are more difficult than what an average fourth grader could read. As selected texts become more difficult, the words are more sophisticated, as is the complexity of the sentence structure. Thus, another indicator of text difficulty is its grammatical complexity, which is measured by the length of the sentence. The Fry readability graph is based on the number of syllables in a word and the number of words in a sentence. It is easy to use and provides an estimate of the reading level of the text (see Figure 9–2). Web sites that can calculate the readability of a selection include the following: http://textalyser.net, http://readability.info/uploadfile.shtml, http://literacynews.com/readability/readability_analyses.php, and http://www.interventioncentral.org/htmdocs/tools/okapi/okapi.php. An example of a Web site that can calculate the readability of a Web site is http://juicystudio.com/services/readability.php#readintro. Numerous software programs can calculate several

Figure 9–2 *The Fry Readability Scale*

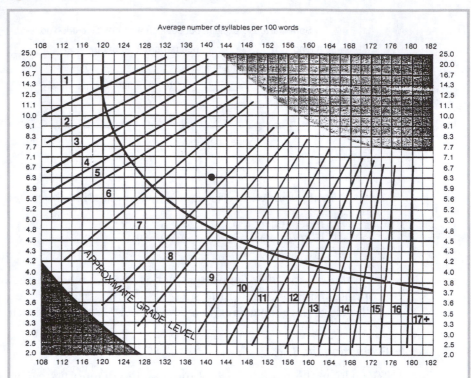

1. Randomly select three (3) sample passages and count out exactly 100 words each, beginning with the beginning of a sentence. Do count proper nouns, initializations, and numerals.
2. Count the number of sentences in the hundred words, estimating length of the fraction of the last sentence to the nearest one-tenth.
3. Count the total number of syllables in the 100 word passage. If you don't have a hand counter available, an easy way is to simply put a mark above every syllable over one in each word, then when you get to the end of the passage, count the number of marks and add 100. Small calculators can also be used as counters by pushing numeral 1, then push the sign for each word or syllable when counting.
4. Enter graph with *average* sentence length and *average* number of syllables; plot dot where the two lines intersect. Area where dot is plotted will give you the approximate grade level.
5. If a great deal of variability is found in syllable count or sentence count, putting more samples into the average is desirable.
6. A word is defined as a group of symbols with a space on either side; thus, *Joe, IRA, 1945,* and *&* are each one word.
7. A syllable is defined as a phonetic syllable. Generally, there are as many syllables as vowel sounds. For example, *stopped* is one syllable, and *wanted* is two syllables. When counting syllables for numerals and initializations, count one syllable for each symbol. For example, *1945* is four syllables, *IRA* is three syllables, and *&* is one.

Source: By Edward Fry. Reprinted from *The Journal of Reading,* December 1977. Reproduction permitted.

formulas at once. Software can be purchased from various companies. Look for options at http://www.readabilityformulas.com.

Leveling Predictable Books

Predictable books generally do not keep sentences short; therefore, the readability formula cannot be used to level this type of book. In predictable books, the sentences may be long but repeated frequently, creating a rhythmic effect. For example, the language pattern "Little pig, little pig, let me come in," is repeated throughout the story *The Three Little Pigs* with a singsong effect. In even easier predictable books, these patterns are repeated every page. The repeated phrases and key pictures help make books easier to read. If the picture depicts the key action or topic that is represented in the text, the page is easier to read because the student can use the picture to figure out the word. For instance, if the page has a picture of a house of straw and the text reads, "The first little pig [a repeated phrase] had a house made of straw," then the student can use the picture as a cue to figure out the word *straw* if it is forgotten. Along with repeated phrases and pictures, familiar experiences and characters such as a dog riding a tricycle or a family eating together also help young readers figure out words. In these cases, they associate a familiar experience with the words on the page. For instance, if the text says, "I can hug my brother," the child can predict the next phrase might be "I can hug my sister." This prediction is based on their experiences with the composition of families and therefore is easier to read. To decide whether a predictable book is easier or harder to read, the diagnostic teacher evaluates the book by asking herself key questions. Let's use "Where can you put a dog?" to think about these questions. The sample book begins, "Where can you put a dog?" followed by a picture of a dog. The next phrase asks, "In a flower pot?" followed by the response, "Oh, no, no!" on the next page, as shown in Figure 9–3. This sequence is repeated throughout the book with different places to put a dog.

Figure 9–3   *Where Can You Put a Dog?*

| Where can you put a dog? | On a flower pot? | Oh, no, no!!! |

Reviewing the book, the diagnostic teacher asks and answers the following questions:

Question	Answer
1. Is the print in a consistent place?	Yes
2. Are phrases repeated?	Yes
3. If key words are changed, can they be predicted easily from the pictures or prior experiences?	Yes
4. Do the phrases sound more like talking/singing?	They sound like talking.
5. Are familiar objects or experiences used?	Most objects are familiar.
6. Do the illustrations provide support for recognizing the words?	Yes
7. Are rhythm and rhyme evident?	The repeated nature of the phrases makes the words easy.

These characteristics can be listed with a Likert scale to estimate the level of difficulty for a predictable book, as shown in Figure 9–4. "Where can you put a dog?" has a familiar topic and commonly used language pattern. The common phrase "Where can you put a dog?" is repeated on almost every page. The pictures represent the words on the page and thus provide clues for the reader when a word is forgotten.

As predictable books become more difficult, the topics are not quite as familiar. The language patterns are less repetitive and include lines that are not repeated in the story. The pictures, however, still provide strong support for figuring out the words. For instance, *Five Little Monkeys Jumping on the Bed* by Eileen Christelow is easy to read, but the beginning of the book contains phrases that are more challenging than the repetition included in the rest of the book.

By the end of first grade through the middle of second grade, the familiar topics are maintained, but the language pattern is varied, such as using a refrain after each new event, as in *I Know a Lady Who Swallowed a Fly* by Charlotte Zolotow. These more difficult books still have fairly familiar topics, but sometimes the characters' actions are fanciful as an old lady who swallowed a fly. The language pattern often develops over several pages, while the illustrations provide support for overall meaning but not specific words.

The predictable books are helpful in initiating reading and are appropriate for young children; however, it is more difficult to find the appropriate level. The following Web site has a list of books on leveling books: http://www.ciera.org/library/instresrc/hot-lists/hot-03.pdfbut. Lists of books also can be very helpful in selecting the appropriate predictable books. Leveled booklists can help with that selection (see appendix C and the following Web sites: http://www.bnkst.edu/literacyguide/books.html and http://www.readinga-z.com/allbooks/index.html).

Figure 9–4 *Predictable Books Evaluation Guide*

1. The print is in a consistent place:

.5	1.0	1.5	2	2.5
all the time	almost all the time	most of the time	some of the time	none of the time

2. Sentence pattern or phrases are repeated:

.5	1.0	1.5	2	2.5
every page	every other page	every 2–3 pages	every 4–5 pages	every 6+ pages

3. Key words are changed in the pattern but can be predicted easily (from pictures or prior experiences):

.5	1.0	1.5	2	2.5
infrequently	occasionally	most of the time	all the time	all the time unfamiliar
easy to predict	easy to predict	easy to predict	not easy to predict	

4. Sentences sound like talking (oral language):

.5	1.0	1.5	2	2.5
all the time	almost all the time	most of the time	blend of oral and written language	book language

5. Familiar objects or experiences are used:

.5	1.0	1.5	2	2.5
all the time	almost all the time	most of the time	sometimes	none

6. Illustrations provide support for recognizing words and patterns:

.5	1.0	1.5	2	2.5
all the time	almost all the time	most of the time	sometimes	none

7. Rhythm and rhyme are evident:

.5	1.0	1.5	2	2.5
in entire story	most of the story	on repeated phrases	sometimes	not included

More to Consider When Selecting Material

Reading ease is not the only consideration when selecting material for students. Other key aspects, such as interest, topic familiarity, and book length, are important considerations as the diagnostic teacher selects material to use during the diagnostic lesson.

Interest

Interest is crucial in selecting books. If the topic and/or story line is interesting and engaging, then the book is usually easier to read. Students can be drawn into a text when characters are interesting and readily befriended, words provoke strong images, and stories have unanticipated twists (Schallert & Reed, 1997). As mentioned in chapter 2, expository text written in an engaging style is easier to read because students are more readily involved with proselike vignettes than academic facts (Reed, Schallert, & Goetz, 1992). Interest is a crucial factor in finding the appropriate book for struggling readers. Check this online site: http://news.bbc.co.uk/2/hi/uk_news/education/2494637.stm.

Choice

One of the best ways to determine interest is by letting the student choose the book. When students believe they can make choices about the books they read, they are more likely to be interested in the books and the activities surrounding them (Deci, Vallerand, Pelletier, & Ryan, 1991). By presenting several books with mini–book talks, the diagnostic teacher can encourage the reader to choose the book that looks the most interesting. Having books accessible to young children encourages them to choose among multiple titles and allows them to define their interests and set their own purposes. Arranging books in tubs or displaying them on low-level shelves can assist readers in choosing books.

Background Knowledge of the Reader

Closely tied to both choice and interest is the background knowledge of the reader. A reader's interest in a particular textual selection may show a growing knowledge about the topic, "signaling an optimal match between interest and knowledge" (Schallert & Reed, 1997, p. 73). For example, a student who has hiked in the mountains will probably be more interested in reading *Beardance* by Will Hobbs than students who have spent most of their life in the city. Students' background knowledge helps them define their interests and inform their choices.

Length of the Book

The attention span of many struggling readers is relatively short; therefore, as the diagnostic teacher selects books, she looks for texts, such as chapter books, that are short. Reading two short books instead of one long book will be more appealing to a struggling reader. The length of the text does influence readers' perceptions of their ability to read the text and, in turn, their attention and motivation while reading. Many readers believe they can read a short book and understand it as a whole, while a long book would be more difficult for them. The diagnostic teacher understands these aspects of student perception and their effect on the types of material selected.

Summary

Finding instructional materials is an essential task of the diagnostic teacher. As she plans lessons, the diagnostic teacher thinks about materials and their influence on the student's learning. When material is too difficult, a student cannot construct meaning or flexibly use reading strategies; therefore, the diagnostic teacher selects instructional material that will allow the student to construct meaning and demonstrate his strengths. Knowledge about instructional materials facilitates the diagnostic teacher's decision making and enables teachers and students to adapt instruction.

10

Literacy Coaching and Teacher Development

Constructivist theories in literacy have brought changes to the way teachers develop their practice. No longer will the one-day workshop with no follow-up be sufficient (International Reading Association [IRA], 2005). Teacher development is viewed as an active process where the teachers engage in instruction and reflection in order to advance their understanding of teaching reading. Literacy coaching is a cyclic process where teachers and coaches collaborate to improve student learning. In this process, literacy coaches observe classroom instruction and discuss possible alternatives for instructing students. As the coaches watch teachers implement new techniques, they scaffold the teachers' new learning and language use. Both the literacy coach and teacher record observations and collect data to analyze student growth. Next, they reflect on what occurred continually focusing on student learning. If student learning does not occur, they recycle and start the process again. Thus, the literacy coach plays a key role in providing ongoing support for literacy instruction and reflecting on practices with teachers. The support they provide is aimed at the teachers' efforts to use research-based literacy strategies within the classroom. As all teachers discuss and reflect on reading instruction, they develop a **community of practice**. In a community of practice, literacy teachers have an identity defined by a shared interest: to teach all children to read. Within the community of practice, the teachers add to their shared knowledge base. This shared knowledge implies a commitment to teaching reading and therefore a shared expertise that distinguishes literacy educators from others.

Shared Expertise in Reading

Although teachers continually develop expertise in reading, there is a knowledge base for reading that is important for continual teacher development (IRA, 2005). Drawing from several sources (Braunger & Lewis, 2005; Gambrell, Malloy, & Mazzoni, 2006), the following is a list of five elements of knowledge bases that are elaborated on in this book:

1. Reading is a construction of meaning with text. It is an active process of using background knowledge along with the text (see chapter 1).
2. Engagement and social interactions in reading are keys in successfully learning to read and developing as a reader (see chapter 2).

3. Reading involves complex thinking as students engage in reading authentic informational passages and stories (see chapter 2).
4. Continuous monitoring and assessment of reading is vital to student learning (see chapters 5 and 7).
5. Children develop literacy strategies and skills through a variety of literacy opportunities, models, demonstrations, and abundant reading (see chapter 9).

These are knowledge bases that form a basic expertise in reading.

However, within a constructivist context, teachers continually rethink their instruction using their shared expertise. They use current knowledge and develop new insights that will improve student learning. Kennedy (1998) found that when teachers focused on student learning rather than approaches to instruction, they did advance student learning. Furthermore, the current focus on student learning and teacher effectiveness has demonstrated that effective teachers can advance reading even with struggling readers. A collaborative group of teachers working in low-poverty schools increased student learning when they used higher-level questions that focused on relating the reading passages to students' background knowledge, making predictions before and during reading, summarizing what was read, and discussing the theme (Taylor, Pearson, Peterson, & Rodriguez, 2003). Other research has found that the more students are engaged in literacy interaction, the higher their achievement (Guthrie & Wigfield, 2000). A characteristic of classrooms with increased student learning is one where students are highly engaged. These attributes focus on teacher and student behaviors rather than instructional techniques and require sustained support throughout each year. The literacy coach, as a member of the school community, can provide sustained, ongoing, and intensive support through frequent encounters with teachers.

Cycle of Literacy Coaching

As literacy coaches visit teachers' classrooms, they establish themselves as part of the classroom milieu. They learn the students' names and become an extra set of eyes to observe students' responses and learning in the classroom. As this roaming time is occurring, the coach and the teacher discuss the class's individual differences and what could possibly improve student learning. After a few weeks, the coach and the teacher sit down for a *preconference* that occurs before a formal observation. In this conference, they discuss student learning and any assessment data that have been collected and collaboratively plan ways to increase student learning. The next day, the teacher tries out the agreed-on procedures while the literacy coach continues to observe the classroom interactions and student learning. *During the lesson*, the literacy coach collects observational data and later analyzes it for patterns of student engagement. Immediately after teaching, the classroom teacher jots down observations. Later that day, the literacy coach and the teacher jointly discuss what happened, focusing on student learning in a *postconference*. Together they reflect on the information they both collected (observations and jottings) and discuss specific aspects of student learning. Thus, the literacy coach and the teacher engage in thoughtful discussions about what occurred in the classroom as well as the teacher behaviors that promote student learning. In this process, they engage in reflective dialogue. They sustain their reflective dialogues about student engagement and the instructional events that encouraged it. Although the conversation can get off track, both redirect their focus on student learning. This continuous focus helps teachers develop their craft. Thus, the literacy coach and the classroom teacher take part in joint analysis and problem-solving strategies to figure out what instructional adjustments would further enhance the students' engagement and subsequent learning. When instructional decisions are made, sometimes the literacy coach models the classroom instruction so that the teacher can see "instruction in action" and observe the students' response to the instructional activities. Other times, the coach supports the teacher with scaffolds in the midst of instruction. The literacy coach and the teacher continually reflect on instruction and plan new ways to improve teaching. This is a cycle of literacy coaching. It is a means for continuous teacher development that results in student learning. Further information about literacy coaching and a place to share expertise and experiences can be found at http://www.literacycoachingonline.org.

 ## Developing Collaboration

In the initial interaction that occurred between one literacy coach and a classroom teacher, they developed collaborative interactions to jointly solve problem issues in classroom learning. Because the focus of the initial interactions was on student learning, they established a common goal. Each step of the way, they began to work together using open discussions. As they continued to work together, they shared their views of reading instruction, relying heavily on their knowledge base yet accepting each other's points of view. They often talked about their personal views of teaching. Within these conversations, they began to see that collaboration added value to the instructional decision making. Thus, they began a journey of learning to collaborate rather than remaining isolated in their classroom.

As the classroom teacher and the literacy coach continued their journey, they searched for others who would join them. They wanted to share their discoveries, so they developed reflective discussion groups. The teachers consider ideas from each other and begin to express their new insights. This deepened their understanding of how students learn. For example, one teacher brought the case of Angela before the collarative group. Now in fourth grade, Angela was having trouble comprehending what she read. The literacy coach, with his knowledge of struggling readers, began the discussion with queries about Angela and her current instruction. Each teacher has had varied interactions with Angela, from classroom instruction to playground duty. Many of them had noticed that Angela was very literal in her understanding of the world. This was supported by comments from the classroom teacher, who had found that Angela read word by word so as to remember everything in the text. By the time she finished reading, she could repeat only what was in the last part of the text. The team thoughtfully considered instructional options that would advance Angela's understanding. They decided that the classroom teacher could use more questions that prompted Angela to use her background knowledge so that she would realize that comprehension was not simply repeating the text. Angela began to respond to the instruction. Thus, as teachers reflected with others, they recognized that the discussion group was leading them forward as they reconsidered their ideas about Angela and her learning. Reflective discussion helps teachers rethink their teaching with others, building on the group's expertise. As they reflected on their teaching and personal perspectives, they developed mutual respect for each other and the expertise being shared. The reflective discussions stayed focused on teaching and promoted deep thinking. As they matured as a collaborative group, the teachers accepted not only one another's points of view but also one another's unique personality. This respect for individual perspectives and unique personalities is the cornerstone of collaboration.

 ## The Learning Community

As teachers reflect about students' learning and discuss those reflections in collaborative groups, they create a **learning community**. Although the focus of student learning is paramount, they also discuss their own teaching and their beliefs about literacy learning. According to Neufeld and Roper (2003), besides student learning, a feature of teacher development includes forming collaborative groups that share their knowledge and practice with each other. Within this context, teachers develop and adapt their ideas in tandem with their changing practice.

Within the learning community, literacy coaches provide the ongoing leadership and expertise for teacher development. When an entire group of teachers are involved in a learning community, both teacher and student learning occur (Richardson & Anders, 2005). The literacy coach, along with others, such as the diagnostic teachers, the learning specialist, and other teacher-leaders, use reflective discussions within a learning community. They build relationships that enable them to learn from each other, taking time to sustain productive conversations. These discussions are powerful, but they are not enough to sustain ongoing professional development. A learning community is just that. It is a community that focuses on tackling innovative concepts about instruction. This means that members of the learning community not only discuss teaching but also study the latest developments in reading instruction.

The literacy coach's role is influenced by the teachers' existing beliefs about literacy instruction. These beliefs, in turn, affect their practices and their willingness to change their practice. Therefore, coaching alone is not powerful enough to change beliefs and values. Rather, coaching, along with other aspects of teacher development, increases receptivity to innovative thinking.

Forms of Studying Reading Instruction

Two approaches to studying reading instruction (study groups and teacher research groups) are prevalent today. These groups stem from questions teachers encounter within their classrooms and school. Together, individuals in the school select the topics for study groups and teacher research based on student learning, collected data, and teacher needs and interests.

Study Groups

As teachers are eager to meet the changing needs of society, these groups emerge out of the learning community. Study groups are organized around a particular theme or topic. After collaboratively selecting a topic (i.e., assessment, strategy instruction, curriculum integration, and so on), the group decides on how to proceed. Study groups have typically revolved around discussing books related to a chosen topic. Having everyone read the same professional book develops a common language around the theme selected. In these situations the literacy coach facilitates group discussion about topic selection and resource development. For instance, Larkin Elementary School wanted to focus on comprehension. The teachers had a well-developed knowledge base about decoding but wanted to know more about comprehension instruction and student learning. Angela had heightened their attention to the challenges of comprehension instruction. In the first year, all teachers read and discussed the book *Mosaic of Thought* (Keene and Zimmermann, 1997). As the faculty read the book, they began to implement suggested practices, and their classroom language changed. The teachers began to ask more "connection" questions, such as "How did you make that connection? What were you connecting? What did Angela say in the group?" This change helped students with their comprehension, yet the teachers wanted more. The following year, they used a structured study group program on comprehension (IRA Literacy Study Groups Reading Comprehension Module [2003]; for further information, see http://www.reading.org/publications/bbv/books/bk9200) that included books, a reflective journal, and a facilitator's guide. As they continued, the teachers built on their knowledge of comprehension and began to ask higher-level questions, increasing students' understanding and reading achievement as measured on a standardized test. They also increased their knowledge about how their students constructed meaning. Their discussions in the study groups increased their commitment to each other so that their talk changed from "Where are you going tonight for dinner?" to "What kind of connection is Johnny making with the novel?" In this way, they held each other accountable for making changes in their classrooms.

In other study groups, the literacy coach organizes book clubs to help teachers use deeper thinking, discussion, and strategic processing in their classrooms. For example, Flood, Lapp, Ranck-Buhr, and Moore (1995) used book clubs to focus on culture diversity, a theme. Everyone related to the instructional program (teachers, administrators, consultants) read multicultural literature. As they discussed the books, each shared their beliefs and ideas about varying cultures. The discussions led teachers to create an environment that honored diverse viewpoints and beliefs. In another teacher study group, a group of secondary teachers who were using the recitation format (teacher asks a question and the students answer it) formed a book club. Eskridge (2002) found that the teachers talked extensively about their personal connections to characters in trade books. In fact, personal stories that helped the teachers understand the books were retold frequently. Realizing how they used their personal experiences and feelings when they discussed the books, they developed book clubs in their secondary classrooms. As they had done in their book club, they encouraged their students to tell personal stories as they discussed their understanding. This changed the instructional context from recitation to a more open and shared one. As this occurred, the students were more engaged and on task when they read books and stories in class.

Teacher Research Groups

Effective professional development is often embedded in inquiry and supported by teacher reflection (Neufeld & Roper, 2003). Usually, teacher action research begins by studying innovative ideas. In these groups, the teachers actually try out the procedures or techniques and collect student data. Teacher research groups include a group of teachers who are committed to the process of classroom research and sharing their findings with each other. Teacher research starts with an issue or questions. In light of the action research questions, the teachers develop a miniexperiment or research project. Teachers plan how they will investigate the issues or questions and what information they will gather. They collect this information during and after teaching. After instruction, teachers review and analyze both their observations and the informational data. Finally, teachers reflect on how the instruction improved or hindered student learning. For example, a group of first-grade teachers at Larkin Elementary School decided to engage in teacher research projects. Each of them was going to try out a new technique based on their class needs. This teacher research group met weekly to discuss how their research was progressing. For instance, Juan, a kindergarten teacher, decided to use interactive writing (see part 2) during morning meeting. As he used this each morning, he began to change his expectations about what kind of writing a kindergarten student could accomplish as well as his definition of writing. These professional changes occurred because Juan analyzed his observations of student learning. At critical points, he collected data and observations, then analyzed them. In the teacher research group, Juan initially discussed his observations, telling about the children's writing performance and showing examples. Later, however, Juan examined his beliefs and expectations about young children's writing. During each interactive writing experience, his students learned more about writing and written language. This knowledge advanced their understanding about reading and writing. Juan no longer believed that most kindergarten children could write only strings of letters in a random fashion. He began to see how purposeful interactions with writing enhances student learning. Trying out interactive writing also changed his views about the amount and kind of writing kindergarten children can do. Teacher research is a powerful tool for teacher development.

Responding to Struggling Readers Using Classroom Based Teams

Because of their knowledge base about struggling readers and adapting instruction, literacy coaches and reading specialists have always supported the learning of struggling readers. These teacher-leaders have worked in and out of classrooms to provide specified instruction for these readers. This is an important and continuing role for these individuals.

Within the developing learning community, the teachers are ready to respond to initiatives in a professional manner. As they have always done, literacy coaches are positioned to take the lead in bringing fresh views to the learning community. They provide professional resources and a variety of instructional materials (see chapter 9). They also take the lead when encountering reform efforts. In fact, many literacy coaches are taking the lead in forming Early Intervening Teams for the Response to Intervention Initiative in Special Education. For example, in a school that was developing the Early Intervening Team, the literacy coach gathered the classroom teacher, other related teachers, the special education teacher, and the parent together to discuss Angela's lack of progress in reading. Although the team was now larger than the previous one, the instructional team realized that the simple adjustment of supporting Angela using her background knowledge was not enough to change her reading strategies. They looked at recent assessment data and the observation notes the classroom teacher had taken. After discussing Angela's profile in more depth, they agreed on after-school tutoring focusing on fluency and comprehension instruction, having the classroom teacher support the comprehension strategies through explicit teaching, and having the special education teacher monitor progress weekly. The parent was going to work on fluency by using echo reading (see modification #1 under "Impress Method" in part 2) at home. Because the instructional team had thoroughly reviewed Angela's profile and shared perspectives, Angela profited from the instructional plan. The team found that with these adjustments, Angela could stay in her classroom for reading instruction. This type of team problem solving is grounded in the learning community where collaborative inquiry and reflection are valued.

Criteria for a Teacher Development Context

Teacher development that is ongoing and sustained is very different from the one-shot workshops of the past. Literacy coaches, teachers, and administrators who want to create this support for teacher development need parameters for developing this yearlong experience. Criteria for this evolving notion of teacher development are being developed. Teacher development improves student learning when the following criteria are implemented. These are adapted from a paper by Neufeld and Roper (2003). Teacher development

1. is grounded in inquiry, reflection, and experimentation, which are teacher driven;
2. is collaborative, involving a sharing of knowledge and a focus on teachers' communities of practice rather than on individual teachers;
3. is sustained, ongoing, intensive, and supported by modeling, coaching, and collaborative problem solving of teaching dilemmas;
4. is coupled with and resulting from teachers' work with their students; and
5. occurs in a community of practice.

The learning community continues to develop as the literacy coach supports teachers when they encounter challenges in their teaching.

Summary

Literacy coaching and teacher development are critical ways to advance teachers' knowledge of instructional practice. This ongoing form of professional development changes not only practice but also beliefs and values about literacy and literacy instruction. Literacy coaching and teacher development occur within collaborative learning communities where teachers discuss their practice and share their expertise.

11 Selecting Techniques

Knowing *how* instruction occurs supports the diagnostic teacher while she modifies her instruction. She thinks about the techniques she uses and their influence on learning. By classifying techniques according to several critical characteristics, the diagnostic teacher can select instructional techniques that match the students' learning. Therefore, this chapter classifies each teaching technique in the following ways:

1. The point at which the technique is implemented during the lesson
2. The type of text being read
3. The mode of response
4. The targeted reasoning strategy
5. The targeted reading skill
6. The information source
7. The type of structure (explicit or implicit teaching) embodied in implementing the technique
8. The cognitive process emphasized during implementation

The classification serves two functions for the diagnostic teacher: (a) to help select techniques that fit the readers' patterns, and (b) to help focus instructional modifications during the reading event.

Initially, the diagnostic teacher selects a technique and analyzes its underlying characteristics. This analysis increases her effectiveness in implementing and creating alternative instruction. However, many teachers seem to be hesitant to change their routines even if they are not working well for individual students. Often teachers resist change because they lack knowledge about why one technique may be more effective in certain situations. This chapter and part 2 provide reasons why a given technique might be more effective under certain conditions. Knowledge about techniques allows teachers to make instructional changes that facilitate student learning.

The instructional techniques, which are described in detail in part 2, can be used either as a part of the guided reading lesson to support authentic reading activities or as part of a specific strategy or skill lesson to focus on areas of concern. The orchestration of the techniques depends on the strengths and needs of a particular reader. Thus, the classification of the diagnostic teaching techniques is divided into three major categories. In the first, the techniques are classified according to their implementation within the instructional framework, and they fit appropriately during guided contextual reading (see chapter 4). To select appropriate techniques for this part of the diagnostic teaching session, the teacher asks herself the following questions:

- Do I want to focus on print or meaning processing to advance student understanding of the entire passage?
- At what point during the guided reading lesson will the student need support in order to construct meaning?
- What techniques will best suit the type of text I am using?
- Can using more writing or discussion build on the strengths of the learner?

The second major category deals with the selection of techniques to encourage students' use of weaker areas, and these techniques fit appropriately during the elements of strategy and skill instruction (see chapter 4). Here the diagnostic teacher selects techniques that work on learner needs by showing students how to use their strengths when reading becomes difficult. To select appropriate techniques, the teacher asks herself the following questions:

- Would a strategy that the student is not using be helpful to her? If so, how should I approach instruction so that he can use the new strategy in combination with the strategies he already uses?
- Does the student have a skill he is not using when he reads? If so, how should I mediate learning so that he incorporates the skill, using his strengths?

The third major category deals with the specificity of implementation. For instance, a reader might need a great deal of teacher direction. In this case, the diagnostic teacher uses Table 11–7 on explicit instruction and narrows her previous options. To differentiate her selection of techniques, the teacher asks herself the following questions:

- If the student is overrelying on an information source, can I match reliance with an instructional technique and show him how to integrate information sources?
- What kind of teacher support does the student need? Does he need to work on his own, or does he need more teacher direction?
- If the student is compensating for deficits by using a strength in cognitive processing, can I match this strength in order to show him how to use his weaker area in combination with his strength?

Diagnostic teaching techniques from different views of reading have been classified according to these key questions so that the diagnostic teacher can match the students' strengths and needs and design lessons that mediate learning for each student. The diagnostic teacher selects techniques according to the classifications described in this chapter using the diagnostic hypotheses for Jenny (see chapter 6), the third grader who is experiencing difficulty in fluent oral reading.

Classifying Techniques for Guided Contextual Reading

When considering the instructional framework, the diagnostic teacher selects techniques that support reading an entire story. The diagnostic teacher thinks about the element of guided contextual reading and considers how instruction will occur as the student reads a particular selection. Selecting appropriate techniques facilitates a student's learning by supporting the student when he can no longer learn independently. In other words, the instructional lesson is a planned exchange between independent student learning and teacher-guided learning. If the teacher intervenes with appropriate techniques, she can move the student to more complex reading level.

First, the diagnostic teacher identifies the focus of instruction for the students. Most students read silently during guided contextual reading because the focus of this session element is constructing meaning. Thus, the diagnostic teacher uses meaning processing techniques. However, some students need to focus on print processing because once they can read the words, they will comprehend. In these cases, the diagnostic teacher uses print processing techniques but stresses meaning construction. Techniques can be classified, therefore, according to whether the instructional focus is on print processing or meaning processing. These techniques are then further classified by (a) instructional framework, (b) type of text, and (c) mode of response. Each of these variables is discussed in turn.

Classifying Techniques by Instructional Framework

The diagnostic teacher needs to analyze the instructional framework. Several critical points in the lesson influence decision making about the instructional framework for guided contextual reading. Techniques to increase story understanding can supplement instruction either before, during, or after reading the text. Sometimes it is most appropriate to provide instruction prior to reading so that the students readily construct meaning with text. For example, students might need instruction in word meanings or word identification as related to the story. Before reading, some students will need assistance to think about how what they already know will help them interpret text.

Another critical point in the instructional framework is during the reading of the text. During this part of the lesson, the teacher needs to encourage students' inferencing, elaboration, and monitoring of text comprehension. In these instances, she intervenes during reading to build reading strategies such as self-questioning, summarization, visualizing difficult parts, and organizing the information.

The final critical point in the instructional framework is after reading the selection. To mediate learning here, the diagnostic teacher provides instruction in integrating the text with personal experiences as well as organizing the information. He may also need to reinforce word recognition strategies or develop fluency. In any case, the diagnostic teacher can promote student learning by using techniques at the critical points within the instructional framework.

Classifying Techniques by Type of Text

The selection of appropriate techniques also depends on the type of text (narrative or expository) that students will be reading. Techniques are often developed for a specific kind of text format. For example, story maps (see "Story Mapping" in part 2) are designed for narrative text and teach elements of story grammar, while reciprocal teaching (see "Reciprocal Teaching" in part 2) is designed for expository text and teaches summarizing through the use of topic sentences. Techniques are most effective when used with the appropriate kind of text. The classification of techniques in Tables 11–1 and 11–2 is based on three instructional

TABLE 11–1 *Classifying Techniques by Instructional Framework–Meaning Processing*

	Narrative	Expository
Before	Direct Experience Approach Collaborative Reading Experience–Text Relationship Guided Reading Imagery Instruction Shared Reading Semantic Mapping	Contextual Processing Concept Mapping Direct Experience Approach Experience–Text Relationship Feature Analysis Grid Graphic Organizers Imagery Instruction K-W-L Semantic Mapping Thematic-Inquiry Approach Visualization
During	Directed Reading-Thinking Activity Guided Reading Questioning the Author Prediction Strategy Instruction ReQuest Say Something Story Drama Story Maps Think-Aloud Approach	Concept-Oriented Reading Instruction Group Investigation Technique Internet Inquiry Reciprocal Teaching ReQuest SQ3R
After	Directed Reading-Thinking Activity Experience–Text Relationship Questioning the Author Journal Writing Literature Discussions Retelling Question–Answer Relationships Story Drama Story Maps Summary Experience Approach Vocabulary Self-Collection Strategy	Cloze Instruction Concept Map Experience–Text Relationship Feature Analysis Grid Group Investigation Approach Internet Inquiry Journal Writing K-W-L Metaphors Question–Answer Relationships Question-Generation Strategy Semantic Mapping Summarization Thematic-Inquiry Approach Vocabulary Self-Collection Strategy

Note: Only the techniques that support meaning processing are classified. The lesson frameworks of strategy instruction, explicit teaching, implicit teaching, and sustained silent reading are not classified.

TABLE 11–2   *Classifying Techniques by Instructional Framework—Print Processing*

	Narrative	*Expository*
Before	Collaborative Reading	Contextual Processing
	Directed Reading Activity	Semantic Mapping
	Decoding by Analogy	Language Experience Approach
	Guided Reading	
	Language Experience Approach	
	Sight Word Approach	
	Synthetic Phonics	
	Talking Books	
During	Impress Reading	Collaborative Reading
	Guided Reading	Process Writing
	Language Experience Approach	
	Shared Reading	
	Talking Books	
After	Analytic Phonics	Cloze Instruction
	Chunking	Multisensory Approaches
	Decoding by Analogy	Repeated Readings
	Directed Reading Activity	Word Sorts
	Framed Rhyming Innovations	
	Multisensory Approaches	
	Readers Theater	

Note: Only the techniques that support meaning construction are classified. The lesson frameworks of strategy instruction, explicit teaching, implicit teaching, and sustained silent reading are not classified.

decisions: the instructional focus (meaning or print processing), the type of text (expository or narrative), and the phase of instruction in which guided instruction is most appropriate (before, during, or after the lesson). The teacher thinks about the framework of the diagnostic teaching session. He must decide how to orchestrate instruction for guided contextual reading. Therefore, he evaluates the underlying strengths and needs of the student and predicts at which points within the guided reading lesson she will profit most from mediated instruction. Augmenting instruction at critical points during the lesson enhances text interpretation. He returns to her analysis of the extended passage to look at monitoring and summarization strategies and to her evaluation of the data from the student's informal reading inventory (see chapter 5). Using her interpretation, she refers to Tables 11–1 and 11–2 to select an appropriate technique to support instruction.

> Within the guided reading lesson, which process (print or meaning processing) do I need to use for interpreting text?
>
> What type of text (narrative or expository) am I using?
>
> At what point during the guided reading lesson (before, during, or after) will the student need support?

Diagnostic Hypothesis

During guided contextual reading, Jenny needs to read silently. Prior to reading the story, she does need assistance in recognizing new vocabulary words. However, she does not need instruction during the story because she monitors comprehension. After instruction, the diagnostic teacher needs only to reinforce word recognition. The student also shows a preference for reading expository text.

Classifying Techniques by Mode of Response

An additional decision about the instructional framework is the kind of response mode that will be used. Readers' responses can be either oral or written. The diagnostic teacher considers the students' interaction patterns by asking herself, "Will discussing or writing advance this student's reading? Which mode is this student's strength?" Whether the response is in written format or discussion format changes the task. Some students prefer to write about what they read, while others prefer to discuss what they read. Both processes are constructive and facilitate reading growth.

Writing and Reading

Writing and reading are supportive processes that can enhance each other. Writing about what was read facilitates reading. First, writing requires learners to reconstruct their understanding and thus prompts a more thoughtful response. The students can later use this written record of their thoughts to reflect on and analyze their thinking, and it allows the diagnostic teacher to discuss students' interpretations with them. Writing brings inner thoughts into the open for verification and facilitates discussing personal interpretations.

Writing also facilitates reading because it reinforces the constructive process. Reading and writing require similar processes: both readers and writers make plans about how they are going to construct meaning; both monitor their understandings to see whether they are making sense; both revise their thinking by rereading, using what was written and comparing it to what they know; and both elaborate what was written, making connections between what was written and what is known to create new ideas. In these ways, both reading and writing are constructive processes in which one facilitates the other.

In addition, writing facilitates reading because both systems use the same written conventions. Both use letters grouped together to form words, words grouped together to form sentences, and so on. The way the groups are formed follows certain patterns or conventions. Writing heightens students' awareness of how to use these conventions when they read. For instance, a young writer trying to spell *mother* thinks about how that word looked in the book *Are You My Mother?* Writing heightens an awareness of the visual features of words. Writing facilitates reading through three avenues: reflective thinking, constructing meaning, and using written conventions.

Discussion and Reading

Discussing what students read does facilitate reading growth. When students verbalize their understanding of what they read, they reconstruct the text so that they can communicate their understanding to others. This constructive process is not simply a recall process. Readers think to themselves, "What is important, and how do I communicate it to the others in the group? What did I learn that I want to share with this group? Did I think of something in a new light that would help others understand?" In fact, the meaning of students' interpretations has been found to change during the discussion. As students share their thinking, they coconstruct meaning through social interaction. In ongoing discussions, meaning seems to be negotiated moment by moment as students rethink and discuss their understanding.

Social interaction facilitates reading, therefore, because it provides a vehicle for talking about the strategies, plans, and processes of meaning construction (Vygotsky, 1978). In other words, thinking about what is read is facilitated by conversations that encourage students to elaborate and explain their thinking. Within the social situation, the teacher also explains and elaborates on her thinking. This process allows the student to use tools for thinking (words, plans, strategies, ideas, and so on). The teacher responds, encouraging a refinement of thinking (use of tools) and showing students how she constructs her answer.

These interactions facilitate students' independent use of literacy processes. As they discuss their thoughts and explain how they construct their answers, the new ideas and strategies that they use become part of their internal thought processes. Through social interaction, students verbalize their thinking, discussing their strategies as well as their ideas. Thus, the verbalized strategies that come to the fore during discussion later become internal mental processes. During discussion, the teacher facilitates reading by discussing interpretations, asking students to justify their interpretations, and sharing her (the teacher's) own thought process. As a result, verbal discussion facilitates reading through three avenues: meaning construction, verbalizing plans and strategies for meaning construction, and making social thinking an internal process.

Conclusions About Mode of Response

The diagnostic teacher thinks about the kind of responses that the student makes. She asks, "Will this student profit from discussing or writing about what he reads?" She realizes that both processes facilitate meaning construction. Writing provides a written record of thoughts so that the student can reflect on how he constructs meaning, while verbal discussion allows the reader to revise ideas on the spot. The diagnostic teacher selects a technique that matches the learner's strengths and needs. She thinks about the mode of response that the techniques demand and refers to Table 11–3 to select one that will support the reader.

Which mode of response (discussion or writing) will better assist the reader in advancing the student's reading?

Diagnostic Hypothesis

For Jenny, whose language comprehension is elaborate and whose verbal abilities are strong, discussion is most appropriate. During guided contextual reading, the diagnostic teacher allows ample time for discussion of the stories that Jenny reads, thus using her strength. Furthermore, for strategy and skill instruction, the diagnostic teacher selects a technique in which Jenny can practice and discuss her fluency.

TABLE 11–3 *Classifying Techniques by Mode of Response*

	Meaning Processing	
	Discussion	*Written Response*
Before	Collaborative Reading Contextual Processing Direct Experience Approach Experience–Text Relationship Group Investigation Approach Listening-Thinking Activity Metaphors Semantic Mapping Visualization	Feature Analysis Grid Imagery Instruction K-W-L Process Writing Semantic Mapping
During	Concept-Oriented Reading Instruction Directed Reading-Thinking Activity Group Investigation Approach Guided Reading Reciprocal Teaching ReQuest Say Something Story Drama Think-Aloud Approach	Generative-Reciprocal Inference Procedure Framed Rhyming Innovations Prediction Strategy Instruction/Logs Process Writing Story Maps
After	Experience–Text Relationship Literature Discussions Question–Answer Relationships Readers Theater Retelling Story Drama	Concept Map Journal Writing K-W-L Process Writing Question-Generation Strategy Story Maps Story Writing Approach Summary Experience Approach Summarization Thematic-Inquiry Approach

 ## Classifying Techniques for Strategy and Skill Instruction

The second major category is designed to help teachers select techniques that work on specific areas that are problematic for students. Although techniques can be used during either guided contextual reading or strategy and skill instruction, the purpose and focus of instruction are different (see chapter 4). During guided contextual reading, the focus is on reading entire stories and understanding the content. The techniques are selected to enhance story or passage understanding. However, during strategy and skill instruction, the diagnostic teacher creates activities that focus on areas of concern. Because no one likes to focus on what one can't do, these lessons are short and use engaging passages. The minilessons or strategy lessons in this part of the diagnostic teaching session focus on strategy deployment during reading. The diagnostic teacher encourages the use of unfamiliar strategies and skills, showing the students how to use their strengths to overcome difficulties. With each lesson, he strives to promote conversations about strategy and skill use. These conversations lead to discussion about how literacy works and how to use strengths to construct meaning with text.

During strategy and skill instruction, the diagnostic teacher identifies students' strategy and skill needs and provides mediated instruction, showing students how a particular skill fits into their repertoire of reading strategies. In other words, the teacher creates an instructional context in which students can explore and talk about how strategies and skills are orchestrated. When selecting activities, the teacher must also remember that students might not use a particular strategy or skill because it relies on a weakness. Instruction that begins with students' strengths is often more effective (for an elaboration of skill strengths and weaknesses, see McCormick, 2007).

For example, Raju uses background knowledge to identify unknown words; however, it is not always an effective strategy. He has a limited ability to manipulate the sounds of language (i.e., he cannot segment sounds and then synthesize them to form words). Therefore, the diagnostic teacher helps Raju develop a large sight vocabulary, using the impress method (see "Impress Method" in part 2). It helps Raju bypass word analysis and use background knowledge and sentence comprehension to identify unknown words.

Although use of phonic knowledge would increase Raju's reading performance, instruction in word analysis is futile unless the student can synthesize and segment sounds. As the student's reading fluency increases, the diagnostic teacher then encourages decoding by analogy, using a prompt: "What would make sense (strength) and sounds like another word you know (weakness)?" This latter instructional task is accomplished easily using repeated readings (see modification #1, "Retrospective Repeated Readings," under "Repeated Readings" in part 2) with a discussion of strategy deployment.

In the preceding example, the diagnostic teacher used Raju's strength to develop a successful reading program. Then she showed Raju how to use a strength in combination with a weaker area when using only his strength would not solve the reading problem. It is often necessary to try a variety of instructional techniques for struggling readers. For example, Duc, a student from Vietnam, is having difficulty with sight-word identification. He is a bilingual student and has limited language development with no skill in sound synthesis. Typical techniques to develop sight-word identification (word walls, language experience, and so on) prove futile until the new words are tied to a conceptual base. Semantic Mapping (see "Semantic Mapping" in part 2) is used to tie background knowledge to the sight words so that the student can associate what the words mean with how the words look.

The following sections elaborate the reasoning strategies and reading skills used during reading. The techniques in Tables 11–4 and 11–5 have been identified according to the targeted reading task developed when the technique is implemented in a diagnostic program.

Classifying Techniques by Reasoning Strategies

Readers strategically reason about what they are reading, applying skills when necessary. As students read, they select, sort, and evaluate the text against what they know. In essence, readers are involved in an active problem-solving process. They predict what is going to be communicated. Then they select and sort important information from the text and relate it to their prior knowledge. Next, they confirm or revise their predictions based on new textual information. Finally, they elaborate their understanding as well as their strategy use. The reasoning process takes place automatically until readers cannot make sense of what they are reading. When readers encounter difficulty, they consciously employ a variety of monitoring strategies to reconstruct meaning. They actively work to regain meaning.

Although students with reading problems exhibit individual variations in the strategies they employ, poor readers are not actively involved in constructing meaning. They view good reading as effortless; consequently, they do not make plans or vary their strategies as they read. Effective readers, however, are active. Before reading, active readers use what they know about the topic, the type of text, the author's purposes and their own purposes to make predictions (Duffy & Roehler, 1987).

Predicting requires wondering what the author is going to say. It occurs before and during reading.

As they read, effective readers remain tentative and revise their predictions frequently, using a variety of reasons for their revisions. They intertwine the sources of information for revision (the text, background knowledge, or both) and the strategies for revisions (ignore the problem and read more, reread to check the facts, read ahead to clarify information, and consult an expert source if necessary). Effective readers stop, reflect, and flexibly shift between reader-based processing ("Does that make sense?") and text-based processing ("What did the text say?"). These actions are called **monitoring** reading.

Monitoring requires checking the text or one's experience to see whether what one is reading is making sense. Monitoring occurs during reading.

Finally, effective readers fit new information into what they know by elaborating relationships among information. In other words, active readers automatically embellish text by drawing unstated inferences and picturing scenes and information as they read. These elaborations help them draw connections among ideas in the text as well as their own knowledge. Furthermore, as they elaborate textual information, they also generate new thoughts, creating new connections among ideas. Thus, elaboration is a generative process in which text prompts readers to enhance their thinking and expand their understanding.

Elaborating requires relating new information to what is known in order to remember it. Thus, the new information becomes part of what is known. Elaborating occurs during and after reading.

Some readers, however, are less active. Their reading can break down in the predicting, monitoring, or elaborating phases of the reasoning process. Some readers do not use what they know to think about what the author might say. They read exactly what the text says without thinking about what it might mean. They need instruction that helps them make predictions about what the text will mean. Other readers venture a guess but hold on to the initial prediction even when the text does not support it. Some readers revise their predictions but change only one part of it, such as the *who, when, where,* or *how* information (Dybdahl & Walker, in press). Some readers rely too heavily on the text or their background knowledge when monitoring their reading. They do not shift between knowledge sources to check their reading. These students need instruction in how to monitor their understanding of text. Other students fail to elaborate the relationship between what they know and the text; therefore, they cannot remember what they read. These readers need instruction in how to reason while they are reading.

Demonstrating reasoning strategies can improve the reading performance of poor readers. However, the diagnostic teacher needs to evaluate the various instructional techniques. Some techniques lend themselves readily to talking about the different strategies of effective reading; others do not. Therefore, diagnostic techniques have been classified here according to the reading strategy that they develop: predicting, monitoring, or elaborating. In addition, techniques can teach the reasoning process related to print processing or meaning processing. Table 11–4 classifies techniques for reasoning while processing print and meaning.

The diagnostic teacher then looks for a strategy that, if learned, will improve this student's reading. He reflects on the strategies that the effective reader uses and evaluates how the student uses them. He returns to the data he has collected about the student's reading and looks at the hypotheses he formed when he analyzed the reading event. He considers whether the situational context or the text is affecting the strategies employed by the reader. If a strategy needs to be taught, the diagnostic teacher uses Table 11–4 to identify techniques that facilitate learning the strategy. Again, he remains tentative in selection until he completes all the diagnostic questions and evaluates several diagnostic lessons.

> Which strategy or strategies (predict, monitor, or elaborate), if learned, will increase the student's reading?

Diagnostic Hypothesis

For Jenny, the diagnostic teacher decides that she needs instruction in monitoring print processing in order to check both what makes sense and what the word looks like. The diagnostic teacher looks for a strategy that will facilitate combining print cuing systems when reading breaks down.

Classifying Techniques by Reading Skills

As readers strategically reason about what they are reading, they apply skills when necessary. Although meaningful interpretation of the text is the ultimate goal of reading instruction, certain tasks consume a major portion of children's thinking capacity as they develop as readers. The knowledge of particular skills is used as students reason about text; however, without the requisite skill knowledge, the reasoning process is hampered. The following explanation will provide a discussion of the major skills involved at a given stage of reading. Even though these skills have been associated with typical techniques, each skill can be developed through a variety of ways. The diagnostic teacher selects the technique that mediates learning for the particular student (see Table 11–5 on page 184).

Stage 1

For beginning readers, the major task is the association of oral language with its written equivalent. Young children have learned to communicate by using oral language within a situational context. To read, however, they must infer the communicative intent of printed words. The new task places demands on learners. They must learn that printed words represent both a concept and spoken words. Therefore, the task of young readers is to develop this functional concept of printed language as well as the recognition of letters and sounds.

TABLE 11–4   *Classifying Techniques by Reasoning Strategy*

	Print Processing	*Meaning Processing*
Prediction	Collaborative Reading Decoding by Analogy Framed Rhyming Innovations Guided Reading Impress Method Language Experience Approach Listening-Thinking Activity Shared Reading Sound Boxes Summary Experience Approach Talking Books	Cloze Instruction Concept Map Directed Reading-Thinking Activity Graphic Organizers Experience–Text Relationship Imagery Instruction K-W-L Listening-Thinking Activity Prediction Strategy Instruction ReQuest Semantic Mapping SQ3R Thematic-Inquiry Approach
Monitoring	Chunking Collaborative Reading Language Experience Approach Paired Reading Shared Reading Approach Readers Theater Repeated Readings Retrospective Miscue Analysis Shared Reading Word Walls	Directed Reading-Thinking Activity Generative-Reciprocal Inference Procedure Prediction Strategy Instruction Reciprocal Teaching Story Maps Think-Aloud Approach Visualization
Elaboration	Analytic Phonics Decoding by Analogy Making Words Making and Writing Words Phonogram Approach Repeated Readings Retrospective Miscue Analysis Synthetic Phonics Word Sorts	Concept-Oriented Reading Instruction Experience Text Relationship Group Investigation Approach Internet Inquiry K-W-L Literature Discussions Prediction Strategy Instruction Question–Answer Relationships Question-Generation Strategy Readers Theatre Reciprocal Teaching Retelling Semantic Mapping Story Drama Story Maps Summarization

Note: The techniques listed are the most effective; however, other techniques can be used. See individual techniques in part 2.

TARGETED SKILLS FOR STAGE ONE

Word Identification

Based on

- Knowing how to use prior knowledge to construct knowledge about print
- Ability to remember the visual form (visual memory)
- Knowing how to use the initial letter and word length to figure out words

Typical techniques

- Language experience approach
- Shared reading approach

As these concepts of print develop, children begin to associate meaning with written words in stories. They automatically recognize a group of words at sight. They say, "I know a word that starts with *h* and is the same length, so this word must be *hat*." The development of a sight-word vocabulary indicates that children are reasoning about the relationship between graphic symbols and meaning. Whether children use sounds, visual features, or background knowledge, their major task is to develop sight-word knowledge, which generally consumes a major portion of their thinking through the middle of the first-grade reading level.

Stage 2

As students can read more words and longer stories, reading changes from a predominantly oral, shared experience to silent reading and discussion. Thus, the reader begins to focus on text-based information, particularly on the patterns in words and stories. Because students can read longer stories, they encounter unfamiliar words that are not contained in their sight vocabularies. Therefore, emerging readers

TARGETED SKILLS FOR STAGE TWO

Word Analysis

Based on

- Knowing how to blend sounds (phonemic synthesis)
- Knowing how to divide words into their sounds (phonemic segmentation)
- Knowing how to use decoding analogies

Typical techniques

- Decoding by analogy
- Sound boxes

Literal Comprehension

Based on

- Understanding patterns in stories (story organization)
- Knowing how determine what's important in the story to retell
- Connecting background knowledge with text

Typical techniques

- Retelling
- Story maps

develop new ways to figure out unfamiliar words. In addition to experiential knowledge and sight-word knowledge, they begin to use sound analogies to decode words (i.e., "I know a sight word that looks similar to this new word; I will try substituting the sounds to see whether the new word makes sense in the story"). This stage of reading development is marked by the ability to use the alphabetic principle, namely, the understanding that words are made of sounds and letters that have a consistent pattern. Therefore, young readers match these patterns to known sight words. This process is decoding by analogies.

As students begin to figure out many words independently, they are able to read longer stories; silent reading, therefore, becomes more efficient than oral reading. Thus, in order to communicate what they read, they retell the story, focusing on what the text said. This process places a high demand on literal comprehension because the learner's attention is focused on the logical development of a story line. Students begin to focus on the patterns of stories or how stories are organized (characters, problem, events, resolution) so that they can remember and retell more readily.

These skills occupy children's thinking capacity through the end of second grade, where techniques dealing with word analysis and literal comprehension are most appropriately employed.

Stage 3

As learners encounter extended passages and chapter books where word meanings are embedded in complex sentence structures, the simple strategies of using known sight words, decoding by sound analogy, and thinking about the facts of a story are no longer sufficient. Because sentences are longer and more complex, students must focus on the

---

TARGETED SKILLS FOR STAGE THREE

Fluency

Based on

- Instinctly connect how words look with what words mean
- Knowing how to break sentences into thought units
- Knowing how and using background knowledge to predict sentence meaning

Typical techniques

- Chunking method
- Readers theater

Sentence Comprehension

Based on

- Knowing how and using sentence structure to develop word meanings
- Knowing how and using sentence structure to decode words
- Prediction of sentence meaning to increase fluent reading

Typical techniques

- Story writing
- Contextual processing

forms of the sentences and match them with what they know about word and story meaning. This leads to increases in fluent word identification, allowing more thinking capacity for word, sentence, and idea meaning. Using sentence structure enhances fluent reading because the student breaks sentences into meaningful phrases. Likewise, students become more adept at using their background knowledge to predict sentence meaning. Sentence comprehension also enhances print processing because students must use sentence context as well as decoding by analogy to figure out unknown words. Using sentence context to figure out unknown words and simultaneously associating appropriate word meanings becomes a major task for these readers. This stage occupies students' thinking capacity through the middle of the fifth-grade reading level, where techniques developing fluency and sentence comprehension are most appropriately employed along with the students' continuing development of the tasks involved in literal comprehension.

Stage 4

As students read more difficult text, they find the strategies that deal primarily with textual information are no longer sufficient. In texts at this level of difficulty, authors develop complex ideas that require an interpretation of text-based information within a reader's personal worldview. Therefore, readers must be able to strategically shift between text-based and reader-based processing, synthesizing their understanding. At this stage, students have an increasing need to develop and use a meaning vocabulary, or word meaning. Readers must think about what each new word might mean, form a tentative word meaning, and then integrate this

TARGETED SKILLS FOR STAGE FOUR

Meaning Vocabulary

Based on

- Integration of background knowledge with textual meaning
- Constructing word meaning by analyzing likenesses and differences
- Constructing word meaning by analyzing sentence context to elaborate definitional knowledge

Typical techniques

- Semantic mapping
- Feature analysis grid

Nonliteral Comprehension

Based on

- Knowing how to synthesize background knowledge with textual information
- Self-monitoring and Self-questioning
- Making connections

Typical techniques

- Think-aloud approach
- Story drama

knowledge with how the textbook used this word. Likewise, they read for a variety of purposes and monitor their own understanding of text, questioning what is important to remember and how ideas and concepts fit together. This stage of development continues through the middle grades, where techniques emphasizing vocabulary knowledge and nonliteral comprehension are orchestrated with developing literal comprehension.

Stage 5

As readers develop, they begin to link information from a variety of sources into a cohesive point of view or a series of premises. This synthesis requires an increasing reflective stance that involves evaluating various positions to form a point of view. Further development at this stage involves realizing that a point of view is only one perspective on an issue. When you begin an inquiry, you suspend judgment, using multiple sources and consider multiple perspectives dealing with an issue or problem. This stage then involves more complex and critical thinking.

Thus, taking into account the appropriate stage for each reader, the diagnostic teacher looks for a skill that, if learned, will increase this student's reading. He reflects on the major skills of reading and evaluates their influence on this reader's performance. He looks at the level of performance that is at the borderline range and matches it with the targeted skills for that reading level. Then he checks previous instructional experiences to evaluate their influence on the targeted skill. Basically, he asks, "Has this student received instruction in this skill and is still not proficient?" If a skill needs to be taught, the diagnostic teacher uses Table 11–5, "Classifying Techniques by Reading Skills," to identify techniques that facilitate learning that skill.

TARGETED SKILLS FOR STAGE FIVE

Inquiry

Based on

- Knowing how to summarize and organize information from multiple sources
- Knowing how to reorganize information to support a premise or point of view
- Knowing how to reflect and analyze others' points of view and one's own point of view

Typical techniques

- Literature discussions
- Internet inquiry

The instructional techniques in this book have been analyzed as to the major skill developed. Within each major area, the techniques differ, but each technique can increase the specific skill mentioned. The diagnostic teacher checks the chart to identify how to work with the targeted skill.

Diagnostic Hypothesis

For Jenny, whose borderline range is around the middle of second grade, the teacher decides that instruction in phonics is not appropriate because of her attempts and subsequent failures in using decoding. Jenny's literal comprehension is well developed and thus not the best choice for instruction now. Only when she reads text with just one-seventh of the words correct did she ever miss a question. Therefore, the teacher decides to work on reading fluency, a skill that is at the third-grade level (i.e., the next-higher level).

Which skills, if learned, would increase this student's reading?

TABLE 11–5 *Classifying Techniques by Reading Skills*

	Word Identification	Word Analysis	Fluency	Meaning Vocabulary	Sentence Comprehension	Literal Comprehension	Nonliteral Comprehension	Inquiry Thinking
Alternate Writing					*	*	*	
Analytic Phonics		*						
Chunking			*		*			
Cloze Instruction				*	*	*		
Collaborative Reading	*		*					
Concept-Oriented Reading Instruction						*	*	*
Concept Map				*		*	*	*
Contextual Processing				*	*			
Decoding by Analogy	*	*						
Direct Experience Approach				*				
Directed Reading Activity	*			*		*	*	
Directed Reading-Thinking Activity						*	*	
Experience–Text Relationship				*		*	*	
Feature Analysis Grid				*				
Framed Rhyming Innovations		*		*	*			
Generative-Reciprocal Inference Procedure						*	*	
Graphic Organizers						*	*	*
Group Investigation Approach						*	*	*
Guided Reading	*		*			*		
Imagery Instruction						*	*	*
Impress Method	*		*					
Interactive Writing	*	*						
Internet Inquiry						*	*	*
Journal Writing							*	*
K-W-L						*	*	
Language Experience Approach	*		*					
Listening-Thinking Activity						*	*	
Literature Discussions							*	
Making Words	*	*						
Making and Writing Words	*	*						

Continued

TABLE 11–5 *Continued*

	Word Identification	Word Analysis	Fluency	Meaning Vocabulary	Sentence Comprehension	Literal Comprehension	Nonliteral Comprehension	Inquiry Thinking
Metaphors				*			*	*
Multisensory Approaches	*	*						
Paired Reading	*		*					
Phonogram Approach		*						
Prediction Strategy Instruction						*	*	*
Process Writing					*	*	*	
Question–Answer Relationships						*	*	*
Question-Generation Strategy							*	*
Questioning the Author						*	*	*
Readers Theater			*			*	*	
Reciprocal Teaching						*	*	*
Repeated Readings	*	*	*					
ReQuest						*	*	
Retelling						*	*	
Retrospective Miscue Analysis	*	*			*			
Say Something						*	*	
Semantic Mapping				*		*	*	*
Sentence Combining				*	*			
Shared Reading Approach	*		*					
Sight Word Approach	*							
Sound Boxes		*						
SQ3R						*	*	
Story Drama						*	*	
Story Maps						*	*	
Story Writing Approach					*	*	*	
Summarization						*	*	*
Summary Experience Approach	*		*			*		
Synthetic Phonics		*						

TABLE 11–5   *Continued*

	Word Identification	Word Analysis	Fluency	Meaning Vocabulary	Sentence Comprehension	Literal Comprehension	Nonliteral Comprehension	Inquiry Thinking
Talking Books	*		*					
Thematic Inquiry Approach						*	*	*
Think-Aloud Approach						*	*	*
Visualization				*			*	
Vocabulary Self-Collection Strategy				*		*	*	
Word Sorts	*	*						
Word Walls	*	*		*				

Note: (a) These classifications represent common uses for the techniques. Techniques can be adapted to accommodate the task demands of related skill areas; thus, word attack technique (synthetic phonics) might be used to establish a sight word vocabulary. (b) The lesson frameworks of strategy instruction, explicit teaching, implicit teaching, and sustained silent reading are not classified.

Conclusions About Reading Strategies and Skills

After the diagnostic teacher evaluates the student's reading level and formulates hypotheses about how the student reads, she plans the strategy and skill lessons. Using the data collected, the diagnostic teacher identifies skills, strategies, or both that are inhibiting reading performance. She reviews the strategies employed by the reader as well as skill development. Then she selects an appropriate technique that will focus instruction on the targeted concern in order to improve the student's reading performance.

 ## Classifying Techniques for Increased Specificity

The tables in this section are used in conjunction with the other tables. They increase the specificity of the previous selections. Readers demonstrate strengths and preferences that can be used to enhance active reading. Techniques that focus on critical areas for readers' progress are classified in this section in three ways: (a) by sources of information, (b) by type of structure, and (c) by strengths in cognitive processing.

Basically, reading is an interactive process in which readers use various sources of information (reader based and text based) at the same time to construct meaning with text. However, techniques differ according to which information sources are emphasized during instruction. Some techniques emphasize reader-based sources of information, while others stress text-based sources of information. In addition, the type of structure needed during the diagnostic lesson varies depending on the strengths and preferences of the struggling reader. Some students profit from a structured, direct approach to the material, while other students prefer to structure their own learning and discover rules. Techniques differ in how they structure the learning task. Finally, readers exhibit strengths in cognitive processing. Some readers use successive processing of information (a step-by-step analysis), while others prefer to use simultaneous processing (thinking about multiple relationships at the same time). These strengths can be matched with appropriate techniques, thus enhancing reading.

The techniques have been classified according to these characteristics, enabling the diagnostic teacher to select techniques that match the students' strengths as she is teaching a new task. As the task is learned, she can select techniques that have a more integrative instructional approach. The diagnostic teacher can thus use learner strengths to show students how to regain meaning when text interpretation breaks down. The following discussion and tables elaborate these areas.

Classifying Techniques by Sources of Information

Students vary the use of information sources as they read, depending on the situation and their purposes for reading. Because active–constructive reading depends on combining all available sources of information, readers use reader-based sources (topic knowledge, rhetorical knowledge, phonological knowledge, and so on) and text-based sources (letters, pictures, words, and so on) as needed to construct meaning.

Sometimes readers employ reader-based processes to predict what the text will say, using their own knowledge. These predictions frame the text-based processing and are subsequently confirmed or revised. The degree to which the reader engages in reader-based processing depends on the purposes for the task. For example, one Saturday afternoon a young teen was reading a novel. As he read, he embellished the story, making inferences from his own life and rapidly predicting what the characters would do next. Thus, the young teen used a great deal of reader-based information as he read. However, at other times, readers choose to engage in text-based processing where they defer evaluation until they have read enough textual information to form a conclusion. When readers encounter unfamiliar information, when previous predictions have been disproved, when reading new directions, or when text fails to make sense, students use more text-based processing. For example, on the next Saturday afternoon, this same young teenager was taking a college entrance examination. As he read the test directions, he read and reread the printed page, focusing on the information exactly as it was stated in the text. In this case, he used the text predominantly as an information source.

Effective readers perpetually shift between information sources to select, combine, and restructure data from the text and their personal knowledge. However, struggling readers often experience a deficit in either a skill or a strategy that causes them to shift away from one information source. They compensate by using their strength and thus eliminate a need to use their deficient knowledge source (Stanovich, 1986). Therefore, ineffective readers circumvent, using their weaker information sources, and, as a result, often depend on a single source related to their strength.

Some readers have a wealth of general and topic knowledge that they use continually as they read. They employ reader-based processes to predict what the text will say, using their topic knowledge and paying little attention to the text. Their approach inhibits the development of knowledge sources dealing with the conventions of print. Because these readers overrely on reader-based processing of the content, they fail to develop knowledge sources dealing with the text. For example, Sandy entered first grade with poor phonemic awareness, as many potentially poor readers do

(Juel, 1988). This weakness inhibited his understanding of phonics and slowed his progress in the basal reader program that was used in the classroom. Therefore, Sandy used his strength of background knowledge to figure out words. When this strategy did not work, he made up the text by looking at the pictures. Thus, Sandy began to overrely on his reader-based strength, inhibiting his strategic meaning construction.

> Some struggling readers overrely on reader-based information, making inferences from topic knowledge when a more careful reliance on the text is warranted.

Other struggling readers, however, learn phonics easily and believe reading is accurately calling a string of words. When asked comprehension questions, they give answers using the exact words in the text even when inferences from topic knowledge are more appropriate. They have come to believe that meaning is found in the text. But as stories become more complex, they find that simply repeating sentences from the text does not result in understanding. For example, Danni rapidly reads words, seldom needing to monitor his understanding. This strategy seemed to work well when he read novels where the plot was similar to his own experiences. However, as he began reading content-area texts, he became lost. He could read the words, but he failed to check his understanding and elaborate on new word meaning. Danni continued to passively read words and repeat text-based definitions (his strength) without relating ideas. This approach inhibited his development of strategic reading.

> Some struggling readers overrely on text-based information, repeating text segments when inferences from background knowledge are more appropriate.

Instructional decision making is facilitated by knowing which information sources the struggling reader is using and then matching those with particular techniques so that readers demonstrate their strength. After several successful reading experiences, the diagnostic teacher chooses techniques that encourage strategically combining information sources. The techniques have been classified by the source of information that is emphasized during instruction: (a) reader based and (b) text based. Some techniques initially ask students to use their prior knowledge, while other techniques ask students to use the information in the text.

Reader-Based Sources

When selecting approaches that focus on using reader-based information sources, the diagnostic teacher identifies techniques that initially have the students use their background knowledge in relation to the content of the story. In using these techniques, the diagnostic teacher continually asks students to think about what they know in order to create an expectation about what the text may say. For example, when using the directed reading-thinking activity (see part 2), the teacher asks the students to predict what the story might be about. Then, after reading sections of the story, the teacher asks the students whether their predictions were on the right track or whether they would like to keep, add to, or change predictions. Thus, throughout the discussion, the teacher focuses on using reader-based inferencing to construct story understanding. Likewise, when the language experience approach is used (see part 2), students are asked to tell a story that is then recorded on a piece of paper. The story constructed from the students' own words becomes the text, and the students are continually asked to refer to what they said (reader-based source) when they cannot figure out a word.

Text-Based Sources

When selecting approaches that focus on using text-based information sources, the diagnostic teacher identifies techniques that initially ask students to use text-based information. In using these techniques, the diagnostic teacher focuses on how the information in the text explains and describes major characters, events, and ideas. For example, in the story mapping approach (see part 2), the diagnostic teacher asks students to identify the setting (characters and place), the problems, the events that lead to the problem's resolution, and then write this information on a visual framework (see "Story Mapping" in part 2) for the story. The focus is on putting the text-based information on the story map. Likewise, when the synthetic phonics approach is used (see part 2), students are asked to look closely at words and sound them out letter by letter. The students are continually asked to refer to the text when problems in print processing occur.

Conclusions About Sources of Information

Effective readers do not operate using either reader-based information or text-based information sources exclusively but rather strategically combine these sources of information. What is necessary when reading is a flexible interplay between these sources. To help students develop more efficient use of both sources of information, the diagnostic teacher begins by using the reader's strength (reader-based inferencing or text-based inferencing) and gradually introduces a merging of both sources of information by using scaffolding statements that prompt the student to combine sources. To expedite the selection of teaching techniques, Table 11–6 analyzes teaching techniques in terms of the major tasks and information sources. The teacher evaluates the students' use of information sources and analyzes the requisite task to be taught. He then selects a technique and constructs a diagnostic lesson to verify the appropriateness of the technique.

What source of information (text based, reader based, or both) does the student tend to use?

Diagnostic Hypothesis

As she reads, Jenny uses reader-based sources of information, embellishing text with her wealth of knowledge. She predicts what the words are and the meaning is, using her background knowledge. She seldom checks the text to confirm or revise her interpretation but continues to read, using what she knows, even though referring to the text would allow her to correct her miscues that affect her comprehension. The strategy has inhibited Jenny from developing print processing strategies that would facilitate her reading. Thus, Jenny overrelies on reader-based sources of information, particularly as reading becomes more difficult, failing to develop a flexible use of text-based and reader-based cues to figure out unfamiliar words in the text.

Classifying Techniques by Type of Structure

Instructional decision making also includes an analysis of how mediated instruction will occur. The diagnostic teacher thinks about how she will mediate learning. She asks what kind of structure (explicit or implicit) will be necessary for students to regulate their own learning. Learners differ in how they approach the reading event. Some readers are active, while others are passive.

TABLE 11–6   *Classifying Techniques by Sources of Information*

	Reader Based	*Text Based*
Word Identification	Collaborative Reading Guided Reading Interactive Writing Language Experience Approach Listening-Thinking Activity Shared Reading Approach	Multisensory Approaches Echo Reading[*] Impress Method[*] Sight Words
Word Analysis	Framed Rhyming Innovations Language Experience Approach Interactive Writing Making and Writing Words Retrospective Miscue Analysis Sound Boxes Word Sorts	Analytic Phonics Making Words Multisensory Approaches Decoding by Analogy Phonogram Approach Synthetic Phonics
Fluency	Chunking[*] Language Experience Approach Paired Reading Readers Theater Summary Experience Approach	Cloze Instruction Impress Method[*] Repeated Readings
Sentence Comprehension	Readers Theater Framed Rhyming Innovations Process Writing Story Writing	Contextual Processing Cloze Instruction Sentence Combining
Vocabulary	Direct Experience Approach Feature Analysis Grid Metaphors Semantic Mapping Visualization Vocabulary Self-Collection Strategy	Contextual Processing Cloze Instruction
Literal Comprehension	Experience–Text Relationship Guided Reading K-W-L Questioning the Author Retelling Say Something Story Writing Summary Experience Approach Visualization	Graphic Organizers Question–Answer Relationships Reciprocal Teaching ReQuest[*] Story Maps Summarization
	Reader Based	*Text Based*
Nonliteral	Concept-Oriented Reading Instruction	Question–Answer Relationships

190

TABLE 11–6 *Continued*

	Reader Based	Text Based
Comprehension	Experience–Text Relationship Generative Reciprocal Inference Procedure	Questioning the Author Reciprocal Teaching
Group Investigation Approach	Summarization Internet Inquiry Imagery Instruction Literature Discussions Prediction Strategy Instruction Process Writing Story Drama Think-Aloud Approach*	
Inquiry	Imagery Instruction Literature Discussions Question-Generation Strategy* Group Investigation Technique Thematic-Inquiry Approach	Graphic Organizers Question–Answer Relationships Summarization

*These techniques utilize both reader-based and text-based sources of information but focus slightly more on one or the other.

Note: The lesson frameworks of strategy instruction, explicit teaching, implicit teaching, directed reading activity, directed reading-thinking activity, and sustained silent reading are not classified.

Active Readers

Active readers are problem solvers. They select key characteristics by sampling several alternatives and flexibly shifting among sources of information. As they solve these problems, active readers use strategies for print and meaning processing. This may be an inherent way to process information, or it may be developed through the social interactions that students experience daily. Often the more active, independent learners have had numerous experiences with schoolbook language. To communicate socially, these students use a wide variety of words to describe events and elaborate descriptions to justify their actions. Through previous social interactions, they become more active and explicit when they solve verbal problems.

Passive Readers

Passive learners, however, learn by watching how other students and the teacher solve the problem. They have difficulty distinguishing between the situational context of learning (such as teacher praise and peer approval) and the task of learning. They approach problem solving as a spectator and remain passive toward their own process of learning, preferring to follow the teacher's model whenever possible. The passive stance may be an inherent way to process information, or it may be a result of the daily social interactions.

Often the more passive students have relied on shared understandings during their social interactions. Communication is often limited to information that refers to events or ideas that are known to the listener; therefore, passive learners use less precise words and nonverbal language to communicate meaning. They rely on their listeners to infer meaning based on shared understandings rather than speaker explanations. When learning demands a more active verbal stance, these students are unfamiliar with the elaborate language that can be used to justify their actions. They remain passive, therefore, preferring to follow the teacher's model to solve problems.

Previous Experiences

For both active and passive students, previous experience with the task being taught affects the need for explicit instruction. If students have not had prior experiences related to the task, they might need some explicit instruction in the new task. If they have had prior experiences and *failed,* they might profit from explicit instruction that is different from the initial instructional context.

The diagnostic teacher analyzes the students' need for explicit instruction by evaluating how active they are when solving the reading problem. If the students are active and have positive experiences with the task, the diagnostic teacher chooses a task that focuses on implicit instruction (students read texts rich in language and figure out the underlying consistency as the teacher guides inquiry). However, if students are passive and have few positive experiences with the task, the diagnostic teacher chooses a technique that focuses on explicit instruction (students are directly informed of what they are learning, provided a model, and given directed practice).

Explicit Instruction

In explicit instruction (see "Explicit Teaching" in part 2), the diagnostic teacher precisely states what is to be learned and models the thinking process that accompanies this new strategy or skill. Students are given reasons why the new strategy or skill will help them read better (Duke & Pearson, 2002). Minilessons are constructed to show them how to use the reading strategy or skill, with the teacher modeling the steps of the task. Guided practice with a high level of teacher feedback is then provided. The feedback explicitly explains when and where students would use the strategy or skill. In the explicit teaching model, however, a gradual release of teacher-directed instruction allows students to direct their own learning. The diagnostic teacher identifies students who initially lack control of their own learning, then he explicitly teaches the new strategy. Finally, he plans for the independent use of the strategy.

EXPLICIT INSTRUCTION

Based on

- Reasons for learning
- Teacher modeling of how it works
- Collaborative practice
- Students take control

Typical techniques

- Reciprocal teaching
- Question–answer relationships

Implicit Instruction

Implicit instruction (see "Implicit Teaching" in part 2) is characterized by an emphasis on the text, the reading event, and the student as informant. Large quantities of text are read, requiring students to use the targeted strategy or skill. Students apply the strategy or skill to make sense of what is read without consciously understanding the principle. Because the situational context has been carefully arranged, students can readily decide which mistakes make a difference in understanding. From these choices, they reason about text interpretation. The teacher plays the role of

IMPLICIT INSTRUCTION

Based on

- Immersion in reading
- Teacher as linguistic inquirer
- Scaffolding thinking, using student responses
- Student generation of rules and ideas

Typical techniques

- Language experience
- Literature discussions

linguistic inquirer, asking students, "How did you know that . . . ?" This role allows students to generate their own rules for text interpretation.

Conclusions About Type of Structures

The diagnostic teacher thinks about the student's reading performance and the information he has collected. He asks, "What kind of mediated instruction, implicit or explicit, will facilitate learning for this student?" In other words, does the student want direction on how to complete the tasks? Does he appear to need direct, explicit information before he attempts a reading task, or does he want to control his own learning? The teacher theorizes about the kind of mediated instruction the student needs in order to change his reading behavior. The diagnostic teacher predicts whether implicit (student-discovered strategies) or explicit (teacher-directed learning) instruction will result in a greater change in reading performance. The teacher matches the hypothesis with an appropriate technique using Table 11–7.

In order to advance reading, what kind of mediated instruction (implicit or explicit) will be needed?

Diagnostic Hypothesis

For Jenny, the decision is clear-cut. She prefers to control the decision making when she reads. During the retelling, for example, she stated, "I'm not saying this in order." She also made the self-evaluation about a statement that it "might not be right," showing that she has control over her comprehension, although not over word recognition. Consequently, a more implicit technique to develop fluency is selected that will allow Jenny to control her reading strategies and assess her progress.

Classifying Techniques by Strengths in Cognitive Processing

Individual differences in problem solving influence how students build their models of meaning as they read. A multitude of theoretical frameworks exists for studying individual differences; however, a model of dichotomous thinking referred to as simultaneous and successive cognitive processing seems to relate more appropriately to literacy interactions (Das, 1999). This model refers to *how* students solve problems, recognizing and restructuring information in a problem-solving situation such as reading.

As students read, they vary their cognitive processing depending on the nature of the reading task (i.e., they flexibly shift between simultaneous and successive processing). For example, when constructing a main idea from the text, readers organize important information (successive processing) while drawing relationships among the information (simultaneous processing).

When reading requires a step-by-step analysis of text, readers use successive processing and sequentially order the information to solve the problem. Reading tasks such as phonic decoding and sequencing story events require that readers recognize and structure information in a step-by-step sequence. This problem-solving process is referred to as **successive processing**.

TABLE 11–7 *Classifying Techniques by Type of Structure*

	Implicit	Explicit
Word Identification	Collaborative Reading Impress Method Language Experience Approach Listening-Thinking Activity Shared Reading Approach Summary Experience Approach Talking Books	Interactive Writing Multisensory Approaches Sight-Word Approach Word Walls
Word Analysis	Analytic Phonics Framed Rhyming Innovations Interactive Writing Making Words Making and Writing Words Repeated Readings Retrospective Miscue Analysis Sound Boxes Word Sorts	Phonogram Approach Synthetic Phonics Decoding by Analogy Responsive Repeated Reading Under Repeated Readings
Fluency	Impress Method Language Experience Approach Paired Reading Readers Theater Talking Books	Chunking Repeated Readings (with teacher mediation)
Sentence Comprehension	Alternate Writing Cloze Instruction Framed Rhyming Innovations Process Writing Retrospective Miscue Analysis	Contextual Processing Sentence Combining Story Writing
Meaning Vocabulary	Cloze Instruction Direct Experience Approach Feature Analysis Grid Semantic Mapping Visualization Vocabulary Self-Collection Strategy	Contextual Processing Experience–Text Relationship Metaphors Word Walls
Literal Comprehension	Alternate Writing Concept-Oriented Reading Instruction Group Investigation Approach Internet Inquiry K-W-L Readers Theater ReQuest	Concept Map Graphic Organizer Reciprocal Teaching Story Maps Summarization

TABLE 11–7 *Continued*

	Implicit	*Explicit*
	Retelling	
	Say Something	
	Story Writing	
Nonliteral Comprehension	Imagery Instruction	Experience–Text Relationship
	Journal Writing	Generative-Reciprocal Inference Procedure
	Literature Discussions	Question–Answer Relationships
	Internet Inquiry	Reciprocal Teaching
	Questioning the Author	Think-Aloud Approach
	Prediction Strategy Instruction	
	Readers Theater	
	Story Drama	
	Visualization	
InquiryIqIn	Imagery Instruction	Graphic Organizers
	Internet Inquiry	Question–Answer Relationships
	Question-Generation Strategy	Reciprocal Teaching
	Questioning the Author	Summarization
	Thematic-Inquiry Approach	

Note: (a) The lesson frameworks of strategy instruction, explicit teaching, implicit teaching, directed reading activity, directed reading-thinking activity, and sustained silent reading are not classified. Of these, explicit teaching and the directed reading activity are explicit techniques. (b) Teacher implementation can change any technique to make it more or less explicit or implicit.

On the other hand, when reading requires the analysis of several ideas at the same time, readers use simultaneous processing; they relate ideas according to a general category to solve the problem. Reading tasks such as predicting the author's purpose and interpreting character motives draw heavily on organizing many aspects of information around their most important characteristics. This process is referred to as **simultaneous processing**.

Students can be identified as having strengths in one of these ways of processing information. A *simultaneous* preference refers to the propensity to think about multiple relationships among ideas, relating the most important characteristics. Students who prefer simultaneous processing build their models of meaning using large, inclusive categories of meaning. A noticeable characteristic of these students is their well-developed ability to manipulate visual information. These readers often draw visual diagrams or pictures to organize information. Students with a strength in simultaneous processing look for the coherent patterns of text by tying together the underlying relationships implied by the author. They use a minimal amount of textual information and rely heavily on their background knowledge to interpret text. They often comment, "Oh, yeah, that's like a. . . ." Their language is noticeably less precise and characterized by a tendency to draw images with words rather than use specific definitional language.

> Simultaneous processing strength means that the student thinks first about the overall meaning and then organizes the parts as they relate to the entire meaning.

At the word identification level, these readers prefer using the semantic cuing system over the graphophonic or syntactic cuing system because they have a high need to create meaning from what they read. The preference often precludes their making a careful analysis of the text.

A ***successive*** preference refers to the propensity for developing sequential, logical relationships with words. Students who prefer successive processing tend to develop models of meaning by arranging information in a logical, hierarchical sequence. They develop meaning from precise words that are logically organized to form definitional language. Students with a successive processing strength look for the logical organization of the text to gain meaning. After reading a text, they can recall the sequence of story events but often cannot tie together events to form a main idea. Because they rely heavily on textual information to fill in unstated meanings, their models seldom reflect personal application of the text. They organize information according to its function; therefore, their comments are flooded with precise text-based references.

At the word identification level, successive readers prefer using the graphophonic or syntactic cuing system because they rely on the logical relationships among and within words. This preference often precludes using the overall meaning of the text to decode words, creating a word-bound reader. They forget to think about the overall meaning of the selection and to relate the textual information to their previous experiences.

> Successive processing strength means that the student thinks about the parts first and then orders the parts to form a literal understating.

Instructional decision making is facilitated by knowing which cognitive process is used in the various techniques. The techniques have been classified by their simultaneous or successive framework. Some techniques initially ask students to consider the overall meaning before analyzing the parts. Other techniques ask readers to learn and use the parts before constructing the general meaning.

Simultaneous Framework

When selecting approaches that use a simultaneous framework, the diagnostic teacher identifies techniques that focus on the overall meaning of text. In using these techniques, the diagnostic teacher continually redirects attention by asking how things make sense within the entire passage. Specific facts are presented to show relationships to the overall meaning and to one another. These procedures require the synthesis of information, which is characteristic of simultaneous processing. For example, the shared reading approach (see "Shared Reading Approach" in part 2) requires students to move from understanding the whole (memorizing the story) to identifying the parts (single words). Selecting techniques that focus on simultaneous processing, the diagnostic teacher also evaluates whether learning is mediated through a visual array of the relationships, through tactile/kinesthetic experiences, or through visualization. Techniques that have this focus ask students to look at multiple relationships simultaneously.

> **SIMULTANEOUS FRAMEWORK**
>
> Based on
>
> - Multiple relationships among pieces of information
> - Visual display of information
> - Overall generalization
>
> Typical techniques
>
> - Shared reading approach
> - Imagery instruction

Successive Framework

When selecting approaches that use a successive framework, the diagnostic teacher identifies techniques that focus on discrete parts that form meaning when grouped together. In these techniques, the diagnostic teacher gradually presents the sequential parts of the task, leading students to an overall understanding (see "Story Mapping" in part 2). These procedures require that new bits of information are evaluated individually and gradually arranged in a sequence that forms meaning. For example, the instructional emphasis of synthetic phonics (see "Synthetic Phonics" in part 2) moves from knowing the parts (single letter sounds) to sequencing these sounds into words (sound synthesis) and finally to reading the words in stories. Selecting techniques that focus on successive processing, the diagnostic teacher also evaluates whether learning is mediated through auditory/verbal information, functional analysis, or analysis of small amounts of information. Each of these techniques requires a successive processing of individual sections within the text.

SUCCESSIVE FRAMEWORK

Based on

- Small, discrete parts
- Step-by-step arrangement
- Verbalizing function

Typical techniques

- Synthetic (explicit) phonics
- Question–answer relationships

Conclusions About Strengths in Cognitive Processing

Effective readers do not operate exclusively in either the simultaneous or the successive mode. What is necessary for fluent reading is a flexible interplay between simultaneous and successive processing of text. Efficient readers flexibly shift between a successive analysis of the textual elements and a simultaneous relating of textual and nontextual information to construct a model of meaning. However, inefficient readers often rely too much on their strength in cognitive processing, thus inhibiting fluent reading performance.

To develop more flexible text processing, the diagnostic teacher begins instruction using readers' strengths in cognitive processing (teach new reading strategies using the strength) and gradually introduces a more integrated processing of text by showing them how to incorporate their weaknesses into their reading repertoires. Thus, the diagnostic teacher initially uses students' strengths in cognitive processing to mediate learning before introducing other strategies.

The sensitive teacher—understanding the problem-solving demands of the tasks of reading, readers' preferences, and the various ways to teach reading—can modify instruction to facilitate students' learning. In other words, if fluency is an identified inhibiting behavior in the initial assessment, a technique that develops fluency would be chosen. Furthermore, if the student's cognitive processing appears to proceed from the overall meaning to the isolated parts (simultaneous understanding), a technique that develops fluency from a simultaneous perspective, such as Reader's Theatre, would be selected. The teacher looks at the data he collected and asks, "Does the reader use simultaneous or successive strategies to regain meaning?" Using Table 11–8, he then selects a technique that matches the student's processing style and will remedy the inhibiting reading behaviors.

What processing sequence (simultaneous or successive emphasis) does the student seem to prefer?

TABLE 11–8 *Classifying Techniques by Sequence of Cognitive Processing*

	Simultaneous	Successive
Word Identification	Collaborative Reading Guided Reading Impress Method Language-Experience Approach Listening-Thinking Activity Shared Reading Approach Summary Experience Approach Word Sorts	Making Words Multisensory Approaches Sight Words Word Walls
Word Analysis	Decoding by Analogy Framed Rhyming Innovations Impress Method Interactive Writing Language Experience Approach Repeated Readings	Analytic Phonics Making Words Making and Writing Words Multisensory Approaches Phonogram Approach Sound Boxes Synthetic Phonics Word Analogy Strategy Word Probe Strategy
Fluency	Impress Method Language Experience Approach Paired Reading Readers Theater Repeated Readings	Chunking Cloze Instruction Retrospective Miscue Analysis
Sentence Comprehension	Framed Rhyming Innovations Readers Theater Process Writing Story Writing	Cloze Instruction Contextual Processing Sentence Combining
Vocabulary	Direct Experience Approach Metaphors Semantic Mapping Thematic-Inquiry Approach Visualization Vocabulary Self-Collection Strategy	Cloze Instruction Contextual Processing Feature Analysis Grid Word Walls
Literal Comprehension	Concept-Oriented Reading Instruction Graphic Organizers Experience–Text Relationship Guided Reading Question-Generation Strategy Semantic Mapping Story Maps* Story Writing Summary Experience Approach Visualization	Question–Answer Relationships Reciprocal Teaching ReQuest Summarization

TABLE 11–8 *Continued*

	Simultaneous	Successive
Nonliteral Comprehension	Concept Map Concept-Oriented Reading Instruction Experience-Text-Relationship Imagery Instruction Internet Inquiry Journal Writing K-W-L Literature Discussions Semantic Mapping Story Drama	Generative-Reciprocal Inference Prediction Strategy Instruction Question-Answer Relationships Questioning the Author Reciprocal Teaching Think-Aloud Approach
Inquiry	Concept Map Concept-Oriented Reading Instruction Imagery Instruction Internet Inquiry Graphic Organizers Group Investigation Approach Question-Generation Strategy Semantic Mapping Thematic-Inquiry Approach	Question–Answer Relationships Questioning the Author Reciprocal Teaching Summarization Think-aloud Approach

*These techniques are less simultaneous than the others in the list.

Note: (a) The lesson frameworks of strategy instruction, explicit teaching, implicit teaching, directed reading activity, directed reading-thinking activity, and sustained silent reading are not classified. Of these, explicit teaching and the directed reading activity are more successive than simultaneous. (b) Teacher implementation can change any technique to make it more or less simultaneous.

Diagnostic Hypothesis

Jenny appears to use simultaneous processing. She relates stories to what she already knows and often makes word substitutions that fit the overall meaning of the text. Although she has a successive strength in comprehension (excellent literal comprehension), she does not have these same successive strengths in word analysis. Her miscues often reflect letter and syllable reversals. Jenny needs techniques that encourage her to integrate simultaneous and successive processing rather than over-rely on a single process.

 **Summary**

Putting the Parts Together for Jenny

Reviewing Jenny's case, the teacher reaches the following conclusions. Jenny needs instruction in fluency (a skill) and self-correction (a strategy). Jenny also views her poor fluency as subject to forces outside her control, thus increasing her negative attribution of reading failure. She likes expository text and has a high need for stories to make sense. In fact, she over-relies on reader-based processing of text, often making her interpretation fit pictures or a miscue rather than referring back to the text. However, she prefers to control her own learning (implicit instruction) whenever she can. She also has a tendency to prefer material presented with the overall theme first (simultaneous), before learning the details.

When the diagnostic teacher looks at all the hypotheses, she selects a text that contains expository passages of interest to the student (predominantly science stories) to use during guided contextual reading. Prior to instruction, she introduces key vocabulary words using webbing (see part 2), allowing Jenny to elaborate her knowledge about the concepts. During the lesson, the teacher uses collaborative reading where she reads the story aloud and then has Jenny read it on her own (implicit instruction). After the lesson, Jenny presents science facts to the class. She is allowed to use the assigned reading or her own research efforts.

To help Jenny attribute her success to effective strategies and to lead her to more flexible strategies when reading errors occur, a   of repeated readings (see "Repeated Readings" in part 2) is used in strategy and skill instruction. After Jenny reads a short informational passage for the first time, the teacher plans an intervention in which efficient strategies are discussed. The teacher demonstrates the following self-statement consistent with implicit instruction: "What would make sense and start with a _____?" This procedure allows Jenny to assume increasing responsibility for her own oral reading fluency while permitting her to use the overall meaning (simultaneous processing) of the selection to correct her miscues, thus respecting her natural preference for using prior experience and situational context to self-correct. Charting the repeated readings also helps Jenny attribute her increasing fluency to her own efforts and ability, reversing her negative attribution in word recognition.

Reviewing Technique Selection

The teacher's selection of a technique reflects the diagnostic hypotheses about a student's learning at that particular time. To select the most appropriate technique, the diagnostic teacher analyzes each technique according to its instructional features. First, the diagnostic teacher thinks about the instructional framework during guided contextual reading and selects techniques that will lead the student to interpret whole stories meaningfully. She thinks about the students' print and meaning processing and how she will advance their overall reading by supporting reading before, during, or after instruction. She also thinks about the type of text students are reading and selects techniques that are appropriate for that type of text. She thinks about students' preferences and decides whether more writing or discussing will advance story understanding.

Next, the diagnostic teacher selects techniques to encourage students to use strategies and skills that are inhibiting the reading process. She thinks about the element of strategy and skill instruction and selects techniques that work on weaknesses by showing students how to use their strengths to support their weaknesses.

Finally, the diagnostic teacher refines her selections by checking the selection against students' strengths and needs so she can use these during instruction. She uses the following criteria: source of information, type of mediated instruction, and cognitive processing. She thinks about the sources of information on which students rely: reader based or text based. The diagnostic teacher matches their assessments with instructional techniques that show them how to integrate information sources while at the same time use their strength. Then she decides on the type of structure that is needed: explicit or implicit. Providing the appropriate type of mediated instruction in the learning situation enhances students' reading performance. The diagnostic teacher decides which technique matches the students' strengths in cognitive processing. Some techniques incorporate a successive, serial approach to instruction, while others incorporate a global, simultaneous approach. For hard-to-teach students, instruction using their processing strength facilitates the learning of new information.

Throughout her instruction, the diagnostic teacher makes instructional modifications that increase each student's reading performance. To date, no single instructional sequence or instructional framework has proven effective for struggling readers. However, teachers vary in their preferences for teaching, and these preferences often dictate how they conduct the diagnostic session. Effective teachers remember that student learning is accomplished not by a mindless implementation of instructional techniques but by understanding the variables in the process of reading. Therefore, the diagnostic teacher needs to employ a variety of techniques to meet the individual needs of struggling readers, identify the key features of these techniques, and evaluate how these features affect reading acquisition.

PART TWO

The Instructional Techniques

In this part, 69 instructional procedures are presented to help teachers design programs for struggling readers. The instructional procedures, or techniques, include a variety of instructional formats, approaches, methods, and specialized techniques. The techniques represent a variety of ways to encourage proficient reading. Each technique is discussed in two parts: (a) a simple procedural description followed by (b) an explanation of specific diagnostic applications.

In field use, this part may be used in the following manner. First, the diagnostic teacher consults the general description and its steps. In order to make instructional modifications, the diagnostic teacher needs to evaluate how she instructs the lesson. Consequently, part 2, "Instructional Techniques," describes the steps in implementing each technique, thus facilitating a comparison of how instruction occurs when using various techniques. After outlining the steps, she evaluates at what point she modified instruction to mediate learning. She reflects on her reasons for deviating from the steps. Then the diagnostic teacher may turn to the second section of each technique. This section describes the learner patterns in which the technique produces success. Using this information will assist the teacher as she tries to match an appropriate instructional technique to the needs of an individual student. After she has selected a technique, the teacher uses a diagnostic teaching lesson to evaluate her hypothesis (see chapter 7).

The Information for Each Technique

Initially, the explanation is presented in simple terminology and is constructed to assist teacher–parent collaboration. The following topics are included:

- *Description.* In an effort to simplify communication, a two- or three-sentence description is presented. This description can be used in report writing or communicating with parents and the public.
- *Targeted Reading Levels.* Many techniques were developed for use with students at a particular stage in reading development. This section will facilitate selecting a technique that matches the reading level of the student.
- *Predominant Focus of Instruction.* This section delineates the critical focus of each technique. Techniques can be placed on a continuum of various instructional features that are stressed during implementation. For example, most techniques have both an oral discussion and a written component; however, one of

these aspects will predominate. It must be remembered that the significance of this emphasis depends on the learner's strategies, his task knowledge, and the situational context. In this section, the predominant focus is delineated according to the charts in chapter 10. The following list represents the selected areas:

1. Print or meaning processing
2. Instructional phase (before, during, or after reading) in the lesson
3. Response mode emphasized (oral or written)
4. Strategy emphasized (prediction, monitoring, or elaboration)
5. Skill emphasized (word identification, word analysis, fluency, sentence comprehension, word meaning, literal comprehension, nonliteral comprehension, or inquiry procedures)
6. Source of information (text based or reader based)
7. Type of instruction (explicit or implicit)
8. Type of cognitive processing (successive or simultaneous)

- *Procedures.* This section is a sequential enumeration of the process of instruction for each technique. This explanation serves two purposes. First, it facilitates implementation of the technique so that experimenting with new methods of instruction is not overwhelming. Second, using the steps of instruction, the diagnostic teacher can analyze at what step the student has incorporated the desired reading behaviors. This knowledge facilitates modifying instruction to increase its effectiveness.

The next section specifies the diagnostic applications of each technique and includes the following elements:

- *Basic View of Reading.* Techniques have developed from various views of learning. As individuals formulate views of how learning occurs, they propose teaching techniques that support their views. Therefore, instructional techniques reflect theories about how individuals learn. An assumption of this part is that the diagnostic teacher can match how a student is learning by monitoring how a student reacts to a particular technique. The major views are text based, which focuses instruction on text-based processing; reader based, in which instruction is focused on reader-based processing; interactive, with instruction focused on combining reader-based and text-based processing; and socio-interactive, in which instruction is focused on shared meaning construction (see chapter 1).
- *Patterns of Strengths and Strategies.* This section looks specifically at what the student is asked to do when the teacher implements the technique. The underlying strengths and strategies that are necessary for the student to profit from this instructional technique are then presented.
- *Learner Patterns That Produce Increased Engagement.* Techniques can be used in different ways to engage students in literacy. This section analyzes the technique as it would be integrated into instruction with different learners. How the technique is implemented is matched to the corresponding learner patterns. Learner patterns (see chapter 10 for further explanation) that are highlighted in this section include the following:

1. *Active readers,* who independently solve reading problems by reorganizing new information around its key features. They predict, monitor, and elaborate what they read, using both the text and what they know.

2. *Passive readers,* who rely heavily on cues from their environment to decide what is important to remember. They prefer to follow a teacher's model when predicting, monitoring, and elaborating what they read. When reading, they use they often use a single source of information.
3. *Readers who have a simultaneous processing strength* and think first about the overall meaning, then organize the parts as they relate to the entire meaning.
4. *Readers who have a successive processing strength* and think about the parts first, then order the parts to form the general meaning.

Described first are the learner patterns that represent how the technique matches students strengths. For these students, the technique can be used to modify the basic lesson during guided contextual reading or for strategy and skill instruction (see chapter 4 for further explanation of these features of the diagnostic teaching session). The items designated by an asterisk, which appear second, represent how the technique would be used to develop a weaker source during strategy and skill instruction.

- *Using the Technique as a Diagnostic Teaching Lesson.* This section provides a short checklist to focus the evaluation of a student's success when the technique is used. If the answers are "yes," the technique facilitates learning for this particular student.
- *Evidence Base.* This section includes references for the evidence base for each technique. Evidence base means that the instructional technique has been proven to be a reliable and valid support for children. In these studies, the data are systematically collected and analyzed. The results are then published in a referenced source.
- *Web Sites.* This section includes a couple of Web sites where you can find further information and suggestions for classroom practice. At the time of this writing, the Web sites were current. However, the Web is an ever-changing source of information.

Ways to Use These Techniques

The techniques in this part are arranged alphabetically so they can be used as a resource rather than procedures to be memorized. The alphabetical arrangement facilitates locating a technique that was selected in chapter 11.

These pages have been used by preservice teachers, in-service teachers, special education teachers, literacy coaches, and school psychologists in many different ways. Preservice teachers follow the procedures step-by-step as they learn how to teach in different ways. Then they read why they are doing what they are doing. When students do not succeed with a particular technique, these teachers analyze what they asked them to do by reading the second section. This assessment helps preservice teachers understand how students are different. In-service teachers use chapter 11 extensively to choose several techniques. As they identify what technique works best, they also identify their students' strengths. The literacy coach, special education teachers, and school psychologists, on the other hand, use chapter 11 to match assessment data with particular techniques. They look up each technique to verify which might be the most beneficial. Then they collaborate with teachers to decide on the appropriate techniques for their class.

1 Alternate Writing   *Targeted Reading Levels 4–8*

Description   Alternate writing is the composition of a story among a group of students and a teacher. Writing for a specified amount of time, each person alternately continues the development of a cohesive story line. Each person's contribution to the story line must build on prior information in the composition and must lead to the next event.

Text   Students' and teacher's writing

Predominant Focus of Instruction

1. Processing focus: meaning
2. Instructional phase: strategy lesson
3. Response mode emphasized: written discourse
4. Strategy emphasized: elaboration
5. Skill emphasized: sentence comprehension
6. Source of information: reader based
7. Type of instruction: implicit
8. Type of cognitive processing: successive

Procedure

1. The teacher selects topics of interest to the students. As the procedure is used, an increasing variety of text types and subject areas need to be included.
2. Using the story starter or topic selected, the teacher begins writing and continues developing the story line for 2 minutes. In a small group, an overhead can be used.
3. The story is passed to the next student. This student writes for 2 minutes.
4. In order to continue the story, each student must read the previous text and create text that maintains the story theme and moves the story to its conclusion.
5. When the story is completely written, the teacher reads the story as a whole.
6. The teacher revises her own parts of the story for coherence and grammatical clarity. As she is revising, she thinks out loud, "Will this make sense to my reader?"
7. The teacher encourages students to revise their writing for coherence and grammatical clarity.

Modifications

1. A story map can be developed prior to writing so that each student adds information that will fit the story map (see "Story Mapping" in this part).
2. A word processing program can be used, and students can write and revise the story on the computer.
3. Cartoons and comic books can be used as a framework for the story line.
4. This technique can be used in pairs, small groups, and tutoring situations.
5. This technique can be easily adapted to a writing center where students add to the story when they attend that center. Students initial their additions.
6. Alternate writing can also be used to create an informational text about specific topics.

Further Diagnostic Applications

Basic View of Reading   Reading and writing are socio-interactive processes in which the reader's ideas are shaped by group members. He uses prior knowledge to construct and monitor understanding, asking himself what would fit the story and be meaningful to group members. Through writing, the reader becomes sensitive to how stories are constructed so that they make sense.

Patterns of Strengths and Strategies Alternate writing is most appropriate for students who have facility with writing and prefer to communicate through writing rather than discussing. This approach helps students develop a sense of the text structure and approach text as a communication between reader and writer.

Learner Patterns That Produce Increased Engagement

1. For successive learners who write well but do not understand that reading is a communication process, this technique provides a tool for talking about the communicative intent of the author.
2. For simultaneous learners who write and read for self-understanding and meaning but do not realize that the text is a contractual agreement between reader and writer, this technique provides a tool for talking about what needs to be in a text in order to make it understandable to a reader.
*3. For learners who have verbal difficulty and who need to participate in writing a story to understand story structure, this technique provides an experience in developing writing fluency in a group setting, which is less threatening.

Using the Technique as a Diagnostic Teaching Lesson   For alternate writing to be effective, a majority of the following statements must be answered in the affirmative:

Yes   *No*

_____   _____   1. The student writes fluently and can construct text that makes sense.

_____   _____   2. The student prefers to write what he thinks rather than contribute to a discussion.

_____   _____   3. The student can retell a cohesive story and has an intuitive sense of story structure.

Evidence Base

Lingnau, A. H., & Mannhaupt, G. (2003).Computer supported collaborative writing in an early learning classroom. *Journal of Computer Assisted Learning; 19,* 186–194.

Lopez-Reyna, N. A. (1997). The relation of interactions and story quality among Mexican American and Anglo American students with learning disabilities. *Exceptionality, 7,* 245–261.

Web Sites

http://www.writingproject.org
http://senior.billings.k12.mt.us/6traits

---

*Indicates a technique that can be used to remediate a weakness.

2 Analytic Phonics   *Targeted Reading Levels 1–2*

Description   Analytic phonics (sometimes referred to as implicit phonics instruction) is an approach to teaching decoding that is based on drawing phonic relationships among words that have the same letters. Using familiar words, the student identifies the sounds of letter clusters by using known words. In other words, the student says, "I already know a word that begins like this new word. I will match the sounds in that word with the sounds in the new word." In analytic phonics, letter cluster(s) from the beginning, middle, and ending of words are used.

Text   Known words and new words that have some of the same sounds

Predominant Focus of Instruction

1. Processing focus: print
2. Instructional phase: after reading
3. Response mode emphasized: oral discussion
4. Strategy emphasized: elaboration
5. Skill emphasized: word analysis
6. Source of information: text based
7. Type of instruction: implicit
8. Type of cognitive processing: simultaneous to successive

Procedure

1. The teacher selects a text that contains an abundance of the letter sounds to be taught.
2. The teacher presents known words that represent the targeted sound or sound cluster. For example, she places these words on the board: *green grass grow.*
3. She asks the student to identify how these words are alike. The student responds, "They all have the letters *gr* at the beginning."
4. The teacher directs attention to the sounds by saying, "How does the *gr* sound in these words?"
5. If the student cannot figure out the sound, the teacher says, "Try the *gr-r-r* sound as in *green, grass,* and *grow.*"
6. The student reads a text with words that have the *gr* sound, such as the following:

    In the land of the gremlins, there were gobs of green grapes as big as Grandpa. One baby gremlin loved to eat the green grapes. He began to grow and grow and grow. So his mother said, "You cannot eat anymore. You have grown too big." This made the gremlin grumpy. He growled and growled. He grabbed a great big green grape and gobbled it up.

7. The teacher draws attention to how the student used the strategy by identifying initial letter sounds.

Further Diagnostic Applications

Basic View of Reading   Learning to read is a text-based process in which the student makes inferences about the phonic relationships within words. When a student can read an abundance of words that contain a consistent phonic relationship, he will infer the phonic rule for the target words and similar words. This process is called *implicit* or *analytic phonics.*

Patterns of Strengths and Strategies   Analytic phonics is most appropriate for students who can segment words into their sounds and readily make phonic inferences about the consistency of sounds in words. This technique builds on their strengths and allows them to develop the strategy of decoding.

Learner Patterns That Produce Increased Engagement

1. For simultaneous learners who can segment words into their sounds and have established a word identification vocabulary, this technique matches their strengths in knowing the whole word before the parts and finding the patterns between what they know and what is new.
2. For active readers who do not respond to the direct instruction of other decoding approaches, this technique allows them to develop their own rules for how phonics works.
3. For learners who have an overriding need for meaning and purpose, this technique uses letter clusters using known words to develop strategies for decoding.

Using the Technique as a Diagnostic Teaching Lesson   For analytic phonics to be effective, a majority of the following statements must be answered in the affirmative:

Yes	No	
_____	_____	1. The student is effective at phonemic segmentation.
_____	_____	2. The student has a well-established recognition vocabulary that facilitates making phonic inferences to new words.
_____	_____	3. The student can draw sound cluster similiarities between known words and new words.

Evidence Base

Christensen, C. A., & Bowey, J. A. (2005). The efficacy of orthographic rime, grapheme-phoneme correspondence, and implicit phonics approaches to teaching decoding skills. *Scientific Studies of Reading, 9,* 327–349.

Web Sites

http://www.ltscotland.org.uk/5to14/specialfocus/earlyintervention/issues/phonics.asp
http://www.indstate.edu/soe/blumberg/reading/rd-word.html#ana

3 Chunking   *Targeted Reading Levels 4–8*

Description   Chunking is a technique to encourage the student to read phrases of language that represent meaning rather than separate words. Chunking facilitates comprehension and fluency by grouping words into thought units rather than word-by-word reading.

Text   All kinds

Predominant Focus of Instruction

1. Processing focus: print and meaning
2. Instructional phase: during reading
3. Response mode emphasized: oral production
4. Strategy emphasized: prediction
5. Skill emphasized: fluency and sentence comprehension
6. Source of information: text based and reader based
7. Type of instruction: explicit
8. Type of cognitive processing: successive to simultaneous

Procedure

1. The teacher chooses a passage at an instructional reading level that will take about 3 minutes to read.
2. The teacher tapes the student reading the passage.
3. The teacher and the student echo read the passage using meaningful phrases. In other words, the teacher reads a sentence modeling appropriate chunks of the sentence, and the student repeats the same sentence using the phrasing. The example that follows illustrates the sequence:

   Text: The bright girl liked to read stories about horses.

   Student reading: The/bright/girl/liked/to/read/stories/about/horses.

   Teacher modeling: The bright girl/liked to read/stories about horses.

   Student echoing: The bright girl/liked to/read stories/about horses.

   Teacher comment: I liked the way you chunked "read stories." Did it make more sense to you to read it that way?

4. The teacher and student continue reading the entire passage. When possible, the teacher increases the number of sentences chunked before the student repeats the model.
5. As the student's ability to chunk thought units increases, the teacher ceases to model the chunking, and the student reads the passage on her own.
6. The teacher tapes the reading of the passage again.
7. The teacher and the student compare fluency, intonation, and phrasing.

Modifications

1. For the extremely slow reader, the teacher may incorporate oral chunking experiences as an intervention with multiple, timed, silent readings.
2. For the beginning reader, chunking a language experience story by writing phrases from the story on 3- by 5-inch cards is an effective technique.

Further Diagnostic Applications

Basic View of Reading   Reading is an interactive process whereby a reader thinks about how the words of the text are combined to form the ideas the author intended to convey.

Patterns of Strengths and Strategies   Chunking is most appropriate for students who have facility with word identification and reflect a successive, text-based processing. Chunking of text encourages these students to connect the underlying thought with the text as they are reading.

Learner Patterns That Produce Increased Engagement

1. When chunking, successive learners who have difficulty relating what is written in the text to their own thoughts must use understanding of the meaning to group the words together.
2. For passive readers who read words without thinking of their meaning, chunking uses recognizing the words (a strength) to understand how the words create meaning (a weakness).
*3. For learners who are word bound because of an overemphasis on phonics or oral accuracy, chunking increases fluency and speed.
4. For extremely slow readers who think about every word, chunking encourages thinking about groups of words rather than individual words.

Using the Technique as a Diagnostic Teaching Lesson   For chunking to be effective, a majority of the following statements must be answered in the affirmative:

Yes   *No*

_____   _____   1. The student has accurate word identification skills.
_____   _____   2. The student can model the teacher's chunking of words.
_____   _____   3. The student transfers the chunking to new text.

Evidence Base

Young, A., & Bowers, P. (1995). Individual difference and text difficulty determinants of reading fluency and expressiveness. *Journal of Experimental Child Psychology, 60,* 428–454.

Rasinski, T. V. (1990). Investigating measures of reading fluency. *Educational Research Quarterly, 14,* 37–44.

Web Sites

http://www.pde.state.pa.us/reading_writing/cwp/view.asp?a=196&q=98178
http://www.educationoasis.com/curriculum/Reading/glossary_reading_terms.htm
http://www.resourceroom.net/readspell/2002_automaticity.asp

4 Cloze Instruction   *Targeted Reading Levels 4–12*

Description   The instructional cloze is a technique that develops comprehension by deleting target words from a text. It encourages the student to think about what word would make sense in the sentence and in the context of the entire story.

Text   Coherent paragraphs and stories

Predominant Focus of Instruction

1. Processing focus: meaning
2. Instructional phase: after reading
3. Response mode emphasized: written
4. Strategy emphasized: prediction and monitoring
5. Skill emphasized: sentence comprehension and word meaning
6. Source of information: text based with some reader based
7. Type of instruction: implicit
8. Type of cognitive processing: successive

Procedure

1. The teacher selects a text of 200 to 400 words.
2. The teacher decides on the target words, such as nouns or verbs or targeted sight words.
3. The teacher systematically deletes the words from the paragraph and inserts a blank for the deleted word.
4. The student is instructed to read the entire passage to get a sense of the entire meaning.
5. The student is then instructed to fill in the blanks in the passage.
6. When the student finishes filling in the blanks, the answers are evaluated as to the similarity of meaning between the deleted word and the supplied word.
7. The student reviews his choices and talks about what strategies he used to decide on the word choices.

Modifications

1. An oral cloze can be used to develop predictive listening in the young child.
2. A cloze exercise can be constructed from language experience stories in order to develop the ability to predict a word by using prior knowledge (what I said) and the text (how I said it).
3. Cloze can be adapted so that pairs of students work together to decide what word fits in the text. This activity causes a discussion and justification of word choices.

Further Diagnostic Applications

Basic View of Reading   Reading is an interactive process of verifying text expectation by using knowledge of how language works (sentence structure) and what the passage means (overall contextual meaning).

Patterns of Strengths and Strategies   The cloze procedure relies on a well-developed sense of the redundancy of language and a manipulation of sentence structure. For students who have verbal fluency, this technique facilitates comprehension by encouraging the combination of overall text meaning and sentence sense.

Learner Patterns That Produce Increased Engagement

1. For successive learners who have become word bound during the process of initial reading instruction and need to increase the use of context to construct meaning, this technique increases the ability to figure out what words are from the sentence context.
2. For successive learners who tend to read isolated words rather than using the context and asking what would make sense, this technique helps readers think about what groups of words mean.
3. For simultaneous learners who need to use both sentence structure and overall meaning to read text effectively, this technique focuses attention on sentence meaning.

Using the Technique as a Diagnostic Teaching Lesson   For cloze instruction to be effective, a majority of the following statements must be answered in the affirmative:

Yes   *No*

_____   _____   1. The student fills in the blanks with some degree of certainty.

_____   _____   2. The student has verbal facility that supplements his performance on the cloze.

_____   _____   3. The student begins to use not only *word* knowledge but also *world* knowledge to complete the cloze.

Evidence Base

Gipe, J. P. (1978–1979). Investigating techniques for teaching word meanings. *Reading Research Quarterly, 14,* 624–644.

Henry, G., & Hincq, M. F. (1975). The cloze procedure as a means of instruction. *Scientia Paedagogica Experimentalis, 1,* 189–206.

Web Sites

http://www.utpjournals.com/jour.ihtml?lp=product/cmlr/592/592_TCL_Steinman.html
http://www.education.tas.gov.au/english/cloze.htm

5 Collaborative Reading   *Targeted Reading Levels 2–5*

Description   In the collaborative reading technique, the challenge of unfamiliar selections is supported by reading together and sharing interpretations as with young children in shared reading. The teacher begins reading the story aloud and then invites the student to follow. They discuss what the story could be about as they read the story to develop an understanding of the story while reading together. Using his understanding of the story, the student reads the new selection on his own with only minimal support from the teacher.

Text   Easy chapter books

Predominant Focus of Instruction

1. Processing focus: meaning and print
2. Instructional phase: before reading
3. Response mode emphasized: oral discussion
4. Strategy emphasized: prediction
5. Skill emphasized: literal comprehension and word identification
6. Source of information: reader based
7. Type of instruction: implicit
8. Type of cognitive processing: simultaneous

Procedure

1. The teacher selects a chapter book to read.
2. The teacher and students discuss what they think the book will be about based on the title.
3. The teacher reads the story aloud modeling appropriate intonation. (If the student is reading well, then the first read is not necessary, but the teacher can ask the following questions as she and the student read together.) As the teacher reads, she stops and asks,

   What do you think will happen next?

   Do you agree with what the main character did?

4. After the first reading the teacher asks open-ended questions that encourage a higher level of engagement in the selection, such as

   Which part of the story did you like best?

   What would you change in the story?

5. When reading the story a second time together, the teacher keeps a fluent pace and invites the student to join in the reading.
6. After the second reading, the student and teacher review the troublesome phrases and ideas.
7. On the third reading of the story, the student reads alone. The teacher prompts the student if he needs help.

Further Diagnostic Applications

Basic View of Reading   Reading is a socio-interactive process in which the reader's background knowledge and how he discusses the story with others help him understand the story and recognize the words. When the teacher reads the story aloud and discusses it with the child, she creates an expectation for the words in the text. The student then uses reader-based processing (i.e., what the text means) to figure out unfamiliar words. The ultimate goal is a reader who will simultaneously apply the decoding skills of reading while comprehending text.

Patterns of Strengths and Strategies   Collaborative reading is most appropriate for intermediate students who have a simultaneous strength and have a high drive for meaning when reading. For these students, the approach uses their strengths of listening and thinking, then it asks them to use these strengths to recognize words.

Learner Patterns That Produce Increased Engagement

1. For simultaneous learners with a high listening comprehension and minimal (second-grade) word identification skills, this technique uses their strengths in listening and thinking to develop an anticipation of what the text will say and facilitates word identification.
*2. For passive learners with adequate listening comprehension skills and minimal word identification skills, the teacher needs to emphasize self-talk when revising miscues.
*3. For extremely word-bound, successive readers who lack fluency, this technique uses what students remember about the story to develop expectations for what words will look like.

Using the Technique as a Diagnostic Teaching Lesson   For collaborative reading to be effective, a majority of the following statements must be answered in the affirmative:

Yes   No

_____ _____ 1. The student can listen to and remember stories read aloud.
_____ _____ 2. The student follows the teacher's model during choral reading.
_____ _____ 3. The student reads fluently after hearing the page or pages.

Evidence Base

Mathes, P. G., Torgesen, J. K., Clancy-Menchetti, J., Santi, K., Nicholas, K., Robinson, C., et al. (2003). A comparison of teacher-directed versus peer-assisted instruction to struggling first-grade readers. *Elementary School Journal, 103,* 459–79.

Reutzel, D. R., Hollingsworth P. M., & Eldredge, J. L. (1994). Oral reading instruction: The impact on student reading development. *Reading Research Quarterly, 29,* 40–62.

Web Sites

http://www.busyteacherscafe.com/units/fluency.htm
http://www.gisd.k12.nm.us/reading/bestprac.html

6 Concept Mapping

Targeted Reading Levels 7–12

Description   The concept mapping technique is designed to show relationships among information by creating a network of concepts. Stemming from science education, concept mapping uses nodes that represent the concept and links of complex relationships. These maps help students learn the new concepts and propositions and embed them in existing cognitive structures.

Text   Expository text

Predominant Focus of Instruction

1. Processing focus: meaning
2. Instructional phase: before reading
3. Response mode emphasized: oral discussion
4. Strategy emphasized: elaboration
5. Skill emphasized: literal and nonliteral comprehension
6. Source of information: text based
7. Type of instruction: explicit
8. Type of cognitive processing: simultaneous

Procedure

1. The teacher chooses a chapter from a textbook.
2. The teacher selects key concepts.
3. The teacher arranges the concept into nodes (ideas) and links (relationship among ideas) to show their interrelationships. She labels the node and sometimes the links.
4. The teacher strives to show the relationships and the overall structure of the complex concept so as to increase understanding.
5. The teacher presents the concept mapping on a PowerPoint slide show or constructs it while talking using mapping software. As she presents the concept map, she explains the relationships.
6. Students discuss the impact of the interrelationships.
7. The students read the chapter referring as needed to the concept map.
8. After reading the selection, the students may return to the concept map to refine and elaborate on relationships among attributes.

Further Diagnostic Applications

Basic View of Reading   Reading is an active process in which learners extend their understanding of complex concepts by understanding the relationships among ideas. By constructing a concept map of complex relationships, the teacher shows how information is related prior to reading.

Patterns of Strengths and Strategies   The concept mapping technique is appropriate for students who profit from a visual organization of complex relationships. It is especially useful for the highly visual students who profit from seeing relationships in order to tie them together.

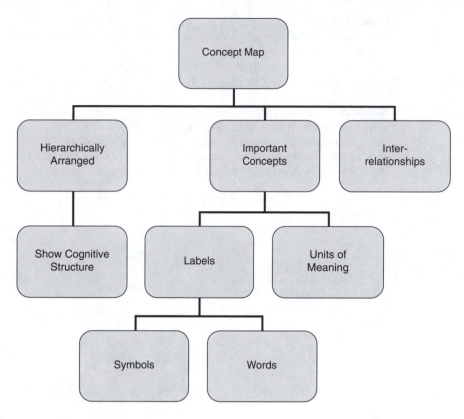

Note. Made with PowerPoint software.

Learner Patterns That Produce Increased Engagement

1. For simultaneous readers who think in visual patterns, concept maps help relate and elaborate topic knowledge through the network of relationships.
*2. For readers who read without relating what they know to the attributes and conceptual knowledge, concept maps help them to see the relationships that develop a concept and use what they know to interpret the information.
*3. For passive readers who read new concepts without seeing the relationships among complex ideas surrounding a concept, concept mapping helps them focus on the relationships among constructs.

Using the Technique as a Diagnostic Teaching Lesson   For concept mapping to be effective, a majority of the following statements must be answered in the affirmative:

Yes   *No*

_____   _____   1. The student can easily see the connecting relationships on the map.

_____   _____   2. The student understands how the nodes and links work.

_____   _____   3. The student discusses complex relationships.

Concept Mapping 6

Evidence Base

Derbentseva, N., Safayeni, F., & Cañas, A. J. (2007). Concept Maps: Experiments on dynamic thinking. *Journal of Research in Science Teaching, 44,* 448–465.

Willeman, M., & MacHarg, R. (1991). The Concept Map as an Advance Organizer. *Journal of Research in Science Teaching, 28,* 705–711

Web Sites

http://users.edte.utwente.nl/lanzing/cm_home.htm
http://depts.gallaudet.edu/englishworks/reading/mapping.html
http://www.learningcommons.uoguelph.ca/Fastfacts-ConceptMapping.pdf
http://www.education-world.com/a_tech/tech164.shtml

7 Concept-Oriented Reading Instruction

Targeted Reading Levels 5–12

Description   Concept-oriented reading instruction is designed to improve students' learning in content areas. It shows them how to connect new knowledge to what is already known and how to demonstrate their learning in fascinating ways.

Text   Expository text

Predominant Focus of Instruction

1. Processing focus: meaning
2. Instructional phase: before, during, and after reading
3. Response mode emphasized: discussion
4. Strategy emphasized: elaboration
5. Skill emphasized: literal, nonliteral comprehension, inquiry thinking
6. Source of information: text based and reader based
7. Type of instruction: implicit
8. Type of cognitive processing: simultaneous

Procedure

1. The teacher introduces the conceptual theme and discusses what students know about the theme.
2. The teacher leads students through a hands-on experience designed to activate their prior knowledge and engage them in the theme.
3. Students write observations in journals or chart information and reflect in journals.
4. The teacher leads a discussion about the activity, data collected, observations, and reflections. The teacher encourages students to ask questions that will further their inquiry.
5. The teacher introduces search strategies for inquiries. For example, the teacher might explain how to identify what they want to learn; how information is organized and presented in books, in the library, and on the Internet; and how to get information from books to formulate generalizations about queries.
6. The students self-select books and other materials to read and review to find answers to questions.
7. The students are engaged in reading material for an extended period of time.
8. To help students comprehend, integrate, and organize information, the teacher models comprehension strategies, such as developing images or graphics, rereading to clarify, and identifying key ideas.
9. Students are grouped into idea circles based on topics and text selected.
10. Students pool information and sources to gain a conceptual understanding from multiple texts.
11. Students share what they have learned using various media such as debates, written reports, PowerPoint presentations, dramas, and graphics.

Further Diagnostic Applications

Basic View of Reading   Reading is a socio-interactive process where students work together to create meaning. Through sharing information in a small group, students define and elaborate conceptual understanding.

Patterns of Strengths and Strategies   Concept-oriented reading instruction is most appropriate for students who can discuss ideas in a small group and can reorganize information from multiple sources.

Learner Patterns That Produce Increased Engagement

1. For self-directed readers who profit from discussing information and ideas, concept-oriented reading instruction helps these students integrate and elaborate understanding.
2. For simultaneous learners who profit from discussing and following a model of strategic processes, concept-oriented reading instruction helps these students read and organize information in an elaborate fashion.
*3. For readers who are bound by the text and believe that reading means getting the answers right, concept-oriented reading instruction helps these students organize information and use strategies for understanding the material.

Using the Technique as a Diagnostic Teaching Lesson   For concept-oriented reading instruction to be effective, a majority of the following statements must be answered in the affirmative:

Yes   No

_____ _____   1. The student can share information in the group.
_____ _____   2. The student is engaged when reading expository text and using multiple sources of information.
_____ _____   3. The student can follow an oral demonstration of strategic reading.

Evidence Base

Guthrie, J. T., Van Meter, P., McCann, A. D., Wigfield, A., Bennett, L., Poundstone, et al. (1996). Growth of literacy engagement: Changes in motivation and strategies during concept-oriented reading instruction. *Reading Research Quarterly, 31*(3), 306.

Web Sites

http://www.cori.umd.edu
http://www.teach.virginia.edu/go/clic/nrrc/cori_r10.html

8 Contextual Processing

Description   Contextual processing is a technique used to develop new word meanings as they are found in the context of a selected story. This technique shows students how to use context to figure out what new vocabulary words mean.

Text   Paragraphs three to four sentences long, where the meaning of new vocabulary is apparent from the surrounding context

Predominant Focus of Instruction

1. Processing focus: meaning
2. Instructional phase: before or after reading
3. Response mode emphasized: oral discussion
4. Strategy emphasized: monitoring and elaboration
5. Skill emphasized: word meaning and sentence comprehension
6. Source of information: text based
7. Type of instruction: explicit
8. Type of cognitive processing: successive

Procedure

1. The teacher selects unfamiliar key vocabulary words to teach.
2. The teacher finds a passage in the text where the meaning of the word is apparent from the surrounding context. If such texts are not available, she creates her own three-sentence paragraph.
3. She writes the paragraph on the overhead or chalkboard.
4. She reads the paragraph aloud to the students.
5. The students reread the paragraph silently.
6. The teacher asks the students about the meaning of the word found in the paragraph, asking, for example, "What does the paragraph tell you about the word . . . ?"
7. The teacher uses the students' answers to probe further understanding, asking, "Why did you think that?"
8. The teacher asks students to write down what the new word might mean.
9. The teacher has students think of other similar situations in which they could use the word. She asks, "Who else might be . . . ? or Where else might you . . . ?"
10. The students think of other words with similar meanings.
11. The students record target words and a personal definition in their vocabulary journals.

Modification   The teacher can increase the explicitness of the technique by modeling how to figure out the meaning of the word using the surrounding words in the paragraph. The teacher models step 6 (what the paragraph told her), step 7 (why she thought that), and step 8 (how she came up with the meaning).

Further Diagnostic Applications

Basic View of Reading   Reading is an interactive process in which the readers use what they know about the words in the story to elaborate word meaning.

Patterns of Strengths and Strategies   Contextual processing has students figure out unfamiliar word meanings from the context; therefore, it is most appropriate for students who have facility with sentence meaning but do not use their knowledge to figure out what new words mean.

Learner Patterns That Produce Increased Engagement

1. For successive learners who have the ability to use sentences to figure out how to pronounce new words but do not use their sentence knowledge to expand word meanings, this technique starts with their strengths and then asks them to use sentence knowledge and background knowledge to elaborate word meaning.
2. For passive learners who read the words without actively thinking about what they mean in the new context or other contexts, this technique encourages them to think actively about what words mean. The modification of modeling may be needed.
3. For simultaneous learners who do not use the sentence context to figure out word meanings, this technique encourages them to use context as well as what they know to figure out new word meanings.

Using the Technique as a Diagnostic Teaching Lesson   For contextual processing to be effective, a majority of the following statements must be answered in the affirmative:

Yes   *No*

_____   _____   1. The student can use sentence comprehension to facilitate learning new word meanings.

_____   _____   2. The student learns to use information from sentences to define the word easily.

_____   _____   3. The student can use words to define new meanings and does not need a direct experience.

Evidence Base

McKeown, M. (1985). The acquisition of word meaning from context by children of low ability. *Reading Research Quarterly, 20,* 482–496.

Web Sites

http://ol.scc.spokane.edu/jstrever/comp/fall100/context_clues.htm
http://www.scc.losrios.edu/~langlit/reading/contextclues/intro1.htm
http://www.learner.org/jnorth/tm/ReadStrat19.html

9 Decoding by Analogy   *Targeted Reading Levels 1–4*

Description   The decoding by analogy technique is an approach to teaching phonics in which children are taught a strategic process of using word patterns they know to figure out unfamiliar words.

Text   Individual words

Predominant Focus of Instruction

1. Processing focus: print
2. Instructional phase: skill lesson
3. Response mode emphasized: oral
4. Strategy emphasized: monitoring
5. Skill emphasized: word identification and word analysis
6. Source of information: text based
7. Type of instruction: explicit
8. Type of cognitive processing: simultaneous to successive

Procedure

1. The teacher explains that sometimes individuals use words they know to figure out unfamiliar words.
2. The teacher models how to find familiar letter patterns in unfamiliar words. For instance, when reading the word *stain,* the student could identify *ain* as a pattern in *rain,* a familiar word.
3. Next, she models the self-talk that she uses to try out the sounds from *rain* in the unfamiliar *stain.*
4. Then she has the student try out the strategy on a series of unknown preselected words. These words share letter patterns with familiar words.
5. The teacher posts a set of key words that have common word patterns, such as the *at* in *cat,* and *ay* in *hay.* She uses picture clues next to the words to help readers remember the key word.
6. On a regular basis, the children read texts which have words with familiar spelling patterns.

Modifications

1. The Word Detective Program is a decoding-by-analogy approach that includes self-talk and self-evaluation. During the process of learning decoding analogies, the teacher models the decoding process and the self-talk she uses to figure out the words using analogies. Her self-talk follows the chart below. After learning a new word, the students fill out the chart.

    Talk to Yourself Chart

    1. The word is _____.

    2. Stretch the word. I hear _____ sounds.

    3. I see _____ letters because _____.

4. The spelling pattern is _____.

5. This is what I know about the vowel _____.

6. Another word in the key word list with the same vowel sound is_____.

2. The decoding-by-analogy technique is enhanced when teachers focus on common word patterns. Thirty-three common word patterns are listed in the following box (Stahl, 1998).

ack	ain	ake	ale	all	ame	an	ank
ap	ash	at	ate	aw	ay		
eat	ell	est					
ice	ing	ink	ip	ir	ick	ide	
ight	ill	in	ine				
op	or	ore	ock	oke			
uck	ug	ump					

Further Diagnostic Applications

Basic View of Reading   Learning to read is an interactive process. By developing procedures to figure out words, the student uses the text first to sound out the word and then relates the new word to familiar words with the same language pattern.

Patterns of Strengths and Strategies   The decoding by analogy strategy is most appropriate for students who can segment words into their sounds and match those sounds to the letters in the word. This technique builds on their strength and allows them to develop a system for decoding by analogy to key words.

Learner Patterns That Produce Increased Engagement

1. For successive learners who can match sounds to letters, this technique helps develop a system for using what they know to figure out new words.
2. For simultaneous thinkers who readily use what they know but need help focusing on letter pattern cues to figure out words, this technique matches the familiar with the unfamiliar in decoding words.
3. For passive learners who need explanations to understand how to decode unfamiliar words, this technique provides a tool to build word identification.

Using the Technique as a Diagnostic Teaching Lesson   For the decoding by analogy strategy to be effective, a majority of the following statements must be answered in the affirmative:

Yes   *No*

_____ _____   1. The student knows initial consonants and blends.
_____ _____   2. The student can match sounds to letter clusters.
_____ _____   3. The student applies analogies to both known and unknown words.

Evidence Base

Gaskins, I. W., Ehri, L. C., Cress, C., O'Hara, C., & Donnelly, K. (1996–1997). Procedures for word learning: Making discoveries about words. *The Reading Teacher, 50,* 312–327.

Greaney, K. T., Tunmer, W. E., & Chapman, J. W. (1997). Effects of rime-based orthographic analogy training on the word recognition skills of children with reading disability. *Journal of Educational Psychology, 89,* 645–651.

Walton, P. D., & Walton, L. M. (2002). Beginning reading by teaching in rime analogy: Effects on phonological skills, letter-sound knowledge, working memory, and word-reading. *Scientific Studies of Reading, 6,* 79–115.

White, T. G. (2005). Effects of systematic and strategic analogy-based phonics on grade 2 students' word reading and reading comprehension. *Reading Research Quarterly, 40,* 234–255.

Web Sites

http://www.readwritethink.org/lessons/lesson_view.asp?id=157
http://www.glenorchy.tased.edu.au/literacy/whole_to_parts_phonics.htm
http://www.sedl.org/cgi-bin/mysql/buildingreading.cgi?showrecord=8&l=description

10 **Direct Experience Approach** *Targeted Reading Levels: All levels; necessary for young children*

Description   Direct experience is an approach in which actual situations are used to develop word meanings. The actual object is manipulated or the event enacted in order to develop an understanding of a concept. During the activity, the teacher and students use the new word (label) as they actually experience the concept. This approach associates the word label with the word concept.

Text   The object or event in a situational context

Predominant Focus of Instruction

1. Processing focus: meaning
2. Instructional phase: before reading
3. Response mode emphasized: oral discussion
4. Strategy emphasized: elaboration
5. Skill emphasized: word meaning
6. Source of information: reader based
7. Type of instruction: implicit
8. Type of cognitive processing: simultaneous

Procedure

1. The teacher makes a list of target words that are not well developed in the students' meaning vocabularies.
2. She secures the objects that these words represent or plans an excursion where the student would use the words. To develop an understanding of the word *sour,* for example, the teacher brings lemons to class.
3. The teacher constructs a situation in which to use the object. In the example, students would taste the lemons.
4. The students use the objects in the situation and describe the experience. In the example, students could describe how the lemons tasted.
5. The students identify other objects that are similar and tell how they are alike and then how they are different. In the example, students could contrast the taste of the lemon with a pickle, a doughnut, and a hamburger.
6. The students identify other objects that are different and tell how they are different and then how they may be alike. In the example, the students would think of other fruits that are sour and those that are not sour.
7. The teacher writes the words on a card or the chalkboard so that meaning can be associated with what the words look like.

Modifications

1. Science experiments use activities to develop a concept and follow the activity with a labeling and recording of the information; therefore, they develop meaning through a direct experience.
2. Simulation of social studies concepts provides an activity in which words describing a concept are used in a situational context, and therefore students develop meaning through a direct association between the concept and the actions.

Further Diagnostic Applications

Basic View of Reading   Reading is a socio-interactive process in which a conceptual understanding of words is based on generalizations from specific events that the reader has encountered. Therefore, word meanings are based not only on categorical relationships but also on the knowledge of specific events each person has had. Definitions are developed as the student uses language in social situations.

Patterns of Strengths and Strategies   Direct experience is appropriate for students who learn through kinesthetic involvement in learning. Concrete objects build a store of specific instances for the students to develop definitional language. For these students, the approach matches their underlying preference for developing meaning within the context of situations rather than by verbal descriptions devoid of actions.

Learner Patterns That Produce Increased Engagement

1. For simultaneous learners who use past experiences rather than specific definitional knowledge to construct meaning, direct experience shows them how to label the environment.
2. For kinesthetic and English Language learners, the direct experience helps them to develop verbal and concept meaning simultaneously.
3. For passive learners who use word labels without understanding the underlying conceptual meaning of the words, direct experience makes the connections between the words they use and the underlying conceptual meaning.

Using the Technique as a Diagnostic Teaching Lesson   For the direct experience approach to be effective, a majority of the following statements must be answered in the affirmative:

Yes	*No*	
_____	_____	1. The student uses specific examples when defining words.
_____	_____	2. The student uses *like a* statements rather than definitional language.
_____	_____	3. The student finds manipulative activities meaningful and not boring.

Evidence Base

Bringle, Ro. G., & Hatcher, Ju. A. (1999). Reflection in service learning: Making meaning of experience. *Horizons, 77,* 179–85.

Speaker, Ka. Mc. (2001). Interactive exhibit theory: Hints for implementing learner-centered activities in elementary classrooms. *Education, 121,* 610–615.

Web Sites

http://olc.spsd.sk.ca/DE/PD/instr/experi.html
http://ws.cs.ubc.ca/~kla/index.php?page=Links
http://en.wikipedia.org/wiki/Kinesthetic_learning

11 Directed Reading Activity   *Targeted Reading Levels: All levels*

Description   A directed reading activity is an instructional format for teaching reading in which the teacher assumes the major instructional role. The teacher develops background knowledge, introduces new words, and gives the students a purpose for reading. Then she directs the discussion with questions to develop reading comprehension. Finally, she reinforces and extends the skills and knowledge developed.

Text   Graded stories in basal readers or content-area textbooks

Predominant Focus of Instruction

1. Processing focus: print and meaning
2. Instructional phase: before and after reading
3. Response mode emphasized: oral discussion
4. Strategy emphasized: elaboration
5. Skill emphasized: word identification and literal comprehension
6. Source of information: text based
7. Type of instruction: implicit
8. Type of cognitive processing: successive

Procedure

1. The teacher develops readiness for reading:
   a. The teacher presents new vocabulary words in oral and written context. Students are asked what these new words mean and directed to remember the words by their distinctive visual features.
   b. The teacher develops appropriate background knowledge so that students will understand the general setting of the story.
   c. The teacher gives the students a purpose for reading by telling them to read to find out a particular thing or concept. She develops purposes that require students to read the entire story before an answer is resolved.
2. The students read the story silently.
   a. If necessary, the teacher divides the passage into sections. After the students read a section, the teacher asks a variety of questions emphasizing literal and nonliteral understanding.
   b. The teacher asks the students to support their answers by reading the appropriate sections in the text.
3. The teacher reinforces and extends concepts introduced.
   a. Activities to reinforce word recognition and word meanings are used to develop independence in reading.
   b. Activities that develop a creative response are assigned.
   c. Activities that require students to relate the meaning to their own experiences and to other information are used.

Further Diagnostic Applications

Basic View of Reading   Reading requires recognizing words and then associating meaning with these new words. Initially, therefore, reading is a text-based process.

However, when new words have been learned and purposes have been set, students can read with comprehension.

Patterns of Strengths and Strategies   A directed reading activity is a flexible approach for instructing children to read. Following this format, the text can be narrative or expository, short or long, or interrupted or read as a whole. However, it must be remembered that the directed reading activity is just that, reading directed by the teacher and not the student. Therefore, it is most appropriate when a substantial amount of teacher direction is needed in order to construct meaning.

Learner Patterns That Produce Increased Engagement

1. For active readers who need new words presented before they read so that word recognition does not interfere with comprehension, this approach introduces new words to facilitate comprehension.
2. For passive readers who need the teacher to direct their attention to important word identification and comprehension cues, the teacher can use this format.

Using the Technique as a Diagnostic Teaching Lesson   For the directed reading activity to be effective, a majority of the following statements must be answered in the affirmative:

Yes   *No*

_____   _____   1. The student comprehends the story and is fairly active when he reads.

_____   _____   2. The student needs his attention directed to recognizing words in isolation and context.

_____   _____   3. The student is more comfortable answering questions than retelling the story.

Evidence Base

Schmitt, M. C. (1988). The effects of an elaborated directed reading activity on the metacomprehension skills of third graders. *National Reading Conference Yearbook, 37,* 167–181.

Schmitt, M. C., & Baumann, J. F. (1990). Metacomprehension during basal reader instruction: Do teachers promote it? *Reading Research and Instruction, 29,* 1–13.

Web Site

http://www.nea.org/reading/directedreading.html

12 Directed Reading-Thinking Activity

Targeted Reading Levels:
All levels

Description A directed reading-thinking activity (DRTA) is an instructional format for teaching reading that includes predicting what the author will say, reading to confirm or revise those predictions, and elaborating responses. Teachers and students discuss both strategies and responses.

Text Can be applied to all narrative and expository texts

Predominant Focus of Instruction

1. Processing focus: meaning
2. Instructional phase: during and after reading
3. Response mode emphasized: oral discussion
4. Strategy emphasized: prediction and monitoring
5. Skill emphasized: nonliteral comprehension
6. Source of information: reader based and text based
7. Type of instruction: implicit
8. Type of cognitive processing: simultaneous

Procedure

1. The teacher asks the students to predict what will happen in the story by using the title and any available pictures.
2. She continues her questioning by asking the students why they made their predictions.
3. The students read to a turning point in the story.
4. The teacher asks the students whether their predictions were confirmed.
5. The teacher asks the students to support their answers, using the information in the text, and explain their reasoning.
6. The teacher then asks the following questions:

   What do you think is going to happen next?

   Why do you think that?

7. The students read to the next turning point in the story.
8. The teacher repeats steps 4, 5, 6, and 7.
9. When they are finished reading, the teacher and the students react to the story as a whole.
10. The teacher leads the students to analyze the story in relation to other stories, personal experiences, and the author's purpose.
11. The teacher discusses the strategies that were used to understand the story.
12. The teacher reviews the meaning of any key vocabulary words.

Further Diagnostic Applications

Basic View of Reading Reading is an active thinking process in which readers predict, confirm, and revise their interpretation, using important textual information. The reflective thought process focuses on not only what was understood but also how it was understood.

Patterns of Strengths and Strategies   A DRTA is appropriate for students who readily engage in constructing meaning as they read. They use what they already know to predict what will happen and then select important information from the text to justify their responses. The teacher discusses not only what the students think but also how the students think.

Learner Patterns That Produce Increased Engagement

1. For active readers who use what they already know and the text to construct meaning, a DRTA allows this reader to construct meaning with guidance from the teacher.
2. For simultaneous readers who use what they already know to understand passages but have difficulty justifying their responses with information from the text, this technique requires readers to justify their thinking with information from the text.

Using the Technique as a Diagnostic Teaching Lesson   For a DRTA to be effective, a majority of the following statements must be answered in the affirmative:

Yes   *No*

_____   _____   1. The student directs and monitors his own learning when reading.

_____   _____   2. The student uses appropriate text-based and reader-based inferences when evaluating predictions.

_____   _____   3. The student is more comfortable summarizing the story than answering questions.

Evidence Base

Schorzman, E. M., & Cheek, E., Jr. (2004). Structured strategy instruction: Investigating an intervention for improving sixth-Graders' reading comprehension. *Reading Psychology, 25,* 37–60.

Web Sites

http://www.nwrel.org/learns/resources/middleupper/drta.pdf
http://www.justreadnow.com/strategies/drta.htm
http://www.indiana.edu/~l517/DRTA.htm

13 Experience–Text–Relationship

**Targeted Reading Levels:
All levels**

Description Experience–text–relationship (ETR) is specifically designed to use children's experiences to teach new concepts and new words in the story. In this technique, the teacher spends time showing students the relationships between what they know and what they are reading, both before and after reading. It is specifically designed for use with students from various cultures (Au, 1993).

Text Stories with an interesting theme or plot that can sustain an in-depth discussion

Predominant Focus of Instruction

1. Processing focus: meaning
2. Instructional phase: before and after reading
3. Response mode emphasized: oral discussion
4. Strategy emphasized: elaboration
5. Skill emphasized: literal and nonliteral comprehension
6. Source of information: reader-based phasing to text based
7. Type of instruction: implicit
8. Type of cognitive processing: simultaneous

Procedure

1. The teacher chooses an appropriate text.
2. The teacher reads the selected passage to decide the theme, topic, and important points.
3. The teacher thinks about what the students know related to the theme, topic, and important points.
4. The teacher formulates general questions that will initiate a discussion about what the students know.
5. The teacher begins the instruction with a general discussion of what the students know. (This step is the *experience phase* of the lesson and is student initiated.)
6. The teacher uses the information generated to tie the students' experiences directly to the story. She uses pictures and information that come directly from the story. (This step is teacher directed.)
7. She asks the students to make a prediction based on the discussion (student input).
8. Then, if necessary, the teacher sets other purposes for reading (teacher input).
9. The students read a portion of the story to see whether their predictions are right. This activity begins the *text phase* of the lesson.
10. The teacher returns to predictions and asks the students what they have learned so far about these predictions.
11. The teacher sets additional purposes.
12. The teacher calls attention to important information in the text if necessary.
13. The teacher alternates periods of silent reading and discussion until the entire story has been read.
14. When the entire story has been read, the teacher directs a discussion of the key ideas in the story.
15. She then compares the key ideas in the text to the key experiences of the students by returning to the information gained during the experience phase of the lesson. This process is called the *relationship phase* and is teacher directed.
16. The teacher then contrasts the key ideas in the text with the students' experiences.

17.   The teacher summarizes the main relationships after the discussion is complete.
18.   Finally, the teacher recommends that the students use the ETR steps when they read on their own.

Modification   From this technique emerge instructional conversations, which are used widely with English-language learners and other diverse populations. Instructional conversations have less structure on exactly how to do the conversation but focus on the aspects of the instructional conversation. The conversational elements are a challenging, non-threatening climate; responsiveness to students; discussion with connected interchanges; and turn taking. The instructional elements are a thematic focus, using background knowledge, promoting complex language use, proving statements, and sometimes direct teaching.

Further Diagnostic Applications

Basic View of Reading   Reading is an interactive process in which the learners use what they know to interpret what the text says. Readers need assistance learning how to figure out what they know that is useful to interpret the text. They need assistance in making connections between this information and what the text says.

Patterns of Strengths and Strategies   The ETR technique is appropriate for students who need assistance in bringing their background knowledge to the text. It is especially useful for multicultural students who experience a gap between the way they talk about their experiences and the way an author describes those same experiences. This technique helps these students relate their own language and experiences to the text.

Learner Patterns That Produce Increased Engagement

1.   For passive learners who read text without relating what they know, ETR focuses on the students' experience during every step of the lesson.
2.   For passive learners who will not venture a guess while reading, ETR gives them the tools to make a guess.

Using the Technique as a Diagnostic Teaching Lesson   For ETR to be effective, a majority of the following statements must be answered in the affirmative:

Yes   *No*

_____   _____   1. The student can orally express what he knows.

_____   _____   2. The student can make a prediction.

_____   _____   3. With teacher assistance, the student can see the relationship between his experience and what the text says.

Evidence Base

Kucan, L., & Beck, I. L. (2003). Inviting students to talk about expository texts: A comparison of two discourse environments and their effects on comprehension. *Reading Research and Instruction, 42,* 1–31.

Many, J. E. (2002). An exhibition and analysis of verbal tapestries: Understanding how scaffolding is woven into the fabric of instructional conversations. *Reading Research Quarterly, 37,* 376–407.

Web Sites

http://www.ncela.gwu.edu/pubs/ncrcdsll/epr2
http://www.cal.org/resources/digest/ncrcds03.html

14 Explicit Teaching

Targeted Reading Levels: Depends on the strategy or skill being taught

Description Explicit teaching is a lesson framework that directly instructs a student in the strategies and skills of reading. The lesson framework is based on making the task relevant to the student and directly teaching the task through examples and modeling. The teacher systematically plans activities to increase independent application of the strategy or skill.

Text Text chosen or constructed to teach the targeted task

Predominant Focus of Instruction

1. Processing focus: print or meaning
2. Instructional phase: before and during reading
3. Response mode emphasized: oral discussion
4. Strategy emphasized: monitoring
5. Skill emphasized: depends on task
6. Source of information: depends on task, most often the text
7. Type of instruction: explicit
8. Type of cognitive processing: successive

Procedure

1. The teacher selects the strategy or skill to be taught.
2. The teacher selects a series of texts to illustrate the strategy or skill.
3. The teacher introduces the strategy or skill. For example, she may choose finding the main idea in paragraphs.
4. She explains the reason why learning this strategy or skill will facilitate reading performance. In this example, she may say that finding the main idea is important because it helps us remember facts using one idea rather than many different facts.
5. She asks students how this strategy is like other strategies or skills that they have learned. This approach helps them understand the reasons for learning a particular skill. In this example, she may say, "We already studied how to identify key vocabulary words. How did this help us?" The students and teacher discuss how these words were often what the text was mainly about.
6. The teacher explains the process of the strategy or skill. For example, she may say, "When deciding on a main idea, you think to yourself, 'What does each sentence tell about and how is the information alike?' How the information is alike becomes the main idea."
7. The teacher demonstrates how to think when one uses the strategy or skill. A sample demonstration might include the steps that follow.
   a. The teacher puts a three- or four-sentence paragraph on an overhead or the chalkboard.
   b. She summarizes each sentence aloud.
   c. She tells how each sentence is related to the main idea.
   d. She explains that the way the sentences are alike is what the paragraph is mostly about, or the main idea.
8. The students and the teacher do the next example together. The students talk through the new example, explaining what they are doing, why they are doing it, and how they are doing it. The teacher explains her thinking to clarify any steps in the process.

9. The students do the next example by talking through how they complete the task. Then the students tell how this task will help them read.
10. The teacher provides feedback about what the students say by modeling how she would have completed the task.
11. The students read more paragraphs and use the newly learned task on their own.

Further Diagnostic Applications

Basic View of Reading   Reading is an interactive process in which readers monitor their reading using both text and background knowledge. Reading instruction, therefore, should explicitly teach the student to use reading strategies and skills independently.

Patterns of Strengths and Strategies   Introducing the new strategy or skill, the approach systematically leads students through the reasoning process related to the strategy or skill. It takes the separate parts, explains them, and then integrates the parts into the whole task. It is most efficient for the passive or successive learner who profits from seeing how to fit the parts of reading into the whole process.

Learner Patterns That Produce Increased Engagement

1. For simultaneous learners who need to be shown how to control their own learning, mediation would be very short.
2. For passive learners who do not actively use a particular strategy or skill when reading independently, explicit instruction teaches the strategy or skill by showing them how to use it when they are reading.
3. For successive learners who need to be shown exactly how the strategies of reading affect the entire reading process, explicit instruction shows them how the parts fit into the whole.
4. For inattentive learners who approach reading in a trial-and-error fashion and don't understand the exact strategies and skills necessary for consistent reading performance, explicit instruction gives them a system for approaching learning.

Using the Technique as a Diagnostic Teaching Lesson   For explicit teaching to be effective, a majority of the following statements must be answered in the affirmative:

Yes   *No*

_____ _____   1. The student learns from the examples what the process is and how it works.

_____ _____   2. The student improves his ability to do the strategy or skill.

_____ _____   3. The student can explain how the process works in new situations.

Evidence Base

Simmons, D. C., Fuchs, L. S., & Fuchs, D. (1995). Effects of explicit teaching and peer tutoring on the reading achievement of learning-disabled and low-performing students in regular classrooms. *Elementary School Journal, 95,* 387–408.

Web Sites

http://www.ciera.org/library/presos/2001/2001MRACIERA/nduke/01cmndk.pdf
http://olc.spsd.sk.ca/DE/PD/instr/strats/explicitteaching/index.html

15 Feature Analysis Grid   *Targeted Reading Levels: All levels*

Description   A feature analysis grid is a technique to develop word meanings by graphing the major characteristics of target words. Key words are compared as to how they are alike and how they are different.

Text   Isolated words that are associated in categories

Predominant Focus of Instruction

1. Processing focus: meaning
2. Instructional phase: before and after reading
3. Response mode emphasized: oral discussion
4. Strategy emphasized: elaboration
5. Skill emphasized: word meaning and literal comprehension
6. Source of information: reader based
7. Type of instruction: explicit
8. Type of cognitive processing: successive

Procedure

1. The teacher selects categories and words to analyze.
2. The teacher makes a feature analysis grid with a column of words to analyze.
3. The teacher and the students discuss the characteristics of the first word.
4. The teacher adds the characteristics across the top of the grid, indicating the important characteristics with a plus in the respective squares of the grid.
5. The teacher and the students then discuss the second target word.
6. The teacher and the students evaluate this word according to the important features on the grid. The teacher puts a plus on those characteristics that the second target word has and a minus on those that it does not have.
7. The teacher adds any new important characteristics, indicating those with a plus in the appropriate square on the grid. The teacher and the students discuss any uncertain responses. In the example, deserts consist mainly of sand, but there are some snow deserts.
8. The teacher and the students discuss how the two words are alike and how they are different.
9. The procedure is repeated for other words. The teacher adds important characteristics as needed.
10. The teacher adds other words that are prevalent in the students' oral vocabularies to make comparisons between what is new and what is already known.

Modifications

1. A rating scale (1 to 3) can be used to show the relative importance that each characteristic contributes to the meaning of the words.
2. The technique can be used as a prewriting activity for a comparison paragraph among words and concepts.

Further Diagnostic Applications

Basic View of Reading   Reading is an interactive process that is based on what the reader already knows about the words used in the text. Comprehension is facilitated by understanding the specific attributes of the words used in a passage.

Patterns of Strengths and Strategies   The feature analysis grid is most appropriate for students who have a well-developed background of experiences but who overgeneralize word meanings, failing to see the likenesses and differences between specific definitional meanings. For these students, the graphic representation of important characteristics organizes the prior knowledge into specific linguistic categories.

Learner Patterns That Produce Increased Engagement

1. For successive learners who have difficulty drawing comparisons among word meanings but have verbal fluency and analyze individual words by their major features, this technique allows them to compare and contrast the major features of words at the same time.
2. For divergent thinkers who notice features other than the major characteristics but easily understand the grid and the relationships among word meanings, this technique focuses that attention on the key features of the words.
3. For passive learners who do not think about the differences among words, this technique helps them think and talk about how words are alike and different.

Using the Technique as a Diagnostic Teaching Lesson   For a feature analysis grid to be effective, a majority of the following statements must be answered in the affirmative:

Yes   *No*

_____   _____   1. The student understands the purpose of the grid and can visualize the negative and positive aspects of the important characteristics.

_____   _____   2. Using the grid, the student develops a clear understanding of the attributes of the target words.

_____   _____   3. The student understands likenesses and differences.

Evidence Base

Bos, C. S., Anders, P. L., & Filip, D. (1985). Semantic feature analysis and long-term learning. *National Reading Conference Yearbook, 34,* 42–47.

Bos, C. S., Anders, P. L., & Filip, D. (1989). The effects of an interactive instructional strategy for enhancing reading comprehension and content area learning for students with learning disabilities. *Journal of Learning Disabilities, 22,* 384–390.

Web Site

http://skyview.vansd.org/REmerson/CD%20Version/Thinking%20And%20Organizing/Semantic%20Feature%20Grid.doc

16 Framed Rhyming Innovations   *Targeted Reading Levels K–3*

Description   The framed rhyming innovations approach is the rewriting of a predictable book that has rhymes that are spelled the same (rime) using a structured frame. The teacher and student rewrite the predictable book using the frame but changing key words.

Text   Predictable books

Predominant Focus of Instruction

1. Processing focus: print
2. Instructional phase: after reading
3. Response mode emphasized: writing
4. Strategy emphasized: prediction
5. Skill emphasized: word identification, word analysis, and sentence comprehension
6. Source of information: reader based and text based
7. Type of instruction: explicit
8. Type of cognitive processing: simultaneous

Procedure

1. The teacher selects a familiar predictable book that can be easily rewritten and has rhyme. For instance, *I Was Walking Down the Road* by Sarah Barchas can easily be rewritten and has rhyming phrases.
2. The teacher prepares a frame for rewriting the predictable book. For *I Was Walking Down the Road,* she would write,

   Complete frame

   I was walking down the road.

   Then I saw a little toad.

   I caught it.

   I picked it up.

   I put it in the cage.

   Frame for innovation

   I was _____.

   Then I _____.

   I caught it.

   I picked it up.

   I put it in the cage.

3. The teacher and the student read the predictable book.
4. The teacher presents the frame for the innovation.
5. The teacher and student reread the complete frame first.
6. The teacher prompts the student for each blank in the frame. She might say, "What are you going to pick up?" The student suggests a frog and writes the word in the blank. "Then I saw a little frog."

7. After the student decides what is going to be picked up, he generates a rhyming word to go with it that makes sense in the first sentence.

frog

dog

log

8. The student rewrites the first line. In this case he thinks of something that fits with "I saw a little frog." The student said, "I was running with my dog." He writes this line below the frame and rewrites the rest of the phrase.
9. This procedure is repeated several times so that the student can make his own book.
10. The student and teacher make a book based on the rewriting of the framed predictable book.

Modifications

1. *Reviewing writing for misspellings*. One of the best ways to learn about print is to look at the students' own writing. The teacher and the student look at the story to find those words that are misspelled, and then the teacher helps the student figure out the spelling by using sound boxes (see "Sound Boxes" in this part).
2. *Reviewing writing for word families*. When the teacher asks the student to generate words that rhyme with a particular word, the teacher can extend these patterns by showing how the spelling pattern is part of longer words. For the *og* sound cluster, these words could be initially suggested: *frog, dog, log, jog, hog*. Then the teacher shows how these little words are also in longer words, such as *doggy, froggy, logging, hogging, jogger, hotdog, underdog*.

Further Diagnostic Applications

Basic View of Reading   Reading is an interactive process. By using story patterns that rhyme, students have to use their own knowledge about rhymes in words and synthesize sounds to make words that rhyme and rime. But they also have to make sure the word fits with the story pattern. This approach will facilitate word identification, word analysis and sentence comprehension.

Patterns of Strengths and Strategies   The framed rhyming innovations approach is most appropriate for students who have facility with language and phonemic awareness. If the student uses his own language and sense of phonic analogies, then this approach matches his own way for figuring out words.

Learner Patterns That Produce Increased Engagement

1. For simultaneous learners who readily think of the rhymes in words and see the analogous relationship among words, this approach uses the strength of seeing patterns to develop decoding processes.
2. For extremely creative verbal students who easily think of words that will fit the story, this approach increases the knowledge of word patterns and phonic analogies.

Using the Technique as a Diagnostic Teaching Lesson   For the framed innovations approach to be effective, a majority of the following statements must be answered in the affirmative:

Yes   No

_____ _____ 1. The student can segment sounds.

_____ _____ 2. The student applies analogies to both known and unknown words.

_____ _____ 3. The student can easily think of rhyming words that fit in the predictable frame.

Evidence Base

Christensen, C. A., & Bowey, J. A. (2005). The efficacy of orthographic rime, grapheme–phoneme correspondence, and implicit phonics approaches to teaching decoding skills. *Scientific Studies of Reading, 9,* 327–349.

Smith, M., Walker, B., & Ahrens, I. (2007). Using literature to support phonemic awareness and phonics for struggling readers. In B. Walker & C. Dybdhal (Eds.), *Supporting struggling readers in classrooms and tutoring Norwood, MA;* Christopher Gordon Publishing.

Walton. P. D. (2002). Beginning reading by teaching in rime analogy: Effects on phonological skills, letter-sound knowledge, working memory, and word-reading strategies. *Scientific Studies of Reading, 6,* 79–115.

Web Sites

http://www.readwritethink.org/lessons/lesson_view.asp?id=216
http://www.readwritethink.org/lessons/lesson_view.asp?id=131
http://www.readwritethink.org/lessons/lesson_view.asp?id=157

16

Framed Rhyming Innovations

17 Generative-Reciprocal Inference Procedure

Description   The generative-reciprocal inference procedure (GRIP) is an instructional procedure for teaching children how to make inferences in both reading and writing. It involves reading and writing short paragraphs that require making an inference. After the teacher models the inferencing procedure, students, in pairs, write and exchange paragraphs that require an inference.

Text   Constructed by students and teacher

Predominant Focus of Instruction

1. Processing focus: meaning
2. Instructional phase: during reading
3. Response mode emphasized: written
4. Strategy emphasized: prediction and monitoring
5. Skill emphasized: nonliteral comprehension
6. Source of information: reader based
7. Type of instruction: explicit
8. Type of cognitive processing: successive phasing to simultaneous

Procedure

1. The teacher selects a short paragraph to model how to make an inference.
2. The teacher puts the paragraph on the board or an overhead projector and highlights key words as the paragraph is read aloud. For example,

   Dennis looked surprised. He had not intended it to happen. It was just that getting the dog food was difficult because it was behind the table. "It was my new lamp," said Mrs. Wilson. "I just purchased it yesterday."

   What had Dennis done?

3. The teacher explains that an inference is figuring out the key idea that is not in the text by using the key words that are in the text.
4. The teacher justifies how she figured out the inference by explaining how she used the text clues together with what she knew.
5. The teacher uses several more example paragraphs, letting the students make and justify the inference until they understand the procedure. The suggested sequence is the following:
   a. The teacher marks key words, the students make the inference, and the teacher explains the justification.
   b. The students mark the key words; the teacher makes the inference and explains the reasons.
   c. The students mark the key words and make the inference; the teacher explains the reasons.
   d. The students mark the key words, make the inference, and explain their reasoning.
6. Students write their own inference paragraphs in pairs, starting by creating a list of five or more key words.

Generative-Reciprocal Inference Procedure

17

7. The students write the paragraph without telling the inference.
8. In groups of four (two pairs), the students exchange paragraphs.
9. The students mark key words, make an inference, and explain their thinking to one another.
10. The students discuss their thinking, giving each other feedback about the inferencing process.

Further Diagnostic Applications

Basic View of Reading   Reading is a socially constructed process in which learners use what they know to interpret what is written in the text. Readers need assistance learning how to identify key words in the text that can be used to predict unstated information and meaning. They also need assistance justifying how the text information and what they know support the inference.

Patterns of Strengths and Strategies   The GRIP technique is appropriate for students who need assistance in identifying key words that can be used in making inferences by using these words and what they already know.

Learner Patterns That Produce Increased Engagement

1. For passive learners who read text without figuring out the unstated ideas needed to interpret text, GRIP helps focus how information in the text can suggest ideas not directly stated in the text.
2. For passive learners who do not identify important textual information to make inferences, GRIP shows them how selecting key information can facilitate thinking.

Using the Technique as a Diagnostic Teaching Lesson   For GRIP to be effective, a majority of the following statements must be answered in the affirmative:

Yes   No

_____ _____   1. The student has facility with written communication.

_____ _____   2. The student can work collaboratively.

_____ _____   3. With teacher assistance, the student can select important information and see how it supports an inference.

Evidence Base

Reutzel, D. R., & Hollingsworth, P. M. (1988). Highlighting key vocabulary: A generative-reciprocal procedure for teaching selected inference types. *Reading Research Quarterly, 23,* 358–378.

18 Graphic Organizers

Targeted Reading Levels 3–12

Description The graphic organizer technique is designed to provide a visual representation of the key words in content-area readings. By conceptually arranging the key words in a chapter, the teacher and students develop an idea framework for relating unfamiliar vocabulary words and concepts.

Text Expository text

Predominant Focus of Instruction

1. Processing focus: meaning
2. Instructional phase: before reading
3. Response mode emphasized: oral discussion with graphic information
4. Strategy emphasized: elaboration
5. Skill emphasized: word meaning literal comprehension, and inquiry thinking
6. Source of information: text based
7. Type of instruction: explicit
8. Type of cognitive processing: simultaneous

Procedure

1. The teacher chooses a chapter from a textbook.
2. The teacher selects key vocabulary words and concepts.
3. The teacher arranges the key words into a diagram that shows how the key words interrelate.
4. The teacher adds a few familiar words to the diagram so students can connect their prior knowledge with the new information.
5. The teacher presents the graphic organizer on the chalkboard, an overhead transparency, or using PowerPoint. As she presents the organizer, she explains the relationships.
6. Students are encouraged to explain how they think the information is related.
7. The students read the chapter referring as needed to the graphic organizer.
8. After reading the selection, the students may return to the graphic organizer to clarify and elaborate concepts.

Modifications

1. Students can generate their own graphic organizers after they read the chapter. In this situation, graphic organizers are an implicit instructional technique. The herringbone technique is an excellent example. The herringbone diagram uses the outline of a fishbone to help students organize their thoughts in a simple, visual way.
   As students read, they put down the supporting details like who, what, where, and when or just writing the important points of an expository piece on the scales of the fishbone. Then the students review the the supporting details and collapse them onto the spine of the herringbone as they construct the main idea. This Web site has multiple examples: http://www.enchantedlearning.com/graphicorganizers/fishbone.
2. Students can work in cooperative learning groups to construct a graphic organizer after they read. This adds a socio-interactive aspect to the technique.

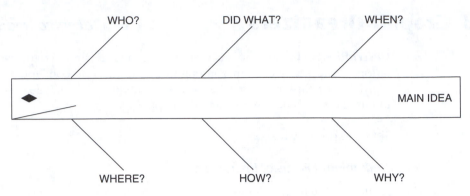

Note. This is the fishbone diagram.

Further Diagnostic Applications

Basic View of Reading   Reading is an active process in which learners use what they know to elaborate and extend what the text says. By constructing a visual map of word relationships, the teacher helps create an idea framework prior to reading the information.

Patterns of Strengths and Strategies   The graphic organizer technique is appropriate for students who profit from a visual framework relating unfamiliar words and ideas to known information. It is especially useful for the highly visual students who profit from seeing relationships in order to tie them to what they are reading.

Learner Patterns That Produce Increased Engagement

1. For simultaneous readers who think in visual images by relating patterns of information, graphic organizers help relate and elaborate topic knowledge.
*2. For readers who read without relating what they know to the text, graphic organizers help them relate what they know to unfamiliar concepts.
*3. For passive readers who read words without defining their meaning or conceptualizing how words relate, graphic organizers help them focus on new word meanings and concepts.

Using the Technique as a Diagnostic Teaching Lesson   For graphic organizers to be effective, a majority of the following statements must be answered in the affirmative:

Yes	No	
_____	_____	1. The student can easily see the visual relationship of key words.
_____	_____	2. The student refers to the organizer as he reads.
_____	_____	3. The student can organize the information learned.

Evidence Base

Alvermann, D., & Booth, P. (1986). Children's transfer of graphic organizer instruction. *Reading Psychology, 7,* 87–100.

DiCecco, V. M., & Gleason, M. M. (2002). Using graphic organizers to attain relational knowledge from expository text. *Journal of Learning Disabilities, 35,* 306–320.

Robinson, D. H., & Kiewra, K. A. (1995). Visual argument: Graphic organizers are superior to outlines in improving learning from text. *Journal of Educational Psychology, 87,* 455–467.

Web Sites
http://www.enchantedlearning.com/graphicorganizers/tchart
http://www.edhelper.com/teachers/graphic_organizers.htm
http://www.eduplace.com/graphicorganizer
http://www.writedesignonline.com/organizers

18 Graphic Organizers

19 Group Investigation Approach   *Targeted Reading Levels 4–12*

Description   Group investigation uses cooperative groups to plan and execute extended projects. By focusing their questions, investigations, and responses within the project group, the students use their interests to focus their learning and assist one another in learning the content information.

Predominant Focus of Instruction

1. Processing focus: meaning
2. Instructional phase: before, during, and after reading
3. Response mode emphasized: oral discussion
4. Strategy emphasized: elaboration
5. Skill emphasized: literal, nonliteral comprehension, and inquiry
6. Sources of information: reader based with some text based
7. Type of instruction: implicit
8. Type of cognitive processing: simultaneous

Procedure

1. The teacher provides an overview of the topic, framing the topic with various interesting questions (e.g., What can we learn from Native American cultures in Montana?) and suggestions about avenues to explore.
2. The students and teacher scan various information sources: speakers, films, texts, magazines, TV specials, Web resources, and so on.
3. The students meet in buzz groups to generate what they would like to investigate.
4. The groups compare their lists, eliminating repetitions and finally creating a common list of questions to investigate.
5. This common list is classified into several key categories with subtopics.
6. Research groups are organized around the subtopics. Students join groups according to their interest.
7. The groups plan the investigation, recording the topic, group members, roles (coordinator, resource persons, recorder, and so on), and the subquestions each member or pair are investigating.
8. The groups clarify the scope of investigation and list possible resources.
9. The groups carry out the investigation by summarizing information and sharing this information in reporting sessions during class work times.
10. The groups prepare a final response, focusing on what is most important to present to the whole class and how to present this information.
11. The teacher and students can prepare summary questions to be used as an evaluation of student learning.
12. Students reflect on what they learned by writing or discussing the important aspects of their learning.

Further Diagnostic Applications

Basic View of Reading   Reading, thinking, and composing are socio-interactive processes in which the social context influences what students view as important and interesting to learn about a topic. Through sharing their investigations in small groups, students focus and elaborate their understanding of a subject area.

Patterns of Strengths and Strategies   The group investigation approach is appropriate for students who can discuss their ideas in a group, which encourages them to seek more information to clarify uncertainties, thus giving them more control over their learning. The conversations help these students connect new learning to their experiences.

Modification   The entire process can be conducted through Web searches as teachers focus on how to use Internet information effectively.

Learner Patterns That Produce Increased Engagement

1. For self-directed readers who profit from sharing their ideas in a group, group investigation helps these students clarify and elaborate their ideas.
2. For readers who profit from pursuing individual interests but also need a group to focus personal interests and to complete ideas, group investigation uses interests and group interaction to encourage elaboration.
3. For readers who tend to focus on irrelevant textual information and narrow personal experiences, group investigation helps these students focus on important information and verbalize important ideas in a group.

Using the Technique as a Diagnostic Teaching Lesson   For group investigation to be effective, a majority of the following statements must be answered in the affirmative:

Yes	*No*	
_____	_____	1. The student can share information in a group.
_____	_____	2. The student likes expository text so that he finds it engaging enough to pursue answers to questions.
_____	_____	3. The student can generate questions to investigate.

Evidence Base

Matthews, M. W., & Cobb, M. B. (2005). Broadening the interpretive lens: Considering individual development along with sociocultural views of learning to understand young children's interactions during socially mediated literacy events. *Journal of Literacy Research, 37,* 325–364.

Web Sites

http://www.readwritethink.org/lessons/lesson_view.asp?id=416
http://www.inquiry.uiuc.edu/php/units.php

Guided Reading

20 Guided Reading   *Targeted Reading Levels 1–6*

Description   Guided reading is used to develop reading abilities by having children read "just right" trade books that provide a slight challenge as the teacher provides a model for how to read the particular book. With the teacher model and guidance, the student assumes more independent reading behaviors.

Text   Leveled trade books

Predominant Focus of Instruction

1. Processing focus: print and meaning
2. Instructional phase: before, during, and after reading
3. Response mode emphasized: discussion
4. Strategy emphasized: prediction and monitoring
5. Skill emphasized: word recognition and literal comprehension
6. Source of information: text based and reader based
7. Type of instruction: implicit
8. Type of cognitive processing: simultaneous

Procedure

1. The teacher assesses the children's reading performance using leveled books. Their instructional level is reached when they have 90% accuracy in word recognition.
2. Students are placed into guided reading groups based on their instructional level. As the year progresses, children are regrouped based on reading level.
3. For younger children, the teacher pages through the book discussing the pictures.
4. The teacher guides the learning by reading the book aloud and discussing the book with the children.
5. Children are supported as they read along with the teacher. Young children are encouraged to use their finger to point to the words as they read.
6. Children are focused on print concepts and reading the text using multiple readings. These strategies involve predicting, sampling, confirming, cross-checking, and self-correcting using the cuing system.
7. Children reread the text while the teacher listens to the children reading orally. The teacher prompts children to use cues to figure out words.
8. Children engage in retelling the story to each other while the teacher guides them to focus on what happened in the beginning, middle, and end.
9. Children engage in projects that extend their story understanding.
10. Children take guided reading books home to read to family members.

Further Diagnostic Applications

Basic View of Reading   Reading is a socio-interactive process in which children read with the teacher to create meaning. Through sharing information in a small group, children refine their use of print strategies and their understanding.

Patterns of Strengths and Strategies   Guided reading is most appropriate for students who can learn to read in a small group and readily understand how to figure out words.

Learner Patterns That Produce Increased Engagement

1. For successive readers who profit by following the teacher's model, guided reading helps these students integrate the cuing systems.
2. For simultaneous learners who profit from hearing the whole story read at once, guided reading instruction helps these students create an expectation for the printed words.
*3. For readers who are bound by the text and believe that reading means getting the words right, guided reading helps these readers think about the overall meaning and use this understanding to self-correct mistakes.

Using the Technique as a Diagnostic Teaching Lesson
For guided reading instruction to be effective, a majority of the following statements must be answered in the affirmative:

Yes   *No*

_____ _____ 1. The student can follow the teacher's model and looks at the words as the teacher reads them.

_____ _____ 2. The student can follow an oral demonstration of strategic print processing.

_____ _____ 3. The student can model the teacher's use of multiple cuing strategies.

Evidence Base

Reistma, P. (1988). Reading practice for beginners: Effects of guided reading, reading-while-listening, and independent reading with computer-based speech feedback. *Reading Research Quarterly, 23,* 219–235.

Web Sites

http://teacher.scholastic.com/professional/teachstrat/guidedreading.htm
http://www.msrossbec.com/literacy_index.html
http://www.hubbardscupboard.org/guided_reading.html

21 Imagery Instruction

Targeted Reading Levels K–Adult

Description   Imagery instruction uses sensory images related to the story line to increase active comprehension and activate background knowledge about (a) situations and characters in a story or (b) key concepts in expository text.

Text   Narrative text or concepts in expository text

Predominant Focus of Instruction

1. Processing focus: meaning
2. Instructional phase: before reading
3. Response mode emphasized: oral discussion
4. Strategy emphasized: prediction and monitoring
5. Skill emphasized: nonliteral comprehension
6. Source of information: reader based
7. Type of instruction: implicit (can be adapted to explicit)
8. Type of cognitive processing: simultaneous

Procedure

1. The teacher selects a text.
2. To begin the lesson, the teacher has the students relax in their chairs.
3. The teacher uses imagery prompts such as "When you read this story or passage, I want you to make pictures or scenes about it."
4. The teacher can create a guided imagery. See below.
5. The students read the text.
6. Sometimes the teacher stops the students during reading so they can draw a picture of what they are seeing.
7. When they are finished reading, the students can share their images with a partner.

Modifications

1. Using guided imagery rather than a prompt.
   a. The teacher identifies key events and characters or key concepts, depending on the type of text.
   b. The teacher writes a guided journey that uses these key items. In the journey, the teacher intersperses calming statements with the story events and character descriptions or the key concepts. The following is an example that might be used prior to reading:

   Close your eyes. . . . and relax in your chair. . . . Now listen to the noises in the room. . . . Can you hear them? Feel the temperature of the room. . . . Now turn the noises of this room into the sounds of a meadow. . . . What kind of day is it? You can hear a river. . . . Begin walking toward the river. . . . You are closer. . . . closer. . . . closer to the river. . . . As you reach the river. . . . you see a boat. . . . Walk toward the boat. . . . You get in the boat and begin to float . . . down . . . down . . . down the river you float. . . . The current or waves begin to rush faster. . . . faster . . . faster. . . You see rocks and boulders ahead . . . You are steering the boat through the rapids. . . . I will leave you now. . . . When you have finished your journey . . . you may return to this room . . . and open your eyes.

    c. To begin, the teacher has the students relax in their chairs and think of sounds and smells relating to the setting. Then she reads the prompt or the journey in a calm, serene voice, interspersing action statements with calming statements.

    d. After several minutes, the teacher tells the students to return to the classroom when they have completed their journeys in the mind.

2. The guided imagery can form the basis for a dictated language experience story. The teacher uses a list of targeted sight words to compose the guided imagery (see "Language Experience Approach" in this part).

3. The motor imaging technique is specifically designed to develop word meanings by using images and movements related to the key attributes of a word. This technique ties together actions, images, and words.

Further Diagnostic Applications

Basic View of Reading   Reading is an active process that uses personal images (reader-based inferencing) to create meaning. As the students read, they form an expectation for meaning that is represented by images of specific events.

Patterns of Strengths and Strategies   Imagery instruction is a technique for students who prefer to create images while they read. It is appropriate for the reflective, simultaneous thinker who refers to specific events and images when discussing text. Using guided imagery helps these learners translate images into a verbal response.

Learner Patterns That Produce Increased Engagement

1. For simultaneous thinkers who use images to construct meaning that often changes the meaning to fit their images, this technique helps them see how their own ideas and images affect comprehension.

2. For extremely imaginative thinkers who enjoy sharing their images and comparing them to the text, this technique allows them to use this strength when comprehending.

3. For simultaneous reflective thinkers who use images instead of words when thinking, this technique allows images to be connected with words.

*4. For passive readers who do not check what they know, learning to image can increase their elaboration and monitoring of what they read.

*5. For extremely literal thinkers who seldom construct images, imagery instruction provides a support for them to construct images before reading, thus increasing their understanding.

Using the Technique as a Diagnostic Teaching Lesson   For imagery instruction to be effective, a majority of the following statements must be answered in the affirmative:

Yes	*No*	
_____	_____	1. The student constructs a coherent and logical ending to the guided journey.
_____	_____	2. The student reads with increased involvement, comparing his images with the text.
_____	_____	3. The student does not overly rely on the images and make the text fit his predictions.

Evidence Base

Gambrell, L. B., & Bales, R. J. (1986). Mental imagery and the comprehension-monitoring performance of fourth- and fifth-grade poor readers. *Reading Research Quarterly, 21,* 454–464.

Gambrell, L. B., & Jawitz, P. B. (1993). Mental imagery, text illustrations, and children's story comprehension and recall. *Reading Research Quarterly, 28,* 264–276.

Web Sites

http://www.readingonline.org/research/Sadoski.html
http://www.readwritethink.org/lessons/lesson_view.asp?id=139
http://www.understandmore.com/research.htm

22 Implicit Teaching

Target Reading Levels: All levels

Description   Implicit teaching is a nondirective approach to instruction in which the teacher creates an instructional situation that stimulates thinking about specific reading tasks. The teacher participates only as a cognitive inquirer, asking the student, "How did you know that?" The student makes generalizations because he is immersed in a literate context.

Text   Authentic texts selected to demonstrate the strategy or skill that is targeted for instruction

Predominant Focus of Instruction

1. Processing focus: print or meaning
2. Instructional phase: after reading
3. Response mode emphasized: oral discussion
4. Strategy emphasized: elaboration
5. Skill emphasized: depends on child, environment, and scaffolds (prompts)
6. Source of information: reader-based phasing to text based
7. Type of instruction: implicit
8. Type of cognitive processing: depends on child and task

Procedure

1. The teacher decides on the targeted learning outcome.
2. The teacher strategically arranges the physical environment so that students can discuss with the teacher what they read in a relaxed atmosphere.
3. In prominent places in the room, the teacher arranges attractive books or printed materials that incorporate the strategy or skill.
4. The teacher creates a social activity that causes the students to use the targeted strategy or skill in a meaningful way.
5. When the students use print to make sense of their environment, the teacher asks, "How did you know that?"
6. The teacher creates the expectation of the learning outcome by discussing the learning outcome informally. She says, "Did you notice . . . ?"
7. When appropriate, the teacher demonstrates reading the text for meaning and enjoyment. She says, "When I read that I thought . . . "
8. The teacher creates a similar experience that causes the students again to use the targeted strategy or skill in a meaningful way.

Comment: Implicit instruction is an instructional format in which the teacher assumes an indirect role in mediating learning. This type of instruction is associated with a whole language environment in which the children are more actively involved in directing their own learning. Techniques fall along a continuum, ranging from *teacher directed* to *student directed*. Implicit instruction has less teacher-directed instruction and more student participation in the learning activity.

Further Diagnostic Applications

Basic View of Reading   Reading is a socio-interactive process in which readers use what they know to make sense of the situational context. Reading instruction, therefore, should consist of creating a situational context in which students can use and discuss print to make sense of their environment.

Patterns of Strengths and Strategies This format engages students in literate activities in which they construct meaning with text. The teacher asks a student what he did to make sense of his environment. The student who actively restructures his environment so that it makes sense learns easily through this method.

Learner Patterns That Produce Increased Engagement

1. For active learners who need learning activities to make sense, this method allows them to use thinking strategies in natural learning environments.
2. For active learners who prefer to learn without teacher direction, this method allows them to direct their own learning.
3. For simultaneous learners who need to experience the whole before understanding the parts, this method allows them to use the socio-interactive experience to understand the parts of reading.

Using the Technique as a Diagnostic Teaching Lesson For implicit teaching to be effective, both of the following statements must be answered in the affirmative:

Yes   *No*

_____ _____ 1. The student actively explores the context to make sense of his reading.

_____ _____ 2. The student can explain his reasons for the way language works.

Evidence Base

Maranzana, E. M. (1998). Toward a theory of reading acquisition as a synthesis of implicit and explicit learning. *Dissertation Abstracts International Section A: Humanities and Social Sciences, 58* (7–A), 2624.

Web Sites

http://olc.spsd.sk.ca/DE/PD/instr/strats/readmeaning/index.html
http://olc.spsd.sk.ca/DE/PD/instr/strats/inquiry/index.html

23 Impress Method

Targeted Reading Levels K–5

Description   The impress method uses unison oral reading between the teacher and the student. The teacher and student sit side by side, with the teacher reading out loud slightly louder and ahead of the student, modeling fluent and expressive oral reading.

Text   Self-selected text is recommended

Predominant Focus of Instruction

1. Processing focus: print
2. Instructional phase: during reading
3. Response mode emphasized: oral production
4. Strategy emphasized: prediction
5. Skill emphasized: fluency and word identification
6. Source of information: reader based
7. Type of instruction: implicit
8. Type of cognitive processing: simultaneous

Procedure

1. The student and the teacher select a text that is near the student's frustration-level reading and about 200 words long.
2. The teacher and the student read the text in unison. The teacher reads slightly ahead of, and slightly louder than, the student.
3. The teacher sits on the right side of the student and reads with the student.
4. The teacher moves her finger along the line of print so that the student's eyes can follow the reading.
5. The student's eyes follow the line of print as he reads.
6. As the student gains success through understanding the context, the teacher gradually lets him take the lead.
7. At this time, the teacher releases her lead in reading; however, she supplies difficult words when needed.

Modifications

1. Echo reading is similar to the impress method; however, the teacher reads a line of a story, and the student echoes her model by reading the same line, emulating her intonation and phrasing.
2. Unison choral reading can be used with a group of students.
3. The textual characteristics seem to influence the effectiveness of impress reading. Rhythmic and repetitive texts seem to increase the student's participation. A good source is Shel Silverstein's *Where the Sidewalk Ends*.

Further Diagnostic Applications

Basic View of Reading   Reading is a text-based process of accurate and automatically identifying words. Thus, automatic word identification precedes understanding.

Therefore, accurate word identification is increased by unison reading, with the teacher modeling fluent oral reading.

Patterns of Strengths and Strategies   The impress method is most appropriate for students who make a series of miscues without using passage meaning to self-correct the miscues, which is often the result of reading at frustration level for an extended period of time. In the impress method, the student follows the teacher's model and emulates her fluent, accurate, oral reading.

Learner Patterns That Produce Increased Engagement

1. For simultaneous learners who rely heavily on background knowledge when reading orally and who do not attend to graphic cues, the impress method establishes accurate identification of words through use of the overall textual meaning and unison reading.
2. For nonfluent readers who are not fluent because of a heavy emphasis on phonic instruction, this method can rapidly increase oral reading fluency by providing a model of fluent reading.
*3. For nonreaders who have not established a sight vocabulary, this technique can develop the student's sight vocabulary, particularly when high-interest material is used.

Using the Technique as a Diagnostic Teaching Lesson   For the impress method to be effective, a majority of the following statements must be answered in the affirmative:

Yes   No

_____ _____ 1. The student is sufficiently motivated to read along with the teacher.
_____ _____ 2. The student begins to track with the teacher and follows the model.
_____ _____ 3. An increase in sight word accuracy and fluency is a result of using the method.

Evidence Base

Flood, J., Lapp, D., & Fisher, D. (2005) Neurological impress method plus. *Reading Psychology, 26,* 147–160.
Heckelman, R.(1969). A neurological-impress method of remedial-reading instruction. *Academic Therapy, 4,* 277–282.

Web Sites

http://www.sil.org/lingualinks/literacy/otherresources/glossaryofliteracyterms/WhatIsTheNeurological ImpressMe.htm
http://www.sil.org/lingualinks/literacy/ImplementALiteracyProgram/UsingEchoReading.htm
http://www.nellieedge.com/articles_resources/Resources_Neuro.htm
http://www.ops.org/reading/fluencystrategies.htm

24 Interactive Writing

Targeted Reading Levels K–2

Description Interactive writing is a collaboration between the teacher and her students where they jointly write text. The teacher models writing words as students engage in composing text. Interactive writing provides children with opportunities to hear sounds in words and connect those sounds with corresponding letters. Interactive writing is a unique opportunity to help children see the relationship between reading and writing.

Text Collaborative teacher and student written text

Predominant Focus of Instruction

1. Processing focus: meaning
2. Instructional phase: during reading
3. Response mode emphasized: written discourse
4. Strategy emphasized: elaboration
5. Skill emphasized: word analysis and sentence comprehension
6. Source of information: reader based
7. Type of instruction: implicit
8. Type of cognitive processing: successive

Procedure

1. The teacher and students jointly discuss a book or experience and decide on a topic to write about. As they compose the text, the teacher acts as the facilitator modeling, adding, summarizing, and combining the children's ideas.
2. As the students begin telling or retelling the story or experience, the teacher begins writing and talking aloud about the words she is writing.
3. The teacher asks a student to take over writing the next couple of words as the students continue telling the story or experience.
4. As they continue, the teacher takes the pen back and talks aloud about the sounds as she spells a word.
5. She invites another child to continue writing the letters as all students sound out the words and the student writes the word as it is spelled out.
6. As they are writing the words, the teacher discusses the words. The students and teacher alternately share the pen.
7. When the story is completely written, the teacher reads the story as a whole and discusses story construction.

Modifications

1. A story map can be developed prior to writing so that each student adds information that will fit the story map (see "Story Mapping" in this part).
2. Cartoons and comic books can be used as a framework for the story line.

Further Diagnostic Applications

Basic View of Reading Reading and writing are socio-interactive processes in which the reader's ideas and knowledge about written conventions can be learned in group interactions and teacher modeling. Through writing, the reader becomes sensitive to written conventions such as letter formation, phonics, spelling, sentence sense, and how stories are constructed so that they make sense.

Patterns of Strengths and Strategies   Interactive writing is most appropriate for students who have facility with telling a story and like to write. This approach helps students develop a sense of the language structures and approach text as a communication between reader and writer.

Learner Patterns That Produce Increased Engagement

1. For successive learners who write well but do not understand that reading and writing are communication processes, this technique provides a tool for talking about reading and writing.
2. For simultaneous learners who do not understand print conventions, this technique provides a tool for talking about how words work.
3. For learners who have verbal difficulty and need to learn how to figure out words, this technique provides an experience in writing words in an interactive group setting, which is less threatening.

Using the Technique as a Diagnostic Teaching Lesson   For interactive writing to be effective, a majority of the following statements must be answered in the affirmative:

Yes	No	
_____	_____	1. The student can form some of the letters and knows letter names.
_____	_____	2. The student prefers to write rather hear sounds in words.
_____	_____	3. The student can tell about the written conventions he is learning.

Evidence Base

Craig, S. A. (2003). The effects of an adapted interactive writing, intervention on kindergarten children's phonological awareness, spelling, and early reading development. *Reading Research Quarterly, 38,* 438–440.

Web Sites

http://www.stanswartz.com/IAW%20excerpt.pdf
http://www.brentwood.k12.ca.us/garin/interactivewriting.htm

25 Internet Inquiry

Targeted Reading Levels 4–12

Description   An Internet inquiry project is where students formulate exploratory questions, locate information on the Internet, and then build knowledge that ultimately reflects their answers to the original questions.

Text   Expository text on the Web

Predominant Focus of Instruction

1. Processing focus: meaning
2. Instructional phase: before and after reading
3. Response mode emphasized: discussion and writing
4. Strategy emphasized: elaboration
5. Skill emphasized: literal, nonliteral comprehension, and inquiry thinking
6. Source of information: text based and reader based
7. Type of instruction: implicit
8. Type of cognitive processing: simultaneous

Procedure

1. The teacher and the students select a topic that is interesting and somewhat familiar to explore.
2. They begin by asking or framing meaningful target questions.
3. As students write these questions, they can place them on an I-chart (inquiry chart; Hoffman, 1992) so that they can keep focused on the target questions (see below).

Topic	Question 1	Question 2	Question 3	Interesting Information
What We Know				
Keyword Source				
Keyword Source				
Keyword Source				
Keyword Source				

4. The teacher and the students brainstorm information they already know about the questions. This information is put on the I-chart.
5. Students develop a search strategy for locating multiple sources of information. Using the Web, the students examine their questions for key words. They try to develop a key word pool to improve the likelihood of locating useful information.
6. The teacher and students place the keywords in Web search tools (e.g., Google, Dogpile, Yahoo!) to locate information.
7. The teacher and the students decide if the Web information is important and accurate by evaluating the Web resources collected and comparing it to their questions.
    a. Students decide if the information at the Web site is related to their target questions.
    b. Students decide if the Web site was constructed by an expert, organization, or qualified person or group that has the specialized knowledge needed.
    c. Students evaluate the information by cross-checking information among Web sites for each question.
8. The teacher and the students ascertain whether they are missing important information. If they are, the students return to the search again and locate new sites.
9. Students go back to the target question and construct responses to their questions. Students synthesize the information for each question into summaries and put the summaries on the I-chart.
10. Students decide how to communicate the information. Responses can vary and include Web presentations, PowerPoint presentations, videos, and so on.

Modifications

1. Teachers can make this procedure more explicit by adding more scaffolding. Struggling readers will need scaffolding; however, this technique provides opportunities for these readers to participate in whole-class activities.
2. Internet inquiry can be conducted in small, collaborative groups. In these groups, partners take a question and search the Web to find multiple sources of information. The group synthesizes the information to create a response. The group activity is very supportive of struggling readers.
3. Instead of an I-chart, some teachers use the K-W-H-L sheet, where students list Web sources in the "How" column.

Further Diagnostic Applications

Basic View of Reading   Reading is an active process where students use Web sites to create responses to target questions. By reviewing Web site information, students redefine and elaborate conceptual understanding related to the target questions.

Patterns of Strengths and Strategies   Internet inquiry instruction is most appropriate for students who can use the Web search engines, collect information, and synthesize information from multiple sources.

Learner Patterns That Produce Increased Engagement

1. For self-directed readers who profit from reading and responding to information and ideas, Internet inquiry instruction helps these students integrate and elaborate on understanding.

2. For simultaneous learners who enjoy using the Web and its multiple sources, Internet inquiry helps these students read and organize information in an elaborate fashion.

*3. For readers who are bound by the text and believe that reading means getting the answers right, Internet inquiry instruction helps these students evaluate the authenticity of Web sites and demonstrates that the Web sites, like books, are composed by fallible authors.

Using the Technique as a Diagnostic Teaching Lesson   For Internet inquiry instruction to be effective, a majority of the following statements must be answered in the affirmative:

Yes   *No*

_____   _____   1. The student can find information on the Web.

_____   _____   2. The student is engaged when reading and viewing on the Web.

_____   _____   3. The student can synthesize multiple sources of information into a coherent whole.

Evidence Base

Hoffman, J. (1992). Critical reading/thinking across the curriculum: Using I-charts to support learning. *Language Arts, 69,* 121–127.

MacGregor, S. K., & Yiping, L. (2004). Web-based learning: How task scaffolding and Web site design support knowledge acquisition. *Journal of Research on Technology in Education, 37,* 161–175.

Web Sites

http://olc.spsd.sk.ca/DE/PD/instr/strats/inquiry/index.html
http://www.missouri.edu/~elpajs/c444/html/group_inquiry_project.html
http://inquiry.uiuc.edu/

26 Journal Writing   *Targeted Reading Levels: All levels*

Description   Journal writing is a written response from students of their understanding and exploration of ideas related to reading or a particular unit of study. In notebooks, students write about their reactions to new information, ask questions, elaborate on new understandings, and so on. The teacher responds to these ideas with questions, comments, and personal reactions. Through multiple journal entries, the students and the teacher carry on a written conversation.

Text   Self-generated written responses

Predominant Focus of Instruction

1. Processing focus: meaning
2. Instructional phase: after reading
3. Response mode emphasized: written discourse
4. Strategy emphasized: elaboration
5. Skill emphasized: nonliteral comprehension
6. Source of information: reader based
7. Type of instruction: implicit
8. Type of cognitive processing: simultaneous

Procedure

1. The teacher secures writing notebooks. She can use bound composition notebooks, student-made books of stapled pages, or loose-leaf notebooks.
2. The teacher explains that a journal is a written explanation of the student's thinking. It is like writing a letter to the teacher.
3. She tells the students she will comment personally on what is written.
4. The teacher shows the students an example from a journal. (The teacher first secures permission from the writer.)
5. She tells the students that they are to write about the focus topic.
6. The students and teacher write in their journals.
7. The teacher reads what the students write.
8. The teacher responds with questions or comments that encourage elaboration of the topic.
9. The students read the teacher's comments.
10. The students write a response or elaborate on new information.
11. The journal cycle continues.

Modifications   Many modifications can be made for journal writing. Some common ones are described in the following list:

1. Dialogue journals are a personal communication between the teacher and the student. There is no designated topic but rather a personal written exchange, like writing a letter to a friend. With it, students write important things about their life to their teacher. Although this kind of dialogue journal is more effective for some students than others, it is recommended as part of the diagnostic teaching session because it releases the structured format of directed and guided instruction.
2. Learning logs are specific journals about a unit of study. The teacher comments are to focus the students on aspects of their study, such as selecting and narrowing a

topic, gathering information, organizing the information, elaborating on and integrating concepts, and evaluating the information learned.

3. In double-entry journals, notebook pages are divided in half. On the left-hand page, the student makes notes, diagrams, clusters, and observations, while on the right-hand page, the student integrates this information into a coherent written understanding.

Further Diagnostic Applications

Basic View of Reading   Reading is an active, reader-based process in which readers' personal understanding focuses thinking. Both reading and writing are constructive processes that are influenced by the desire to communicate ideas.

Patterns of Strengths and Strategies   Journal writing is most appropriate for simultaneous, nonverbal students who enjoy communicating ideas through writing rather than talking. In this technique, ideas and understandings are communicated without an oral explanation or eye contact.

Learner Patterns That Produce Increased Engagement

1. For simultaneous learners who need time to express their ideas in words, writing allows them to think through ideas without noticeably lengthy pauses.
2. For visually oriented readers who prefer to communicate ideas through writing rather than talking, journal writing allows them to put thoughts into words without talking.
*3. For passive readers who do not realize that reading and writing are constructive processes, this technique allows them to experience reading and writing as communicating meaning.
*4. For text-bound readers who do not use personal understanding of the world to interpret information, journals show them how a writer uses personal understanding to compose text.

Using the Technique as a Diagnostic Lesson   For journal writing to be effective, a majority of the following statements must be answered in the affirmative:

Yes   No

_____   _____   1. The student can produce written text fairly easily.

_____   _____   2. The student likes to communicate his ideas in writing.

_____   _____   3. The student uses the teacher's model to correct his own writing errors.

Evidence Base

Cantrell, R. J., Fusaro, J. A., & Dougherty, E. A (2000). Exploring the effectiveness of journal writing on learning social studies: A comparative study. *Reading Psychology, 21,* 1–11.

Shang, H. (2005). Email dialogue journaling: Attitudes and impact on L2 reading performance. *Educational Studies, 31,* 197–212.

Web Sites

http://www.gmu.edu/departments/writingcenter/handouts/puller.html
http://www.readwritethink.org/lessons/lesson_view.asp?id=313
http://712educators.about.com/cs/writingresources/a/journals.htm

27 K-W-L   *Targeted Reading Levels 3–12*

Description   K-W-L is a technique used to direct students' reading and learning of content-area text. Before the text is read, students write what they already know about the topic as well as questions that they would like to explore. After the text is read, students write what they learned about the topic.

Text   Especially suited for expository text but can be applied to all text

Predominant Focus of Instruction

1. Processing focus: meaning
2. Instructional phase: before and after reading
3. Response mode emphasized: written with some discussion
4. Strategy emphasized: prediction and elaboration
5. Skill emphasized: literal and nonliteral comprehension
6. Source of information: reader-based phasing to text based
7. Type of instruction: implicit
8. Type of cognitive processing: simultaneous

Procedure

1. The teacher chooses an appropriate topic and text.
2. The teacher introduces the K-W-L worksheet (see the accompanying figure).
3. The students brainstorm ideas about the topic.
4. The teacher writes this information on a chart or chalkboard.
5. Students write what they know under the K ("What I Know") column.
6. Together, the teacher and students categorize the K column.
7. Students generate questions they would like answered about the topic and write them in the W ("What I Want to Learn") column.
8. Students silently read the text and add new questions to the W column.
9. After reading, the students complete the L ("What I Learned") column.
10. The students and teacher review the K-W-L sheet to tie together what students knew and the questions they had with what they learned.

Modifications

1. The K-W-L Plus technique extends the after-reading phase to include organizing the information through webbing or graphic organizer and then writing a summary.
2. The information known and learned can be combined to form a book.
3. The technique can be modified to include a column for students to discuss "How" they learned new information (KWHL).

Further Diagnostic Applications

Basic View of Reading   Reading is a socio-interactive process in which learners share what they know to elaborate and extend what the text says. Readers need experience relating what they know, the questions they have, and what they have learned from text in order to actively construct meaning.

K-W-L Technique

What I Know	What I Want to Learn	What I Learned

Note. Adapted from "K-W-L: A Teaching Model That Develops Active Reading of Expository Text" by Donna Ogle, 1986, *The Reading Teacher, 39,* 564–570. Copyright 1986 by International Reading Association. Adapted by permission.

Patterns of Strengths and Strategies   The K-W-L technique is appropriate for students who need to talk and write about the topic prior to reading. It is especially useful for students who need to see concretely what they know in order to tie it to what they are reading.

Learner Patterns That Produce Increased Engagement

1. For self-directed readers who do not readily elaborate what they learn, K-W-L helps these students expand and elaborate topic knowledge.
*2. For passive readers who read without relating what they know to the text, K-W-L helps tie together what they know and the text.
*3. For passive readers who need to see what they learned in relation to what they know, the K-W-L helps them assess the understanding they have developed through reading.

Using the Technique as a Diagnostic Teaching Lesson   For K-W-L to be effective, a majority of the following statements must be answered in the affirmative:

Yes   *No*

_____   _____   1. The student easily writes what he knows.

_____   _____   2. The student develops at least one question that he wants answered.

_____   _____   3. The student can organize the information learned.

Evidence Base

Cantrell, R. J., Fusaro, J. A.,& Dougherty, E. A. (2000). Exploring the effectiveness of journal writing on learning social studies: A comparative study. *Reading Psychology, 21,* 1–11.

Ogle, D. (1986). A teaching model that develops active comprehension of expository text. *The Reading Teacher, 39,* 564–570.

Web Sites

http://www.ncrel.org/sdrs/areas/issues/students/learning/lr2kwl.htm
http://www.ncrel.org/sdrs/areas/issues/students/learning/lr1kwlh.htm
http://www.squires.fcps.net/library/research/kwl.htm

28

28 Language Experience Approach   *Targeted Reading Levels K–3*

Description   The language experience approach (LEA) is a technique used for beginning reading instruction in which the child dictates a story to the teacher. The story becomes the text for instruction, and a collection of the stories becomes the child's first reader.

Text   The child's own language

Predominant Focus of Instruction

1. Processing focus: print
2. Instructional phase: before and during reading
3. Response mode emphasized: oral discussion
4. Strategy emphasized: prediction and monitoring
5. Skill emphasized: word identification
6. Source of information: reader based
7. Type of instruction: implicit
8. Type of cognitive processing: simultaneous

Procedure

1. The teacher engages students in dialogue about a particular topic. A stimulating, engaging, and concrete topic tends to elicit more language from the students.
2. The students dictate a story while the teacher serves as secretary for the class.
3. Using leading questions, the teacher guides the students to develop a story line by using questions such as these: "What happened next? Is this what you wanted to say? How can you make a story using this information?"
4. The students and the teacher read the story simultaneously to revise any statements or phrases that are unclear to the students. The story is to follow the natural language patterns of the students.
5. Then the teacher and the students read the story *repeatedly* because repetition of the entire story will encourage a predictive set for the story.
6. The students are asked to read the story independently.
7. Activities to reinforce word identification are constructed from the story.
8. Chunk cards are developed using the words in the story. These cards are made by dividing the entire story into meaningful phrases that are written on cards.
9. Initially, these chunk cards are flashed in the order in which they appear in the story. Later, they are mixed up. This activity maintains the sense of the whole while the whole is being broken into parts.
10. Stories are collated into anthologies that create the initial reading material for the student.
11. As words are repeatedly read in context, the teacher checks them off a word list but does not assess this knowledge in isolation.

Modifications

1. The extremely imaginative, creative learner can use guided imagery as a medium for creating stories. The teacher designs a guided imagery journey that incorporates targeted sight words. For instance, if the targeted sight words are *balloon, climb, sky,* and *wind,* the journey might contain the events that follow.

Close your eyes and imagine that you are walking on a narrow pathway.... The wind is blowing gently as you walk softly down the path.... You come to an open meadow, and you see a hot-air balloon.... A wise teacher offers to take you for a ride in the sky.... You climb into the basket.... You soar up ... up ... up ... in the sky. I will leave you now.... You can finish the journey in your mind.... When you have finished your journey ... you may return to the classroom and open your eyes.

Then follow these steps:

    a. When all the students have opened their eyes, they share their journeys in pairs. This activity allows them to verbalize the images.

    b. The students dictate the journey while the teacher serves as secretary for the class (or individual student).

    c. The students are reminded that the stories represent what happened in their imaginations. Their stories represent their images, just like a published story represents an author's images.

2. For English language learners, teachers can create several experiences around a theme like hunting. For example, with native American students, a buffalo hunt was used. The next experience was a deer hunt, then a lion hunt, and so on.

3. The extremely concrete learner can use field trips and science activities as a medium for creating stories.

4. The learner who has difficulty developing a coherent story can use wordless picture books to boost his confidence in developing a story.

Further Diagnostic Applications

Basic View of Reading   Reading is an active, reader-based process. By reading their own story, students can infer the consistency of printed language patterns. Because the story is based on their experience, they continually use this experience to remember the words.

Patterns of Strengths and Strategies   Language experience is most appropriate for students who have facility with language and are simultaneous, reader-based thinkers. If a student predicts from his own experiences rather than the words in the text, then language experience matches his strategies (using what he knows); therefore, this technique facilitates word learning by asking the student to identify words using his own experiences.

Learner Patterns That Produce Increased Engagement

1. For simultaneous thinkers who use prior knowledge to construct meaning, often resulting in overpredicting or guessing without identifying words, LEA uses the student's strength (using prior knowledge) to facilitate word identification.

2. For extremely verbal, creative students whose verbalization interferes with the mundane task of looking at words, LEA uses the strength (verbalization) to facilitate word identification.

3. For students who are unwilling to take a guess unless they are certain the response will be correct, LEA provides a text that allows the student to make a safe guess, using both what is on the page and what they remember was written.

4. For learners who have had an overemphasis on phonics, language experience can increase their fluency.

Using the Technique as a Diagnostic Teaching Lesson For LEA to be effective, a majority of the following statements must be answered in the affirmative:

Yes   *No*

_____ _____ 1. The student can remember the story he told.

_____ _____ 2. The student tells a fairly coherent story.

_____ _____ 3. The student remembers the story well enough to predict the words she does not remember.

_____ _____ 4. The student responds correctly when prompted, using the preceding context and story theme.

Evidence Base

Moustafa, M. (1987). Comprehensible input plus the language experience approach: A longterm perspective. *Reading Teacher, 1,* 276–286.

Freeman, R. H., & Freeman, G. G. (1987). Reading acquisition: A comparison of four approaches to reading. *Reading Psychology, 8,* 257–272.

Stauffer, R. (1970). *The language experience approach to teaching reading.* New York: Harper & Row.

Web Sites

http://www.sasked.gov.sk.ca/docs/ela/e_literacy/language.html

http://www.sil.org/lingualinks/literacy/otherresources/glossaryofliteracyterms/WhatIsTheLanguage ExperienceApp.htm

http://www.literacyconnections.com/InTheirOwnWords.php

29 Listening-Thinking Activity   *Targeted Reading Levels: All levels*

Description   A listening-thinking activity (LTA) is an instructional format for developing predictive listening and comprehension. It involves predicting what will happen, talking about what happened, and talking about how you know what is happening. As the teacher reads aloud, she communicates the message by adding intonation and gestures to facilitate understanding.

Text   An interesting, well-written text; picture storybooks are excellent

Predominant Focus of Instruction

1. Processing focus: meaning
2. Instructional phase: before and during reading
3. Response mode emphasized: oral discussion
4. Strategy emphasized: prediction and monitoring
5. Skill emphasized: listening comprehension
6. Source of information: reader based
7. Type of instruction: implicit
8. Type of cognitive processing: simultaneous

Procedure

1. Using the title of the story, the teacher has the students brainstorm what the story might be about.
2. She reads to a turning point.
3. She asks the students to talk about what they are thinking, using "I wonder" statements. The teacher can also demonstrate her thinking.
4. The teacher asks the students to tell what has happened so far to make them curious. The teacher adds her own interpretation.
5. The teacher and the students review previous predictions. Then they decide whether they still want to keep all the predictions.
6. The students revise predictions or make new predictions.
7. The teacher alternates reading and discussing until the end of the story.
8. The teacher uses nonverbal cues from the students (such as their facial expressions and attentiveness) to check their understanding. When students are confused, the teacher stops to discuss the story line and how they arrived at their interpretations.
9. The teacher and the students discuss the story as a whole, relating various interpretations.

Modification   The teacher can demonstrate predicting using the first several stopping points. She uses the following steps:

1. The teacher models her questions about what is happening thus far in the story: "I wonder why the author said . . . ?"
2. The teacher summarizes what she has read so far, relating it to the *I wonder* statements.
3. From the summary, she develops a prediction or bet. She says, "Oh, I know, I bet . . . "

Listening-Thinking Activity

29

Further Diagnostic Applications

Basic View of Reading   Reading is a socio-interactive process in which students think about what they read, using what they know and the text. Then they share predictions and thinking with class members. Listening is also an active process in which students interpret the passage as they listen. In a listening activity, the interpersonal communication occurs during reading when the teacher can use nonverbal cues such as gestures and intonation to convey the author's message.

Patterns of Strengths and Strategies   An LTA is appropriate for developing readers who need the added input of social interaction to learn new strategies. This technique allows the teacher to demonstrate these active reasoning strategies and to check students' understanding.

Learner Patterns That Produce Increased Engagement

1. For passive readers who like group work and need to learn how to make predictions, LTA provides a short lesson in which students can be involved in making predictions and discussing their thinking.
2. For passive readers who need to check their understanding, LTA provides a short lesson in which the teacher can demonstrate comprehension monitoring.
*3. For students with severe reading disability, this technique allows students to practice active thinking strategies without having to read the words. LTA leads students to more active thinking strategies that they can use.
*4. For simultaneous readers who need to experience the steps of active thinking to clarify their thinking, LTA provides such an opportunity.

Using the Technique as a Diagnostic Teaching Lesson   For LTA to be effective, a majority of the following statements must be answered in the affirmative:

Yes   No

_____   _____   1. The student listens to stories and can remember what was read.

_____   _____   2. The student can construct an oral response after listening.

_____   _____   3. The student likes listening to stories that are read orally.

Evidence Base

Aarnoutse, C. A., van den Bos, K. P., & Brand-Gruwel, S. (1998). Effects of listening comprehension training on listening and reading. *Journal of Special Education, 32,* 115–126.

Garner, J. K. & Bochna, C. R. (2004). Transfer of a listening comprehension strategy to independent reading in first-grade students. *Early Childhood Education Journal, 32,* 69–74.

Web Sites

http://www.rockingham.k12.va.us/English/shared/Directed%20Listening%20Thinking.pdf
http://members.tripod.com/~emu1967/DLTA.htm
http://www.siu.edu/~arc/chapter8.html

30 Literature Discussions   *Targeted Reading Levels K–12*

Description   Literature discussions are used to develop personal responses to literature by having students share their interpretations in a discussion group. By talking about the literature, students integrate the author's ideas and concepts with their own.

Text   Authentic children's literature

Predominant Focus of Instruction

1. Processing focus: meaning
2. Instructional phase: after reading
3. Response mode emphasized: oral discussion
4. Strategy emphasized: elaboration
5. Skill emphasized: nonliteral comprehension
6. Source of information: reader-based
7. Type of instruction: implicit
8. Type of cognitive processing: simultaneous

Procedure

1. The teacher introduces several books by giving short summaries or book talks.
2. The students choose a book to read over the next 2 days or week.
3. After the books are read, the students reading the same book gather into a literature discussion group.
4. The discussion is open ended, with the teacher beginning with an invitation such as "Tell me about this book" or "What was your favorite part?"
5. At the end of the discussion time, the group decides what they will talk about the next day.
6. As the students become familiar with this format, the teacher becomes less involved in the discussion and lets the students take the lead.
7. The teacher's role in discussion includes these activities:
   a. Listening closely and focusing on students' ideas
   b. Supporting thinking and reflection by saying, "Let's think more about that"
   c. Keeping the discussion focused on a theme
   d. Pointing out literary elements (characters, setting, and so on) and strategies (using background knowledge) and encouraging students to discuss them
8. At the conclusion of the discussion, group members can present their interpretation to the class as a "book talk."

Modifications

1. In literature circles, group members take specific roles during the discussion, like director of discussion, illustrator, question maker, clarification monitor, and so on.
2. To add a writing component, students can keep a literature log (see "Journal Writing" in this part) so they can more easily share their ideas.
3. For some groups, the teacher may continue in the literature discussion as a group member.

Further Diagnostic Applications

Basic View of Reading   Reading is a socio-interactive process in which the social context affects individual interpretation of text. Through sharing ideas in a peer group, students define and elaborate on their ideas.

Patterns of Strengths and Strategy   The literature circle technique is appropriate for students who can discuss their ideas freely in a group. The dialogue helps these students elaborate on their understanding of literature and connect that understanding to their experiences.

Learner Patterns That Produce Increased Engagement

1. For self-directed readers who profit from sharing ideas in a group, literature discussion help these students verify and create interpretations.
2. For self-directed readers who like to share personal feelings about text but need time to reflect on ideas before discussing, literature discussions help these students connect their personal feelings with the text.
*3. For readers who are bound by the text and believe that reading means getting right answers, literature discussion allows these students to verbalize ideas in a safe context and see how their peers think about a story.

Using the Technique as a Diagnostic Teaching Lesson   For literature discussions to be effective, both of the following statements must be answered in the affirmative:

Yes	No	
_____	_____	1. The student can share interpretations in a group.
_____	_____	2. The student likes narrative text so that he finds it engaging enough to make a response.

Evidence Base

Allen, J., Möller, K. J., & Stroup, D. (2003). "Is this some kind of soap opera?": A tale of two readers across four literature discussion contexts. *Reading and Writing Quarterly: Overcoming Learning Difficulties, 19,* 225–251.

Möller, K. J. (2004). Creating zones of possibility for struggling readers: A study of one fourth grader's shifting roles in literature discussion. *Journal of Literacy Research, 36,* 419–460.

Morrow, L. M. (1992). The impact of a literature-based program on literacy achievement, use of literature, and attitudes of children from minority backgrounds. *Reading Research Quarterly, 27,* 250–275.

Web Sites

http://www.literaturecircles.com
http://www.literaturecircles.com/article1.htm
http://home.att.net/~TEACHING/litcircles.htm
http://www.sedl.org/cgi-bin/mysql/buildingreading.cgi

31 Making Words

Targeted Reading Levels 1–4

Description Making words is used to help readers develop the ability to spell words and apply this knowledge when decoding. In this procedure, students learn to make a six- or seven-letter word as they make smaller words. This activity is used to increase the students' decoding skills.

Text Letter cards

Predominant Focus of Instruction

1. Processing focus: print
2. Instructional phase: skill instruction
3. Response mode emphasized: oral
4. Strategy emphasized: monitoring
5. Skill emphasized: word identification and word analysis
6. Source of information: text based
7. Type of instruction: implicit
8. Type of cognitive processing: successive

Procedure

1. Before beginning, the teacher decides on the final word in the lesson and makes a list of the shorter words that can be made from its letters. She picks 10 to 15 words that include (a) words that can be sorted for the patterns, (b) words of different lengths to provide challenging and easy work, (c) a proper name so they can be reminded to use capital letters, and (d) words with familiar meanings. She writes all the words on cards and orders them from shortest to longest so the order emphasizes letter patterns.
2. The teacher places the larger letter cards in a pocket chart or along the chalk ledge and gives the student a set of letters.
3. The teacher and student review the letter cards.
4. She tells the student to take two letters and make the first word. She says the word and uses it in a sentence. For example:
   Using the word "battle," the teacher would say use two letters to make the word "at."
5. The teacher has the student make the other words, indicating the number of letters needed, and cues the student as to whether to change one letter, change letters around, or use all the letters. For example:
   In the same example, she says add the letter "b" to the beginning of the word "at" and what does it spell? Then she says add the letter "l" to the beginning of the word "at" and "e" to the end of it, what do these letters spell?
6. The teacher reviews all the words in the lesson, saying and spelling each word and putting it on an index card.
7. The words are then sorted (see "Word Sorts" in this part) for phonic patterns. For example, all the words beginning with the same letter would be one sort, rhyming words are another sort, and so on.

Further Diagnostic Applications

Basic View of Reading Learning to read means understanding how letters work within a word. Readers need to use their knowledge of letter patterns to figure out new words;

therefore, reading is an interactive process. By listening closely to a word pronounced, the student can match the letters to the sounds in the words.

Patterns of Strengths and Strategies   The making-words approach is most appropriate for students who can segment words into their sounds and match those sounds to the letters in the word. This technique builds on their strength and allows them to develop a system for decoding.

Learner Patterns That Produce Increased Engagement

1. For simultaneous thinkers who readily use what they know and manipulate visual information, this technique promotes understanding the sound relationships in words.
*2. For passive learners who are phonetically aware but need to focus on letters in words, this technique uses their strength of sound knowledge to enhance the decoding process.
*3. For successive learners who can match sounds to letters, this technique helps them develop a system for using what they know to figure out words.

Using the Technique as a Diagnostic Teaching Lesson   For the making-words approach to be effective, a majority of the following statements must be answered in the affirmative:

Yes   *No*

_____   _____   1. The student can segment sounds.

_____   _____   2. The student can match sounds to letters.

_____   _____   3. The student applies decoding analogies to both known and unknown words.

Evidence Base

Cunningham, P. M., & Cunningham, J. W. (1992). Making words: Enhancing the invented spelling-decoding connection. *The Reading Teacher, 46,* 106–107.

Reutzel, D. R., & Smith, J. A. (2006). Words to Go! Evaluating a first-grade parent involvement program for "Making" words at home. *Reading Research and Instruction, 45,* 119–159.

Web Sites

http://www.wfu.edu/academics/fourblocks/block1.html

http://www.readingcenter.buffalo.edu/center/research/word.html

http://www.readwritethink.org/lessons/lesson_view.asp?id=150

http://www.k111.k12.il.us/lafayette/Fourblocks/templates_-_making_words.htm

32 Making and Writing Words   *Targeted Reading Levels 2–6*

Description   Making and writing words is used to help readers think about and write words using letters and letter patterns. In this procedure, students either think about the sounds in easy and hard words that are pronounced by the teacher or match hints provided by the teacher. In this way this procedure works on spelling, decoding, and vocabulary knowledge.

Text   Making and writing words worksheet

Predominant Focus of Instruction

1. Processing focus: print
2. Instructional phase: skill instruction
3. Response mode emphasized: written
4. Strategy emphasized: predicting and monitoring
5. Skill emphasized: word analysis
6. Source of information: text based
7. Type of instruction: implicit
8. Type of cognitive processing: successive

Procedure

1. In planning the lesson, the teacher decides on the final word in the lesson and makes a list of the shorter words that can be made from its letters. She picks 10 to 15 words that include (a) words that can be sorted for the patterns, (b) words of different lengths to provide challenging and easy work, and (c) words with familiar meanings. She makes a list of the consonants and vowels that will be used.
2. The teacher instructs the students to write the consonants and vowels in the appropriate place on the making and writing words worksheets (see accompanying figure).
3. The teacher either pronounces or gives cues for two- and three-letter words. For example the teacher might say, "In box number one write a three-letter word that means a fury animal." The students would write *cat*.
4. The teacher gives clues for the other boxes. For example, she might say, "In the next three boxes, write words that belong to the *at* family."
5. The teacher works with the class through the remaining words she had planned.
6. The final word is always the "challenge word." Students are challenged to use all the letters to write the final word in the final box.
7. The teacher then asks students to write *transfer words,* which are words that are difficult but use the knowledge gained in the initial boxes.
8. Finally, the students cut out each box to form individual word cards to be used in word sorts (see "Word Sorts" in this part). For example, the students may sort all words in the *at* family.

Further Diagnostic Applications

Basic View of Reading   Reading involves understanding how letters work within a word. Readers use their knowledge of letter patterns to figure out new words; therefore, reading is an interactive process. By listening to clues about words, the students can

Making and Writing Words

Vowels	Consonants

1	6	11
2	7	12
3	8	13
4	9	14
5	10	15

T-1	T-2	T-3

Source. Rasinski, Timothy. (1999). Making and writing words. *Reading Online,* an electronic journal of the International Reading Association. Reprinted with permission. Available at http://www.readingonline.org/articles/art_index.asp?HREF=/articles/words/rasinski_index.html.

predict what the word might mean or be and then figure out the letter and letter patterns to write the word.

Patterns of Strengths and Strategies   The making and writing words approach is most appropriate for students who can segment words into their sounds, who match those sounds to the letters in the word, and who are highly verbal. This technique allows them to develop a system for decoding.

Learner Patterns That Produce Increased Engagement

1. For successive thinkers who readily use letter pattern knowledge and write easily, the technique promotes understanding the sound relationships in words.
*2. For passive learners who are phonetically aware but need to focus on letters, the technique asks students to write the sounds in the words they know.
*3. For simultaneous thinkers who readily think about what they know, the technique offers a visual way to think about sounds in words.

Modification   Rather than writing unrelated words, the activity can focus on letter patterns. The teacher selects multisyllabic words and identifies their letter patterns and individual letters. The teacher then writes the letters and letter patterns in the boxes rather than vowels and consonants.

Using the Technique as a Diagnostic Teaching Lesson   For the making and writing words approach to be effective, a majority of the following statements must be answered in the affirmative:

Yes   *No*

_____   _____   1. The student can segment sounds.

_____   _____   2. The student can match sounds to letters.

_____   _____   3. The student has sufficient verbal language to understand semantic clues given.

Evidence Base

Rasinski, T., & Oswald, R. (2005). Making and writing words: Constructivist word learning in a second-grade classroom. *Reading and Writing Quarterly: Overcoming Learning Difficulties, 21,* 151–163.

Rasinski, T. (1999). Making and writing words. *Reading Online.* Retrieved September 1, 2002, from http://readingonline.org/articles/words/rasinski.html

Web Sites

http://www.readwritethink.org/lessons/lesson_view.asp?id=150
http://www.ohiorc.org/ohiorc_resource_display.aspx?recId=142

33 Metaphors   *Targeted Reading Levels 4–8*

Description   Metaphors are used to relate words and concepts to already-known objects by identifying their likenesses and differences. For young children, common concrete objects can be used to develop metaphors.

Text   Isolated words or concepts

Predominant Focus of Instruction

1. Processing focus: meaning
2. Instructional phase: after reading
3. Response mode emphasized: oral discussion
4. Strategy emphasized: elaboration
5. Skill emphasized: word meaning
6. Source of information: reader based
7. Type of instruction: implicit
8. Type of cognitive processing: simultaneous

Procedure

1. The teacher selects a key word or concept from the assigned text.
2. The teacher creates a metaphor that describes the key attributes of the word or concept.
3. The teacher describes how the metaphor is like the key word and how it is different from the key word. For example, "A cloud is a puddle in the sky. It is like a puddle because a cloud is made of water droplets. A cloud is not like a puddle because the water droplets have become water vapor. It is not like a puddle because it is in the sky and not on the ground."
4. Then the students create a metaphor within a particular class. For example, "What can you think of that is like a volcano?"
5. The students decide on a metaphor. For example, "A dragon is like a volcano."
6. The students explain the similarity. For example, "A dragon is like a volcano because they are both hot and spit fire."
7. The students explain how it is different from the metaphor. For example, "A dragon is not like a volcano because it is a make-believe animal. It has four legs and can run very, very fast."
8. The students discuss the meaning of the words.

Modification   A brainstorming or listing of options in group situations can facilitate understanding of metaphors. In this situation, students would justify their metaphors and decide on one or two metaphors to use as the concept is developed in class.

Further Diagnostic Applications

Basic View of Reading   Reading is an interactive process in which a reader's prior knowledge influences his comprehension of the text. Word knowledge is based on conceptual knowledge that is related by analogous relationships among prior experiences.

Patterns of Strengths and Strategies   Metaphors are most appropriate for students who have facility with verbal language but draw unspecific relationships among concepts. The words *like a* are often prevalent in their conversations. For these students, creating metaphors elaborates the relationships they draw between what they already know and the new information.

Learner Patterns That Produce Increased Engagement

1. For simultaneous learners who relate many concepts at once but are often unaware of the relationship or the precise words used to associate the concepts, this technique helps label and categorize word relationships.
2. For highly verbal students whose facility with words needs to elaborate the analogous relationships between what they already know with new words, this technique helps relate what they know into more inclusive categories.
3. For successive learners who use words without drawing relationships between the word concepts and the word labels, this technique helps explain relationships among words and experiences.

Using the Technique as a Diagnostic Teaching Lesson   For metaphors to be effective, a majority of the following statements must be answered in the affirmative:

Yes   *No*

_____   _____   1. The student understands how a metaphor is constructed and can readily draw analogous relationships.

_____   _____   2. The student can rationally explain the similarities and differences of the metaphors he creates.

_____   _____   3. The student creates more elaborate definitions of words as a result of explaining the relationships.

Evidence Base

Delain, M. T., Pearson, P. D., & Anderson, R. C. (1985). Reading comprehension and creativity in black language use: You stand to gain by playing the sounding game! *American Educational Research Journal, 22,* 155–173.

Readence, J. E., Baldwin, R. S., & Rickelman, R. J. (1983). Instructional insights for metaphors and similes. *Journal of Reading, 27,* 109–112.

Web Sites

http://exchanges.state.gov/forum/vols/vol34/no1/p8.htm
http://www.teachersmind.com/metaphors1.htm

34 Multisensory Approaches   *Targeted Reading Levels K–3*

Description   Multisensory approaches or VAKT (visual/auditory/kinesthetic-tactile) techniques reinforce learning by having students trace letters and words to learn the word. Relying on tactile-kinesthetic reinforcement, these techniques provide a multisensory stimulation for word learning.

Text   Varies with approach; however, a generic VAKT can be used to reinforce any word that is difficult to learn

Predominant Focus of Instruction

1. Processing focus: print
2. Instructional phase: before reading
3. Response mode emphasized: written production
4. Strategy emphasized: elaboration
5. Skill emphasized: word identification
6. Source of information: text based
7. Type of instruction: explicit
8. Type of cognitive processing: successive

Procedure

1. The teacher selects the key words to be learned and writes them with a crayon on cardboard or large paper. (A rough surface is better for the tactile reinforcement.)
2. The teacher models writing the word one letter at a time, saying the letter name, syllable, or letter sound.
3. The student traces each word letter by letter, saying either the letter name or the letter sound. Then the student says the entire word.
4. The procedure is repeated with each word until the word can be written (not copied) from memory.
5. At any point that an error is made, the procedure is stopped, and the teacher models the correct form of writing and saying the word.
6. This structured presentation continues until the student has mastered a sight vocabulary sufficient to read the stories.

Modifications   Many variations of the generic VAKT exist. The following approaches are a few examples of how the variations can be used to differentiate instruction.

1. The Fernald Technique moves from self-selected word learning to creating personal stories from individual word banks. Words are presented by syllables, maintaining more of a sense of the whole than other VAKT procedures. Therefore, the technique is highly personalized and motivational for students who like to structure their own language.
2. The Orton-Gillingham-Stillman Method, the Herman Method, the Cooper Method, the Spaulding Method, and the Distar use the generic VAKT (mainly writing letter sounds to make words) to reinforce the sounds of letters and require the student to blend sounds of letters to form words. Therefore, words are selected that are decodable and follow an extremely structured presentation of phonic generalizations. This variation is most appropriate for students who guess at words and have poor visual memory but can blend sounds to form words. Thus, if they can't remember a word, they can sound it out in order to recognize it.

Further Diagnostic Applications

Basic View of Reading   Reading is a text-based process in which readers learn a words through repetitious, multisensory reinforcement of letters in words before reading complete stories.

Patterns of Strengths and Strategies   Multisensory approaches are most appropriate for students who have strong tactile-kinesthetic preferences for learning and exhibit difficulty in initial word learning. This approach focuses the attention of the learner to the key features of each word.

Learner Patterns That Produce Increased Engagement

1. For successive learners with tactile-kinesthetic preferences who have difficulty remembering words that have been taught, this technique reinforces those words that are difficult to learn.
2. For extremely passive learners with tactile-kinesthetic preferences who do not attend to the key features of words but instead make wild guesses, this technique draws attention to what words look like and the key features of the words.
3. For simultaneous learners who have difficulty remembering key words, multisensory techniques reinforce words that are difficult to remember.

Using the Technique as a Diagnostic Teaching Lesson   For multisensory techniques to be effective, a majority of the following statements must be answered in the affirmative:

Yes	*No*	
_____	_____	1. The student guesses at words without using their graphic or phonic cues.
_____	_____	2. Tracing the word facilitates recognition of words or sounds.
_____	_____	3. Tracing the words focuses the student's attention on the key features of words.

Evidence Base

Doyle, B. A., & Valente, B. (2002). Labels needn't stick: "At-risk" first graders rescued with appropriate intervention. *Journal of Education for Students Placed at Risk, 7,* 327–332.

Web Site

http://www.indstate.edu/soe/blumberg/reading/rd-word.html#multi

35 Paired Reading

Targeted Reading Levels K–5

Description   The paired reading technique uses joint reading aloud between two individuals. They sit together and read a story aloud simultaneously. One individual (another adult or student) serves as a model of fluent reading.

Text   Stories and poems

Predominant Focus of Instruction

1. Processing focus: print
2. Instructional phase: during reading
3. Response mode emphasized: oral reading
4. Strategy emphasized: prediction
5. Skill emphasized: fluency
6. Source of information: reader based
7. Type of instruction: implicit
8. Type of cognitive processing: simultaneous

Procedure

1. The student and the teacher select a text that is interesting and not too long. The paired reading needs to be short.
2. Before beginning, the teacher and the student decide on a sign for the student to give when he is ready to read on his own and one for when he needs help.
3. The teacher and the student read the text in unison.
4. The teacher sets a pace that is appropriate for the text, modeling intonation and phrasing.
5. The teacher can move her finger along the line of print if necessary.
6. As the student gains success, he signals the teacher to stop reading aloud.
7. The student continues on his own.

Modifications

1. This technique is effective with peer tutoring when the teacher can divide the class into two groups and establish pairs for reading matching the top student in the first half with the top in the second half and so on. Some teachers call this approach *partner reading*.
2. The pairs or partners can rate each other's fluency using a modified fluency scale (see Chapter 5 for fluency scale).

Further Diagnostic Applications

Basic View of Reading   Reading is a socio-interactive process in which fluency is developed as students read along with others. Using a model of a more fluent reader, the student readily integrates word recognition and comprehension as he reads.

Patterns of Strengths and Strategies   Paired reading is most appropriate for students who read slowly but accurately. The paired reading provides a model of fluent reading and increases the student's reading rate at the same time.

Learner Patterns That Produce Increased Engagement

1. For learners who rely heavily on background knowledge when reading orally, paired reading allows them to attend to letters and meaning simultaneously.
2. For highly social students who like to interact with others and follow their model, this technique lets them use this preference while practicing reading.
*3. For nonfluent readers who are word bound because of a heavy emphasis on phonic instruction, this method can increase reading fluency.

Using the Technique as a Diagnostic Teaching Lesson   For the paired reading technique to be effective, a majority of the following statements must be answered in the affirmative:

Yes   *No*

_____   _____   1. The student likes to read along with someone.
_____   _____   2. The student begins to take over the reading.
_____   _____   3. The student becomes more fluent and expressive.

Evidence Base

Fiala, C. L., & Sheridan, S. M. (2003). Parent involvement and reading: Using curriculum-based measurement to assess the effects of paired reading. *Reading Psychology in the Schools, 40,* 613–626.

Topping, K. J. (1992). The structure and development of the paired reading technique. *Journal of Research in Reading, l (15),* 120–136.

Van Keer, H., & Verhaeghe, J. P. (2005). Effects of explicit reading strategies instruction and peer tutoring on second and fifth graders' reading comprehension and self-efficacy perceptions. *Journal of Experimental Education, 73,* 291–329.

Web Sites

http://www.sil.org/linguaLinks/literacy/ImplementALiteracyProgram/UsingPairedReading.htm
http://www.dyslexia.ie/paired.htm

36 Phonogram Approach

Targeted Reading Levels 1–3

Description   The phonogram approach is a structured program to introduce phonic principles by use of sound clusters within words. As whole words are introduced, the student is directed to look at the sound clusters in the words. Then the student finds similar letter clusters in new words and associates them with the known cluster words.

Text   Isolated words that have the same word patterns and text that contains these patterns

Predominant Focus of Instruction

1. Processing focus: print
2. Instructional phase: after reading
3. Response mode emphasized: oral discussion
4. Strategy emphasized: elaboration
5. Skill emphasized: word analysis
6. Source of information: text based
7. Type of instruction: explicit
8. Type of cognitive processing: generally successive but does look at patterns (simultaneous)

Procedure

1. The teacher presents isolated words that contain the letter cluster. For the *an* sound cluster, these words could be presented:

fan	can	candy
man	pan	fancy
ran	Stan	candle

2. The teacher pronounces the whole word and identifies letter names and letter sounds of that target cluster. For example,

   "In the word *fan,* the letter *f* goes '*f-f-f*' and the letters *a–n* go '*an*.'"

3. The teacher pronounces the letter sound or cluster sounds and asks the student for its name. For example,

   "In the word *fan,* what letter goes '*f-f-f*'?"

   "In the word *fan,* what letters go '*an*'?"

4. The teacher pronounces the letter name or cluster and asks the student for its sound. For example,

   "In the word *fan,* what sound does the *f* make?"

   "In the word *fan,* what sounds do *a-n* make?"

5. The teacher asks the student, "What is the word?"

6. Steps 2, 3, 4, and 5 are continued until the pattern is learned.
7. The teacher presents the words in sentences, and the student reads the sentences. For example,

   "The man canned the fancy candy."

   "Stan ran to fan the candle."

8. If a word cannot be decoded, the teacher directs the student to the letter cluster and asks for its name and sound. For example,

   "Look at the word. Where is the *a-n*? What sounds do they make? What's the first letter? What sound does it make?"

9. The teacher returns to the list of words and asks the student, "How are *can, candy,* and *canopy* alike, and how are they different?"

Modifications

1. Similar to the phonogram approach is the linguistic method, an approach for instructing a beginning reader that is also based on word patterns. The word families introduced have a minimal contrast in the word patterns (*cat, mat, fat*). Therefore, this approach emphasizes decoding by visual analogy and does not emphasize sound analogies. The teacher introduces the words before the story by having the students spell each new word and then asking how the word patterns are alike and how they are different. Then the students read the text that uses the word pattern:

   The cat is fat.

   The cat is on the mat.

   The fat cat is on the mat.

   Therefore, this approach is more implicit than the phonogram approach.
2. The target words can be selected to teach the word patterns that are causing the student difficulty.
3. The target words can be selected to teach a particular letter sound. For example, if short *a* words are difficult for the student, the teacher can choose the patterns of *an, at, am, ab,* and *ap* so the student can generalize the concept of short *a* without separating the individual letter sound from its pattern.

Further Diagnostic Applications

Basic View of Reading   Reading is a text-based process in which the student must learn to decode printed words before he can read for meaning. As such, the learner is explicitly taught the analogous sound relationships to enhance decoding.

Patterns of Strengths and Strategies   Looking for sound clusters in whole words is most appropriate for a simultaneous learner. For this student, the approach facilitates word identification by using the similarity among sounds in already known words.

Learner Patterns That Produce Increased Engagement

1. For simultaneous learners who need direct instruction in forming phonic analogies among the words they already know and new words they encounter, this technique uses their strength in identifying patterns.
2. For older students who need to add a decoding strategy to supplement contextual analysis, this technique helps them use what they know about context and word identification.

Using the Technique as a Diagnostic Teaching Lesson   For the phonogram approach to be effective, a majority of the following statements must be answered in the affirmative:

Yes	*No*	
_____	_____	1. The student can segment sounds.
_____	_____	2. The student applies the analogies to both known and unknown words.
_____	_____	3. The student applies the strategy when reading connected text and encountering an unknown word.

Evidence Base

Glass, G. & Burton, E. (1973). How do they decode: Verbalization and observed behaviors of successful decoders. *Education, 94,* 58–63.

Savage, R., Carless, S., & Stuart, M. (2003). The effects of rime- and phoneme-based teaching delivered by Learning Support Assistants. *Journal of Research in Reading, 26,* 211–233.

Web Sites

http://www.readwritethink.org/student_mat/student_material.asp?id=3
http://www.readwritethink.org/lessons/lesson_view.asp?id=795

37 Prediction Strategy Instruction *Targeted Reading Levels 4–12*

Description   Prediction is a technique where readers explain their active reading strategies as they read. At designated points, the students make a prediction and a reason for their prediction. As they read, they evaluate new information in relation to their previous predictions.

Text   Narrative and expository text

Predominant Focus of Instruction

1. Processing focus: meaning
2. Instructional phase: during reading
3. Response mode emphasized: oral discussion
4. Strategy emphasized: prediction and monitoring
5. Skill emphasized: nonliteral comprehension
6. Source of information: reader based
7. Type of instruction: implicit
8. Type of cognitive processing: simultaneous

Procedure

1. The teacher selects interesting passages so that the readers can make predictions.
2. She decides on key turning points in the passage and marks them for the students. As the students read, the students stop to discuss their predictions.
3. The students ask if they want to revise, change, or add to their prediction.
4. After the story is read, how the students revised and expanded their predictions is discussed.
5. The students discuss how their interpretation developed through the story.
6. The students discuss the influence of personal understanding on comprehension.

Modifications

1. *Prediction Logs* Instead of discussing orally, the teacher uses a written account of the students' thinking. After each section, the students write their predictions on the prediction logs. The written record is used as a basis for discussing the story. Finally, the students write a reaction to the discussion, telling how their comprehension developed.
2. *Prediction Mapping* For students that need a visual representation of their active reading process, teachers can use a prediction map, which uses a conceptual flowchart to visually map the prediction and revision process. Using the title, the students and teacher make a prediction and place it in the center of the oval on the left side of the page *(see the accompanying figure)*. Next, the teacher demonstrates her thinking by saying, "I predict _____ is going to happen next." And she adds her prediction to the map as well as the textual information and what she knows to support her prediction.

Prediction Mapping

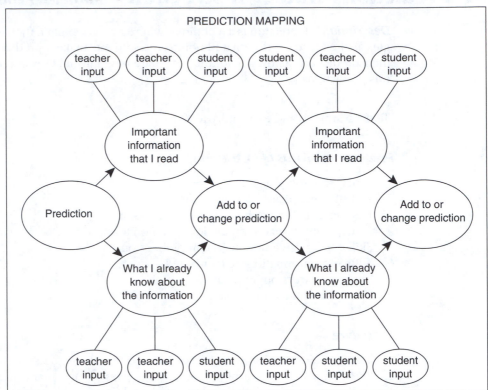

Source. From "Right-Brained Strategies for Teaching Comprehension" by Barbara J. Walker, 1985, *Academic Therapy, 21*, p. 137. Copyright 1985 by PRO-ED, Inc. Reprinted by permission.

Further Diagnostic Applications

Basic View of Reading   Reading is a socio-interactive process in which readers build a model of meaning based on textual and nontextual information and then revise this model during a discussion. As a result of predicting and revising and the subsequent discussion, readers build a model of meaning; they predict, monitor, and evaluate their interpretation in relation to the context of the situation.

Patterns of Strengths and Strategies   Prediction is most appropriate for reflective students who need to evaluate how they form a model of meaning. They often do not realize what information they use from the text and what they already know. Furthermore, they have difficulty thinking about how they form ideas as well as discussing them in a group. Predictions provide a method for analyzing how they construct meaning.

Learner Patterns That Produce Increased Engagement

1. For simultaneous, reflective learners who understand the passage but do not understand how they construct a response, prediction logs provide a record of thoughts so that they can analyze them.

*2. For passive learners who need to actively engage in forming and revising a model of meaning, predictions logs and maps can help them elaborate their understanding during reading.

Using the Technique as a Diagnostic Teaching Lesson   For the prediction technique to be effective, a majority of the following statements must be answered in the affirmative:

Yes	No	
_____	_____	1. The student can make a prediction.
_____	_____	2. The student can give a rationale for predictions.
_____	_____	3. The student will discuss his thinking in a group.

Evidence Base

Afflerbach, P. (1990). The influence of prior knowledge and text genre on readers' prediction strategies. *Journal of Reading Behavior, 22,* 131–148.

Spears, M. W., & Gambrell, L. B. (1991). Prediction training and the comprehension and composing performance of fourth-grade students. *National Reading Conference Yearbook, 40,* 239–245.

Web Sites

http://www.readwritethink.org/lessons/lesson_view.asp?id=292
http://www.manatee.k12.fl.us/sites/elementary/palmasola/rctextfea1.htm

38 Process Writing

Targeted Reading Levels: All levels

Description   Process writing was developed to engage all children, regardless of age, in a writing and composing process. There are five stages: prewriting (idea gathering), drafting (composing), revising (improving the draft), editing (correcting mechanical errors), and publishing (sharing with others). Student of all ages move back and forth among these stages; thus, writing is not a one-shot process and continues over multiple days. Using this process, students begin to understand that what they read is composed by an author like they are.

Text   Self-generated written responses

Predominant Focus of Instruction

1. Processing focus: meaning
2. Instructional phase: during writing followed by reading
3. Response mode emphasized: written discourse
4. Strategy emphasized: elaboration
5. Skill emphasized: literal and nonliteral comprehension
6. Source of information: reader based
7. Type of instruction: implicit
8. Type of cognitive processing: simultaneous

Procedures

1. The teacher secures writing folders. She can use a manilla folder or have students make one with construction paper.
2. The teacher explains that learning to write is a process that involves writing every day. The students write every day and put their written work in a folder. This is the prewriting stage of the process.
3. The drafting process (*composing a rough draft*) is usually the next step. The students choose an idea or ideas from their writing folder to write a draft. They use their ideas from prewriting folders to create a draft piece of work.
4. After the rough draft or sloppy copy is composed, the students begin to revise their draft, the next step in process writing. This includes adding and deleting words and ideas, changing ideas, and moving ideas around so that the writing makes more sense. Revising is hard work.
5. Sometimes, teachers model for students how to revise. They take a letter or something they have written and put it on a screen. Then they demonstrate revising their own writing.
6. Some teachers use a technique called Author's Chair to promote more revision and some editing. The author brings a draft piece to a group of students and reads the piece aloud, noticing if his classmates can follow the text. In this way, the revision process for word use and idea development continues.
7. To start the editing phase, the students reread their work looking for mechanical mistakes that occur while thinking about ideas and organization. Students can use the word CUPS (C *C*apitalization, U Grammar *U*sage, P *P*unctuation, and S *S*pelling) to help them remember what they are looking for when proofreading their paper.

8. After they proofread their writing, the students take the piece to the editor's table. This usually includes other students, parents, or the teacher. These individuals proofread the written work and make suggestions.
9. Finally, the final draft is ready for sharing with the entire community. The step is known as the publishing phase of process writing. Although there are multiple ways to publish work, teachers often create books (folded paper, computer book, and so on)
10. As students celebrate their published works, they begin to view themselves as authors.

Note: Adapted from http://wind.prohosting.com/bstone38/writingprocess.htm.

Further Diagnostic Applications

Basic View of Reading   Reading is an active, reader-based process in which readers' personal understanding focuses thinking. Both writing and reading are constructive processes that are influenced by the desire to communicate ideas.

Patterns of Strengths and Strategies   Process writing is most appropriate for simultaneous, verbal students who enjoy communicating ideas through writing. In this technique, they demonstrate their ideas by writing and revising a piece of work.

Learner Patterns That Produce Increased Engagement

1. For simultaneous learners who need time to express their ideas in words, process writing allows them to think through ideas over time.
2. For visually oriented readers who prefer to communicate ideas through writing rather than talking, process writing allows them to put thoughts into words.
3. For passive readers who do not realize that reading and writing are constructive processes, this technique allows them to experience reading and writing as an author.
4. For text-bound readers who do not use personal understanding of the world to interpret information, process writing show them how a writer uses personal understanding to compose text.

Using the Technique as a Diagnostic Lesson   For process writing to be effective, a majority of the following statements must be answered in the affirmative:

Yes   *No*
_____ _____ 1. The student can write (produce letters) fairly easily.
_____ _____ 2. The student likes to communicate his ideas in writing.
_____ _____ 3. The student uses group processes to influence his ideas and to correct writing errors.

Evidence Base
Lipson, M. Y., Mosenthal, J., & Daniels, P. (2000). Process writing in the classrooms of eleven fifth-grade teachers with different orientations to teaching and learning. *Elementary School Journal, 101,* 209–231.

38

Process Writing

Pressley, M., Wharton-McDonald, R., & Mistretta-Hamptston, J. (1998). Literacy instruction in 10 fourth- and fifth-grade classrooms in upstate New York. *Scientific Studies of Reading, 2,* 159–194.

Web Sites

http://www.planet.eon.net/~bplaroch/index.html
http://www.angelfire.com/wi/writingprocess
http://www.planet.eon.net/~bplaroch/index.html

39 Question-and-Answer Relationships

Description   The question-and-answer relationships (QAR) technique is used to identify the type of response necessary to answer a question. Questions are the most prevalent means of evaluating reading comprehension; therefore, knowledge about sources of information required to answer questions facilitates comprehension and increases a student's ability to participate in teacher-directed discussion and answer questions in textbook exercises.

Text   Any text on which questions can be based

Predominant Focus of Instruction

1. Processing focus: meaning
2. Instructional phase: after reading
3. Response mode emphasized: oral discussion
4. Strategy emphasized: monitoring and elaboration
5. Skill emphasized: literal and nonliteral comprehension
6. Source of information: text based with some reader based
7. Type of instruction: explicit
8. Type of cognitive processing: successive

Procedure

1. The teacher selects a text that can be the basis of different kinds of questions.
2. She introduces "right there" and "on my own" sources of information:
   a. "Right there" means that the answers are "right there" on the page, and the words from the text can be used to answer the question. The teacher points out that this source is often used in answering a teacher's questions and in completing textbook exercises.
   b. "On my own" means that the students must fill in missing information, using what they know about what is in the text to answer the question. In this instance, the students must realize that they are "on their own" and use their own experience when they answer the question.
3. The teacher completes an example lesson identifying the kind of answer that is required by the question as well as giving the answer itself. She models the strategy of finding answers to questions and identifying the sources of information used.
4. The teacher introduces the "think and search" QAR. Here the student must read the text carefully and then "think and search" different parts of the text to find the answers that fit together to answer the question.
5. Then the teacher introduces "author and you" sources of information. In this response, the students need to think about what they know, what the author tells them, and how this information fits together.
6. The teacher completes an example lesson, identifying the kind of answer that is required by the questions as well as the answer. She models by using all four sources of information (*right there, think and search, author and you,* and *on my own*) and telling why and how the answers were obtained.
7. The students complete a third example lesson using a paragraph, the questions, and the answers. The students as a group identify the QAR. The students talk about reasons for a particular answer and the strategy used to obtain the answer.

8. The students complete a fourth example lesson using a paragraph, the questions, and the answers. Individually, the students identify the QAR. Then the students tell why they chose an answer based on textual and nontextual information and the strategy used to obtain the answer.

9. Steps 5, 6, and 7 are extended to longer passages in progressive steps until the procedure can be used with basal readers or content-area texts.

Further Diagnostic Applications

Basic View of Reading   Reading is a socio-interactive process in which a reader's interpretation of text is based on textual and nontextual information. As they share their thinking, readers construct answers to questions, shifting between the text and what they know. Therefore, not only do students figure out answers to questions, but they also know the source of information they are using to construct the answer.

Patterns of Strengths and Strategies   QAR is most appropriate for students who rely heavily on one source of information to answer questions or who cannot answer questions. The technique requires these students to distinguish when it is appropriate to use more of their background knowledge and/or textual information to answer questions.

Learner Patterns That Produce Increased Engagement

1. For passive learners who are unaware of the various sources of information used to answer questions, this technique increases their active reading by asking them to evaluate how they got an answer.

2. For learners who rely heavily on background knowledge about the subject to answer questions, this technique shows them when and how they can use background knowledge effectively and when they need to use the text.

3. For successive text-bound learners who do not use what they already know to answer questions, this technique shows them how to fill in missing information using what they know.

Using the Technique as a Diagnostic Teaching Lesson   For QAR to be effective, a majority of the following statements must be answered in the affirmative:

Yes   No

_____   _____   1. The student can understand the differences between reader-based answers and text-based answers.

_____   _____   2. The student can explain which source of information was used when he answered the question.

_____   _____   3. The student elaborates his responses to questions.

Evidence Base
Raphael, T. E., & Pearson, P. (1985). Increasing students' awareness of sources of information for answering questions. *American Educational Research Journal, 22,* 217–235.

Web Sites
http://www.itrc.ucf.edu/forpd/strategies/stratqar.html
http://www.readwritethink.org/lessons/lesson_view.asp?id=227
http://www.kimskorner4teachertalk.com/readingliterature/readingstrategies/QAR.htm
http://www.readingquest.org/strat/qar.html

40 Question-Generation Strategy   *Targeted Reading Levels 4–12*

Description   Writing postreading questions uses student-generated questions to develop an understanding of the important information in the text. By deciding what to ask in their questions, students think about what is important in the text.

Text   Narrative or expository

Predominant Focus of Instruction

1. Processing focus: meaning
2. Instructional phase: after reading
3. Response mode emphasized: written
4. Strategy emphasized: elaboration
5. Skill emphasized: literal and nonliteral comprehension
6. Source of information: reader based because the student writes the question but can be text based if the student uses only the text
7. Type of instruction: initially explicit, then rapidly moves to implicit
8. Type of cognitive processing: simultaneous

Procedure

1. The teacher selects a text at the appropriate level.
2. She discusses how to write questions:
    a. A question has an answer.
    b. A good question begins with a question word like *who, what, when, where,* or *why.*
    c. A good question asks about important information in the story.
3. The teacher selects a short paragraph and models writing questions about the important information in the text.
4. The students write questions after they read a short paragraph.
5. The students answer their questions.
6. The students compare their questions and answers with the teacher's questions and answers.
7. The teacher gives feedback about the importance of the questions.
8. The students write questions about the important information in their assigned text.
9. Other students answer the questions.
10. The students compare their questions and answers with the teacher's questions and answers.

Modifications

1. Instead of step 2, the teacher uses story grammar questions (e.g., "Who was the leading character?"). Then she has the students make story-specific questions (see "Story Mapping" in this part).
2. Instead of step 10, the teacher allows the students to share their questions and answers in small groups, which makes the technique more social.
3. The teacher uses postgenerated questioning with book reports. After reading a book, the student writes his questions on cards. Then other students who have read the same book can use the cards to answer questions about the book.

Further Diagnostic Applications

Basic View of Reading   Reading is an interactive process in which the reader selects important textual information by constructing questions using his background knowledge and selected information.

Patterns of Strengths and Strategies   Postgenerated questioning is most appropriate for students who have facility with word identification and word meaning but have difficulty studying for tests. For these students, this approach requires them to read text in order to formulate questions about the important information in the text.

Learner Patterns That Produce Increased Engagement

1. For successive learners who know the meanings of words but depend on teacher questioning to interpret the important information, this technique helps students become more independent by having students write the questions before comparing them with the teacher's questions.
2. For simultaneous learners who have not learned to ask themselves questions to monitor what they need to remember, this technique encourages students to monitor their understanding by asking themselves questions.
*3. For passive learners who try to remember all the details rather than focusing on the important information, by writing and comparing questions they begin to think about what is important to remember.

Using the Technique as a Diagnostic Teaching Lesson   For the question-generation strategy to be effective, a majority of the following statements must be answered in the affirmative:

Yes	No	
_____	_____	1. The student can recognize and understand the individual words in the text.
_____	_____	2. The student begins to ask himself what information is important enough to remember.
_____	_____	3. The student rehearses important information.

Evidence Base

Commeyras, M., & Sumner, G. (1998). Literature questions children want to discuss: What teachers and students learned in a second-grade classroom. *Elementary School Journal, 99,* 129–152.

Davey, B., & McBride, M. (1986). Effects of question-generation on reading comprehension. *Journal of Educational Psychology, 22,* 2–7.

King, J. R., Biggs, S., & Lipsky, S. (1984). Student's self-questioning and summarizing as reading study strategies. *Journal of Reading Behavior, 15,* 205–218.

Web Sites

http://www.interventioncentral.org/htmdocs/interventions/rdngcompr/qgen.php
http://www.designedinstruction.com/research/brief_ed_03-1.pdf

41 Questioning the Author

Targeted Reading Levels 4–12

Description Questioning the author is designed to have students grapple with and reflect on what the author is trying to say. Understanding comes from viewing reading as a conversation between the readers and the author (another person's ideas written down). By posing questions to the author, the students engage in a dynamic discussion about the author's ideas.

Text Narrative or expository

Predominant Focus of Instruction

1. Processing focus: meaning
2. Instructional phase: during and after reading
3. Response mode emphasized: oral or written
4. Strategy emphasized: monitoring and elaboration
5. Skill emphasized: literal and nonliteral comprehension
6. Source of information: reader based because students have to think about what the author might have meant
7. Type of instruction: more explicit than implicit
8. Type of cognitive processing: simultaneous

Procedure

1. The teacher selects a text at the appropriate level.
2. She plans how to approach the text.
   a. She identifies the major understandings students might construct from the passage and anticipates their problems.
   b. She decides where to stop reading and initiate a discussion by segmenting the passage before reading.
   c. She decides on the kinds of queries.
3. She decides on initiating questions that focus on the author and the major concepts the author wants readers to learn.
   a. What is the author trying to say here?
   b. What is the author's message?
   c. What is the author talking about?
4. Following reading a section, the teacher uses a second set of queries that focus on what the author meant when he wrote the text.
   a. What does the author mean here?
   b. Does the author explain this clearly?
5. Continuing on, the teacher uses a third set of queries that helps the students focus on making connections.
   a. Does this make sense with what the author told us before?
   b. How does this connect to what the author told us here?
6. Finally, the teacher uses a set of questions to focus on the author's reasons for including certain information.
   a. Does the author tell us why?
   b. Why do you think the author tells us this now?
7. Between the queries, the students read and discuss responding to the teacher queries.
8. The teacher repeats the queries in steps 3, 4, 5, and 6 section by section.

9. After reading the entire text, the students reflect on their responses and the author's work.

Modification   The queries can be modified to focus on narrative text. The following questions can be used:

1. Given what the author has already told you about this character, what do you think he's up to?
2. How does the author let you know that something has changed?
3. How does the author settle this for us?

Further Diagnostic Applications

Basic View of Reading   Reading is an interactive process in which the reader responds to queries about what the author meant. Using "author questions," the students construct a rational for the author's point of view and clarity of writing.

Patterns of Strengths and Strategies   Questioning the author is most appropriate for students who have facility with word identification and word meaning but have difficulty understanding text because they do not think about the author, a real person who wrote the text. For these students, this approach requires them to think about what authors were thinking when they wrote the text.

Learner Patterns That Produce Increased Engagement

1. For successive learners who know the meanings of words but depend on teacher questioning to interpret the important information, this technique helps students become more independent by thinking about the author's purpose for writing a text and the information they decide to include.
2. For simultaneous learners who have not learned to question the author's intentions, this technique provides queries that will reveal underlying reasons for including information.
3. For passive learners who believe everything in the text because the text is always right, this technique demonstrates to them that an author wrote the text and that an author is fallible; therefore, sometimes what the author wrote does not align with a reader's point of view.

Using the Technique as a Diagnostic Teaching Lesson   For the questioning the author technique to be effective, a majority of the following statements must be answered in the affirmative:

Yes	No	
_____	_____	1. The student can recognize and understand the individual words in the text.
_____	_____	2. The student begins to understand that an author wrote a text.
_____	_____	3. The student participates in the discussion.

Evidence Base

Almasi, J. F., McKeown, M. G., & Beck, I. L. (1996). The nature of engaged reading in classroom discussions of literature. *Journal of Literacy Research, 28,* 107–146.

Beck, I. L., McKeown, Ma. G., Sandora, C., Kucan, L., & Worthy, J. (1996). Questioning the author: A yearlong classroom implementation to engage students with text. *Elementary School Journal, 96,* 385–415.

Web Sites

http://www.readingquest.org/strat/qta.html
http://www.fcrr.org/FCRRReports/PDF/QuestioningAuthorFinal.pdf

42 Readers Theater

Targeted Reading Levels 2–5

Description   Readers theater is a dramatic interpretation of a play script through oral interpretive reading. The story theme and character development are conveyed through intonation, inflection, and fluency of oral reading.

Text   Scripts designed for the appropriate number of readers

Predominant Focus of Instruction

1. Processing focus: print and meaning
2. Instructional phase: after reading
3. Response mode emphasized: oral
4. Strategy emphasized: elaboration
5. Skill emphasized: fluency and nonliteral comprehension
6. Source of information: reader based and text based
7. Type of instruction: implicit
8. Type of cognitive processing: simultaneous

Procedure

1. The teacher selects a narrative text at the appropriate reading level and constructs a play script.
2. The teacher presents a brief description of the characters, setting, events, and problem.
3. The students select or are assigned appropriate parts to read.
4. The students preview the scripts silently.
5. The students practice reading the script until they are fluent.
6. Standing in a line in front of a seated audience, the students read the scripts orally.
7. No props or costumes are used.
8. The students convey the story line by their intonation and phrasing.
9. Listeners must use their imaginations to interpret the story line.

Modifications

1. A readers theater can be developed from the text that the students are reading. It provides additional reinforcement for word recognition. For example, when deciding how to write a script from a preprimer, the students and teacher reread parts of the text numerous times as they write the scripts on chart tablets.
2. Having the students write a readers theater script from a story can also improve comprehension. The students must decide what important dialogue and narration are necessary to understand the story.
3. Different reading levels can be included in a script to allow readers of varying reading abilities to participate in the same activity.

Further Diagnostic Applications

Basic View of Reading   Reading is an active, reader-based process in which the reader interprets the author's intended meaning through oral interpretative reading.

Patterns of Strengths and Strategies Readers theater is most appropriate for students who have a dramatic flair and when given the stage will perform. Often a quiet, less verbal student will perform in a readers theater because the expectation is performance.

Learner Patterns That Produce Increased Engagement

1. For simultaneous learners who communicate through drama and need to develop oral reading fluency, this technique is a natural way to develop fluency for these readers.
*2. For highly efficient decoders who are word bound and do not identify with characters, this technique helps them benefit from the naturalness of character identification forced by the readers theater script.
*3. A student who has difficulty tracking develops a purposeful reason to track when reading *short* readers theater scripts.

Using the Technique as a Diagnostic Teaching Lesson
For readers theater to be effective, a majority of the following statements must be answered in the affirmative:

Yes *No*

____ ____ 1. The student has enough oral reading fluency to convey the message.

____ ____ 2. The student likes to perform.

____ ____ 3. The student becomes more fluent as he identifies with the character.

Evidence Base

Keehn, S. (2003). The effect of instruction and practice through readers theatre on young readers' oral reading fluency. *Reading Research and Instruction, 42,* 40–61.

Rinehart, S. (1999). "Don't think for a minute that I'm getting up there": Opportunities for readers' theater in a tutorial for children with reading problems. *Reading Psychology, 20,* 71–89.

Web Sites

http://www.aaronshep.com/rt
http://www.readwritethink.org/lessons/lesson_view.asp?id=172
http://pbskids.org/zoom/activities/playhouse

43 Reciprocal Teaching

Targeted Reading Levels 5–12

Description   Reciprocal teaching is a technique to develop comprehension of expository text by modeling and practicing how to understand the text. The teacher and students take turns leading a discussion. The teacher provides the initial model by thinking aloud about *how* she constructs a summary, makes up questions, clarifies what is difficult, and predicts what else the text will discuss.

Text   Expository text is preferred.

Predominant Focus of Instruction

1. Processing focus: meaning
2. Instructional phase: during reading
3. Response mode emphasized: oral discussion
4. Strategy emphasized: elaboration
5. Skill emphasized: literal comprehension
6. Source of information: text based
7. Type of instruction: explicit
8. Type of cognitive processing: successive

Procedure

1. The teacher selects a text from a content area.
2. The teacher explains the four tasks: (a) question generating, (b) summarizing, (c) clarifying the difficult parts, and (d) predicting what the next section will discuss.
3. Both the students and the teacher silently read the first section of the text.
4. The teacher talks about the four tasks of reading for that section.
   a. She constructs several good questions.
   b. She constructs a summary of the section, using the main idea and supporting details.
   c. She clarifies difficult parts by stressing vocabulary and organization.
   d. She predicts what the next section will discuss by using the title and headings.
5. The students help revise the summary, answer the questions, clarify unclear parts of the summary and the text, and evaluate the prediction.
6. After modeling, a student becomes teacher. He thinks aloud, using the four steps.
7. The teacher becomes a student and assumes the student's role.
8. Students take turns playing "teacher."
9. Periodically the teacher reviews the four activities with the student.
   a. Rule for good questions: They should be clear and stand by themselves.
   b. Rule for summaries: Look for the topic sentences, make up a topic sentence if there is none, make lists, and delete what is unimportant.
   c. Rule for clarifying: Look for difficult vocabulary, incomplete information, unclear references, and unusual expressions.
   d. Rule for predictions: Use the title and headings, use questions in the text, and use text structures like *two kinds, four levels,* and so on.
10. As the students play "teacher," the teacher does the following:
    a. She provides feedback about the quality of summaries or questions. When necessary, she models her thinking for the student. For example, she might comment, "That was a start on a summary, but I would summarize by adding . . ."

   b. She provides encouragement to the student playing "teacher." For example, she may say, "I liked the way you identified the important information."

Further Diagnostic Applications

Basic View of Reading   Reading is a socio-interactive process in which a reader's interpretation of the text is shaped by discussing ideas with others as well as by the use of the textual and nontextual information. By thinking aloud, the student becomes more aware of how to integrate knowledge sources when reading.

Patterns of Strengths and Strategies   Reciprocal teaching is most appropriate for students who have verbal fluency and experiential knowledge of the topics but need to focus their understanding. These students read and retain information, but the complexities of content-area reading often produce an overload of unorganized facts rather than important related information.

Learner Patterns That Produce Increased Engagement

1. For passive yet verbally fluent learners who need to organize and rethink the text, this technique, with the teacher's model, helps students as they prepare to lead the discussion.
2. For sequential learners who try to memorize a string of unrelated facts rather than focus on the important points and how the facts relate to these points, this technique encourages them to use only the important information in their summary.
3. For passive readers who do not verify information learned, this technique helps them actively summarize text and clarify the difficult parts.

Using the Technique as a Diagnostic Teaching Lesson   For reciprocal teaching to be effective, a majority of the following statements must be answered in the affirmative:

Yes	No	
_____	_____	1. The student has enough expressive language so that constructing a summary is not terribly time consuming.
_____	_____	2. The student can ask good questions.
_____	_____	3. The student can summarize information and convey this information to the group.

Evidence Base

Lederer, J. (2000). Reciprocal teaching of social studies in inclusive elementary classrooms. *Journal of Learning Disabilities, 33,* 91–106.

Le Fevre, D., Moore, D. W., & Wilkinson, I. A. (2003). Tape-assisted reciprocal teaching: Cognitive bootstrapping for poor decoders. *British Journal of Educational Psychology, 73,* 37–58.

Lysynchuk, L., Pressley, M., & Vye, N. (1990). Reciprocal teaching improves standardized reading-comprehension performance in poor comprehenders. *Elementary School Journal, 90,* 469–484.

Palinscar, A. S., & Brown, A. L. (1984). Reciprocal teaching of comprehension-fostering and comprehension-monitoring activities. *Cognition and Instruction, 1,* 117–175.

Web Sites

http://www.greece.k12.ny.us/instruction/ela/6-12/Reading/Reading%20Strategies/reciprocal%20teaching.htm

http://pers.dadeschools.net/prodev/reciprocal_teaching.htm

44 Repeated Readings

Targeted Reading Levels 1–4

Description   The repeated readings technique is the oral rereading of a student-selected passage until accuracy and speed are fluent and represent the natural flow of language. Students must be able to read the selection with some degree of accuracy at the beginning of instruction.

Text   Self-selected

Predominant Focus of Instruction

1. Processing focus: print
2. Instructional phase: after reading
3. Response mode emphasized: oral production
4. Strategy emphasized: monitoring
5. Skill emphasized: fluency and word identification
6. Source of information: text-based phasing to reader based
7. Type of instruction: implicit but can be adapted to explicit
8. Type of cognitive processing: initially successive but rapidly moves to simultaneous

Procedure

1. The student selects a text that he wants to read. The teacher segments the text into manageable passages for oral reading.
2. The teacher makes a copy of the text so she can mark errors as the student reads.
3. The teacher explains that rereading a passage is like practicing a musical instrument or practicing a football play. The repetition helps students read more smoothly and automatically.
4. The student reads the passage orally while the teacher records errors and speed.
5. The errors and speed are charted on a graph.
6. The student practices silently while the teacher listens to other students.
7. The student rereads the passage to the teacher while she records errors with a different-colored pen.
8. The errors and speed are charted on a graph for the second reading. Progress toward the reading goals is discussed.
9. The procedure is continued until a speed of 85 words per minute is reached.
10. Steps 6, 7, and 8 are repeated as needed.

Modifications

1. The teacher can select a text that corresponds to instructional needs.
2. Responsive repeated reading could be conducted where, after the first read, the teacher charts the miscues and then discusses important miscues and sentences where there are multiple miscues. The teacher discusses the important miscues and the process of self-correction. The teacher can suggest that the student say to himself, "Did that make sense?" as well as other correction strategies.
   a. Echo reading (see modification #1 in "Impress Method" in this part) of sentences where the most miscues occur.
   b. Discussion of the author's use of language and intended meaning.

   c. Tape record the readings. Then the student listens to the recording, marks errors, and records his time.
3. Only one or two rereadings are used. All readings are charted.

Further Diagnostic Applications

Basic View of Reading   Reading is both a text-based decoding process and an interactive comprehension process. Comprehension is dependent on the automatic decoding of printed language. Therefore, fluent and accurate decoding are necessary for efficient comprehension. Thus initially, reading is a text-based process.

Patterns of Strengths and Strategies   Repeated readings are most appropriate for students who read word by word and do not use contextual clues to confirm anticipated words as they read. For these learners, the repeated readings encourage the use of overall contextual meaning and sentence structure to predict words and correct mistakes.

Learner Patterns That Produce Increased Engagement

1. For learners who have a great deal of difficulty with word identification because of an overemphasis on isolated word drill, this technique uses the overall textual meaning to increase word recognition accuracy.
2. For simultaneous learners who cannot blend sounds and must rely, therefore, on the context for word identification accuracy, this technique, if progressively difficult text is used, allows students to read more complex text, where words can be recognized by using context rather than what words look or sound like.
3. For successive learners who have become word bound with heavy phonics instruction and need to develop fluency and use of contextual cues for word identification, this technique emphasizes using context to identify words rather than sounding out individual words.

Using the Technique as a Diagnostic Teaching Lesson   For repeated readings to be effective, a majority of the following statements must be answered in the affirmative:

Yes   *No*

_____ _____ 1. The student's errors decrease on a second read.
_____ _____ 2. The student's speed increases on a second read.
_____ _____ 3. The student's pattern of errors includes more self-corrections as fluency increases.
_____ _____ 4. Over several interventions, the student decreases the number of errors on an initial at-sight reading.

Evidence Base
Kuhn, M. R. (2005). A comparative study of small group fluency instruction. *Reading Psychology, 26,* 127–146.
Samuels, S. J. (1979). The method of repeated readings. *The Reading Teacher, 32,* 405–408.

Web Sites
http://www.itrc.ucf.edu/forpd/strategies/stratfluency.html
http://www.sedl.org/cgi-bin/mysql/buildingreading.cgi?showrecord=7&l=description

45 ReQuest   *Targeted Reading Levels 4–12*

Description   The ReQuest (reciprocal questioning) technique develops comprehension by having the teacher and the student take turns asking and answering questions. At turning points in the text, the teacher models effective question-asking strategies. The student, in turn, asks appropriate questions by following the model. The goal is to develop self-questioning strategies for the student.

Text   Particularly suited for narrative text but can be used with expository text

Predominant Focus of Instruction

1. Processing focus: meaning
2. Instructional phase: during reading
3. Response mode emphasized: oral discussion
4. Strategy emphasized: prediction and elaboration
5. Skill emphasized: literal and nonliteral comprehension
6. Source of information: reader based
7. Type of instruction: implicit
8. Type of cognitive processing: successive

Procedure

1. The teacher selects a text that is at the student's reading level and that is predictive in nature.
2. The teacher identifies appropriate points for asking questions.
3. The teacher introduces the ReQuest procedure in terms the student will understand. She tells him that they will be taking turns asking questions about the sentence or paragraph and what it means. The student is to ask questions that a teacher might ask. Then the teacher emphasizes that questions must be answered fully and that they sometimes require support from the text.
4. The student and teacher read the first sentence silently.
5. When the teacher closes her book, the student asks questions. The teacher answers the question, integrating background knowledge and textual information. She also tells how she decided on her answer.
6. Then the teacher asks questions about any important points not mentioned, modeling integrating information and the predictive nature of reading by using questions such as "What do you think will happen next? Why do you think so?"
7. The teacher provides feedback about the student's questioning behavior during the procedure.
8. The procedure is used to develop purposes for reading and employs only the first three or four paragraphs.
9. The student reads the rest of the story silently to see whether he answers his questions.
10. Follow-up discussion and activities can be used.

Further Diagnostic Applications

Basic View of Reading   Reading is a socio-interactive process in which readers' questioning strategies are shaped by discussing questions with others. This shared thinking requires the reader to monitor his behavior by asking himself questions about the important information in the text and answering these questions, using both textual and nontextual information.

Patterns of Strengths and Strategies　The ReQuest procedure is most appropriate for sequential learners who like to ask questions but do not always attend to the text for answers. For these students, the approach matches their desire to ask questions, but it focuses on the relevant information and develops an active question-asking role rather than a passive role.

Learner Patterns That Produce Increased Engagement

1. For successive learners who ask questions and enjoy breaking a story into parts, reading only sections at a time, this technique uses their strength to show them how to elaborate understanding using the text and what they know.
2. For successive learners who ask irrelevant questions when reading and fail to comprehend the main points, this technique focuses attention on asking important questions and justifying answers.
*3. For passive learners who read words fluently but do not ask themselves what the passage means, this technique develops self-questioning and monitoring of comprehension.
*4. For passive readers who read words fluently but do not use prior knowledge to interpret text, this technique asks students to use both textual and nontextual information to ask and answer questions.

Using the Technique as a Diagnostic Teaching Lesson　For the ReQuest technique to be effective, a majority of the following statements must be answered in the affirmative:

Yes　　*No*

_____　_____　1. The student likes to ask questions.

_____　_____　2. The student can answer questions.

_____　_____　3. The student can follow the teacher's model in question-answering behavior.

Evidence Base

King, A. (1991). Enhancing peer interactions and learning in the classroom through reciprocal questioning. *American Educational Research Journal, 27,* 664–668.

Manzo, A. V. (1969). The request procedure. *Journal of Reading, 2,* 123–126.

Web Sites

http://www.sedl.org/cgi-bin/mysql/buildingreading.cgi
http://www2.etown.edu/bap/Resources/recipquest.pdf

46 Retelling

Targeted Reading Levels 1–5

Description　Retelling is a technique in which a reader makes a mental representation of the story and uses it to orally retell the story. The student tells about the characters, setting, problem, main episodes, and resolution.

Text　Narrative but can be applied to all kinds

Predominant Focus of Instruction

1. Processing focus: meaning
2. Instructional phase: after reading
3. Response mode emphasized: oral production
4. Strategy emphasized: elaboration
5. Skill emphasized: literal comprehension
6. Source of information: both reader based and text based
7. Type of instruction: implicit
8. Type of cognitive processing: simultaneous

Procedure

1. Before reading, the teacher explains to the students that she is going to ask them to retell the story when they have finished reading.
2. If the teacher is expecting the students to include specific information, then she should tell the students before reading.
3. The teacher asks the students to retell the story as if they were telling it to a friend who has never heard it before.
4. The students tell the story, noting the important parts: story setting, theme, plot, sequence, and resolution.
5. If the student is hesitant, the teacher uses prompts at the beginning, middle, and end (see step 6).
6. If the student is unable to tell the story, the retelling is prompted step by step: "Once there was . . . who did . . . in the . . . (The character) had a problem. . . . To solve the problem, (the character) . . . first . . . second . . . third. . . . Finally, the problem was solved by . . . and then. . . ."
7. When the retelling is complete, the teacher can ask direct questions about important information omitted.
8. The teacher can also refer the student to the text to reread omitted important information.

Modifications

1. Retelling can be enhanced through the use of feltboards, role playing, and puppets.
2. Retelling can be easily adapted to small group or partner activities in the classroom.

Further Diagnostic Applications

Basic View of Reading　Reading is a socio-interactive process in which the reader reconstructs the story, thinking about what he wants to communicate to the instructional group. His interpretation includes his own perceptions of what is important to remember as well as what he needs to communicate.

46

Retelling

Patterns of Strengths and Strategies The retelling approach is most appropriate for students who have verbal strengths and remember the story long enough to internalize it and retell it. Retelling uses their strength to elaborate textual information.

Learner Patterns That Produce Increased Engagement

1. For readers who like to tell stories but fail to recount the most important events in the passage, retelling uses their strength to draw attention to important textual information.
*2. For readers who are hesitant to communicate their ideas, retelling increases the students' confidence by having them practice reformulating the information they read.
*3. For bilingual readers who become confused because they represent text in two language codes, retelling helps these learners use the text and classroom language to express their ideas.

Using the Technique as a Diagnostic Teaching Lesson For retelling to be effective, both of the following statements must be answered in the affirmative:

Yes   No

_____   _____   1. The student can verbalize some ideas about the story.
_____   _____   2. The student organizes a response that includes some of the story elements.

Evidence Base

Gambrell, L. B., Koskinen, P. S., & Kapinus, B. A. (1991). Retelling and the reading comprehension of proficient and less-proficient readers. *Journal of Educational Research, 84,* 356–362.

Web Sites

http://www.stenhouse.com/pdfs/0383ch13.pdf
http://classroom.jc-schools.net/read/RETELLING.pdf
http://www.waze.net/oea/activities/1
http://www.louisianavoices.org/unit5/edu_unit5w_story_retelling.html

47 Retrospective Miscue Analysis   *Targeted Reading Levels K–5*

Description   The retrospective miscue analysis technique asks students to listen to their miscues and evaluate the strategies they use as well as the strategies they might have used. In the discussion, the student and teacher discuss what good readers do when they encounter problems when reading.

Text   Passages or stories

Predominant Focus of Instruction

1. Processing focus: print and meaning
2. Instructional phase: during reading
3. Response mode emphasized: oral reading
4. Strategy emphasized: monitoring
5. Skill emphasized: word identification
6. Source of information: reader based
7. Type of instruction: implicit
8. Type of cognitive processing: simultaneous

Procedure

1. The teacher selects an interesting text that is near the student's instructional level.
2. Before beginning, the teacher conducts a reading interview.
3. The teacher tapes the student reading the selected text.
4. After the initial session, the teacher codes miscues on a printed version of text and preselects miscues to discuss during retrospective miscue analysis.
5. Sometimes, the teacher may want the student to listen to the tape and stop when he hears a miscue.
6. The teacher and student listen to the tape and mark miscues on a printed version of text.
7. The teacher and student discuss miscues using the following questions taken from Goodman and Marek (1996, p. 45):

   1. Does the miscue make sense?
   2. Does the miscue sound like language?
   3. a. Was the miscue corrected?
      b. Should it have been?
   If the answers to questions 1 and 3a were "No," then ask:
   4. Does the miscue look like what was on the page?
   5. Does the miscue sound like what was on the page?
   For all miscues, ask:
   6. Why do you think you made this miscue?
   7. Did that miscue affect your understanding of the text?

8. As they discuss, the teacher expands the student's responses by asking, "Why do you think that?" or "How do you know?"

Further Diagnostic Applications

Basic View of Reading   Reading is a social process in which understanding the process of reading is developed as students explain their thinking about how reading occurs. As students develop an understanding of the reading process, they begin to revalue themselves as readers.

Patterns of Strengths and Strategies   Retrospective miscue analysis is most appropriate for students who do not integrate the cuing systems; instead, they rely on a single system for figuring out words. As they evaluate their miscues using the structured questions, they explain how to correct miscues based on more than one cuing system.

Learner Patterns That Produce Increased Engagement

1. For highly social students who like to interact with others and discuss their thinking, this technique lets them discuss strategies for figuring out words.
2. For simultaneous learners who rely heavily on background knowledge when reading without attending to text cues, retrospective miscue analysis encourages them to attend to letters and meaning simultaneously.
*3. For word-bound readers who do not use their understanding of the passage to correct miscues, this technique helps them talk about how the meaning and words can be used together to read fluently.

Using the Technique as a Diagnostic Teaching Lesson   For the retrospective miscue analysis technique to be effective, a majority of the following statements must be answered in the affirmative:

Yes	*No*	
_____	_____	1. The student understands how his miscue occurred.
_____	_____	2. The student begins to value his strategy use.
_____	_____	3. The student becomes more strategic.

Evidence Base

Goodman, Y. M., & Marek, A. M. (1996). Retrospective miscue analysis. In Y. M. Goodman & A. M. Marek (Eds.), *Retrospective miscue analysis: Revaluing readers and reading* (pp. 39–49). Katonah, NY: Richard C. Owen Publishers.

Web Sites

http://www.readingmatrix.com/articles/theurer
http://books.heinemann.com/shared/onlineresources/E00720/appendixH.pdf

48 Say Something

Targeted Reading Levels 2–12

Description   Say something is a technique to develop personal responses to literature by having students take turns saying something at intervals during the reading of the story.

Text   Especially suited for engaging, narrative text but can be applied to all text

Predominant Focus of Instruction

1. Processing focus: meaning
2. Instructional phase: during reading
3. Response mode emphasized: oral discussion
4. Strategy emphasized: elaboration
5. Skill emphasized: nonliteral comprehension
6. Source of information: reader based
7. Type of instruction: implicit
8. Type of cognitive processing: simultaneous move toward successive because story sections are used initially

Procedure

1. The teacher and students choose an engaging text.
2. The teacher demonstrates reading with a partner and making a personal response about the text read.
3. The teacher encourages students to challenge and extend the ideas of their partner.
4. The students choose partners for reading.
5. The partners decide whether the reading will be oral or silent.
6. The partners take turns reading and saying something about what they have read.
7. After the students have finished, the teacher leads a group discussion.
8. The teacher puts a central topic in the middle of an overhead or on the chalkboard.
9. The students generate ideas about the topic and discuss how they fit with the author's ideas.
10. After reading several selections in this fashion, the teacher engages students in a discussion of how they use this strategy as they read.

Further Diagnostic Applications

Basic View of Reading   Reading is a social process in which interpretations develop through communicating ideas to others. This sharing enhances and extends text understanding.

Patterns of Strengths and Strategies   The say something technique is appropriate for students who like to talk about what they read as they are reading the text. This dialogue helps social students refine their ideas using their strength.

Learner Patterns That Produce Increased Engagement

1. For self-directed readers who need to talk aloud about their personal feelings, say something allows students to talk about their personal responses to passages.

*2. For quiet students who need to verbalize ideas in a safe environment before discussing those ideas in a large group, the say something technique gives them a chance to try out ideas with a partner.

Using the Technique as a Diagnostic Teaching Lesson   For the say something technique to be effective, a majority of the following statements must be answered in the affirmative:

Yes   *No*

_____   _____   1. The student can talk about the text read.

_____   _____   2. The student can attend to the meaning while reading so that he can make a response.

_____   _____   3. The student can relate personally to his partner.

Evidence Base

Liang, L. A., Peterson, C. A., & Graves, M. F. (2005). Investigating two approaches to fostering children's comprehension of literature. *Reading Psychology, 26,* 387–400.

Web Sites

http://www.learningpt.org/literacy/adolescent/strategies/something.php
http://departments.bcsd.com/cipd/say_something1.htm

49 Semantic Mapping

Levels: All levels

Description   Semantic mapping or webbing develops understanding by visually mapping relationships among words and ideas. The target idea or word is placed in the center of a circle (see figure on next page). The students brainstorm information they already know about the word or idea. Both new information and the students' knowledge of information are arranged around this target idea or word to show relationships between what students already know and the new word or idea.

Text   Key words or ideas; often used to introduce vocabulary words for a story

Predominant Focus of Instruction

1. Processing focus: meaning
2. Instructional phase: before or after reading
3. Response mode emphasized: oral discussion
4. Strategy emphasized: elaboration
5. Skill emphasized: nonliteral comprehension
6. Source of information: reader based
7. Type of instruction: implicit
8. Type of cognitive processing: simultaneous

Procedure

1. The teacher chooses a word or idea that is a key element of what is to be read.
2. She places the word inside a circle in the middle of a blank page or chalkboard.
3. The students and the teacher brainstorm what is already known about this word or idea and place the information in meaningful categories, making a visual array of the relationships.
4. The teacher adds each new idea or word that describes the target idea to the web by drawing lines and new circles that indicate their relationships (see the accompanying figure). For the concept *image,* for example, some relationships involve similes of what an image is like, some suggest the composition of an image, and others look at how an image might be useful.
5. The students read the story.
6. The students and the teacher add additional story information to the semantic map.
7. The students and the teacher discuss new understandings to known concepts and new relationships that were gained by reading.

Modification

1. For the student who needs to build a meaning vocabulary, vocabulary cards can be made with maps on one side of the card and the words in sentences on the reverse side. These words are then reviewed periodically for comprehension.

Further Diagnostic Applications

Basic View of Reading   Reading is an interactive process in which readers use their background knowledge to create semantic relationships between word knowledge (verbal labels) and world knowledge (big ideas).

Semantic Map

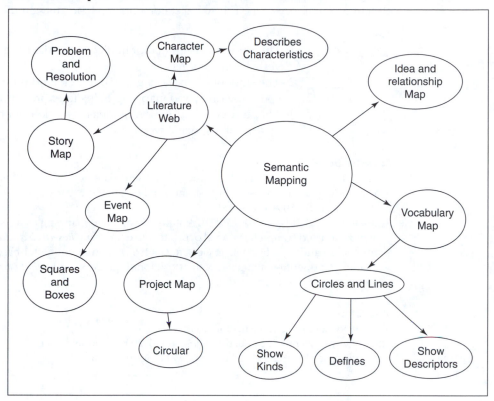

Note. Made with Kidspiration software.

Patterns of Strengths and Strategies Semantic mapping encourages students to use their experiential knowledge to expand their understanding; therefore, it is most appropriate for students who tend to think visually about relationships without describing these relationships in words. This strategy facilitates learning for this student because it begins by showing the visual relationships and then uses words to explain that relationship.

Learner Patterns That Produce Increased Engagement

1. For simultaneous thinkers who perceive visual-spatial relationships rather than definitional relationships, this technique helps students use their visual understanding of relationships to increase their understanding of concepts.
2. For bilingual students who have a well-developed experiential base but need to develop a meaning vocabulary, the semantic mapping of relationships helps them make specific comparisons between the events of their life and the words that are commonly used to express them.
*3. For students with verbal weaknesses who needs to develop a network of meaning, this technique helps them develop verbal relationships among words and the labels used to express those relationships.

Using the Technique as a Diagnostic Teaching Lesson   For semantic mapping to be effective, a majority of the following statements must be answered in the affirmative:

Yes   No

_____ _____ 1. The student has an elaborated experiential base that helps to make verbal connections.

_____ _____ 2. The student often has a general understanding but does not know specific words, and mapping helps to express that understanding.

_____ _____ 3. The student's elaboration of ideas is marked with the word *thing* instead of a specific word.

Evidence Base

Bimmel, P. E., van den Bergh, H., Utrecht, U., & Oostdam, R. J. (2001). Effects of strategy training on reading comprehension in first and foreign language. *European Journal of Psychology of Education, 16,* 509–529.

Ruddell, R. B., & Boyle, O. F. (1989). A study of cognitive mapping as a means to improve summarization and comprehension of expository text. *Reading Research and Instruction, 29,* 12–22.

Sinatra, R., Beaudry, J., Pizzo, J., & Geisert, G. (1994). Using a computer-based semantic mapping, reading, and writing approach with at-risk fourth graders. *Journal of Computing in Childhood Education, 5,* 93–112.

Web Sites

http://www.k12.nf.ca/fatima/semmap.htm
http://www.units.muohio.edu/eap/edt346e/fall_2000/GroupFive/semantic_map.html
http://olc.spsd.sk.ca/DE/PD/instr/strats/webbing/index.html

50 Sentence Combining

Targeted Reading Levels 3–7

Description Sentence combining is a technique designed to help students write and understand complex sentences. The student is shown how to combine short sentences to make increasingly more complex sentences.

Text The student's own writing or short sentences from the text

Predominant Focus of Instruction

1. Processing focus: meaning
2. Instructional phase: after reading
3. Response mode emphasized: oral discussion and written discourse
4. Strategy emphasized: elaboration
5. Skill emphasized: sentence comprehension
6. Source of information: text based
7. Type of instruction: implicit
8. Type of cognitive processing: successive; but using manipulatives adds a simultaneous aspect

Procedure

1. The teacher introduces the concept of combining sentences by using short sentences that the student can read.
2. The teacher explains that simple sentences can be combined and still have the same meaning.
3. She begins by writing sentences on the board, such as these:

   The dog is brown.

   The dog is in the park.

   The dog bit the man.

4. Then she shows the students how to delete repeated words or phrases. For the example in step 3, the following process would take place.
   a. The teacher might say, "If the dog is brown, we can call it a brown dog." On the board, the teacher would write this:

      brown + dog = brown dog

   b. The teacher explains that the sentence can be expanded by adding a phrase to tell where the dog is: "in the park." The teacher then shows the change:

      brown dog + in the park = the brown dog in the park

   c. She also explains that sentences can be further combined by telling what the dog did as the action in the sentence. Therefore, she adds "bit the man" as the action. The teacher writes this:

      The brown dog in the park + bit the man = The brown dog in the park bit the man.

5. The teacher points out to the student that by combining ideas into one sentence, reading and writing become more interesting.

Modifications

1. Phrases can be placed on cards and then combined and recombined to form new sentences.
2. Closed sentence combining, where cued words are provided to indicate how the sentence is combined, can be used to increase sensitivity to a particular sentence structure. For example, the following two sentences might be combined.

   I know_____.

   Chris stole the cookie.

   The teacher supplies the cue word *that,* and the sentences are combined with the following result.

   I know that Chris stole the cookie.

Further Diagnostic Applications

Basic View of Reading   Reading is a text-based process that involves the action of constructing meaning with words in sentences. The sequence of how words are linked in sentences affects reading comprehension; therefore, learning how the words are related in sentences facilitates both reading and writing.

Patterns of Strengths and Strategies   Sentence combining is most appropriate for students who can read short sentences but have difficulty following sentence order in longer sentences. Usually these students have verbal skills but lack the ability to link information in more complex frameworks.

Learner Patterns That Produce Increased Engagement

1. For successive learners who speak in short choppy sentences without using signal words to combine ideas, the technique shows them how short sentences are combined to form longer sentences.
*2. If simultaneous learners have difficulty with sentence order as exhibited by continued failure with a cloze activity, using sentence cards helps these students because they can visually manipulate the words in the sentence.

Using the Technique as a Diagnostic Teaching Lesson   For sentence combining to be effective, both of the following statements must be answered in the affirmative:

Yes   No

_____ _____ 1. The student can easily see the connection between short sentences and the complex sentences.

_____ _____ 2. The student likes to manipulate words and phrases.

Evidence Base
Straw, S., & Schreiner, R. (1982). The effect of sentence manipulation on subsequent measures of reading and listening comprehension. *Reading Research Quarterly, 17,* 339–352.

Wilkinson, P. A., & Patty, D. (1993). The effects of sentence combining on the reading comprehension of fourth grade students. *Research in the Teaching of English, 27,* 104–125.

Web Sites

http://www.learnnc.org/lessons/writing3142003579

http://www.mste.uiuc.edu/courses/ci407su02/students/stansell/strategies_for_sentence_combining.htm

51 Shared Reading Approach   *Targeted Reading Levels K–2*

Description   The shared reading approach is for beginning reading instruction that uses the rhythmic, repetitive sentence patterns in young children's stories. The teacher and children read the story together, creating an expectation for the words in the story. Then the students read the story by themselves.

Text   Predictable books with patterned language, such as

*Run, run, as fast as you can
You can't catch me; I'm the Gingerbread Man.*

Predominant Focus of Instruction

1. Processing focus: print
2. Instructional phase: during reading
3. Response mode emphasized: oral
4. Strategy emphasized: prediction and monitoring
5. Skill emphasized: word identification
6. Source of information: reader based and text based
7. Type of instruction: implicit
8. Type of cognitive processing: simultaneous

Procedure

1. The teacher chooses a predictable book or story.
2. The teacher and the students talk about the story to develop an expectation for meaning.
3. The students tell what they think happens in the story by telling the story page by page, using the pictures.
4. The teacher reads the story, letting the students confirm or revise their thinking about the story. The first reading focuses on comprehension.
5. The teacher reads the story aloud a second time, inviting the student to read along. She moves her finger above the line of print to mark the flow of language. After the second read, the teacher focuses on difficult phrases and repeats them with the class.
6. The teacher continues to read leaving out familiar phrases. The student supplies the missing word in the language pattern.
7. When the student knows the language pattern, he reads the story on his own. The teacher assists him when necessary.

Modification   When the student can predict easily and follows the teacher as she reads, then the teacher can omit steps 3 and 4.

Further Diagnostic Applications

Basic View of Reading   Reading is a social process in which readers use their shared understanding as well as language sense to figure out words. Through rhythmic, repetitious language patterns, the student recognizes the printed forms of words and infers the graphophonic rule system.

Patterns of Strengths and Strategies The shared reading approach encourages the student to associate printed words with the predictive patterns of language; therefore, it is most appropriate for students who laboriously try to decode words to derive meaning from text. Because a repetitive sentence pattern is used in this technique, the student can easily predict both what the words are and what they mean at the same time.

Learner Patterns That Produce Increased Engagement

1. For readers who have facility with verbal language but do not attend to the key features of short similar words found in basal readers, this technique allows them to identify words using the language pattern rather than single words.
2. For learners who need a sense of the whole story before reading, the shared reading approach provides them with a brisk, paced reading of the entire story prior to word identification.
*3. For extremely slow, laborious, letter-by-letter readers, the shared reading approach can restore their sense of the whole and increase fluency because of the predictable language pattern.
*4. For learners who read in a monotone, this approach can restore their sense of rhythm and cadence in reading.

Using the Technique as a Diagnostic Teaching Lesson For the shared reading approach to be effective, a majority of the following statements must be answered in the affirmative:

Yes   No

_____ _____   1. The student identifies the language patterns easily and can complete the oral cloze.

_____ _____   2. The student models the teacher's fluent reading and intonations readily.

_____ _____   3. The student enjoys repetitive language and does not find it boring.

Evidence Base

Johnston, F. R. (2000). Word learning in predictable text. *Journal of Educational Psychology, 92,* 248–255.

Leu, D. J., DeGroff, L. C., & Simons, H. D. (1986). Predictable texts and interactive-compensatory hypotheses: Evaluating individual differences in reading ability, context use, and comprehension. *Journal of Educational Psychology, 78,* 347–335.

Wasik, B. A., & Bond, M. A. (2001). Beyond the pages of a book: Interactive book reading and language development in preschool. *Journal of Educational Psychology, 93,* 243–251.

Web Sites

http://oe.edzone.net/balanced_literacy/shared_reading.htm

http://www.pnglanguages.org/lingualinks/literacy/implementaliteracyprogram/UsingSharedReading.htm

52 Sight-Word Approach   *Targeted Reading Levels K–2*

Description   The sight-word approach is a technique for beginning reading instruction that uses what words mean to develop what the word looks like. Through the use of pictures and oral context, students associate meaning with isolated sight words. Then the teacher can place sight words on individual cards so that the teacher can review and reinforce a recognition vocabulary.

Text   The basic preprimers and primers of published reading series, which contain a regular and controlled introduction of sight words in simple text.

Predominant Focus of Instruction

1. Processing focus: print
2. Instructional phase: before reading
3. Response mode emphasized: oral discussion
4. Strategy emphasized: prediction
5. Skill emphasized: word identification
6. Source of information: text based
7. Type of instruction: implicit
8. Type of cognitive processing: successive but has a simultaneous quality

Procedure

1. The teacher selects a text that has a controlled sight-word vocabulary.
2. She introduces sight words for the story by presenting them in isolation, supplemented by oral context and/or pictures.
3. The teacher reviews the words by placing words on cards and flashing the words in various orders. If the student cannot recall the words, a meaning or semantic prompt is used. If the student cannot recall the word *dog,* the teacher might prompt him by saying, "It rained cats and _____."
4. The student reads the story that contains the words. (The teacher uses the format for directed reading activity or directed reading-thinking activity to direct discussion.)
5. The teacher reinforces sight words by using cloze exercises, games with the word cards, and repetitive reading of stories with the controlled vocabulary.
6. After the student can recognize selected words at sight, the teacher uses analytic phonics (see "Analytic Phonics" in this part) to introduce how to decode new words by using analogies to known sight words. For example, the teacher might write *green, grass, and grow* on the board. She might then ask the students the following series of questions (the appropriate student answers are supplied in parentheses): "How are they alike? (They have *gr* letters.) What can we say about the *gr* sound? (It goes *gr-r-r.*) The next time you see *gr,* what sound are you going to try? (*gr-r-r.*)"

Modifications

1. The teacher can make a word bank by selecting target sight words (including easy words and concrete words) from each lesson and writing them on 3 by 5-inch cards. On the back of the card, she places the word in a sentence taken from the student's own vocabulary or the story.

2. To reinforce sight-word recognition, the teacher can flash the word cards, adding a semantic cue from the story. For example, when the target word *play* is forgotten, the teacher uses the semantic cue, "We like to run and _____."
3. The teacher can chart the number of word cards recognized by recording the student's responses on a graph so that the student can monitor his progress.
4. The teacher uses the word cards to form a word bank of known words that can be used to write and combine sentences. This bank becomes a spelling dictionary of known words for writing during sustained silent writing.
5. Students classify the word cards according to categories and make a feature analysis grid (see "Feature Analysis Grid" in this part).
6. The teacher constructs word sorts (see "Word Sorts" in this part).

Further Diagnostic Applications

Basic View of Reading   Reading is a text-based process in which readers learn the words in the text before they read. As they learn the words, they associate meaning developed through oral context to remember the word. Therefore, learning to read is a process of accumulating enough words recognized at sight so that a student can decode new words in a story by using the written context and applying decoding analogies to known words. Initially, this approach places a high demand on visual feature analysis and phonemic segmentation.

Patterns of Strengths and Strategies   The sight-word approach is most appropriate for students who have developed a systematic way of analyzing the key visual features of words.

Learner Patterns That Produce Increased Engagement

1. For simultaneous learners who attend to the key features of words noticing visual features that are alike and different, presenting the word with a semantic cue helps students focus on meaning and visual cues at the same time.
2. For inattentive learners who attend more to the pictures and context when reading stories than the important features of the words, the sight-word approach isolates the word so that students can identify and remember the key visual features.
*3. For passive learners who need direct instruction in how to select the key features so they can remember what the words look like, the sight-word approach provides a tool for the teacher to talk about what words look like.

Using the Technique as a Diagnostic Teaching Lesson   For the sight-word approach to be effective, a majority of the following statements must be answered in the affirmative:

Yes	*No*	
_____	_____	1. The student easily remembers the sight words taught.
_____	_____	2. The student analyzes the words, noticing visual differences among words.
_____	_____	3. The student can segment sounds so that applying decoding analogies is easy.

Evidence Base

Browder, D. M. (1998). A meta-analysis and review of sight word research and its implications for teaching functional reading to individuals with moderate and severe disabilities. *Journal of Special Education, 32,* 130–153.

Ehri, L. C. (2005). Learning to read words: Theory, findings, and issues. *Scientific Studies of Reading, 9,* 7–18.

King, J. R. (1984). Levels of categorization and sight word acquisition. *Reading Psychology, 5,* 129–138.

Web Sites

http://www.sedl.org/reading/topics/sight.html
http://www.usu.edu/teachall/text/reading/ReadBySight.htm

53 Sound Boxes   *Targeted Reading Levels 1–4*

Description   Sound boxes is a technique to develop print processing. The student writes a sentence by slowly saying the words. The student thinks about the letter sounds and then writes the letters in the words.

Text   Student generated

Predominant Focus of Instruction

1. Processing focus: print
2. Instructional phase: after reading
3. Response mode emphasized: written and oral production
4. Strategy emphasized: prediction and monitoring
5. Skill emphasized: word identification
6. Source of information: reader-based
7. Type of instruction: implicit
8. Type of cognitive processing: simultaneous phasing to successive

Procedure

1. The teacher provides a blank writing book with each page divided in half. The top half is for practice writing, and the bottom half is for sentence writing.
2. Assisted by the teacher, the student composes a brief message (one or two sentences).
3. The sentence is written word by word.
4. If the student is unfamiliar with the printed form of a word, he uses the practice section of the page.
5. The teacher assists by drawing boxes for each letter of the unfamiliar word. For example, the word *dog* would look like this:

```
┌───┐ ┌───┐ ┌───┐
│   │ │   │ │   │
└───┘ └───┘ └───┘
```

6. The student slowly says the sounds and places the letters he knows in the appropriate boxes.

7. The teacher supplies any unknown letters in the appropriate boxes, slowly saying the sounds in the word. In the example, the teacher places an *o* in the middle box and says, "d-d-o-o-g-g."
8. The teacher asks, "Does this look right?"
9. The student evaluates the word and writes it in his sentence.
10. After the sentence is written, the teacher writes it on a sentence strip and then cuts it apart into words.

11. The student reconstructs the sentence, matching the words in his writing book.
12. The sentence is always read in its entirety.

Modifications

1. When a word is unfamiliar to the student, the teacher may want to use magnetic letters before having the student use the writing book. In that case, the student constructs a familiar part and then the teacher supplies other letters.
2. The teacher may use this technique when editing writing during classroom activities.

Further Diagnostic Applications

Basic View of Reading   Reading is an active, reader-based process in which readers predict what words might look like by using their understanding of the graphophonic system (sound segmentation and sound synthesis).

Patterns of Strengths and Strategies   The sound boxes approach is most appropriate for students who write with facility and can predict some letters in a word. By predicting and writing the letters, the students create a personal system for recognizing words.

Learner Patterns That Produce Increased Engagement

1. For simultaneous learners who use only what they know when comprehending text and therefore guess wildly when they come to an unknown word, sound boxes help students focus on the details of printed words as they write a sentence.
*2. For passive learners who do not attempt to figure out unknown words, the students can actively predict letters in words by using sound boxes.

Using the Technique as a Diagnostic Teaching Lesson   For sound boxes to be effective, a majority of the following statements must be answered in the affirmative:

Yes	No	
_____	_____	1. The student can form letters.
_____	_____	2. The student can predict some letter sounds in words.
_____	_____	3. The student wants to communicate a message.

Evidence Base

Joseph, L. M. (2002). Facilitating word recognition and spelling using word boxes and word sort phonic procedures. *School Psychology Review, 31,* 122–129.

Elkonin, D. B. (1988). How to teach children to read. In J. A. Downing (Ed.), *Cognitive psychology and reading in the U.S.S.R.* (pp. 387–426). Oxford: North-Holland.

Web Sites

http://www.readwritethink.org/lesson_images/lesson216/murray.pdf
http://www.u-46.org/dbs/roadmap/files/Appendix/5Elkonin-soundbox.pdf

54 SQ3R

Description   SQ3R is a procedure for studying content-area text that includes the five steps of *survey, question, read, recite,* and *review.* It is designed as a procedure for students to use to monitor their comprehension and learning as they read and study expository text.

Text   Expository

Predominant Focus of Instruction

1. Processing focus: meaning
2. Instructional phase: before, during, and after reading
3. Response mode emphasized: oral discussion
4. Strategy emphasized: elaboration and prediction
5. Skill emphasized: literal comprehension
6. Source of information: text based
7. Type of instruction: explicit but lacks modeling
8. Type of cognitive processing: successive

Procedure

1. The teacher selects a content-area text at an appropriate reading level.
2. She introduces the five steps in a short minilesson.
3. *S—Survey.* The teacher explains how to skim (briefly read) the entire passage to construct an overall framework for the information. She directs the student to use the paragraph headings as key information in understanding the overall framework.
4. *Q—Question.* After the text is surveyed, the teacher directs the student to develop questions that he thinks will be answered in the passage. The teacher helps the student focus on the key concepts of the text as he develops the questions. She directs the student to use paragraph headings and italics to form the questions for each *section.*
5. *R—Read.* The student reads the text section by section to answer the questions posed at the beginning of each section. After a section has been read, the student proceeds to the next step.
6. *R—Recite.* The teacher explains that the student now is to answer the questions he posed for the section just read. The teacher encourages the student to construct an answer rather than read word for word from the text. At this point, the student may need to write down his answer to facilitate recall.
7. The three steps (question, read, and recite) are repeated for each section.
8. *R—Review.* After the last section is read, the student reviews the questions and answers for the entire text. At this time, the student tries to relate the information into an overall framework that will facilitate recall.

Further Diagnostic Applications

Basic View of Reading   Reading comprehension is a text-based process in which information from the text forms the framework for recalling facts and elaborating concepts in content-area texts.

Patterns of Strengths and Strategies　　SQ3R is most appropriate for students who have facility with word recognition and comprehension but lack an overall method for organizing factual information in a content-area text. For these students, the approach provides a systematic method for studying the information.

Learner Patterns That Produce Increased Engagement

1. For students who develop self-control easily, this technique gives them the steps to manage personal learning.
2. For successive learners who question and recall facts without using an organizational framework, the survey and review steps provide a means for relating information into an overall framework.
*3. For passive learners who can use the steps to develop a procedure for studying and remembering text, this technique gives them a tool for active reading.
*4. For successive learners who ask questions but forget to look for the answers, SQ3R gives them a tool for finding answers to important questions in the text.

Using the Technique as a Diagnostic Teaching Lesson　　For SQ3R to be effective, a majority of the following statements must be answered in the affirmative:

Yes	*No*	
_____	_____	1. The student identifies important textual information.
_____	_____	2. The student can construct questions from the subtopics.
_____	_____	3. The student follows the procedures and easily incorporates the steps.

Evidence Base

Adams, A., Carnine, D., & Gersten, R. (1982). Instructional strategies for studying content area texts in the intermediate grades. *Reading Research Quarterly, 18,* 27–55.

Martin, M. A. (1985). Students' applications of self-questioning study techniques: An investigation of their efficacy. *Reading Psychology, 6,* 69–83.

Pauk, W. (1993). *How to study in college* (5th ed.). Boston: Houghton Mifflin.

Web Sites

http://www.ucc.vt.edu/stdysk/sq3r.html
http://www.studygs.net/texred2.htm

54

SQ3R

55 Story Drama   *Targeted Reading Levels 2–6*

Description   Story drama is a method for developing reading comprehension by using the natural dramatic abilities of students. The students think about how a story will end by role-playing scenes from a story that they have read up to a certain point. By taking the roles of the various characters, the students use their knowledge of similar experiences, their affective response to the characters, and key information to act out their interpretation of the story.

Text   Various kinds of literature. Picture storybooks and adventure stories with an intriguing plot lend themselves to dramatic interpretation.

Predominant Focus of Instruction

1. Processing focus: meaning
2. Instructional phase: during reading
3. Response mode emphasized: oral and kinesthetic
4. Strategy emphasized: prediction and monitoring
5. Skill emphasized: nonliteral comprehension
6. Source of information: reader based
7. Type of instruction: implicit
8. Type of cognitive processing: simultaneous

Procedure

1. The teacher selects a story with an intriguing plot.
2. The teacher or the students read until they have enough information about the characters to role-play the story.
3. The teacher assigns the students the character roles from the story.
4. The teacher uses key props to engage the students in the drama in a concrete way.
5. The teacher and the students begin the drama at the point of interruption.
6. The students dramatize their predictions through role playing.
7. In the process of the dramatization, the teacher may stop the drama and have students exchange roles.
8. The students discuss their predictions and the information used to make them.
9. After the dramatization, the students write an ending for the story.
10. Finally, the students finish reading the story.
11. The students discuss and compare both the drama and the story ending.
12. The teacher and the students discuss their personal interpretations evidenced in the drama and how their individual viewpoints influence those interpretations.

Further Diagnostic Applications

Basic View of Reading   Reading is a social process in which the roles students play in the drama shape their personal interpretation and the group interaction focuses their comprehension. Reading requires a personal identification with the story's characters, problems, and events; therefore, the affective purposes of the reader and situational variables influence understanding.

Patterns of Strengths and Strategies   Story drama is most appropriate for students who are extremely expressive, divergent, and simultaneous when thinking. For these students, the powerful influence of personal, kinesthetic imagery is used to analyze the constructive process. This strategy encourages active involvement in analyzing not only the story line and character development but also the effect that personal identification with story characters has on comprehension.

Learner Patterns That Produce Increased Engagement

1. For students who prefer to use dramatic expression and body language to communicate instead of words, story drama uses this strength to aid the student in verbally communicating their ideas about the story.
2. For dramatic, impulsive learners who need to attend to the important information in the text, story drama focuses their attention on character traits and story theme in order to portray a character.
*3. For simultaneous learners who rely too heavily on personal identification with story characters and have difficulty establishing a sense of distance when reading, story drama helps them analyze how their personal identification affects interpretation.
*4. For passive learners who needs to engage in active interpretation of the story line, story drama concretely demonstrates how to be actively involved in a story.

Using the Technique as a Diagnostic Teaching Lesson   For story drama to be effective, a majority of the following statements must be answered in the affirmative:

Yes	No	
_____	_____	1. The student enjoys a dramatic presentation and can easily portray characters.
_____	_____	2. The student makes predictions as a result of the drama.
_____	_____	3. The student analyzes his personal identification with characters more objectively.

Evidence Based

Fizzano, W. J., Jr. (2000). The impact of story drama on the reading comprehension, oral language complexity, and the attitudes of third graders. *Dissertation Abstracts International Section A: Humanities and Social Sciences, 60,* 3908.

Wilhelm, J. D. (1995). The drama of engaged reading: Extending the reader through classroom story drama. *Reading and Writing Quarterly: Overcoming Learning Difficulties, 11,* 335–358.

Web Sites

http://www.readwritethink.org/lessons/lesson_view.asp?id=1024
http://jaie.asu.edu/sp/SPcap.html

56 Story Mapping

Targeted Reading Levels 1–8

Description   Story mapping is a visual representation of the logical sequence of events in a narrative text. The elements of setting, problem, goal, events, and resolution are recorded visually on a sheet of paper.

Text   Any narrative text with a fairly coherent story line

Predominant Focus of Instruction

1. Processing focus: meaning
2. Instructional phase: during or after reading
3. Response mode emphasized: written
4. Strategy emphasized: monitoring and elaboration
5. Skill emphasized: literal comprehension
6. Source of information: text based
7. Type of instruction: explicit
8. Type of cognitive processing: successive but has a visual arrangement (simultaneous)

Procedure

1. The teacher selects a narrative passage of sufficient length so that it has a cohesive story line.
2. The teacher prepares questions to lead students through the story map.
3. The teacher discusses the organization of a story by explaining that every story has a beginning, middle, and an end.
   a. The beginning tells the place and who the characters are.
   b. During the middle of the story, the central character has a problem and makes a plan to solve it. Certain events in the story lead to solving the problem.
   c. The end of the story tells how the character(s) solved the problem.
4. The teacher explains the visual story map (see the accompanying figure) and relates it to story organization.
5. The students read the story.
6. The teacher and the students fill out the map together. The teacher uses the prepared questions to guide the completion of the map.
7. The teacher and the students compare this story with other stories they have read.

Further Diagnostic Applications

Basic View of Reading   Reading is an interactive process in which the reader understands how the elements of a story affect interpretation of the story.

Patterns of Strengths and Strategies   Story mapping is most appropriate for the learner who profits from a visual representation of story organization in order to develop adequate comprehension. Often the abundance of facts overwhelms the young reader, who needs a simple structure such as a story map to apply to stories to help him organize and remember events.

Story Mapping

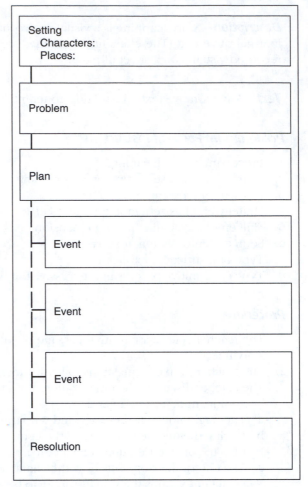

Source. Adapted from *Asking Questions About Stories* by P. David Pearson, Number 15 of the Ginn Occasional Papers. Copyright, 1982, by Ginn and Company. Used by the permission of P. David Pearson.

Learner Patterns That Produce Increased Engagement

1. For simultaneous learners who have difficulty organizing sequential events of the story and remembering factual detail, the story map uses their visual strengths to develop the text-based skill of story development.

*2. For passive learners who have difficulty retelling the story and often leave out key events or characters in the retelling, the story map gives a structure to the retelling.

*3. For fact-bound learners who lack a cohesive sense of story, the map provides them with an overall view of the story.

Using the Technique as a Diagnostic Teaching Lesson   For story maps to be effective, a majority of the following statements must be answered in the affirmative:

Yes   *No*

_____   _____   1. The student understands the story map elements.

_____   _____   2. The student improves his ability to retell the story.

_____   _____   3. The student improves the number of questions about story events he can answer.

Evidence Base

Mathes, P. G., Fuchs, D., & Fuchs, L. S. (1997). Cooperative story mapping. *Remedial and Special Education, 18,* 20–27.

Davis, Z. T. (1994). Effects of prereading story mapping on elementary readers' comprehension. *Journal of Educational Research, 87,* 353–360.

Web Sites

http://www.readwritethink.org/student_mat/student_material.asp?id=8

http://www.onalaska.k12.wi.us/ITLWEB/2story.pdf

http://www.msu.edu/course/cep/886/Reading%20Comprehension/4Learn_Serv_Proj_GroupStMap.html

57 Story Writing Approach   *Targeted Reading Levels 3–6, but can be used at all levels*

Description   Story writing is an instructional format for teaching narrative writing that includes three stages: prewriting, writing, and evaluating. By writing their own stories, students increase their awareness of story parts.

Text   Student's own writing

Predominant Focus of Instruction

1. Processing focus: meaning
2. Instructional phase: after reading
3. Response mode emphasized: written discourse
4. Strategy emphasized: elaboration
5. Skill emphasized: nonliteral comprehension
6. Source of information: reader based
7. Type of instruction: implicit
8. Type of cognitive processing: simultaneous

Procedure

1. The teacher introduces the structure of a story. Stories have a beginning (the characters and place), middle (problems and the events), and an end (solution of the problem).
2. The teacher and the students brainstorm ideas to select a topic and information that might go into the story.
3. Using the information collected, the students write their stories. The teacher emphasizes that the story needs to flow from one idea to the next and make sense.
4. The teacher has the students reread their stories to see whether they make sense. She uses the following questions:
   a. Does the story make sense?
   b. Do I have all the story parts?
   c. Have I left out any information that the reader might need to know in order to understand my story?
5. The students revise any unclear information.
6. The students make a final copy of their stories.

Modifications

1. In prewriting, students can use a visual story map to form the outline of the story.
2. For the student who has a great deal of difficulty, the teacher might use a story frame with only minimal ideas deleted.
3. Guided imagery journeys may be used as a prewriting activity.
4. A story can be composed by a small group of students. Each person writes a segment of the story and then passes the text to the next person. Each student's contribution to the story line must build upon prior information and make sense.
5. Pairs of students can read and edit each other's stories.
6. Instead of step 4, the students can take their stories to the author's circle where students provide input on the three questions.

Further Diagnostic Applications

Basic View of Reading   Reading is an active, reader-based process in which the reader and writer interpret meaning. An author writes a text that allows a clear interpretation by the reader but assumes that a certain amount of inferencing will occur on the part of the reader.

Patterns of Strengths and Strategies   The story writing approach is most appropriate for students who need to write in order to experience how a story is organized so that it makes sense. This approach emphasizes the constructive nature of reading and that the text needs to "make sense."

Learner Patterns That Produce Increased Engagement

1. For simultaneous learners who write and read for self-understanding and meaning but do not realize that a story is a contractual agreement between reader and writer, this technique helps them think about what the author wants them to understand.
*2. For passive learners who do not understand story organization, they learn to attend to story features by writing their own parts of a story.
*3. For readers who rely on background knowledge to interpret text and do not attend to sentence meaning, they become more sensitive to the function that text and sentence structure have on meaning by writing their own stories and listening to others interpret them.

Using the Technique as a Diagnostic Teaching Lesson   For story writing to be effective, a majority of the following statements must be answered in the affirmative:

Yes	No	
_____	_____	1. The student prefers to write what he thinks rather than contribute to a discussion.
_____	_____	2. The student writes fluently and can construct text that makes sense.
_____	_____	3. The student understands the parts of a story well enough to be able to construct a coherent story.

Evidence Base

Lienemann, T. O., Graham, S., Leader-Janssen, B., & Reid, R. (2006). Improving the writing performance of struggling writers in second grade. *Journal of Special Education, 40,* 66–78.

Web Sites

http://pbskids.org/arthur/parentsteachers/lesson/storywriting
http://www.home.duq.edu/~hochman/rdgla.html

58 Strategy Instruction   *Targeted Reading Levels: All levels*

Description   Strategy instruction is an instructional format designed to teach procedures related to print and meaning processing. In such lessons, teachers model their own thinking related to an unfamiliar task, and then ask students to think out loud about how they are completing the task. This instruction is followed by coaching students to ensure self-regulated learning.

Text   Authentic text

Predominant Focus of Instruction

1. Processing focus: print or meaning
2. Instructional phase: before, during, and after reading
3. Response mode emphasized: oral discussion
4. Strategy emphasized: monitoring and elaboration
5. Skill emphasized: depends on focus
6. Source of information: text based and reader based
7. Type of instruction: explicit phasing to self-directed learning
8. Type of cognitive processing: successive, quickly phasing to simultaneous

Procedure

1. The teacher selects the new procedure to be learned.
2. The teacher talks about what the strategy is and what it is like and gives some examples. The use is explained through demonstration. For instance, the diagnostic teacher explains prediction by talking about how the weather forecaster predicts what the weather would be using the information from weather signals and prior experience.
3. The teacher explains why the strategy works when reading.
4. The teacher models the new strategy in authentic texts by talking out loud about how she reads the text, paying particular attention to the targeted strategy.
5. The students use the targeted strategy in authentic texts. They talk out loud about their problem-solving strategies.
6. The teacher supports the "strategic thinking" of the readers. She phases in to coach thinking and phases out to let students use strategies independently.
7. After reading, the students and teacher discuss the strategies they used for text interpretation.
8. Students are asked to assess their strategy deployment and how it affected their text interpretation.
9. The teacher explains when to use the strategy and what to do if its use is not effective.

Further Diagnostic Applications

Basic View of Reading   Reading is an interactive process in which the reader purposely implements strategies and skills he knows to solve problems when interpreting texts.

Patterns of Strengths and Strategies   The strategy instruction format is most appropriate when teaching unfamiliar reading procedures or when students lack particular reading strategies.

Learner Patterns That Produce Increased Engagement

1. This format can be used to teach unfamiliar strategies to active readers. It helps them consolidate strategies.
2. This format is designed for the student who needs a teacher to model strategic reading. By following the teacher's model, the student develops active reading strategies.
*3. This format has been used with passive readers who read words without constructing meaning. Modeling and coaching help passive readers use active reading strategies.

Using the Technique as a Diagnostic Teaching Lesson
For strategy instruction to be effective, a majority of the following statements must be answered in the affirmative:

Yes	No	
_____	_____	1. The student can imitate the teacher's model.
_____	_____	2. The student profits from oral discussion of strategic reading.
_____	_____	3. The student can assess his own strategy use.

Evidence Base

Alfassi, M. (2004). Reading to learn: Effects of combined strategy instruction on high school students. *Journal of Educational Research, 97,* 171–184.

Magliano, J., Todaro, S., Millis, K., Wiemer-Hastings, K., & McNamara, D. S. (2005). Changes in reading strategies as a function of reading training: A comparison of live and computerized training. *Journal of Educational Computing Research, 32,* 185–208.

Reutzel, D. R., Smith, J. A., & Fawson, P. C. (2005). An evaluation of two approaches for teaching reading comprehension strategies in the primary years using science information texts. *Early Childhood Research Quarterly, 20,* 276–305.

Web Sites

http://www.cast.org/system/galleries/download/pdResources/strategy.doc
http://www.hoagiesgifted.org/eric/e638.html

59 Summary Experience Approach   *Targeted Reading Levels K–3*

Description   The student and teacher talk about the material the class is currently reading. Based on the classroom reading material, the student is asked to retell the passage while the teacher records or writes down the retelling. This summary (dictated retelling) becomes material that is read by the student.

Text   Classroom retellings

Predominant Focus of Instruction

1. Processing focus: print and meaning
2. Instructional phase: after listening
3. Response mode emphasized: oral retelling
4. Strategy emphasized: prediction and monitoring
5. Skill emphasized: word identification and literal comprehension
6. Source of information: reader based and text based
7. Type of instruction: implicit
8. Type of cognitive processing: simultaneous

Procedure

1. The teacher checks with the classroom teacher to find out what story is being studied and obtains a copy of the story, book, or book chapter.
2. The teacher engages the student in dialogue about the selection being read in the classroom, asking the student to relate the key ideas.
3. The student is asked to retell the classroom selection while the teacher serves as a secretary and writes down what the student says.
4. Using leading questions, the teacher guides the student to retell the selection by using questions such as, "What happened next?" "What are the important parts?" "How does the passage end?" (For additional prompts, see "Retelling" in this part.)
5. The students and teacher read the dictated summary together to revise any statements or phrases that are unclear. The summary follows the natural language patterns of the student.
6. The teacher and the students read the summary repeatedly so that the repetition of the summary helps the student recognize the words in the summary and the words in the classroom text.
7. Retype the summary and make several copies. Let the students take one copy home to practice.
8. Create a book of story summaries.

Modifications

1. The teacher can use a story map before the retelling to help the students dictate the summary.
2. The teacher can use a story self-assessment (see chapter 8) evaluation to help the student revise and edit the story summary.

Further Diagnostic Applications

Basic View of Reading   Reading is an active, reader-based process. By reading his own summary, the student will learn the key vocabulary words. Because the summary is short and uses his own language structure, the student will be able to remember the words in the summary, which will in turn facilitate understanding the classroom passages.

Patterns of Strengths and Strategies   The summary experience approach is most appropriate for students who have facility with language and are simultaneous reader-based thinkers. If the student uses his own language to retell the story rather than the exact words in the text, then the summary experience matches his own way of expressing and interpreting meaning; therefore, this technique facilitates word learning by asking the student to identify words using his own interpretation of the story.

Learning Patterns That Produce Increased Engagement

1. For simultaneous thinkers who readily think of the main ideas and can retell a passage with ease, the summary experience approach uses the students' strengths (thinking of the main actions or ideas) to facilitate word identification.
2. For extremely verbal students whose verbalization, at times, interferes with focusing on the words in the text, the summary experience approach uses this strength to facilitate recognizing individual words.
3. Students who need to improve comprehension will be able to use their own language to understand complex texts rather than answer direct questions posed by the teacher.

Using the Technique as a Diagnostic Teaching Lesson   For the summary experience approach to be effective, a majority of the following statements must be answered in the affirmative:

Yes   *No*

_____ _____ 1. The student can retell the main actions of the classroom story.

_____ _____ 2. The student can remember how he retold the story well enough to predict the words he does not remember as he rereads his summary.

_____ _____ 3. The student responds when prompted, using the summary and the story theme.

Evidence Base

Daisey, P. (2000). The construction of "how to" books in a secondary content area literacy course: The promise and barriers of writing to learn strategies. In P. E. Linder, W. M. Linek, E. G. Sturtevant, & J. R. Dugan (Eds.), *Literacy at a new Horizon* (pp. 147–159). Commerce, TX: College Reading Association.

Palinscar, A. S., Parecki, A. D., & McPhail, J. C. (1995). Friendship and literacy through literature. *Journal of Learning Disabilities, 28,* 503–510.

Web Sites

http://rice.mentorschools.org/SummaryExperience.html
http://findarticles.com/p/articles/mi_qa4064/is_200310/ai_n9274293/pg_3

60 Summarization

Targeted Reading Levels 6–12

Description   Summarization teaches the student how to write summaries of what he reads. He is shown how to delete unimportant information, group similar ideas, decide on or invent topic sentences, and list supporting details. These procedures culminate in a short paragraph that reflects the most important information.

Text   Most appropriate for expository text

Predominant Focus of Instruction

1. Processing focus: meaning
2. Instructional phase: after reading
3. Response mode emphasized: written discourse
4. Strategy emphasized: elaboration
5. Skill emphasized: literal comprehension and inquiry thinking
6. Source of information: text based to reader based
7. Type of instruction: explicit
8. Type of cognitive processing: simultaneous

Procedure

1. The teacher selects an expository text.
2. She describes a summary as a short version of the text that contains all the important information.
3. The teacher explains that the purpose of writing summaries is to put all the important information together so it can be remembered better.
4. The students read the selection and ask themselves, "What is this mainly about?"
5. The teacher reads her summary of the selection and presents it on the overhead.
6. In the text, the student marks the information the teacher used in the summary.
7. The teacher talks about the rules for writing summaries by telling the students how she wrote her summary.
8. The teacher demonstrates the rule of deleting trivial information. She points out that many writers tell us interesting information that is not a key idea. She tells them to ignore this information when writing a summary.
9. The teacher demonstrates the rule for deleting repeated information. She explains that many writers repeat information to make their point. When writing a summary, students should use an idea only once and ignore repeated information.
10. The teacher demonstrates the rule for combining details into a generalization. When possible, students should combine details that fit into the same category and rename that category with a bigger category. For example, *pigs, horses, cows,* and *chickens* can be renamed to *farm animals*.
11. The teacher demonstrates how to select the topic sentence. She points out that the topic sentence is the author's one-sentence summary. It usually comes at the beginning or the end of the paragraph.
12. The teacher demonstrates how to invent a topic sentence when a paragraph has no summary sentence. In this case, she shows how to organize all the important information into one category. Then she writes a sentence that tells what the paragraph is mainly about. She shows how to think about the important information and relate it.
13. The students write a summary for the demonstration selection and check their summaries individually against the rules.

14. The students compare their summaries in small groups.
15. The students write a summary for another selection.
16. When finished, the students describe how they constructed their summaries.
17. The teacher shows them her summary for the same selection and talks about how she constructed it.
18. The students write summaries for several more selections on their own.

Further Diagnostic Applications

Basic View of Reading   Reading is an interactive process in which the reader decides what is important about the text in order to summarize what it says.

Patterns of Strengths and Strategies   Summarization is most appropriate for students who like to think about what a text says but have difficulty remembering the facts that support this main point. The approach helps such students focus on relating all the textual information that is important to the key idea.

Learner Patterns That Produce Increased Engagement

1. For simultaneous readers who quickly reduce information to the main ideas but need to write out some important details to support the main idea, this technique helps readers understand how details relate to main points.
*2. For successive readers who cannot tie important information together in order to remember information, summarization helps them decide on general categories that relate details.
*3. For successive readers who think everything in the text is important, summarization helps them learn to delete unimportant and repeated information.

Using the Technique as a Diagnostic Teaching Lesson   For summarization to be effective, a majority of the following statements must be answered in the affirmative:

Yes   *No*

_____   _____   1. The student can write fairly fluently; therefore, writing the words on paper does not interfere with the task.

_____   _____   2. The student learns to distinguish what is important and what is unimportant fairly easily.

_____   _____   3. The student learns to group individual information of like categories easily.

Evidence Base

Elosúa, M. R., García-Madruga, J. A., Gutiérrez, F., Luque, J. L., & Gárate, M. (2002). Effects of an intervention in active strategies for text comprehension and recall. *Spanish Journal of Psychology, 5,* 90–101.

Malone, L. D., & Mastropieri, M. A. (1992). Reading comprehension instruction: Summarization and self-monitoring training for students with learning disabilities. *Exceptional Children, 58,* 270–279.

Wood, E. J., Winne, P. H., & Carney, P. A. (1995). Evaluating the effects of training high school students to use summarization when training includes analogically similar information. *Journal of Reading Behavior, 27,* 605–626

Web Sites
http://www.msu.edu/course/cep/886/Reading%20Comprehension/10Learn_Serv_Proj_Summarization.html
http://www.itrc.ucf.edu/FORPD/strategies/stratsummarization.html

61 **Sustained Silent Reading**   *Targeted Reading Levels: All levels*

Description   Sustained silent reading (SSR) is the designation of an uninterrupted time period where both the students and the teacher read self-selected reading materials for their own purposes. The teacher models her own engagement during reading. In turn, the students begin to define their interests and read for their engagement in literacy.

Text   Self-selected

Predominant Focus of Instruction

1. Processing focus: meaning
2. Instructional phase: during reading
3. Response mode emphasized: some oral discussion
4. Strategy emphasized: depends on student
5. Skill emphasized: fluency and nonliteral comprehension
6. Source of information: reader based
7. Type of instruction: implicit
8. Type of cognitive processing: depends on student

Procedure

1. Before beginning SSR, the teacher collects a variety of reading materials that represent a wide range of reading levels and text types (magazines, newspapers, novels, and informational texts).
2. Next, the teacher reads aloud favorite parts of books or talks about books other students have enjoyed in order to stimulate interest.
3. The teacher designates a specific time for reading each day. (After lunch is a good time; students select their books before lunch so they can be ready to read as soon as lunch is over. Another good time is at the end of the day.)
4. The students select their books prior to the designated reading time.
5. The teacher explains the "rule of thumb," which aids in book selection. According to this rule, the student selects a book and reads a page at random. When he reaches the first word he does not know, he places his little finger on it. On the next difficult word, he places the next finger and so on. If he reaches his thumb before the end of the page, the book is too difficult, and he must find another book.
6. The students do not browse and select books during the designated time span.
7. Initially, the teacher sets aside a short time period (5 to 10 minutes) for silent reading and then increases the amount of time each day.
8. The teacher uses a timer to monitor the time so everyone can read.
9. The students read silently for the time period.
10. The teacher and anyone else in the room read silently for the time period.
11. The teacher does not keep records or have students make reports on what they read. The students are in control of what and how much they read.
12. Initially, the teacher allows pretend reading, browsing through books, and looking at pictures. She also initially provides a narrow range of selection choices.

Comment: Although this technique is more effective for some children than others, it is recommended as part of the diagnostic teaching session because it allows students to read for their own purpose and therefore provides them with an experience in which they cannot fail.

Further Diagnostic Applications

Basic View of Reading Reading is an engaging, reader-based process in which the readers' personal interpretations and engagement are the focus. By the teacher's modeling her own engagement in literate activities, she shares "wanting to read."

Patterns of Strengths and Strategies Sustained silent reading is most appropriate for the active, independent reader who enjoys reading for his own purposes rather than the teacher's purposes. In this technique, personal enjoyment is gained while reading for individual purposes.

Learner Patterns That Produce Increased Engagement

1. For successive learners who needs to identify their own reasons for reading, SSR allows them to identify interests and reasons for reading.
*2. For inattentive readers who cannot read long sections of text silently, this technique allows them to increase their attention during silent reading.
*3. For passive readers who view themselves as failures when reading, this technique allows them to feel success when reading because they control the reasons for reading.

Using the Technique as a Diagnostic Teaching Lesson

For SSR to be effective, a majority of the following statements must be answered in the affirmative:

Yes   *No*

_____   _____   1. The student selects books he wants to read.

_____   _____   2. The student observes the rules of silent reading and is not disruptive during that time.

_____   _____   3. The student increases his own task reading time and asks for longer time for sustained silent reading.

Caution: Be persistent in expecting success. Even though some students will pretend to be reading, it is the model and message that they can read what they like that are important.

Evidence Base

Bryan, G., Fawson, P., & Reutzel, D. R. (2003). Sustained silent reading: Exploring the value of literature discussion with three non-engaged readers. *Reading Research and Instruction, 43,* 47–73.

Web Sites

http://www.education-world.com/a_curr/curr038.shtml
http://www.nde.state.ne.us/bmit/Curriculum/sustainedsilentreadingguidelines-columbus.pdf

62 Synthetic Phonics   *Targeted Reading Levels 1–2*

Description   Synthetic phonics teaches sound-symbol relationships (rules) in words to facilitate word identification. The student is systematically instructed to say the letter sounds in words and then blend the sounds together to decode the unknown word. The rapid transfer of decoding principles to new words is expected as the text includes many words that follow the rule.

Text   Decodable words and some isolated drill

Predominant Focus of Instruction

1. Processing focus: print
2. Instructional phase: before reading
3. Response mode emphasized: oral discussion
4. Strategy emphasized: elaboration
5. Skill emphasized: word analysis
6. Source of information: text based
7. Type of instruction: explicit
8. Type of cognitive processing: successive

Procedure

1. The teacher selects phonic rules to be taught.
2. She selects texts and words to illustrate the rule.
3. The teacher directly teaches the letter sounds.

    The letter *s* goes "*s-s-s.*"

    The letter *t* goes "*t-t-t.*"

    The letter *n* goes "*n-n-n.*"

    The letter *m* goes "*m-m-m.*"

    In short words that have a consonant at the beginning and the end and an *a* in the middle, the letter *a* says "*a-a-a.*"
4. The student blends the sounds together to form words.

    S-a-m says "*Sam.*"

    S-a-t says "*sat.*"

5. The student reads the words in a text that uses the sound–symbol relationships that the teacher has introduced.

    Sam is on the mat.

    The man is on the mat.

    Sam sat on the man on the mat.

6. The teacher facilitates the transfer of rules to new words. In the example, she teaches the sounds for *d, h,* and *c.* Then she asks the student to read:

    The man has a hat. The hat is in the sand.

    Sam is a cat. Sam ran in the sand.

Sam ran to the man.

Sam sat on his hat.

The man is mad at Sam. Sam ran.

Further Diagnostic Applications

Basic View of Reading   Reading is a text-based process in which effective reading is based on accurate decoding of words. Learning sounds of letters and sounding out words precedes reading entire passages; therefore, decoding precedes comprehension.

Patterns of Strengths and Strategies   Synthetic phonics is a process of successive blending of sounds, requiring the student to hold a sequence of sounds in their memory while synthesizing the sounds to form a word. Young children who have facility with sound blending and can hold oral sequences in memory will have the greatest success with this method.

Learner Patterns That Produce Increased Engagement

1. For successive learners who have facility with language so that the systematic de-coding of words becomes a tool rather than an end by itself, the synthetic phonics approach facilitates word identification without interfering with fluency.
*2. For passive learners who can blend sounds and profit from direct instruction in the sound system, this technique directly shows them how to decode new words and directs their attention to individual letters.
*3. The successive learner who can blend sounds but has no visual memory can always decode the word he has forgotten. The Distar reading program allows for this approach because more than 99% of the words in the stories are decodable.

Using the Technique as a Diagnostic Teaching Lesson   For synthetic phonics to be effective, a majority of the following statements must be answered in the affirmative:

Yes   No

_____ _____   1. The student can blend sounds.
_____ _____   2. The student can segment sounds.
_____ _____   3. The student can hold a sequence of letter sounds in memory long enough to blend the sounds to form a word.

Evidence Base

Goswami, U. (2005). Synthetic phonics and learning to read: A cross-language perspective. *Educational Psychology in Practice, 21,* 273–282.

Johnston, R. S., & Watson, J. E. (2004). Accelerating the development of reading, spelling and phonemic awareness skills in initial readers. *Reading and Writing, 17,* 327–357.

Web Sites

http://en.wikipedia.org/wiki/Synthetic_phonics
http://www.syntheticphonics.com/synthetic_phonics.htm
http://www.macmillenschools.com/eng/faq/syntheticPhonics.htm

63 Talking Books
Targeted Reading Levels K–5

Description   The talking books method uses CD-recorded readings of selected stories to increase word recognition and reading fluency. The student repeatedly reads along with a CD until he can read the text fluently with comprehension.

Text   Stories that are on a CD

Predominant Focus of Instruction

1. Processing focus: print
2. Instructional phase: during reading
3. Response mode emphasized: oral
4. Strategy emphasized: prediction
5. Skill emphasized: word identification and fluency
6. Source of information: reader based
7. Type of instruction: implicit
8. Type of cognitive processing: simultaneous

Procedure

1. The student selects a text that is interesting to him.
2. The teacher secures or makes a CD of the story.
3. If she makes a CD, she includes the following:
   a. She segments the story so that the student can easily finish a CD in one sitting.
   b. She cues the page numbers so the student can easily find the page.
   c. She records the text, using the natural phrases of language.
4. The student follows the line of print with his finger.
5. The student listens to the tape recording to develop an overall understanding of the story.
6. Then the student listens and reads along with the tape as many times as necessary until he can read the text fluently.
7. The student rehearses the text by himself.
8. The student reads the text to the teacher.
9. The teacher evaluates fluency and comprehension.
10. If the student reads the passage fluently with comprehension, he listens and reads the next segment of the story or another story.

Modifications

1. Teachers can use commercial programs where stories are on CDs. These CDs offer many options for reading the story. Students need to be supervised as they listen to these stories.
2. Currently, there are numerous Web-based read-along stories.

Further Diagnostic Applications

Basic View of Reading   Reading is a reader-based process in which the reader's personal understanding of the story drives the word recognition process. By repeatedly listening to the story, the reader gains an understanding of the story meaning, story structure, and sentence structure. He uses this understanding to facilitate word recognition in the story.

Patterns of Strengths and Strategies   The talking books technique is most appropriate for the beginning reader or the nonfluent reader who easily memorizes stories. This memorization facilitates fluent reading of text and allows students to attend to both meaning and print simultaneously. By memorizing stories, students are exposed to lots of words in context, enabling them to apply phonic knowledge, increase word identification, and self-correct as they meaningfully read text.

Learner Patterns That Produce Increased Engagement

1. For simultaneous learners who rely too heavily on background knowledge and do not self-correct using graphic cues, this technique develops word identification by using the overall textual meaning (a strength) to identify words.
2. For passive readers who read word by word without attention to meaning, this technique restores reading for meaning by having students learn to read whole stories with expression and by allowing students to experience success.
*3. For nonfluent readers who have had an overemphasis of synthetic or explicit phonic instruction and have become word bound, this technique develops reading for overall meaning to increase word identification.
*4. For slow readers who have not developed either decoding skills or word identification, talking books use memorizing whole stories so that students can read lots of words before developing either phonic knowledge or word identification.

Using the Technique as a Diagnostic Teaching Lesson   For talking books to be effective, a majority of the following statements must be answered in the affirmative:

Yes   No

_____   _____   1. The student is sufficiently interested in the text to listen and read the story repeatedly.
_____   _____   2. The student memorizes the story fairly easily, requiring only a minimal number of listen-and-read sessions. (More than a week on the same story is too long.)
_____   _____   3. As the story is read, the student follows the text and associates the words he hears with the words on the page.

Evidence Base

Koskinen, P. S., Blum, I. H., Bisson, S., Creamer, T., Phillips, S. A., & Baker, T. K. (2000). Book access, shared reading, and audio models: The effects of supporting the literacy learning of linguistically diverse students in school and at home. *Journal of Educational Psychology, 92,* 23–36.

Littleton, K., Wood, C., & Chera, P. (2006). Interactions with talking books: Phonological awareness affects boys' use of talking books. *Journal of Computer Assisted Learning, 22,* 382–390.

McKenna, M. C., & Reinking, D. (1997). Using talking books with reading-disabled students. *Reading and Writing Quarterly, 13,* 185–192.

Wood, C. (2005). Beginning readers' use of "talking books" software can affect their reading strategies. *Journal of Research in Reading, 28,* 170–182.

Web Sites

http://www.raz-kids.com/main/Play/id/60/resource/listen_book
http://wiredforbooks.org

64 Thematic-Inquiry Approach   *Targeted Reading Levels 4–12*

Description   The thematic-inquiry approach is a technique to develop an in-depth knowledge of a particular topic through integrating reading and writing activities.

Text   Particularly suited for expository text but can be used with all types

Predominant Focus of Instruction

1. Processing focus: meaning
2. Instructional phase: before and after reading
3. Response mode emphasized: oral discussion, written responses, and alternative modes like PowerPoint
4. Strategy emphasized: elaboration
5. Skill emphasized: literal and nonliteral comprehension
6. Source of information: text based leading to reader based
7. Type of instruction: implicit
8. Type of cognitive processing: simultaneous

Procedure

1. The teacher and students select a topic to be studied.
2. The teacher creates experiences to engage students in a general understanding of the topic.
3. The teacher and students then discuss what they are learning and already know about the topic.
4. The teacher and students brainstorm possible research topics while the teacher records these on a chart or chalkboard.
5. The students select a possible research topic and discuss it in a small group.
6. The teacher discusses research focus with each student elaborating ideas and suggesting possible reference sources.
7. Each student independently researches his special focus related to the topic.
8. Each student takes notes on his special focus area.
9. Each student prepares a presentation on his special focus to share with the class. This presentation can take many response modes: graphic organizer, video, written report, and so on.
10. The teacher and students evaluate their learning.

Further Diagnostic Applications

Basic View of Reading   Reading is an active, reader-based process in which students build topic knowledge, using what they know. What they know is usually related to their individual interests.

Patterns of Strengths and Strategies   The thematic-inquiry approach is appropriate for students who build experiences by pursuing their own interests. In researching their interests, these students build a network of new concepts.

Learner Patterns That Produce Increased Engagement

1. For simultaneous readers who prefer to research topics independently to expand their knowledge, the thematic-inquiry approach allows them to build their own theories and concepts.
*2. For readers who have little prior knowledge about a topic, the thematic experience approach begins by using interest to build a network of ideas on an unknown topic.
*3. For bilingual readers who need to build a network of language to express concepts, the thematic experience approach allows them to make connections in both language codes during the experience.

Using the Technique as a Diagnostic Teaching Lesson   For the thematic experience approach to be effective, a majority of the following statements must be answered in the affirmative:

Yes   *No*

_____   _____   1. The student can easily decide what interests him.
_____   _____   2. The student likes to work independently, researching information about a particular topic.
_____   _____   3. The student can share the information with a group of students.

Evidence Base

Cobb Morocco, C., Hindin, A. M., Mata-Aguilar, C., & Clark-Chiarelli, N. (2001). Building a deep understanding of literature with middle-grade students with learning disabilities. *Learning Disability Quarterly, 24,* 47–58.

Web Sites

http://www.greece.k12.ny.us/instruction/ela/6-12/Reading/annotatedbib6.htm
http://www.vsarts.org/x587.xml
http://www.teach-nology.com/themes

65 Think-Aloud Approach

Targeted Reading Levels: All levels, but most appropriate for 4–12

Description   The think-aloud approach uses the student's thinking to develop active reading. By following the sequence of self-directed questions, the student learns to monitor his understanding as he reads.

Text   Narrative and expository texts

Predominant Focus of Instruction

1. Processing focus: meaning
2. Instructional phase: during reading
3. Response mode emphasized: oral discussion
4. Strategy emphasized: prediction and monitoring
5. Skill emphasized: nonliteral comprehension
6. Source of information: reader based
7. Type of instruction: initially explicit but moves rapidly to implicit
8. Type of cognitive processing: simultaneous but is an interrupted story (successive)

Procedure

1. The teacher decides to think aloud about the active process of predicting and revising a model of meaning.
2. The teacher selects a text that is at the appropriate level and that has a fairly cohesive story line.
3. She decides on key prediction points. A story map (see "Story Mapping" in this part) can facilitate this process.
4. The teacher begins by modeling how to think through the story. She asks herself:

   "What must I do? . . . I must guess what the author is going to say. . . . A good strategy is to use the title. . . . From the title, I bet that. . ."

5. Using another section of the story, the teacher models her plan for betting:

   "Now, let's see what's my plan for betting. . . . To make my bet, I already know that. . . . To prove my bet, I must look for hints in the text . . ."

6. The teacher writes these two aspects on a chalkboard:

   "I already know. . . . Hints from the text . . ."

7. Then, the teacher answers the question: Does my guess make sense?

   "I wonder how it fits? . . . The _____ must be important because the author keeps talking about it. . . . It fits because _____."

8. Using other sections of the story, the teacher writes "oops" on the chalkboard while she models her correction strategies by saying:

   "Oops, that doesn't make sense. . . . I need to check my thinking. . . . So far, I'm right about . . . but wrong about . . ."

9. As she models this strategy, she also models her self-talk related to making a mistake by saying:

    "It's okay to make a mistake. . . . I can change my bet as I get more information. From the new information, I bet that . . . or I wonder whether . . ."

10. Using another section, she models her tentative thinking by saying, "Hmmmm" and writing it on the chalkboard:

    "Hmmm. Sometimes, I am just not sure. . . . Maybe it's . . . or maybe it's . . ."

11. The teacher models confirming her predictions by saying, "I knew it, that sure fits. . . . So far I'm right!"
12. She writes, "I knew it" on the chalkboard. The student and teacher return to step 4 and think aloud.
13. Students read another example passage, talking aloud and using steps 4 to 12.
14. When comprehension breaks down, the teacher models her own thinking rather than asking questions. She says, "When I read that I thought . . ."
15. At the end of the story, the students and the teacher discuss the story content and how they constructed meaning.

Modification   A chart of active reading behaviors can be kept by the teacher or student. In the chart, they assess how many predictions or bets were revised and what sources of information were used.

Further Diagnostic Applications

Basic View of Reading   Reading is an interactive process in which the readers build understanding based on textual and nontextual information. As readers build an understanding, they predict, monitor, and elaborate on their learning.

Patterns of Strengths and Strategies   The think-aloud approach is most appropriate for students who overrely on what they know, failing to monitor reading comprehension and to relate textual information to prior knowledge. For these students, the approach matches their strength of prior knowledge and helps them revise their understanding based on textual information.

Learner Patterns That Produce Increased Engagement

1. For simultaneous learners who understand the story but cannot recall the textual information used to construct their responses, the technique has them check the text, helping to facilitate understanding.
2. For simultaneous learners who do not use self-talk to monitor the sources of information used to construct reponses, this technique encourages the internal dialogue that accompanies effective comprehension.
*3. For passive learners who need to actively engage in forming and revising their interpretations of the text, this technique gives these students a plan for thinking and checking understanding.
*4. For successive learners who know the meanings of words but depend on teacher questioning to interpret the important information in the text, this technique gives them the steps to develop their own questions.

*5. For successive learners who cannot tie story events together, using what they already know and the events, this technique asks students to check both the text and what they know to see whether they fit together.

Using the Technique as a Diagnostic Teaching Lesson   For the think-aloud approach to be effective, a majority of the following statements must be answered in the affirmative:

Yes	*No*	
_____	_____	1. The student can make a prediction.
_____	_____	2. The student can follow the oral discussion of strategic reading.
_____	_____	3. The student learns to use key events to predict outcomes.

Evidence Base

Baumann, J. F., Seifert-Kessell, N., & Jones, L. A. (1992). Effect of think-aloud instruction on elementary students' comprehension monitoring abilities. *Journal of Reading Behavior, 24,* 143–172.

Wilhelm, J. D. (2001). *Improving comprehension think-aloud strategies: Modeling what good readers do.* New York: Scholastic.

Web Sites

http://web.grps.k12.mi.us/academics/5E/thinkaloud.html
http://www.ncela.gwu.edu/practice/itc/lessons/schthinkaloud.html
http://www.itrc.ucf.edu/forpd/strategies/stratthinkaloud.html

66 Visualization

Targeted Reading Levels: All levels

Description   Visualization is an approach for improving word meaning by suggesting to children that they form mental images of words, relating descriptors with the new word.

Text   Key vocabulary words in narrative text or expository text

Predominant Focus of Instruction

1. Processing focus: meaning
2. Instructional phase: before reading
3. Response mode emphasized: nonverbal responses and oral discussion
4. Strategy emphasized: elaboration
5. Skill emphasized: word meaning
6. Source of information: reader based
7. Type of instruction: implicit
8. Type of cognitive processing: simultaneous

Procedure

1. The teacher selects target words for which to develop meanings.
2. The students look at a word and then close their eyes.
3. The teacher reads a definition and *like a* statements and asks the students to form a mental picture of the word. For example, if the target word is *geyser,* the teacher could say, "Think about a geyser like a large whistling teapot just about to boil. The water is bubbling and the pressure is mounting. When enough pressure builds up, the teapot begins to whistle and blow steam into the air. The geyser is like a large teapot in the ground."
4. The teacher and the students discuss their mental pictures.
5. In some cases, the students draw their images.
6. The students read text that uses and elaborates the targeted words.

Further Diagnostic Applications

Basic View of Reading   Reading is an interactive process in which information is stored in images as well as words. Reading involves inferencing from the text by using words and images that are stored in memory.

Patterns of Strengths and Strategies   Visualization is most appropriate for the highly visual, simultaneous learner who initially searches visual images to develop word meanings. This approach activates these students' strength in representing knowledge in its visual-spatial relationships and encourages them to relate this information to definitional knowledge.

Learner Patterns That Produce Increased Engagement

1. For students who have difficulty verbalizing ideas and who code information in images rather than words, visualization links their visual images to verbal descriptions.
2. For passive readers who do not check past experiences to develop word meanings, visualization enhances their active thinking as they elaborate on understanding with images.

*3. For text-based learners who need to relate information to past experiences, visualization offers them a tool to connect textual information with prior knowledge.

Using the Technique as a Diagnostic Teaching Lesson   For visualization to be effective, both of the following statements must be answered in the affirmative:

Yes   No

____ ____ 1. The student sees pictures in his mind and uses these to elaborate his interpretation.

____ ____ 2. The student has difficulty verbalizing ideas and the visualization helps him connect words and images.

Evidence Base

Chan, L. K., Cole, P. G., & Morris, J. N. (1990). Effects of instruction in the use of a visual-imagery strategy on the reading-comprehension competence of disabled and average readers. *Learning Disability Quarterly, 13,* 2–11.

Golden, C., Foley, M. A., Holtz, K., & Lynde, R. (1994). Visualization as a guide for composing. *Reading and Writing, 6,* 197–214.

Web Sites

http://www.mayer.cps.k12.il.us/Strategies_that_Work/STW.htm
http://wilearns.state.wi.us/apps/Default.asp?cid=781

67 Vocabulary Self-Collection Strategy

Target Reading Levels: All levels

Description   The vocabulary self-collection strategy is a technique for developing word meanings by having small groups of students select words they would like to study and tell why they are important to a topic of study.

Text   Selected vocabulary words from a text that has been read by all students

Predominant Focus of Instruction

1. Processing focus: meaning
2. Instructional phase: after reading
3. Response mode emphasized: oral discussion
4. Strategy emphasized: elaboration
5. Skill emphasized: word meaning
6. Source of information: reader based and text based
7. Type of instruction: implicit
8. Type of cognitive processing: simultaneous

Procedure

1. After reading a selected passage, the teacher organizes students into groups of four or five students each.
2. The student groups are to find at least two words they would like to study.
3. In their groups, the students describe the following about words each member would like to study:
   a. Demonstrate where they found the words in the passage.
   b. Discuss what they think the word might mean.
   c. Discuss why the word is important to them.
4. The small groups prioritize the words they would like to study.
5. Each group nominates a word that has not been previously listed with the reasons for learning in a total class discussion.
6. The total class refines definitions and, if necessary, selects words for further study.
7. Students record the final word list along with personalized definitions in their vocabulary journals (see "Journal Writing" in this part).
8. Students revisit their new words, using extension activities such as a feature analysis grid (see "Feature Analysis Grid" in this part).
9. If needed, incorporate vocabulary item into unit tests.

Further Diagnostic Applications

Basic View of Reading   Reading is a social process in which readers' definitional knowledge is shaped by group members' understanding as well as their personal understanding.

Patterns of Strengths and Strategies   The vocabulary self-collection strategy encourages students to use not only their experiences but also the experiences of peers to expand definitional knowledge; therefore, it is most appropriate for students who share and rely on their social interactions for learning. This strategy facilitates learning for

Vocabulary Self-Collection Strategy

67

these students because it allows students to converse about what and how they are learning.

Learner Patterns That Produce Increased Engagement

1. For highly verbal learners who like learning through incidental learning, this technique allows them to use the nuances of personal language to develop definitional knowledge.
2. For highly social learners who like to learn from peers, this technique allows them to learn word meanings as they talk with others in the classroom.
*3. For learners who need to use their personal interest to develop word meanings because previous word learning experiences resulted in negative attributions toward vocabulary development, vocabulary self-collection offers a group setting to share interests.

Using the Technique as a Diagnostic Teaching Lesson   For the vocabulary self-collection strategy to be effective, both of the following statements must be answered in the affirmative:

Yes   No

_____ _____   1. The student converses readily in instructional settings.

_____ _____   2. The student readily identifies words that interest him.

Evidence Base

Haggard, M. R. (1982). The vocabulary self-collection strategy: An active approach to word learning. *Journal of Reading, 26,* 203–207.

Ruddell, M. R., & Shearer, B. A. (2002). "Extraordinary," "tremendous," "exhilarating," "magnificent": Middle school at-risk students become avid word learners with the Vocabulary Self-Collection Strategy (VSS). *Journal of Adolescent and Adult Literacy, 45,* 52–64.

Web Sites

http://www.sedl.org/cgi-bin/mysql/buildingreading.cgi
http://www.readwritethink.org/lessons/lesson_view.asp?id=296

68 Word Sorts

Targeted Reading Levels 1–4

Description   Word sorts are ways to sort word cards that enable the readers to share how they categorize words—for example, on the basis of similar letter patterns, word meanings, or grammatical functions. This technique uses target words to help students review and remember words by categorizing like characteristics.

Text   Isolated words

Predominant Focus of Instruction

1. Processing focus: print or meaning
2. Instructional phase: after reading
3. Response mode emphasized: oral
4. Strategy emphasized: elaboration
5. Skill emphasized: word identification or word meaning
6. Source of information: reader based
7. Type of instruction: implicit
8. Type of cognitive processing: simultaneous

Procedure

1. The teacher or students select target words and write them on word cards (3- by 5-inch cards).
2. Each student collects a box of personalized word cards drawn from language experience stories, basal readers, and/or trade books to form a word bank.
3. To start a lesson, the teacher asks the students to get out their word banks and form small groups or pairs.
4. The teacher demonstrates how to do a word sort by showing the words *one, two, six,* and *ten* and saying, "Why do you think these words go together?"
5. The students respond by saying, "They are numbers."
6. Then the teacher shows them three more word cards (*hat, rat, sat*) and asks, "Why do you think these words go together?"
7. The students respond that all the words have the letters *at* at the end.
8. The teacher explains the process of looking for like characteristics: some groups may have a meaning focus, some may have graphophonic focus, and others may have a grammatical focus such as *go, going, gone*. She asks the students to create groups of words that share the same characteristic (open word sort).
9. Each group explains how their words go together.
10. Next the teacher directs all the groups to find words that share the same letter patterns.
11. Each group explains their categorizations.

Modification   For each group, the teacher can create a set of word cards that have similar letter patterns, word meanings, or grammatical functions. She asks the groups to arrange the cards according to the pattern and be able to tell how the words are alike. This word sort is closed because the teacher chooses the words to reinforce a concept that is being learned.

Further Diagnostic Applications

Basic View of Reading   Reading is a socio-interactive process in which learners share their thinking about how words are categorized based on their meaning, graphophonic similarity, or grammatical function. As students discuss how words are alike, they increase their active thinking.

Patterns of Strengths and Strategies   Word sorts are most appropriate for readers who are developing word identification. For these students, categorizing words according to their distinctive features as well as their meaning enhances decoding by both meaning analogies and decoding analogies.

Learner Patterns That Produce Increased Engagement

1. For simultaneous learners who easily see relationships but often do not look at the word patterns, this approach focuses the student on likenesses among words rather than on their differences.
2. For social learners who learn more readily with a partner or in a group, this approach can be effective because friends help them focus, in this case on distinctive features that are alike in words.
*3. For passive learners who need to select key features so they can remember what the words look like, the sorting provides a tool for talking about how words look alike.

Using the Technique as a Diagnostic Teaching Lesson   For word sorts to be effective, a majority of the following statements must be answered in the affirmative:

Yes	No	
_____	_____	1. The student can identify key visual or meaning features.
_____	_____	2. The student can create analogies among words easily.
_____	_____	3. The student discusses key features with a partner or in a group.

Evidence Base

Joseph, L. M. (2002). Facilitating word recognition and spelling using word boxes and word sort phonic procedures. School *Psychology Review, 31,* 122–129.

Bear, D., Invernizzi, M., Templeton, S., & Johnston, F. (2000). *Words their way: Words study for phonics, vocabulary, and spelling instruction* (3rd ed.). Upper Saddle River, NJ: Merrill/Prentice Hall.

Web Sites

http://www.readwritethink.org/lessons/lesson_view.asp?id=795
http://www.wordsorting.org/Implementation.html

69 Word Walls

Description   Word walls are used to help readers develop their understanding of words. On large sheets of paper, the teacher writes critical and puzzling words for the students. The features of these words are discussed along with their meaning. Students can use the word walls when they write or read during classroom activities.

Text   Single words

Predominant Focus of Instruction

1. Processing focus: print
2. Instructional phase: before and after reading
3. Response mode emphasized: oral
4. Strategy emphasized: elaboration
5. Skill emphasized: word identification and word meaning
6. Source of information: reader based
7. Type of instruction: implicit
8. Type of cognitive processing: successive and simultaneous

Procedure

1. The teacher hangs a long sheet of paper on a wall and titles it, "Word Wall for _____." It could be a story, theme, or skill lesson.
2. The teacher introduces the word wall and writes key words for reading the story large enough for all students to read them.
3. After reading the teacher and students suggest other important story words and then write them on the word wall.
4. If students write the word on the wall, the teacher corrects spelling errors and discusses word features as students use these words when they write.
5. At this time, the teacher reviews spelling and word features as well as meaning.
6. For younger children, the teacher can add a small picture.
7. At the end of a unit, the teacher reviews all the words in the lesson, saying and spelling each word and putting it on an index card. The cards are collated on metal rings and put in the writing center.
8. The words can be sorted (see "Word Sorts" in this part) for phonic patterns. For example, all the words beginning with the same letter would be one sort, then rhyming words would be another sort, and so on.

Further Diagnostic Applications

Basic View of Reading   Learning to read means understanding words that influence stories. Readers need to use their knowledge of word features and word meanings to figure out story understanding; therefore, reading is an interactive process. By studying words, the students can elaborate on their understanding of word meaning and word features.

Patterns of Strengths and Strategies   The word wall approach is most appropriate for students who learn word meaning and word features easily. This technique builds on their strength and allows them to develop a system for analyzing words.

Learning Patterns That Produce Increased Engagement

1. For simultaneous thinkers who readily use what they know and what's important to understanding new information, this technique promotes understanding the relationship words have to meaning.

*2. For passive learners who need help focusing on words to understand text, this technique uses their attention to meaning and word features to enhance reading.

*3. For successive learners who can match sounds to letters but do not think about the meaning of individual words, this technique helps them develop a system for using what they know to figure out word meaning and word features.

Using the Technique as a Diagnostic Teaching Lesson   For the word walls approach to be effective, a majority of the following statements must be answered in the affirmative:

Yes	No	
_____	_____	1. The student can segment sounds.
_____	_____	2. The student can match sounds to letters.
_____	_____	3. The student applies decoding analogies to both known and unknown words.

Evidence Base

Hall, D. P., & Cunningham, P. M. (1992). Reading without ability grouping: Issues in first-grade instruction. *National Reading Conference Yearbook, 41,* 235–241.

Popplewell, S. R., & Doty, D. E. (2001). Classroom instruction and reading comprehension: A comparison of one basal reader approach and the Four-Blocks framework. *Reading Psychology, 22,* 83–94.

Web Sites

http://www.theschoolbell.com/Links/word_walls/words.html
http://www.donjohnston.com/catalog/wordmakerfrm.htm

APPENDIX A

Administering an Informal Reading Assessment

Here are directions for administering an informal reading assessment (IRI).

1. Select texts that sample a range of reading levels, or use a published informal reading inventory.
2. Establish the readability of the text, if necessary.
3. Prepare questions that focus on important information, coherent textual structure, and key concepts. If you use a published informal reading inventory, be sure to check the questions for coherence and importance.
4. Establish rapport quickly and begin assessment.
5. If necessary, use a word recognition list to establish a beginning level for assessment.
6. Start with a passage that you think will be at the student's independent level of difficulty.
7. Have the student read the passage orally.
8. Using the coding system in Table A–1 and Table A–2, record the student's performance as she reads. Both scoreable errors (Table A–1) and recordable errors (Table A–2) are coded. Scoreable errors determine whether a passage was read at the independent, instructional, or frustration level. Recordable errors are additional errors used to evaluate a reader's strategies but are not computed in the error rate.
9. Assess comprehension by asking the prepared questions.
10. Find the oral accuracy score by calculating the error rate (Table A–3) or the percentage of oral accuracy (Table A–4).
11. Compute the comprehension percentage score for the passage by (a) dividing the number of questions answered correctly by the total number of questions asked, and (b) multiplying the resulting decimal number by 100. Example: Brian answered 8 of 10 questions correctly.

$$\text{(a)} \quad 10\overline{)8.00} \quad .80$$

(b) $.80 \times 100 = 80\%$

Substitutions or mispronunciations (the replacement of one word for another): Mark the mispronounced word by drawing a line through it and writing the substitution above the word.

want
"The man ~~went~~ to the store," said Ann.

Omissions (leaving out words): Circle the word omitted.

"The man went to (the) store," said Ann.

Insertions (adding extra words): Draw a carat and write the inserted word above it.

away
"The man went ⌃ to the store," said Ann.

Transpositions (changing the word order): Mark with a ⏝.

"The man went to the store," said Ann.

Prompted words (words that have to be prompted or supplied by the teacher): Write the letter *P* above these words.

P
"The man went to the store," said Ann.

TABLE A-2 *Recordable Errors (not computed in the error rate for an IRI)*

Repetitions (words or phrases that are repeated more than once): Draw a line over the word and write the letter *R* over the line.

R
"The man went to the store," said Ann.

Repeated repetitions (words for phrases that are repeated several times): Draw a line over the word or phrase and mark it with a *2R* over the line.

2R
"The man went to the store," said Ann.

Self-correction: If the child corrects an error, a line is drawn through the previously marked error and the letter *C* is written at the end of the line.

~~want~~ C
"The man went to the store," said Ann.

Pauses: Long pauses that are used to gain meaning are marked with slashes.

"The man / went to the store," said Ann.

Punctuation errors (ignoring punctuation symbols): Draw a circle around the omitted punctuation mark.

"The man went to the store(,)" said Ann(.)"Then he went home."

TABLE A–3   *Calculating Error Rate*

---

1. Determine the number of scoreable errors per passage read.
   Example: Brian made 4 scoreable errors.

2. Estimate the total number of words in the passage read.
   Example: Brian read 86 words.

3. Divide the total number of words by the number of scoreable errors.
   Round off the quotient to the nearest whole number.
   Example:

   $$21 \text{ r } 2 = 21$$
   $$4\overline{)86}$$

4. The quotient determined in Step 3 becomes the denominator in the
   error rate and the number 1 becomes the numerator.
   Example: Brian read the passage with 1 error every 21 running words;
   the error rate is 1/21.

TABLE A–4   *Calculating Percentage of Oral Accuracy*

---

1. Estimate the number of words read.
   Example: Brian read 80 words.

2. Count the number of scoreable errors.
   Example: Brian made 4 errors.

3. Subtract the number of scoreable errors from the number of
   words read.
   Example: 80 words − 4 errors = 76 words

4. Divide the number of words read correctly by the number of
   words read.
   Example:

   $$.95$$
   $$80\overline{)76.00}$$

5. Multiply the resulting decimal number by 100 to find the percentage
   of oral accuracy.
   Example: .95 × 100 = 95%

---

12. Administer another passage on the same level. Have the student read the
    paragraph silently.
13. Assess comprehension by an oral retelling followed by direct questioning.
14. Decide the level of performance for each passage the student read. Use either
    Powell's criteria (1978) from Table A–5 or Betts's criteria (1946) from
    Table A–6. Use fluency rating as well (see Chapter 5).
15. Using the information from step 14, decide how to continue the assessment.
    (a) If the student is reading at an independent level, move her up to the
        next level.

TABLE A–5   *Scoring Criteria by Performance Grade Level Suggested by W. R. Powell (1978)*

Reading Level	Word Recognition Error Rate	Comprehension Percentage
Independent		
1–2	1/17+	80+
3–5	1/27+	85+
6+	1/35+	90+
Instructional		
1–2	1/8–1/16	55–80
3–5	1/13–1/26	60–84
6+	1/18–1/35	65–90
Frustration		
1–2	1/7−	55−
3–5	1/12−	60−
6+	1/17−	65−

Note: From *The Finger Count System for Monitoring Reading Behavior* (pp. 7–11) by W. R. Powell, 1981, unpublished paper. Adapted by permission.

TABLE A–6   *Scoring Criteria Suggested by Betts (1946)*

Reading Level	Word Recognition	Comprehension
Independent	99%+	90%+
Instructional	95%	75%
Frustration	90%−	50%−

    (b) If the student is reading at an instructional level, move her down to the next level to establish independent reading.

    (c) If the student is reading at a frustration level, consider moving her down two levels to establish independent and then instructional reading experiences.

16. Continue using this procedure, alternating between oral and silent reading at each level until a passage is read at frustration reading level for both oral and silent reading.

17. Summarize the results, using the Informal Reading Inventory Summary Sheet, reproduced in Table A–7.

TABLE A–7   *Informal Reading Inventory Summary Sheet*

**Informal Reading Inventory
Summary Sheet**

Student's Name _____ Age _____ Grade _____

Examiner _____ Date _____

IRI Used _____ Form _____

Levels of Performance   **Oral**   **Silent**

Independent Level   ____   ____
Instructional Level   ____   ____
Frustration Level   ____   ____

Level	Fluency Rate	Scoreable Errors Error Rate	Percentage of Comprehension Oral	Silent
pp				
p				
1				
2				
3				
4				
5				
6				
7				
8				
9				
10				
11				
12				

Appendix B

Predictable Book List

Level	Title	Author	Publisher
Beginning of First Grade			
	Look What I Can Do	Aruego, Jose	Scribner
	I Love You, Sun I Love You, Moon	Pandell, Karen, and Tomie de Paola	Putnam
	Do You Want to Be My Friend?	Carle, Eric	Harper Collins
	Have You Seen My Cat?	Carle, Eric	Philomel
	Spider, Spider	Cowley, Joy	Wright Group
	If You Meet a Dragon	Cowley, Joy	Wright Group
	Pancakes for Breakfast	de Paola, Tomie	Harcourt Brace Jovanovich
	Rain	Kalan, Robert	Greenwillow Books
	Brown Bear, Brown Bear	Martin, Bill	Holt, Rinehart, & Winston
	Have You Seen My Duckling?	Tafuri, Nancy	Greenwillow Books
	Cat on the Mat	Wildsmith, Brian	Oxford University Press
	All Fall Down	Wildsmith, Brian	Oxford University Press
	I Went Walking	Williams, Sue	Harcourt Brace Jovanovich
	Seven little monsters	Sendak	Disney

Level	Title	Author	Publisher
Near the Middle of First Grade			
	The Big Toe	Cowley, Joy	Wright Group/Story Box
	It Looked Like Spilt Milk	Shaw, Charles	Harper
	The Chick and the Duckling	Ginsburg, Mirra	Macmillan
	Sam's Cookie	Lindgren, Barbro	Morrow
	Five Little Ducks	Raffi	Crown
	I Love Mud and Mud Loves Me	Stephens, Vicki	Scholastic
	Go Dog Go	Eastman, P. D.	Random House
	The Big Fat Hen	Baker, Keith	Harcourt Brace Jovanovich
	Where's Spot? (also in Spanish)	Hill, Eric	Putnam
	Buzz Said the Bee	Lewison, Wendy	Scholastic
	The Foot Book	Dr. Seuss	Random House
	This old man	Koontz	Studio Child's Play International, LTD
	Six foolish fishermen	Elkin	Children's Press
Middle of the First Grade			
	A Dark Dark Tale	Brown, Ruth	Dial Press
	Have You Seen the Crocodile?	West, Colin	Harper & Row
	Spot's First Walk	Hill, Eric	Putnam
	Five Little Monkeys Jumping on the Bed	Christelow, Eileen	Clarion Books
	Just Like Daddy	Asch, Frank	Prentice Hall
	Mousetrap	Snowball, Diane	Scholastic
	Here are My Hands	Bill Martin, Jr.	
	Rosie's Walk	Hutchins, Pat	Macmillan
	Whose Mouse Are You?	Kraus, Robert	Macmillan
	Just for You	Mayer, Mercer	Dial
	Just Me and My Baby-sitter	Mayer, Mercer	Dial
	Sheep in a Jeep	Shaw, Nancy E.	Houghton Mifflin
	Each Peach, Pear, Plum	Ahlberg, Janet and Allan	Viking Press
	More Spaghetti, I Say	Gelman, Rita	Scholastic

Level	Title	Author	Publisher
	Itchy, Itchy Chicken Pox	Maccarone, Grace	Scholastic
	The Great Big Enormous Turnip	Tolstoy, Alexei	Watts
	Quick as a Cricket	Wood, Audrey	Child's Play International
	Go Dog Go	Eastman, P. D.	Random House
End of First Grade			
	I Was Walking Down the Road	Barchas, Sarah	Scholastic
	Seven Little Rabbits	Becker, John	Scholastic
	Goodnight Moon	Brown, Margaret Wise	HarperTrophy
	Are You My Mother?	Eastman, P. D.	Random House
	Big Dog, Little Dog	Eastman, P. D.	Random House
	Good Night Owl	Hutchins, Pat	Macmillan/Greenwillow
	Lady with the Alligator Purse	Westcott	Houghton Mifflin
	Leo, The Late Bloomer	Kraus, Robert	Windmill Books
	Just a Mess	Mayer, Mercer	Dial
	Jump, Frog, Jump	Kalan, Robert	Greenwillow
	Green Eggs and Ham	Dr. Seuss	Random House
	Hop on Pop	Dr. Seuss	Random House
	Nobody Listens to Andrew	Guilfoile, Elizabeth	Modern Curriculum Press
	Fortunately	Charlip, Remy	Macmillan
	Noisy Nora	Wells, Rosemary	Dial Books for Young Readers
	The Napping House	Wood, Audrey	Harcourt Brace Jovanovich
Between First and Second Grade			
	The Very Busy Spider	Carle, Eric	Philomel Books
	The Very Hungry Caterpillar	Carle, Eric	Philomel Books
	The Little Red Hen	Galdone, Paul	Seabury/Clarion
	The Three Bears	Galdone, Paul	Clarion Books
	The Doorbell Rang	Hutchins, Pat	Greenwillow
	George Shrinks	Joyce, William	Harper & Row
	Mouse Soup	Lobel, Arnold	Harper & Row
	Mouse Tales	Lobel, Arnold	Harper & Row/HarperCollins

Level	Title	Author	Publisher
	Owl at Home	Lobel, Arnold	Harper & Row
	Chicka Chicka Boom Boom	Martin, Bill	Simon & Schuster
	There's Something in My Attic	Mayer, Mercer	Dial
	Little Bear	Minarik, Else	Harper & Row
	The House That Jack Built	Peppe, Rodney	Delacorte/Holiday House
	Oh, Look!	Polacco, Patricia	Philomel
	The Cat in the Hat	Dr. Seuss	Random House
Second Grade			
	Nana Upstairs & Nana Downstairs	de Paola, Tomie	Putnam/Harcourt Brace Jovanovich
	May I Bring a Friend	DeRegniers, Beatrice Schenk	Atheneum
	Over in the Meadow	Galdone, Paul	Prentice Hall
	Danny and the Dinosaur	Hoff, Syd	Harper
	Don't Forget the Bacon	Hutchins, Pat	Greenwillow
	The Very Worst Monster	Hutchins, Pat	Greenwillow
	Frog and Toad Are Friends	Lobel, Arnold	Harper & Row
	Frog and Toad Together	Lobel, Arnold	Harper & Row
	Stone Soup	McGovern, Ann	Scholastic
	If You Give a Mouse a Cookie	Numerhoff, Laura	Harper & Row
	One Fine Day	Hogrogian, Nonny	Macmillan
	Henry and Mudge	Rylant, Cynthia	Aladdin Books
	Chicken Soup with Rice	Sendak, Maurice	Harper & Row
	Caps for Sale	Slobodkina, Esphyr	HarperCollins
	I Know a Lady	Zolotow, Charlotte	Greenwillow

High Interest Series Books

Reading Level	Title	Author
First and Second Grade		
	Clifford, The Big Red Dog	Norman Bridwell
	Jullian Jiggs	Phoebe Gilman
	Arthur books	Marc Brown
	Frog and Toad	Arnold Lobel
	George and Martha	James Marshall
	Little Critters	Mercer Mayer
	Little Bear	Else Minarik
	Amelia Bedilia	Peggy Parish
	Curious George	H. A. Rey
	Henry and Mudge	Cynthia Rylant
	Mr. Putter and Tabby	Cynthia Rylant
	Marvin Redpost	Louis Sachar
	Harry (The Dirty Dog) books	Gene Zion
Second and Third Grade		
	Amber Brown	Paula Danziger
	Pee Wee Scouts	Judy Delton
	Kids of Polk Street School	Patricia Reilly Giff
	Horrible Harry	Suszy Kline
	Kids on Bus 5	Marcia Leonard
	Junie B. Jones	Barbara Park

Reading Level	Title	Author
	Nate the Great	Marjorie Sharmat
	Boxcar Children	Gertrude Warner
	Magic Tree House	Mary Pope Osborne & Others
	Magic School Bus	Joanna Cole & Others
	Time Warp Trio	Jon Scieszka
	Hank the Cowdog	John R. Erickson, Gerald L. Holmes

Online Resources

Informational Material Resources

The following websites have an array of electronic text material to use during instruction. Most can be used with the speech to print software.

Internet Public Library including *KidSpace* for elementary children and *TeenSpace* for adolescents.

Project Gutenberg contains multiple resources online

The World Factbook—provides information on every country in the world.

Blackmask provides the text of the inauguration speeches of every United States president.

Encyclopedias

The Internet's free encyclopedias follow.

www.bartleby.com/65—Columbia Encyclopedia, 6th ed.

www.britannica.com—Britannica encyclopedia

www.education.yahoo.com/reference/encyclopedia

www.encarta.msn.com

www.encyclopedia.com—High Beam Search engine for multiple sites.

www.pantheon.org—The Encyclopedia Mythica

Wikipedia—*www.wikipedia.org*

Infoplease—*www.infoplease.com*

Search Engines

One Key for Kids—*http://www.onekey.com/*

Ask Jeeves—*http://www.askforkids.com/*

Kid's Click—*http://www.kidsclick.org/*

Yahooligans—*http://kids.yahoo.com/*

Dogpile—*www.dogpile.com*

Webcrawler—*www.webcrawler.com*

Yahoo Search—*www.yahoo.com*

Google Search—*www.google.com*

Lists of Books

Choice Reading

http://www.parents-choice.org/readlist.cfm

http://www.ucalgary.ca/~dkbrown/index.html

http://www.factmonster.com (click "Word Wise" then click "All about books")

http://home.comcast.net/~ngiansante/gradeone.html

http://www.library.uiuc.edu/edx/predbook.htm

Predictable Books

http://www.monroe.lib.in.us/childrens/predict.html

http://jefferson.lib.co.us/pdf/predictable.pdf

http://www.earlyliterature.ecsd.net/predictable_books.htm

http://www.selah.k12.wa.us/JC/readabook/literarypatterns.html#anchor618188

http://literacy.kent.edu/Oasis/Pubs/patterns.html

http://www.teachers.net/lessons/posts/2565.html

Chapter Books for Struggling Readers

http://wps.ablongman.com/ab_vacca_areareading_8/0,8848,1221138-,00.html

http://www.isd.net/~bhill/reading/books.htm

http://www.monroe.lib.in.us/childrens/reluctantbib.html

http://the2rs.com/Books_For_Reluctant_Readers/

http://www.ala.org/ala/yalsa/booklistsawards/quickpicks/quickpicksreluctant.htm

Choral Reading Material

http://en.wikipedia.org/wiki/List_of_speeches

http://www.gigglepoetry.com/

http://www.poetry4kids.com/index.php

http://falcon.jmu.edu/~ramseyil/poeform.htm

Readers Theatre Scripts

http://www.teachingheart.net/readerstheater.htm

http://www.scriptsforschools.com/147.html

http://pbskids.org/zoom/activities/playhouse/

http://www.readerstheatre.ecsd.net/collection.htm

Story Books Online

http://www.magickeys.com/books/

http://www.readinga-z.com/allbooks/index.html

http://www.ucalgary.ca/~dkbrown/index.html

http://www.aesopfables.com/

Finding Books at the Appropriate Level

Several websites help find trade books at the appropriate reading as well as interest and specialized topics. Two good ones follow:

Lexile Framework: *http://www.lexile.com*

Book Adventure: *http://www.bookadventure.org* (Click Kid Zone)

Selected Teaching Strategies Websites

There are many websites that describe specific strategies and they are embedded with the techniques. However, some websites focus on multiple strategies for specific targeted areas. These follow.

Comprehension

http://www.literacymatters.org/adlit/intro.htm

http://www.readinglady.com/Comprehension/index.html

http://www.literacy.uconn.edu/compre.htm

http://content.scholastic.com/browse/article.jsp?id=4464

http://literacyleaders.com/Method_Method_Outlines/Comp_Vocab/comp_vocab.html

Graphic Organizers

http://content.scholastic.com/browse/article.jsp?id=2983

http://www.ncrel.org/sdrs/areas/issues/students/learning/lr1grorg.htm

http://www.eduplace.com/graphicorganizer/index.html

http://www.teachervision.fen.com/graphic-organizers/printable/6293.html

http://www.sdcoe.k12.ca.us/score/actbank/torganiz.htm

http://classes.aces.uiuc.edu/ACES100/Mind/c-m2.html

Decoding

http://www.cs.oswego.edu/~borgert/OCM/rdagenda-1.html

http://www.eduplace.com/marketing/nc/pdf/fw_p11-20.pdf

http://www.edb.utexas.edu/readstrong/wordwall.html

Vocabulary

http://www.teachingenglish.org.uk/try/vocabtry/vocab_activities.shtml

http://www.eduplace.com/state/pdf/author/pik_temp.pdf

http://www.readingquest.org/strat/wordmap.html

http://teacher.scholastic.com/products/instructor/nov03_vocab.htm

Fluency

http://www.busyteacherscafe.com/units/fluency.htm

http://wps.prenhall.com/chet_literacy_cluster_1/0,8776,1164830-,00.html

http://www.ops.org/reading/fluency.htm

http://content.scholastic.com/browse/article.jsp?id=4367

Writing and Publishing

The following sites publish stories written by children for online distribution

KidPub site—*http://www.kidpub.org/kidpub/*

Take the Net site *http://www.storiesfromtheweb.org/earlyyears/index.htm*

Writers' Area

http://www.writersarea.com/kids/kids.html

Glossary

active readers Readers who construct or build meaning by shifting between information sources (the text and background knowledge).

alphabetic principle The knowledge that individual sounds in spoken words (phonemes) can be represented by a letter or letter combination.

artifacts Examples of learning that are collected to evaluate learning and are often placed in individual portfolios.

authentic tasks Tasks that represent activities that would actually occur in everyday life.

authentic texts Texts that represent real-life situations such as found in trade books and chapter books.

balanced instructional view Balanced reading instruction grew out of the resolution that neither skills instruction nor whole language could teach everyone to read. As a result, programs have been developed that use both skills and literature circles to teach reading. Balanced reading is much more than that. It is thoughtful reflective teaching that balances literature with informational texts, strategies with skills, explicit instruction with implicit instruction, easy reading with challenging reading, et al. to improve the reading development for all learners.

Community of practice Groups of individuals that share common values about their professional practice. Teachers, literacy coaches, and administrators in a school form a community of practice because they value the school's teaching.

cognitive a kind of mental operations or information processing that deals with operations involved in thinking including creating categories.

compensatory behaviors Readers counteract their weakness by using their dominant strengths and strategies.

constructivist theory A learning theory that posits that knowledge is built on prior experiences or what a learner already knows. It includes an active process of building a model of meaning.

continuous diagnostic assessment An assessment that is conducted from the text that is to be read during instruction.

cue selection When readers pay attention to specific aspects in their reading, like the letters in the words, the grammar of the sentence, or the meaning of the passage, in order to construct meaning with text.

cueing systems The language systems readers use to figure out words. They are the semantic system (dealing with meaning), the syntactic system (dealing with sentence sense), the grapho-phonic system (dealing with letters and sounds) and the pragmatic system (dealing with situational use of language).

decodable text Texts that are restricted to spelling patterns based on systematic letter-sound relationships.

decoding by analogy Using the letter patterns in a known word to figure out an unfamiliar word. For example, I know "sand" so I can figure out "land, brand, and strand."

dynamic assessment Evaluates students' performance as they are being taught and measures adjustments that the teacher makes.

early phonemic stage A stage of spelling development in which students represent whole words with one or more letters that indicate a few of the sounds in words.

elaborating Integrating and drawing relationships between new information and what is known in order to develop a more sophisticated concept.

engagement State of mind of an individual who is participating intensively in an activity. As students engage in literacy activities they become totally involved and passionate about the topic or strategy.

explicit instruction An instructional format in which the student is told what is to be learned and the teacher models the thinking process. As the student learns, the teacher gradually releases control.

familiar text time A part of the teaching session where the students choose books they have already read and know well.

frustration level A level of text that is so demanding and difficult that the reader is unable to construct meaning.

grammatical complexity Refers to organization including clauses and phrases within a sentence.

graphic information In beginning reading, it often refers to the letters found in words. With older students it often refers to diagrams and graphic organizers.

grapho-phonic information or cues The letters and sounds found in words.

guided contextual reading The aspect of the teaching session in which students read connected text at a level where they can construct meaning. It involves no more that 1 error every 14 words and at least 70% comprehension.

high frequency words Words that occur in written language more often than other words.

independent level A level of text that is read easily without the assistance of a teacher.

informal reading inventory An informal assessment that measures print and meaning processing on a series of graded passages establishing independent, instructional, or frustration level.

information source Basis for premises from the text, what the reader knows, and/or the context of the situation to construct meaning with text.

instructional adjustments Changes in instruction that occur as one teaches.

instructional conditions The circumstances under which students profit from instruction.

instructional conversations Discussion that is both instructional (i.e., promotes learning) and conversational, where there is a natural, spontaneous exchange of ideas.

instructional level The level of text that is somewhat challenging and where the reader needs some assistance from the teacher.

interactive view A view of reading that focuses on using what the reader both knows and does to construct meaning with text.

journal writing Students use a notebook to write thoughts and ideas and even compose stories. There is no teacher direction.

letter naming stage The stage of spelling where the sounds of a word are represented by the letter name with more than half the sounds represented.

literal comprehension Understanding explicitly stated information—a form of comprehension that involves "reading the lines" or text-based information.

literacy coaching Supporting classroom teachers as they change their instruction. Coaches observe and analyze teaching, converse with teachers about their practices and suggest alternatives that could improve student learning.

meaning emphasis program A literacy program where the materials and the teacher focus on the meaning of words and stories.

meaning processing The reader's effort to understand the text. Readers construct meaning using a variety of information sources.

mediated reading level   The highest level of instruction that can be reached after instruction.

mediating learning   The process a teacher uses for adjusting instruction so that a reader can understand text fully.

metacognition   Thinking about one's own thinking.

miscue   An oral response that deviates from what the text says.

miscue analysis   An assessment tool for examining miscues in order to analyze cueing patterns.

miscue rate   The number of miscues per running words.

monitoring   Checking the text or one's experience to see if things are making sense.

nonliteral comprehension   Understanding ideas not directly stated in the text. These types of inquiries or questions require a deeper processing of text and the integration of text information with a personal world view.

observations   Looking closely at the student's behaviors while reading and writing. Teachers can use observations as an assessment tool.

on-level assessment   An oral or silent reading of text that is at instructional level followed by an analysis of word recognition (oral only) and comprehension.

onset   The beginning letter-sound(s) in a word.

passive readers   Individuals who read without checking their understanding to see if they are making sense.

passive reading   Reading without checking for understanding.

personalized reading and writing   An instructional aspect of a reading session that allows the student to choose what is read and what is written.

phonemic awareness   Awareness of the individual sounds in words.

phonic cues   The sounds in the words.

phonics program   A reading program in which the materials are designed to focus on the sounds in the words.

phonological awareness   Awareness of sounds in words that develops on three levels; the syllable, the rime-onset level, and the phoneme level.

portfolio   A collection of pieces of work selected to demonstrate students' reading and writing ability.

portfolio reflection   Thoughtful commentary on how the selected piece demonstrates literacy.

pragmatic system   A cue system based on how language is used in various situations.

predictable books   Materials that contain repetitious language patterns and supportive pictures so that students can easily predict the words.

predicting   Making a sophisticated guess about what the author is going to say.

prephonemic stage   The level of spelling development where no letter-sound relationships are present.

print processing   The reader's effort to decode the text.

production demands   The demands the teacher places within an activity for the reader to respond to the text, such as reading orally or writing a summary.

reader-based view   A view of reading that focuses on what the reader does and thinks as a major instructional concern.

response mode   The way the student is asked to respond to what is being read.

rime   Letter patterns that rhyme and contain the same letters. They often follow the initial letter-sound.

scaffolding   Supporting readers as they read, first by modeling, then by prompting as they complete the task, then letting them complete the task on their own.

schema   A framework developed by the reader to label and categorize experiences. Learners actively build schemas and revise them in light of new information. Each person's schema is unique and dependent on personal experiences and thinking processes.

self-assessment   Occurs when students are asked to evaluate their own strategies or their own work.

semantic cue   Meaning-rich words selected by the reader to figure out text meaning.

semantic system   A cue system that uses the meaning of the text.

sentence comprehension   The skill of understanding how the words in a sentence influence meaning.

sentence structure The grammar of a sentence.

sight vocabulary Words that students can recognize rapidly. The first words they learn to recognize.

simultaneous processing The student thinks first about the overall ideas and then organizes the parts.

skill Tasks in reading, such as knowledge of letter sounds.

social context The situation in which reading occurs, including the verbal interactions that happen.

socio-cultural view a view of reading that focuses on using a person's culture and their situational understanding to create a literate community. This view places a premium on interactions with others as major instructional concerns of teachers.

sources of information Essential data from the text, what the reader knows, and/or the context of the situation.

story structure The way stories are formed—that is, the grammar or organization of the story.

strategic processing Using thoughtful plans of actions to comprehend text.

strategy Effortful plans, procedures, or actions for figuring out words or figuring out meaning.

strategy and skill instruction Series of mini-lessons to develop or modify reading strategies and skills.

strategy instruction Lessons on the procedures that readers use when comprehending texts.

student-led conference A meeting with others where students demonstrate their literacy processes and products.

successive processing The student thinks about the parts first and then orders the parts to form meaning or the complete task.

syntactic clues Sentence order clues that show the associations among words in a sentence.

syntactic system A cue system based on how language is put together or the structure of sentences.

task modification Changes the teacher makes in what she asks the student to do in order to ensure a successful reading experience.

teacher investment The amount of support the teacher gives to provide a successful reading experience.

text-based information The information found directly in the text.

text-based view A view of reading that focuses on using the text as the major instructional component of teaching.

text structure The organization of the text. There are text structures for narrative and informational texts.

think-aloud procedures Problem solving out loud as one reads.

visual cues The letters in the words.

word analysis Figuring out how the parts of words work.

word attack The skill of knowing and using decoding knowledge.

word choices The words that the author uses to convey meaning.

word identification The skill of recognizing words.

Bibliography

Afflerbach, P. (2006). Best practices in literacy assessment. In L. B. Gambrell, L. M. Morrow, & M. Pressley (Eds.), *Best practices in literacy instruction.* New York: Guildford.

Alexander, P., & Jetton, T. (2000). Learn from text: A multidimensional and developmental perspective. In M. Kamil, P. Mosenthal, P. D. Pearson, & R. Barr (Eds.), *Handbook of reading research* (Vol. 3, pp. 285–310). New York: Longman.

Allington, R. L. (1984). Oral reading. In P. D. Pearson (Ed.), *Handbook of reading research* (pp. 829–864). New York: Longman.

Allington, R. L. (1995). Literacy lessons in the elementary schools: Yesterday, today, and tomorrow. In R. L. Allington & S. A. Walmsley (Eds.), *No quick fix* (pp. 1–18). New York: Teachers College Press; Newark, DE: International Reading Association.

Allington, R. (2005). *What really matters for struggling readers: Designing research-based programs* (2nd ed.) New York: Longman.

Allington, R. L., & Cunningham, P. M. (2006). *Schools that work: Where all children read and write* (3rd ed.). New York: Allyn/Bacon.

Almasi, J. F. (1996). A new view of discussion. In L. B. Gambrell & J. F. Almasi (Eds.), *Lively discussions! Fostering engaged reading* (pp. 2–24). Newark, DE: International Reading Association.

Au, K. (1993). *Literacy instruction in multicultural settings.* Fort Worth, TX: Harcourt Brace Jovanovich.

Au, K. (2002). Multicultural factors and effective instruction of students of diverse backgrounds. In A. Farstrup & S. Samuels (Eds.), *What research has to say about reading instruction* (pp. 392–414). Newark, DE: International Reading Association.

Barr, R., Blachowicz, C., Bates, A., & Katz, C. (2007). *Reading diagnosis for teachers: An instructional approach* (5th ed.). White Plains, NY: Longman.

Bear, D., Invernizzi, M., Templeton, S., & Johnston, F. (2004). *Words their way: Words study for phonics, vocabulary, and spelling instruction* (3rd ed.). Upper Saddle River, NJ: Merrill/Prentice Hall.

Betts, E. A. (1946). *Foundations of reading instruction.* New York: American Book.

Bottomley, D., Henk, W., & Melink, S. (1997–1998). Assessing children's views of themselves as writer using the Writer Self-Perception Scale. *The Reading Teacher, 5,* 286–296.

Braunger, J., & Lewis, J. P. (2005). *Building a knowledge base in reading* (2nd ed.) Newark, DE: International Reading Association and The National Council of English.

Bus, A. G., de Jong, M. T., & Verhallen, M. (2006). CD-ROM talking books: A way to enhance early literacy? In M. C. McKenna, L. D. Labbo, R. D. Kieffer, & D. Reinking (Eds.), *International handbook of literacy and technology* (2nd ed., pp. 129–142). Mahwah, NJ: Lawrence Erlbaum Associates.

Clay, M. M. (1993). *Reading recovery: A guidebook for teachers in training.* Portsmouth, NH: Heinemann.

Cunningham, P. M., & Allington, R. L. (2007). *Classrooms that work: They can all read and write* (4th ed.). New York: Longman.

Das, J. P. (1999). *PREP: PASS Reading Enhancement Program.* Deal NJ: Sarka Educational Resources.

Das, J. P., Parrila, R. K., & Papadopoulos, T. C. (2000). Cognitive education and reading disability. In A. Kozulin & B. Y. Rand (Eds.), *Experience of mediated learning: An impact of Feuerstein's theory in education and psychology.* (pp. 274–291.) Oxford: Pergamon Press.

Deci, E. L., Vallerand, R. J., Pelletier, L. G., & Ryan, R. M. (1991). Motivation and education: The self-determination perspective. *Educational Psychologist, 26,* 325–346.

Duffy, G. G., & Roehler, L. R. (1987). Teaching reading skills as strategies. *The Reading Teacher, 40,* 414–418.

Duke, N., & Pearson, P. D. (2002). Effective practices for developing reading comprehension. In A. Farstrup & S. Samuels (Eds.), *What research has to say about reading instruction* (pp. 205–242). Newark, DE: International Reading Association.

Dybdahl, C. S. (1983, October). *Comprehension strategies and practices.* Paper presented at the annual conference of the College Reading Association, Atlanta, GA.

Dybdahl, C. S., & Walker, B. J. (in press). *Prediction strategies and comprehension instruction.* In B. Walker, & C. Dybdhal, (Eds.), *Supporting struggling readers in classrooms and tutoring.* Norwood, MA: Christopher-Gordon Publishers, Inc.

Eskridge, E. (2002). Teachers taking the aesthetic stance while practicing discussion of young adult literature. *Dissertation Abstracts International Section A: Humanities and Social Sciences, 63*(10-A), *58*(7-A), 3461.

Feuerstein, R., & Feuerstein, S. (1991). Mediated learning experience: A theoretical review. In R. Feuerstein, P. S. Klein, & A. J. Tannenbaum (Eds.), *Mediated learning experience (MLE): Theoretical, psychosocial and learning implications.* London: Freund Publishing House.

Flood, J., Lapp, D., Ranck-Buhr, W., & Moore, J. (1995). What happens when teachers get together to talk about books? Gaining a multicultural perspective from literature. *The Reading Teacher,* 48, 720–723.

Fountas, I. C., & Pinnell, G. S. (1996). *Guided reading: Good first teaching for all children.* Portsmouth, NH: Heinemann.

Gambrell, L. B., & Jawitz, P. B. (1993). Mental imagery, text illustrations, and children's story comprehension and recall. *Reading Research Quarterly, 28,* 264–276.

Gambrell, L. B., Malloy, J. A., & Mazzoni, S. A. (2006). Evidence-based best practices for comprehensive literacy instruction. In L. B. Gambrell, L. M. Morrow, & M. Pressley (Eds. *Best practices in literacy instruction* (3rd ed., pp. 11–25). New York: Guildford.

Gambrell, L., & Marinak, B. A. (1997). Incentive and instrinsic motivation to read. In J. T. Guthrie & A. Wigfield (Eds.), *Reading engagement: Motivating readers through integrated instruction* (pp. 205–217) Newark, DE: International Reading Association.

Gambrell, L. B., Palmer, B. M., Codling, R. M., & Mazzoni, S. A. (1996). Assessing motivation to read. *The Reading Teacher, 49 (7),* 518–533.

Gaskins, I. W., Ehri, L. C., Cress, C., O'Hara, C., & Donnelly, K. (1996–1997). Procedures for word learning: Making discoveries about words. *The Reading Teacher, 50,* 312–327.

Gillet, J., & Temple, C. (1994). *Understanding reading problems* (4th ed.). Glenview, IL: Scott Foresman.

Gipe, J. P. (2002). *Multiple paths to literacy: Classroom techniques for struggling readers* (5th ed.). Upper Saddle River, NJ: Merrill/Prentice Hall.

Glazer, S. M. (1992). *Reading comprehension: Self-monitoring strategies to develop independent readers.* New York: Scholastic.

Glazer, S. M., & Brown, C. S. (1993). *Portfolios and beyond: Collaborative assessment in reading and writing.* Norwood, MA: Christopher-Gordon.

Goldenberg, C. (1992–1993). Instructional conversations: Promoting comprehension through discussion. *The Reading Teacher, 46,* 316–326.

Goodman, K. (1996). Principles of revaluing. In Y. M. Goodman & A. M. Marek (Eds.), *Retrospective miscue analysis: Revaluing readers and reading* (pp. 13–21). Katonah, NY: Richard C. Owen.

Goodman, Y. M., & Marek, A. M. (1996). Retrospective miscue analysis. In Y. M. Goodman & A. M. Marek (Eds.), *Retrospective miscue analysis: Revaluing readers and reading* (pp. 39–49). Katonah, NY: Richard C. Owen.

Goswami, U. (2000). Phonological and lexical processes. In M. Kamil, P. Mosenthal, P. D. Pearson, & R. Barr (Eds.), *Handbook of reading research* (Vol. 3, pp. 251–268). New York: Longman.

Gunning, T. G. (1998). *Assessing and correcting reading and writing difficulties.* Boston: Allyn & Bacon.

Guthrie, J. T., Van Meter, P., McCann, A. D., Wigfield, A., Bennett, L., Poundstone, et., al. (1996). Growth of literacy engagement: Changes in motivation and strategies during concept-oriented reading instruction. *Reading Research Quarterly, 31* 306.

Guthrie, J. T., & Wigfield, A. (2000). Engagement and motivation in reading. In M. L. Kamil, P. B. Mosenthal, P. D. Pearson, & R. Barr (Eds.), *Handbook of reading research* (Vol pp. 403–422). New York: Lawernce Erlbaum Associates.

Hansen, J. (1995). Literacy portfolios: Helping students know themselves. In J. E. DeCarlo (Ed.), *Perspectives in whole language* (pp. 302–305). Boston: Allyn & Bacon.

Harste, J. Burke, C., & Woodward, V. (1994). Children's language and world: Initial encounters with print. In R. B. Ruddell, M. R. Ruddell, & H. Singer (Eds.), *Theoretical models and processes of reading.* (4th ed., pp. 48–69). Newark, DE: International Reading Association.

Henk, W., & Melink, S. (1995). The Reader Self-Perception Scale (RSPS): A new tool for measuring how children feel about themselves as readers. *The Reading Teacher, 48,* 470–482.

Hidi, S. (2001). Interest, reading, and learning: theoretical and practical considerations. *Educational Psychology Review, 13,* 191–207.

Hidi, S., & Renninger, K. A. (2006). The four-phase model of interest development. *Education Psychologist, 41 (2),* 111–127.

Hiebert, E. H. (1994). Becoming literate through authentic tasks: Evidence and adaptations. In R. B. Ruddell, M. R. Ruddell, & H. Singer (Eds.), *Theoretical models and processes of reading* (4th ed., pp. 391–413). Newark, DE: International Reading Association.

International Reading Association (2004). The Role and Qualification of the Reading Coach in the United States: A position statement of the International Reading Association.

International Reading Association (2003). IRA Literacy Study Groups: Reading Comprehension Module. Newark, DE: International Reading Association.

International Reading Association & National Council of Teachers of English, (1996). Newark, Standards for the English language arts. DE: International Reading Association; Urbana, IL: National Council of Teachers of English.

Irwin, P. A., & Mitchell, J. N. (1983). A procedure for assessing the richness of retellings. *Journal of Reading, 2,* 391–396.

Johns, J. L. (2005). *Basic reading inventory* (9th Ed.). Dubuque, IA: Kendal/Hunt.

Johns, J. L., & Lenski, S. (2001). *Improving reading: A handbook of strategies* (3rd ed.). Dubuque, IA: Kendall/Hunt.

Johnston, P. H. (2004). *Choice words: How our language affects children's learning.* York, ME: Stenhouse Publishers.

Johnston, P. H., & Allington, R. (1991). Remediation. In R. Barr, M. Kamil, P. Mosenthal, & P. D. Pearson (Eds.), *Handbook of reading research* (Vol. 2, pp. 984–1012). New York: Longman.

Jordan, A. (1989). *Diagnostic narrative.* Unpublished journals of lessons. Eastern Montana College.

Juel, C. (1988). Learning to read and write: A longitudinal study of 54 children from first through fourth grades. *Journal of Educational Psychology, 80,* 437–447.

Juel, C. (1998). What kind of one-on-one tutoring helps a poor reader? In C. Hulme & R. M. Joshi (Eds.), *Reading and spelling: Development and disorders*

(pp. 449– 472). Mahwah, NJ: Lawrence Erlbaum Associates.

Kaufman, A. S, & Kaufman., N. L. (1983). *K-ABC Kaufman assessment battery for children: Interpretive manual.* Circle Pines; MN: American Guidance Services.

Keene, E. O., & Zimmermann, S. (1997*). Mosaic of thought: Teaching comprehension in a reader's workshop.* Portsmouth, NH: Heinemann.

Kennedy, M. (1998, April). *The relevance of content in inservice teacher education.* Paper presented at the annual meeting of the American Educational Research Association. San Diego, CA.

Kidspiration: The Visual Way to Think, Write, and Comprehend (2001). Inspiration Software. Beaverton: Oregon

Linnenbrink, E.A. & Pintrich, P. R. (2003). The role of self-efficacy beliefs in student engagement and learning in the classroom. *Reading and Writing Quarterly, 19,* 119–137.

Marek, A. M., & Goodman, Y. M. (1996). Understanding the reading process. In Y. M. Goodman & A. M. Marek (Eds.), *Retrospective miscue analysis: Revaluing readers and reading* (pp. 21–39). Katonah, NY: Richard C. Owen.

Marvuglio, M. J. (1994, Spring). A celebration of learning: Student-led conferences. *Colorado Reading Council Journal,* pp (21–24.)

May, F., & Rizzardi, L. (2002). *Reading as communication* (6th ed.). Upper Saddle River, NJ: Merrill/Prentice Hall.

McCormick, S. (1992). Disabled readers' erroneous responses to inferential comprehension questions: Description and analysis. *Reading Research Quarterly, 27,* 54–77.

McCormick, S. (2007). *Instructing students who have literacy problems* (5th ed.) Upper Saddle River, NJ: Merrill/Prentice Hall.

McKenna, M. C. & Kerr, D. J. (1990). Measuring attitude toward reading: A new tool for teachers. *The Reading Teacher, 43,* 626–639.

Mills, R. E. (1956). An evaluation of techniques for teaching word recognition. *Elementary School Journal, 56,* 221–225.

Mokhtari, K., & Reichard, C. (2002). Assessing students' metacognitive awareness of reading strategies. *Journal of Educational Psychology, 94,* 240–259.

Morrow, L., & Walker, B. (1997). *The reading team: A handbook for volunteer tutors K–3.* Newark, DE: International Reading Association.

Neufeld, B., & Roper, D. (2003). A strategy for developing instructional capacity: Promises and practicalities. Retrieved December 15, 2006, from http://www.annenberginstitute.org/images/Coaching.pdf

Pappas, C., Kiefer, B., & Levstik, L. (2006). *Integrated language perspective in the elementary school: An action approach*. New York: Allyn & Bacon.

Paris, S. G., Lipson, M. Y., & Wixson, K. K. (1994). Becoming a strategic reader. In R. B. Ruddell, M. R. Ruddell, & H. Singer (Eds.), *Theoretical models and processes of reading* (4th ed., pp. 788–811). Newark, DE: International Reading Association.

Pauk, W. (1993). *How to study in college* (5th ed.). Boston: Houghton Mifflin.

Pearson P. D., & Anderson, R. C. (1984). A schema-theoretic view of basic processes in reading comprehension. In P. D. Pearson (Ed.), *Handbook of Reading Research* (pp. 255–291). New York: Longman.

Pearson, P. D. (1985). Changing the face of reading comprehension instruction. *The Reading Teacher, 38,* 724–736.

Pearson, P. D., & Camperell, K. (1994). Comprehension of text structures. In R. B. Ruddell, M. R. Ruddell, & H. Singer (Eds.), *Theoretical models and processes of reading* (4th ed., pp. 448–468). Newark, DE: International Reading Association.

Piaget, J. (1968). *Six psychological studies*, Anita Tenzer (Trans.), New York: Vintage.

Powell, W. R. (1981). *The finger count system for monitoring reading behavior.* Unpublished manuscript.

Powell, W. R. (1984). Mediated (emergent) reading levels: A construct. In J. Niles (Ed.), *Changing perspectives on research in reading language processing and instruction* (pp. 247–251). Rochester, NY: National Reading Conference.

Powell, W. R. (1986, December). *Emergent (mediated) reading levels: A new construct for placement from a Vygotskian view.* Paper presented at the National Reading Conference, Austin, TX.

Pressley, M. (2000). What should comprehension instruction be the instruction of? In M. Kamil, P. Mosenthal, P. D. Pearson, & R. Barr (Eds.), *Handbook of reading research* (Vol. 3, pp. 525–544). New York: Longman.

Rasinski, T. (1999). Making and writing words. *Reading Online,* Retrieved September 1, 2002, from http://readingonline.org/articles/words/rasinski.html.

Rasinski, T. (2001). Making and writing words using letter patterns. *Reading Online,* Retrieved September 1, 2002, from http://readingonline.org/articles/rasinski/MWW_LP.html.

Rasinski, T., & Padak, N. (2004). *Effective reading Strategies: Teaching children who find reading difficult* (2nd ed.). Upper Saddle River, NJ.: Merrill/Prentice Hall.

Rasinski, T., & Padak, N. (2002). *From phonics to fluency: Effective teaching of decoding and reading fluency in the elementary school.* Upper Saddle River, NJ: Merrill/Prentice Hall.

Ray, D. D. (1970). *Ray reading methods test* (Experimental Ed.). Stillwater, OK: RRMT Publications.

Reed, J. H., Schallert, D. L., & Goetz, E. (1992). *Exploring the reciprocal relationship among comprehensibility, interestingness, and involvement in academic reading tasks.* Paper presented at the annual meeting of the American Educational Research Association, San Francisco, CA.

Reutzel, D. R., & Cooter, R. B. (2000). *Teaching children to read: From basals to books* (3rd ed.). Upper Saddle River, NJ: Merrill/Prentice Hall.

Reutzel, D. R., & Cooter, R. (2003). *Strategies for reading assessment and instruction: Helping every child succeed* (2nd ed.). Upper Saddle River, NJ: Merrill/Prentice Hall.

Richardson, V. & Anders, P. L. (2005). Professional preparation and development of teachers in literacy instruction for urban settings. In J. Flood & P. L. Anders (Eds.), *Literacy development of students in urban schools: research and policy*. Newark, DE: International Reading Association.

Roller, C. (1998). *So . . . what's a tutor to do?* Newark, DE: International Reading Association.

Roskos, K., & Walker, B. J. (1994). *Interactive handbook for understanding reading diagnosis.* Upper Saddle River, NJ: Merrill/Prentice Hall.

Roskos, K., & Walker, B. (1998). *Teachers' understanding and adaptation of their discourse as instructional conversation through self-assessment activity.* Paper presented at the annual meeting of the American Educational Research Association, San Diego, CA.

Ruddell, M. R. (2005). *Teaching content area reading and writing* (4th ed.). Hoboken, NJ: Wiley.

Ruddell, R. B., & Unrau, N. J. (1997). The role of responsive teaching in focusing reader intention and developing reader motivation. In J. T. Guthrie & A. Wigfield (Eds.), *Reading engagement: Motivating readers through integrated instruction* (pp. 102–127). Newark, DE: International Reading Association.

Ruddell, R. B., & Unrau, N. J. (2004). Reading as a meaning-construction process: The reader, the text, and the teacher. In R. B. Ruddell & N. J. Unrau (Eds.), *Theoretical models and processes of reading* (5th ed., pp. 1462–1523). Newark, DE: International Reading Association.

Samuels, S. J. (2002). Reading fluency: Its development and assessment. In A. Farstrup & S. Samuels (Eds.), *What research has to say about reading instruction* (pp. 166–183). Newark, DE: International Reading Association.

Sanders, A. (2001). *25 read & write mini books that teach word families*. New York, NY: Scholastic Inc.

Schallert, D. L., & Reed, J. H. (1997). The pull of the text and the process of involvement in reading. In J. T. Guthrie & A. Wigfield (Eds.), *Reading engagement: Motivating readers through integrated instruction* (pp. 68–85). Newark, DE: International Reading Association.

Schunk, D. (2003). Self-efficacy for reading and writing: Influence of modeling, Goal setting, and self-evaluation. *Reading and Writing Quarterly, 19,* 159–172.

Short, K. G., Harste, J. C., & Burke, C. (1996). *Creating classrooms for authors and inquirers*. Portsmouth, NH: Heinemann.

Snider, M. A., Lima, S. S., & DeVito, P. J. (1994). Rhode Island's literacy portfolio assessment project. In S. W. Valencia, E. H. Hiebert, & P. P. Afflerback (Eds.), *Authentic reading assessment: Practices and possibilities* (pp. 71–88). Newark, DE: International Reading Association.

Snow, C. E., Burns, M. S., & Griffin, P. (1998). *Preventing reading difficulties in young children*. Washington, DC: National Academy Press.

Spiegel, D. L. (1998). Silver bullets, babies, and bath water: Literature response groups in a balanced literacy program. *The Reading Teacher, 52,* 114–124.

Stahl, S. (1998). Saying the "P" word: Nine guidelines for exemplary phonics instruction. In R. Allington (Ed.), *Teaching struggling readers* (pp. 208–216). Newark, DE: International Reading Association.

Stanovich, K. E. (1986). Matthew effects in reading: Some consequences of individual differences in the acquisition of literacy. *Reading Research Quarterly, 21,* 360–406.

Stanovich, K. E. (2004). Matthew effects in reading: Some consequences of individual differences in the acquisition of literacy. In R. B. Ruddell, & N. J. Unrau (Eds.), *Theoretical models and processes of reading* (5th ed., pp. 1149–1179). Newark, DE: International Reading Association.

Stowell, L. P., & Tierney, R. J. (1995) Portfolios in the classroom: What happens when teachers and students negotiate assessment? In R. L. Allington & S. A. Walmsley (Eds.), *No quick fix* (pp. 78–96). New York: Teachers College Press; Newark, DE: International Reading Association.

Taylor, B., Harris, L., Pearson, P. D., & Garcia, G. (1995). *Reading difficulties: Instruction and assessment.* New York: McGraw-Hill.

Taylor, B., Pearson, P. D., Clark, K., & Walpole, S. (2002). Effective schools and accomplished teachers: Lessons about primary grade reading instruction in low-income schools. In B. Taylor & P. D. Pearson (Eds.), *Teaching reading: Effective schools, accomplished teachers* (pp. 3–72). Mahwah, NJ: Lawrence Erlbaum Associates.

Taylor, B., Pearson, P. D., Peterson, D. S. & Rodriguez, M. C. (2003). Reading growth in high-poverty classrooms: The influency of teacher practices that encourage cognitive engagement in literacy learning. *Elementary School Journal, 104,* 3–28.

Tierney, R. J., & Pearson, P. D. (1994). A revisionist perspective on "learning to learn from text: A framework for improving classroom practice." In R. Ruddell, M. Ruddell, & H. Singer (Eds.), *Theoretical models and processes of reading* (4th ed., pp. 514–519). Newark, DE: International Reading Association.

Tierney, R. J., & Readence, J. E. (2000). *Reading strategies and practices: A compendium* (5th ed.). Boston: Allyn & Bacon.

Tompkins, G. E. (1998). *Fifty literacy strategies: Step by step.* Upper Saddle River, NJ: Merrill/Prentice Hall.

Turner, J. (1997). Starting right: Strategies for engaging young literacy learners. In J. Guthrie & A. Wigfield (Eds.), *Reading engagement: Motivating readers through integrated instruction* (pp. 183–204). Newark, DE: International Reading Association.

Valencia, S. W., & Place, N. A. (1994). Literacy portfolios for teaching, learning, and accountability: The Bellevue literacy assessment project. In S. W. Valencia, E. H. Hiebert, & P. P. Afflerback (Eds.), *Authentic reading assessment: Practices and possibilities* (pp. 71–88). Newark, DE: International Reading Association.

Vygotsky, L. S. (1978). *Mind in society.* Cambridge, MA: Harvard University Press.

Walker, Barbara. (1990a). A model for diagnostic narratives. In N. Padak, T. Rasinski, & J. Logan (Eds.), *Challenges in reading* (pp. 1–10). Pittsburg, KS: College Reading Association.

Walker, B. J. (1990b). *What research says to the teacher: Remedial reading.* Washington, DC: National Education Association.

Walker, B. J. (1996). Discussions that focus on strategies and self-assessment. In L. B. Gambrell & J. F. Almasi (Eds.), *Lively discussions! Fostering engaged reading* (pp. 286–296). Newark, DE: International Reading Association.

Walker, B. J. (2003a). The cultivation of student self-efficacy in reading and writing. *Reading and Writing Quarterly, 19,* 173–187.

Walker, B. J. (2003b). *Supporting struggling readers* (2nd ed.). Markham, Ontario: Pippin Publishing.

Wigfield, A. (1997). Children's motivations for reading and reading engagement. In J. T. Guthrie

& A. Wigfield (Eds.), *Reading engagement: Motivating readers through integrated instruction* (pp. 14–33). Newark, DE: International Reading Association.

Wilhelm, J. D. (2001). *Improving comprehension think-aloud strategies: Modeling what good readers do.* New York: Scholastic.

Wood, C. (2005). Beginning readers' use of "talking books" software can affect their reading strategies. *Journal of Research in Reading, 28,* 170–182.

Yopp, H. (1995). A test for assessing phonemic awareness in young children. *The Reading Teacher, 49,* 20–29.

Zutell, J. (1988, May). *Developing a procedure for assessing oral reading fluency: Establishing validity and reliability.* Paper presented at 33rd annual convention of the International Reading Association, Toronto.

Zutell, J., & Rasinski, T. (1991). Training teachers to attend to their students' oral reading fluency. *Theory to Practice, 30,* 211–217.

Name Index

Subject Index

Teacher research groups, for reading instruction, 165–166
Teachers. *See also* Diagnostic teachers
    effective, characteristics of, 4–5
    expectations of, 41
Teaching session, 59–60. *See also* Diagnostic teaching
    continuous diagnostic assessment, 61–63
    familiar text time, 61
    guided contextual reading, 61, 63–65
    personalized reading and writing, 69–70
    premises of, 60–61
    process writing time, 68–69
    strategy and skill instruction, 65–68
Team, classroom-based, for struggling readers, 166–167
Techniques. *See* Instructional techniques
Text
    background knowledge and, 22
    classifying instructional techniques by type of, 170–172
    content and, 22
    density of information and, 22
    formats of, 22–23
    grammatical complexity and, 23–24
    organization of, 23
    style and, 23

teaching event and, 22–25
types of, 33
word choices and, 24–25
Text availability, for answers, 21
Text-based view, of reading, 10
Textbooks, 153
Thematic-inquiry approach, 348–349
Think-aloud approach, 350–352
Think-aloud assessments, 99, 107–108, 108, 134
    analyzing silent reading with, 107–114

Visualization approach, 353–354
Vocabulary self-collection strategy, 355–356

Wait time, 40
Word choices, 24–25
Word identification, 86
Word knowledge, 26
Word sorts, 357–358
Word walls, 359–360
Writer Self-Perception Scale (Bottomley, Henk, and Melink), 140
Writing
    personalized, 59, 69–70, 71
    in reading events, 18, 33–34
    in teaching session, 68–69